# Contents

*Contents*

# Acknowledgments

I am indebted to the authors and publishers of the various works from which I have quoted in this book, for permission thus to use copyright material. Each particular reference is made in a footnote on the appropriate page; I hope I have not failed to ask permission of the holders of the copyright in any material I have thus cited. If I have overlooked any, it was an error of omission, and I ask pardon for it.

Four friends read the book in typescript and one in proof, and between them made a very substantial number of suggestions, criticisms and corrections. They are John Burgh; Arthur Davidson, M.P.; Peter Forster; and Brian Inglis. I am very grateful to them for their help, which was of the greatest value.

The book was also read in typescript by Mrs Philippa Fraser-Harrison, of Jonathan Cape Ltd. The fact that this was part of her professional duties in no way diminishes the helpfulness of her many wise and important suggestions, nor my gratitude to her for them.

The final version was typed, in a race with the clock, by Mrs Prudence Hutton, whose sore task did not divide the Sunday from the week. An earlier, and much longer, draft was typed by my former secretary, Sonia Jobson, amid all her other work, and even that represented only a fraction of her assistance; in addition she made countless telephone-calls, looked up countless references, checked countless facts, made me countless cups of tea, and throughout not only kept calm herself, but kept me calm as well. I am deeply indebted to her. I am grateful, too, to Kerry-Jane Ogilvy, who helped with the index and in many other ways.

To all these, and the other friends with whom I discussed the book or parts of it, I now re-iterate my thanks; I emphasize that for any remaining errors, and for all judgments expressed or implied, I am alone responsible.

I am much obliged, too, to Arthur Brittenden, the Editor of the *Daily Mail* (for which I then worked), for so readily agreeing to give me six months' sabbatical leave from the paper to finish the book, and for subsequently, and no less readily, extending this for a further two months.

To Tom Maschler, now Chairman of Jonathan Cape Ltd, and to Graham Watson of Curtis Brown Ltd, my Literary Agent, I owe a debt of a different kind: for their understanding patience with one who must repeatedly have tempted them to wash their hands of him.

Finally, five friends, over a long period, urged—and nerved—me to launch myself on the unknown sea of my first book, after many years of journalism. To three of them—Sidney Bernstein, Alan Moorehead and Woodrow Wyatt—I can now acknowledge my gratitude for their encouragement; I profoundly regret that in the case of the other two—Basil Liddell Hart and Gerald Barry—it is now only to their memory that I can offer my thanks.

B.L.

# 1

# The isle is full of noises

It was a credulous age, perhaps the most credulous ever, and the more rational, the less gullible, the decade claimed to be, the less rational, the more gullible, it showed itself. Never was it easier to gain a reputation as a seer, never was a following so rapidly and readily acquired. Teachers, prophets, sibyls, oracles, mystagogues, avatars, haruspices and mullahs roamed the land, gathering flocks about them as easily as holy men in nineteenth-century Russia, and any philosophy, from Zen Buddhism to macrobiotics and from violence as an end in itself to total inactivity as an end in *it*self, could be sure of a respectful hearing and a group of adherents, however temporary their adherence might prove.

Fashions changed, changed again, changed faster and still faster: fashions in politics, in political style, in causes, in music, in popular culture, in myths, in education, in beauty, in heroes and idols, in attitudes, in responses, in work, in love and friendship, in food, in newspapers, in entertainment, in fashion. What had once lasted a generation now lasted a year, what had lasted a year lasted a month, a week, a day. There was a restlessness in the time that communicated itself everywhere and to everyone, that communicated itself to the very sounds in Britain's air, the stones beneath Britain's feet. These stones shifted as she walked ahead with her once-purposeful stride, so that she began to stumble, then to stagger, then to fall down. Eventually she had fallen down so often that she was not only covered in mud but the laughing-stock of the passers-by. '*Die englische Krankheit*' was a phrase coined in the Sixties by the Germans, and that was not the worst, for Britain even came to be known as 'the sick man of Europe', a title once reserved for the crumbling Ottoman Empire.

Thus diseased, thus befezzed, she rose again and again to her feet, only to fall as often as she rose. The consequence was that she became dazed, and frequently, on rising, began to go backwards under the impression that she was going forwards; in time things grew even worse, and she began to lose all sense of which was which.

Youth would be served; but while established society, with one dropping eye, denounced the young in terms which grew more bitter as the decade wore on, it hastened, with the other, auspicious one, to minister to youth's needs, or supposed needs. Few, at the beginning of the Sixties, would have guessed that the voting age would have been lowered by the end to eighteen; fewer still could have foreseen with how little argument and dissension the change would go through.

Throughout the decade, indeed, ancient citadels, once thought impregnable, were falling at the first shot, and sometimes even at the waving of a musket. The traditional reserve of the British, once thought by other peoples to be indistinguishable from catalepsy, collapsed to such an extent that when, just before the end of the decade, a young couple publicly performed the act of love at an open-air concert in the Isle of Wight, it raised hardly a stir, and what stir it did raise was largely admiring. ('Go on, baby,' the spectators encouragingly cried, 'do your thing'; and others, not present, seemed to share, however fearfully, the same feeling.)

Restraints were being abandoned wholesale; in the last days of the decade a film critic was complaining that the censor (his will sapped, his powers eroded) was discriminating unfairly between the sexes by permitting men to achieve orgasm on screen, but not women; nobody doubted that equality in this matter would be reached before the Seventies were many months old.

Quite right too, if other signs of the times were to be trusted; in fashion, the sexes came closer and closer throughout the decade, until Unisex came upon the scene and began to suggest that the identity of clothing styles implied an identity of sexuality too, until many would fain have called the decade the Androgynous Sixties. That forms of privacy once thought inviolate were no longer so was also suggested by the announcement from the High Priestess of Sixties fashion, Mary Quant, that pubic hair would, in the succeeding decade, become 'a fashion emphasis', a prophecy which was greeted with a good deal of ridicule; it was noticeable, however, that none was so sure of the basis of his ridicule as to deny the possibility.

Certainty had vanished, conviction was vanishing, will itself was crumbling, as those behind cried 'Forward!' and those before cried 'Back!', and both cries were constantly drowned by a mysterious muttering of 'Sideways! Sideways!', which came none knew whence.

The restlessness communicated itself to all levels of society, all ages, all degrees of affluence or poverty, all political and religious persuasions, all fields of endeavour. Eventually it began to seem as though Timon's curse had come true:

> Matrons, turn incontinent!
> Obedience fail in children! Slaves and fools,
> Pluck the grave wrinkled senate from the bench,
> And minister in their steads! To general filths
> Convert, o' the instant, green virginity!
> Do't in your parents' eyes! Bankrupts, hold fast;
> Rather than render back, out with your knives,
> And cut your trusters' throats! Bound servants, steal!
> Large-handed robbers your grave masters are,
> And pill by law. Maid, to thy master's bed,
> Thy mistress is o' the brothel. Son of sixteen,
> Pluck the lin'd crutch from thy old limping sire,
> With it, beat out his brains. Piety and fear,
> Religion to the Gods, peace, justice, truth,
> Domestic awe, night-rest and neighbourhood,
> Instruction, manners, mysteries and trades,
> Degrees, observances, customs and laws,
> Decline to your confounding contraries
> And let confusion live!

Confusion lived all right, in the Sixties. Amid the confusion, those thrived who have always thrived on it. The Sixties saw an outcrop of rogues, large and small, on a gigantic scale; the rogues had little in common with each other but their realization, conscious or instinctive, that there was something in the atmosphere of the times that was propitious to their calling. Some men, for instance, exploited at the beginning of the decade a novel line which in other times might have proved unfruitful: they offered to take money from the public and play roulette with it, promising huge profits.

It might have been expected that these entrepreneurs would be asked why they should not use exclusively their own money, since their rapidly increasing profits would presumably provide them with sufficient working capital and thus enable them to dispense entirely with the administrative problems involved in appeals to the public. On the contrary; from all parts of the country sums large and small were sent, to be staked upon the fortunes of a rolling wheel, of which the only thing that could be demonstrated beyond argument was that the odds in favour of the house were never less than thirty-seven to thirty-six, and frequently more. Sentencing one Littledale, the promoter of such an enterprise who had promised his customers dividends of 100 per cent per annum and who now admitted to defalcations amounting to £22,000, the judge expressed his relief that such a villain was caught at last, but his satisfaction that the trust of the public would no longer be thus abused was short-lived, for within a few months many precisely similar schemes were in operation, neither the operators nor their victims being deterred by the unhappy example of their predecessors.

What put an end to such activities was not the rigour of the existing law at all, but new legislation which for good intentions and unhappy results had not been equalled since the Eighteenth Amendment and the Volstead Act, in the United States, sought to stop people drinking alcohol and resulted in many of them killing one another instead. The Betting and Gaming Act was meant to end the anomalies—of which there was no lack—in the legislation covering gambling in Britain. At the time the bill was being examined by Parliament, it was explained that its purpose was to enable innocent housewives to play whist for sixpences with their friends, and no less innocent vicars to hold raffles and devote the proceeds to the restoration of their churches. It became clear, however, that although the blameless housewife and the deserving vicar had indeed benefited from the new gambling legislation, so had many people far less innocent. All over the country betting-shops appeared, these being the fruits of that part of the Act that made legal, for the first time, off-course cash betting on horse- and dog-racing, thus putting an end at one stroke to the ancient profession of bookie's runner and also to a source of extra income for the undeniably underpaid police force, many of whose members had for years supplemented their income by accepting ten bob or so, at more or less regular intervals, to look the other way when the bookie's runner was running. Many of these betting-shops were owned, and even managed, by most respectable people; others, however, were not, and all, under whichever head they came, were subject to the activities of yet another group, who fell decidedly into the second or less legitimate category, and who realized that a protection racket offered the possibility of an income far more regular, and far less subject to chance, than running the betting-shops themselves. Gangs of these protectors sprang up, and from time to time flung home-made petrol-bombs, often surprisingly effective, through the windows of establishments whose owners or managers had refused to pay the tribute-money.

Much more remarkable, however, was the situation that followed the legalization of casinos, which was also part of the Act. It was stipulated in the legislation that all players should have an equal chance and that the house should have no advantage, making its income solely from the entrance fee or subscription it charged to players; thus roulette could not be played with a zero on the wheel, at any rate if the traditional function of the zero were to be retained.

This provision proving irksome and unprofitable to the casino operators, it was ignored or evaded, and such was the apparent desire of the British to accept the certainty of losing money in the long run in return for the remote possibility of winning it in the short that instead of the players at the casinos insisting that the law should be observed by the proprietors, they co-operated enthusiastically in every scheme the proprietors devised to keep their advantage, a new scheme being thought out every time the courts ruled (in a series of cases brought by, or at the instigation of, a former M.P., Raymond Blackburn, who appeared to take the view that while the legislation existed it should be enforced) that the latest one contravened the law.

In a short time there were some *thousands* of casinos in the country, and their turnover ran into many millions of pounds a week, almost all of which, having been turned over, went into the pockets of the proprietors. It was not long before criminals, in both Britain and the United States, saw the advantages in this situation, and began to take part. Underworld interests in the United States were aroused and soon had a substantial and increasing stake in the British casino industry; some promoters would also fly parties of American gamblers over to play at the British tables.

Gradually the authorities became alarmed at the monster which had grown from their desire to help the housewife and the vicar, and from time to time an American gambling entrepreneur was deported from, or refused entry to, Britain, the most notable of these being George Raft, who observed crossly as he left that just because he had in his film career played many gangsters, it did not mean that he actually was one. The authorities made no reply; Raft was not, however, readmitted.

But this palliative proved quite inadequate, and eventually further, amending, legislation was introduced, and a Gambling Board set up to control and supervise the activities of the casinos and bingo-halls, so that both the criminals on the one hand, and the housewives and vicars on the other, would henceforth have the beady eye of the law far more closely upon them than before. To be the head of this new body the Government appointed Sir Stanley Raymond, who had previously been the chairman of

British Rail, a post in which he had certainly had the opportunity of familiarizing himself with the process of losing money. The death of most of Britain's casinos was confidently forecast, together with the elimination of the criminals from the control of the rest, and certainly Sir Stanley and his board started off with vigour, refusing a licence to some of the oldest and most famous of gambling-clubs, among them Crockford's. But by then the roots had struck deep, and it remained to be seen whether the gambling-fever loosed by the earlier Act would be ended by the second, or whether, as seemed much more likely, the disease would prove more powerful than the cure.

It must be said that Governments in the Sixties were not averse to fostering the gambling instinct in the people. Anxious to encourage lending to the State, by means of National Savings, and struck by the increasing reluctance of people to put their money into an investment of which it was possible to be quite certain that it would in time lose practically the whole of its value, Mr Macmillan had, in 1956, introduced Premium Bonds, which were not only doomed, like other Government securities, to lose their value, but did not even bear any interest, the only point in buying them, therefore, being the fact that, at regular intervals, a very small number of them were selected by lot to receive a prize, which might be as much as £5,000 for a bond that had cost only £1. To the amazement of many, such appallingly unfavourable terms resulted in substantial sales of the bonds. Thus the Macmillan Government, responsible as much as any of its predecessors for the depreciation of the currency, cashed in on the public's growing suspicion of investments which were unlikely to resist the corrosive effects of such depreciation, by offering them an investment that was certain to depreciate even more than most, and found that the public took to it enthusiastically. A more striking example of seething the kid in its mother's milk could hardly be imagined, and it was no wonder either that Mr Wilson, in Opposition when the scheme was instituted, described it with scorn as 'a squalid raffle', or that, on achieving office himself, he hastened to increase the top prize to £25,000.

But the rock on which the foundations of Britain's gambling-habits were laid remained untouched.

> The laws were very comical; to bet was voted lax,
> But your betting was the only thing that nobody could tax

said A. P. Herbert in the Thirties (in the only speech ever to have been made in the House of Commons in verse), and it was still true. As if by some deep instinct, no Government had ever dared to make betting winnings taxable as income, though during the Sixties various levies were imposed on betting, to loud cries of indignation from the bookmakers. The reluctance to tax betting had originally been part of the curious national hypocrisy that involved a refusal to admit that people bet at all (gambling debts, unlike all others, were not recoverable at civil law), and this was still widely believed to be the main cause of the continuing reluctance of Governments in the Sixties to face the prospect of making winners pay income-tax on their winnings as though they had earned them, or even as though they had not. But the moral content had long since disappeared; by the Sixties it was clear that it was fear of popular wrath that stayed Government's hand; and that fear, in turn, stemmed from the realization that Government's failure to prevent, or even materially reduce, the inexorable fall in the value of money through inflation needed a safety-valve, however imaginary it was for most people, and that the safety-valve could only take the form of the possibility of sudden riches. Since it had long been impossible for almost anybody to acquire substantial riches quickly, or even slowly, by the fruits of labour, there was left only the reliance on a windfall from the football pools, which, until a new style of defensive football increased the number of drawn games and thus sharply reduced the size of the biggest prizes, were paying out in some weeks sums of anything up to a third of a million pounds.

Expenditure on betting therefore continued to increase, though the share allocated to different forms of wager varied, and from time to time there was a brief flare of publicity as another beggar mounted his horse of wishes and discovered to his delight that it was real, even though he sometimes fell off with a thud before the steed had galloped far. The decade was littered with the couples whose marriages had ultimately collapsed under the strain of sudden and unprecedented wealth, and even with some hapless individuals who, freed from the restraint imposed by lack of funds with which to do so, proceeded to fulfil what must have been a longstanding subconscious desire by drinking themselves to death. Meanwhile, the churches and other groups altogether opposed to gambling continued to argue the case against it on moral and social grounds, though if they had truly grasped the nature of the problem they might have spent their time and resources campaigning for a stable currency.

Gambling did not by any means exhaust the rogueries of the decade. Other rogues, even more ingenious and enterprising than those who got rich from the casinos and the betting-shops, applied their imagination to the fields of high finance, seeking money from the public for the purposes of straightforward commercial investment, but putting it when received into their own pockets. Others, again, found rich pickings in the field of insurance, and especially motor-car insurance, presumably convincing the public that they had repealed the mathematical laws governing the actuarial basis of their trade, since nothing else could account for the low premiums which they charged. The most notable of these, Dr Savundra, was eventually sent to prison for a very long time, but not before he had persuaded hundreds of thousands of motorists to part with, in all, millions of pounds.

Even agriculture, man's eternal dream of getting back to the land from which his ancestors had come, was not safe from the activities of those who had discovered that the further the twentieth century wore on, the more ready were the people in it to imagine vain things. A Mr Mascall offered to sell pigs to the public, though the pigs were not on view; he thus went, almost incredibly, to the full length of the metaphor, yet the public bought his pigs by the thousand. His scheme was neat: the investor bought pigs; Mascall, it was understood, bred, fed, reared, fattened and sold them, sending the profits regularly and often. Should some investor, unworthily suspicious, demand to see his pigs, a small supply of pigs was kept for show purposes, with metal tags in their ears purporting to bear a number exclusive to the visiting investor but in fact doing duty for many. From the money which the credulous paid for buying the same pigs again and again, Mascall satisfied the first few, lucky, buyers, by sending them sums by way of profits which they found satisfactory, though not nearly so satisfactory as they would have found the sums which their benefactor was applying to his own use. Eventually, the money for satisfying the customers ran out, and shortly afterwards Mascall was run in.

No sooner was one promising avenue closed, however, than a hundred more opened, and Mascall, Littledale and Savundra, if they read of such things in their cells, must have recognized many of their successors as indeed worthy to carry the torch forward. One such scheme was of exquisite simplicity, and had the additional advantage of being almost certainly legal; the promoters would send goods to people who had not ordered them, and shortly afterwards would demand money in payment. A certain proportion always paid, believing that they were obliged to do so, and the tills at the other end rang merrily through the day, and perhaps, at busy seasons, through the night as well.

The Sixties echoed continuously to such things. One enterprising couple sold, for substantial sums, mysterious black boxes covered with wires, lamps and dials. They were supposed to be useful in the cure of a wide variety of diseases, and in the subsequent court proceedings witnesses testified to the beneficial effect the use of these machines had had on them; other, technical witnesses, their testimony felt to be less subjective, declared that the wires, lamps and dials were connected wholly at random, and that the box did not and could not have any effect whatever on its users, beneficial or otherwise. Great was the consternation among the faithful and the sceptical alike when the judge in Philips v. de la Warr ruled that although the box did not in fact bear out the claims made for it, the makers believed that it did, and that in consequence the disappointed among the purchasers could not recover the money they had paid.

It was not only the foolish who were fooled, not only the credulous who believed. Dr Francis Crick, for instance, would never describe himself, and would hardly be described by others, as one of nature's boobies. A Nobel prize-winner in the exacting field of molecular biology, with a third share in one of the most important discoveries ever made in this science (the structure of the DNA molecule, believed to be the ultimate 'building-block' from which life itself is constructed), Crick was appointed one of the first Fellows of Churchill College, Cambridge. (This foundation had been launched with a public appeal for funds, the organizers of which, taking a realistic view of human nature, had thoughtfully caused to be published, at regular intervals, advertisements showing the amount so far collected, with the names of the donors attached, those giving the largest sums being printed at the top.) While Churchill College was building, the question was raised, whether it should have a chapel attached, and those responsible for the project decided that it should. Whereupon some of the Fellows of the as yet non-existent college protested that such pandering to outworn superstition was unjustified, particularly since the money it was to cost (some £30,000) could be better spent. Deadlock ensued, broken by a wealthy Christian philanthropist, the Reverend Timothy Beaumont (subsequently ennobled as Lord Beaumont of Whitley), who offered to meet the entire cost of the chapel, thus simultaneously relieving the foundation's funds of pressure and its Fellows of embarrassment. To the astonishment of many who believed that scientists were rational, Crick refused to be relieved of his embarrassment in this manner, and insisted on resigning his Fellowship if the chapel were built, even at private expense. It was explained to him that he would not be expected to enter it; that no student would be compelled to attend services therein; that it need offend him no more than the existence of Canterbury Cathedral or the Woking Mosque. In vain; Crick, perhaps fearing that cowled monks and wimpled nuns would creep to his room in the dead of night and drag him into the chapel, there to practise upon him hideous rites ranging from baptism to crucifixion, insisted on resigning if the chapel were built. It was, and he did.

There were more elaborately organized forces at work. Scientology, which combined the jargon of pseudo-science with the fanaticism of pseudo-religion, had lain dormant in Britain during the Fifties, but burst forth like some uncontrollably spreading weed during the Sixties. Its founder, Ronald Hubbard, was about as plainly daft as it is given to men to be, believing passionately that the entire psychiatric profession of the world is engaged in a gigantic conspiracy to destroy not only all those who have dared to criticize it but thousands who have never done anything at all, and has in consequence transformed psychiatric hospitals and other institutions into concentration-camps, where the inmates are tortured and murdered by the thousand, and a constant stream of new victims is admitted, to undergo torture and murder in turn. The movement in its early days had concentrated on the pseudo-scientific side of its work, claiming to be able to transform the minds and lives of those who would sign up for the courses of treatment and instruction it offered and pay the substantial sums involved. Later, the movement began to call itself the Church of Scientology, and was registered as such in the State of California, a move which had the incidental advantage of bringing it within the ambit of laws which granted substantial fiscal advantages to organizations that could plausibly claim to be religious; the adherents were thus no doubt reinforced in their view that they were smiled upon by the Lord, or at any rate the State of California.

The cult gained adherents at an alarming, though considering the nature of the decade unsurprising, rate, protests about its harmful effects gathering volume throughout the decade until, shortly before its end, an official inquiry was set up on the orders of the Minister of Health, who had just been directly accused, in the organization's journal, of mass murder.

The delights of scientology proving too tame for some – much as it is argued (though also denied) that the 'soft' drugs presently seem too tame for their users, so that they graduate, with fatal effect, to the 'hard'—a group broke away from the parent body, for all the world as if determined to repeat the history of Christianity down to the last detail, and went into business separately under the name of The Process. Its beliefs and practices were even more bizarre than those of Scientology, and after more than one of its adherents had suffered nervous breakdown, and some fierce public criticism of it had been voiced, those in charge thought it best to move from Britain to more congenial climates.

One avenue was closed in the Sixties, and for this one relief the gullible could be thankful (though it is a well recognized fact that the gullible are seldom thankful to those who suppress the gull-catchers; not only are a fool and his money soon parted, but the fool at any rate has rarely been known to thank the man who brings it back): though Moral Re-Armament still existed, it was heard from little. Early in the decade it ventured on a spectacular and comic action in Edinburgh; at the Festival, a theatrical 'happening' had been staged, in which for a few seconds a glimpse was caught, by exceptionally wide-awake members of the audience, of a girl who might well, according to some who saw the event, have been naked. Local M.R.A. members began an agitation, and eventually brought a prosecution against the organizers for an indecent exhibition, several of them going into the witness-box to declare that they had seen a naked girl and been profoundly shocked. One of them, from his demeanour, suggested that the sight of a naked girl might well have shocked him, or even unhinged his reason entirely, but he rather weakened this Saint-Anthony-like impression by claiming to be a journalist and, on being pressed as to the nature of his journalism, producing as the only example he could actually remember a letter he had once had printed in the *Scotsman*. The action resulted in the acquittal of all concerned. Moreover, at the decade's end it was difficult to remember the holy rage, so few years previously, over the naked girl at Edinburgh, for the abolition of the Lord

Chamberlain's power to censor plays, and the virtual abdication of the Board of Film Censors', resulted in a rush of nudity to stage and screen, and after a time it began to seem that hardly a play could be put on without the exposure of pudenda of various kinds, and hardly a film screened without its obligatory ration of pubic hair. Finally, as was inevitable, the habit spread to the audience, and a young lady at a concert in the Albert Hall took off all her clothes, though it was noted ungallantly that what she thus revealed would hardly have inflamed the passions of the man in the Edinburgh witness-box, and the suspicion grew that she had found it necessary to undress in public because she could find few to care whether or no she undressed in private.

* * *

The more credulous the age became, the more it was said to be a rationalist, a sceptical time, without roots or faith, in which the people would not willingly deprive themselves of any of the comforts and pleasures of the flesh, not even for the hope of salvation or the fear of damnation. Those who deplored such a state of affairs cried woe, while their opponents denied that it was really happening, and these were quite right, for in fact it had been a long time since so many flagellant orders were on the roads, scourging themselves for the sake of Christ, even though in some cases it was a very dubious Christ. Jehovah's Witnesses, awaiting the Last Day with the quiet kind of satisfaction that a man gets in the dry season when he knows his neighbour's house is not insured against fire, increased their numbers daily, so that their regular ritual gatherings, which at the beginning of the decade took place in a small hall in the middle of London, by the end of it would fit into nothing smaller than Wembley Stadium. At every street corner Jehovah's devotees were to be found, selling copies of the *Watchtower*, with its biblical injunctions to refrain from everything that the sinful world offered, and its attendant promise of eternal bliss made even better by the scent of roast flesh from the sinners down below. On Sunday mornings worldly lie-a-beds would be disturbed by ominous knockings at their door, to find further Witnesses, with more *Watchtowers*, at the step, these for some reason usually women, and invariably, the wickedness of the world being what it was, in pairs; the conversion-rate was never disclosed, but must, if the evidence of Wembley Stadium was anything to go by, have been considerable.

Even more austere was the practice of another sect, the Exclusive Brethren, who had broken away from the long-established Plymouth Brethren on the grounds that these had let the world corrupt the pure faith. The Exclusives took with an awful and undeviating literalness the Biblical command: 'Be ye not equally yoked together with unbelievers'; and their proselytizing, together with the results that flowed from it, caused demands to be made for the leader of the sect, an American, to be barred from Britain, though these were refused by the authorities. The Exclusive Brethren were forbidden by the tenets of their faith to have any social contact with anyone not of the order, to eat or sleep with any such, to let any child born in the truth play with any outside, to own radio sets, television sets, dogs or cats, to visit theatres, cinemas or public-houses, to study at universities, or to belong to any kind of organization that included the un-Exclusive—even, it transpired, the Automobile Association. A series of case-histories was revealed in each of which much misery had been caused by the Brethren's doctrines. Exclusive husbands had parted from non-Exclusive wives and vice versa, families had broken up, parent been set against child and child against parent; in some cases the pressures had been such as to cause suicides, whereat Parliament itself became disturbed at the growing popularity of the cult, though to little effective purpose, and its influence only began to wane when the American leader of it visited Britain once too often, was set upon by a number of those who had seen their marriages or homes disintegrate under its influence, and narrowly escaped with his life. He returned hastily to the United States, whence there presently came an announcement that some of the harsher rules of the order were to be relaxed, though this was the worst possible news for some, who sought not relaxation but ever-fiercer harshness, and a breakaway organization rapidly appeared which rejected the easier life ordered by the parent body. The criers of woe continued, however, to declare that nobody in the country cared any more for anything but their own pleasure, and were widely reported, though the scepticism with which such cries would have been greeted by the new and even more Exclusive Brethren, had they heard about them, was unfortunately diminished by the fact that they were also forbidden to read newspapers.

The prophets of doom and woe, those who declared that the end was at hand, and that sinful man was to be punished for his sin, every now and again during the decade seemed even to the more sceptical to have cause to believe they were right. And occasionally the lesson was learnt in circumstances of such appalling but inevitable atavism that it was indeed tempting to draw from it conclusions about earthly crime and heavenly punishment.

In the midst of this advanced century the country reverted to the most ancient ritual of all, buried for centuries beneath layer after layer of civilization, so that it would have been thought beyond the reach of even the most determined archaeologist of the mind. All over England men made burnt offerings to gods of their forgotten past, as man had done since even before he was fully man. 'Thou shalt burn the whole ram upon the altar: it is a burnt offering unto the Lord: it is a sweet savour, an offering made by fire unto the Lord.' Thus spake Exodus, with the evident approval of the Lord, and thus, thousands of years later, the ancient urge stirred in men's souls, and pyres of burnt offerings were made to a God who had turned his face from them:

> Although we started to make the pyre on Sunday morning, it took until Wednesday to complete it. We used 450 bales of straw, three lorry-loads of tyres, 200 gallons of oil, 250 railway sleepers and 45 tons of coal ... Ninety yards long and twenty feet wide, it burned for three days.[1]

[1] Ralph Whitlock, *The Great Cattle Plague* (John Baker, London, 1968), Ch. V, p. 61.

Moses would have admired, Aaron marvelled, to see the resources of modern technology thus harnessed, to outdo the puny efforts of the Old Testament, and to fill the nostrils of the Lord with the sweet savour, made perhaps more sweet with straw, tyres, oil, railway sleepers and coal; for on the pyre here described one hundred and forty of the finest Friesian cows were piled, together with proportionate numbers of calves, and burned for an offering, that the Lord might be pleased to lift his hand from man and turn away the plague.

The plague was foot-and-mouth disease, and the Lord seemed to have it in for the cattle-farmers of Britain. Every year for forty-five years the plague had returned, despite the burnt-offerings, but now it had come as never before, stalking the land like some invisible sickle wielded by a mad farm-hand. Descriptions of its progress are indistinguishable from those of the Black Death.

> In a way, the farms first stricken by the plague were the lucky ones. They at least knew the worst. For those which escaped to begin with, the tension built up unbearably. For weeks they lived in a state of siege, taking every conceivable precaution but knowing that all their efforts might be in vain. The disease was capricious. It would sweep by them, taking in most of their neighbours in a broad swathe; then, several weeks later, would double back and strike at random a farm here and there that had hitherto escaped.[1]

Scientific farming, or at least the alliance of bureaucracy with agriculture, meant that the figures of the beasts sacrificed as burnt-offerings were recorded with ghastly precision; in the fifty-five days during which the epidemic raged, there were

[1] Ibid., p. 64. Cf. Philip Ziegler, *The Black Death* (Collins, London, 1969), Ch. VIII, p. 137: 'The infection no longer advanced regularly from point to point but sprang up simultaneously in a hundred places; reaching its peak, for no reason that can be established, in Norfolk and Suffolk before Cambridgeshire; in Hampshire before Surrey: in Warwickshire before Worcestershire. By July it was spreading across the northern counties, by the end of the year nowhere had been spared. Through winter and summer, through flood and drought; against old and young, weak and strong; the disease went imperviously on its way.'

slaughtered 15 goats, 77,592 sheep, 98,527 pigs and 180,664 cattle—a total of 356,798 beasts, greater by three times than the highest total ever previously recorded. Foot-and-mouth disease had been known in Britain for one hundred and thirty years, and in all that time no method of dealing with it had ever been devised other than the slaughter of the whole herd in which even one scapegoat had been found with the infection. It was a salutary reminder, in a decade which one would have thought needed no such reminders but clearly did, that man was not yet in control of his environment. While the disease was at its height, while the sky over the farming counties of England and Wales was dark with the smoke from the pyres on which hecatombs of cattle were burning to illustrate how helpless, with all the resources of civilization, man still was, Dr Edmund Leach, Provost of King's College, Cambridge, was delivering the Reith Lectures on the B.B.C. radio, saying in the first words of the first of the series:

> Men have become like gods. Isn't it about time that we understood our divinity? Science offers us total mastery over our environment and over our destiny, yet instead of rejoicing we feel deeply afraid. Why should this be?[1]

It is possible that the Cheshire farmer who recounted the slaughter of all the livestock on all his five farms, and ended with an account of the strange and empty nature of his days, saying: 'We now hear radio programmes we never had time to hear before and we watch television for hours on end, but the one thing we cannot get used to is to go through the day without having a cow to milk, a calf to tend or even an old sow to feed',[2] may even, in his unaccustomed and unwelcome leisure, have heard Dr Leach's broadcasts. If so, what he thought of them has not been recorded.

Nor was it only the animals who were reminded, in the Sixties, that all flesh is as grass, and that however far man

[1] Edmund Leach, *A Runaway World?* (B.B.C., London, 1968), Ch. I, p. 1.

[2] Whitlock, op. cit., Ch. V, p. 68.

imagined he had got by then towards the complete control of his environment, there were still plenty of open doors through which uncertainty might enter. The outrageous metaphor of Poe's *Masque of the Red Death* might have been taken as the sign-manual of the decade. Disease, poverty, hunger, the pollution of air, water and soil, the congestion of cities, sporadic violence springing as much from psychological inadequacy as from causes social, economic or political – these afflictions, and a thousand more, dogged man's footsteps throughout the Sixties, as most of them had dogged him for centuries before, those which were new being frequently the result of a rash acceptance of science's offer to man of total mastery over his environment. If there was any moral to be drawn it was surely that if there were those who thought that the rainbow had been reduced to mathematics, the rainbow might yet have some surprises in store, and that it might be some time before man was total master of his environment, and even more time before he could behave like a god.

This lesson had also been learnt (or, more precisely, not learnt) even earlier in the decade when, in 1960 and 1961, a series of nightmare malformations of newly born children began to be recorded. Some were delivered without upper limbs, some without lower, some without either; others had hands joined directly to their shoulders, or feet growing directly from their hips; almost all were in other respects entirely normal, especially in their minds, so that they were all too soon to realize in what tragic way nature had jested with them, unlike the child stunted in mind and body alike, spared (we like to think) even the ability to be unhappy.

It presently came to light, however, that it was not nature who had so cruelly treated these children but man, and scientific man at that, for when sufficient of the deformed children had been born for a common cause of their deformations to be sought, it was eventually found that the mothers had in common the fact that they had, while pregnant, taken a mild and supposedly harmless drug called thalidomide, marketed in Britain (by the reputable Distillers' Company) under the name Distaval, and that this drug had produced the terrible effects on the children within the womb. Its sale was presently stopped in Britain and the other countries in which it had become popular, with the exception of the United States, a country with far more rigorous standards of testing, where new medical discoveries are concerned, than Britain, and in which sales of the drug had never been permitted in the first place. The thalidomide disaster might also have been taken as a warning against a too ready assumption that man was in complete control of himself and his environment. There is no evidence that it was, however, and a good deal that it wasn't, as the rest of the decade continued to resound to claims for new 'wonder-drugs' that were supposed to be going to put an end to any number of diseases that had once ravaged the world, but which were shortly relegated to the discard of man's unsuccessful experiments, like—the *locus classicus* of all such ventures up blind alleys—cortisone, which had been hailed on its first appearance as an infallible cure for rheumatism, arthritis and any number of related diseases, but which was eventually admitted, even in the gullible Sixties, to be little, if any, more use in the treatment of such ailments than aspirin.

Some were alarmed, in this decade so full of turnip-ghosts, at menaces entirely of their own devising, much as Pooh and Piglet had been so terrified by the tracks in the snow, which to them betokened rapidly increasing numbers of fierce woozles and fiercer wizzles, but which Christopher Robin pointed out were their own footprints, and seemed to be multiplying only because they were going round and round in circles and thus leaving two fresh sets of tracks at every circuit. Most alarming of these turnip-ghosts, and perhaps the most significant, was the horror of fluoride, and in particular of its addition by local authorities, under medical advice, to the water supply, so that everyone in the district would have to swallow his dose of fluoride whether he would or no.

The insistence on purity in the water supply, and the fear of its contamination, went deep, and a long way into the past, and on the way down and back it became inextricably mixed with other and odder things. The early exponents of racial purity, for instance, from whom Hitler had drawn much inspiration, were as insistent on the necessity of keeping the water uncontaminated as they were on the importance of keeping the blood undefiled; the belief may be traced back even further, to the medieval legend that the Jews were in the habit of poisoning wells from which Christians drew their water (Barnabas, in Marlowe's *Jew of Malta*, proudly boasts of doing this), from which its descent to modern anti-Semitism is not difficult to follow. It was, for instance, curious and noteworthy that the most extreme of all the British followers of Hitler's theories, Arnold Leese, divided his energies almost equally between calling for the extermination of the Jews and insisting on the purification of the water supply. Blood and water, so often in human history used together in ritual, so often symbolic, so often dominant in men's minds, came together again in the Sixties, and produced one of the strangest campaigns ever waged at the borders of sanity; for though of course it was not at all true that all the anti-fluoride campaigners stood politically on the very far Right, it *was* true that most of the extremist right-wing groups did insist that fluoridation was a wicked plot, almost certainly devised by the Jews to bring about the enfeeblement, and loss of virility, of the Gentiles, so that they might go the more easily about their nefarious programme of conquest from within.

Amid all this, what tended to be forgotten was the mild purpose of adding, in areas deficient in natural fluoride, minute amounts to the water supply. It was the preservation and improvement of the nation's teeth, since it had been shown that the appallingly high incidence of dental caries could be much reduced if greater care were taken of the teeth in childhood, and that remarkable results in such care and preservation had been achieved by the fluoridation of water. This reasonable argument, however, had no effect on the strictly non-rational fears of the campaigners against fluoride, who managed at the same time to argue that fluoride had no such beneficial effect on teeth, that it did but that the beneficial effect was far outweighed by harmful side-effects, and that the argument from the effects was anyway irrelevant, as the only thing that should be considered was the inalienable right of the people not to have substances other than water pouring out of their taps without their having been consulted in the matter.

This last, it must be said, was a reasonable point, and had the campaigners concentrated on it they might have got further, though it is doubtful whether even then they would have got very far, for the certainty of the authorities that they knew what was good for the people, and their determination to see that the people got it, were forces that by the Sixties had become so strong as to make almost impossible any effective resistance.

* * *

Talismans, charms, amulets and runic stones with wondrous powers abounded; a man would wear a copper bracelet to ward off rheumatism, for instance, and, when he found that he did not contract rheumatism, took this as triumphant vindication of the efficacy of the device. Another, no less insistent on his rationality, would fit a short length of steel chain to the back of his motor-car; this dangled down and touched the ground as the car sped along, and was supposed to ward off car-sickness, as the bracelet rheumatism. What such things had in common was a pseudo-scientific basis; this gave the believer a feeling of superiority over the heathen who, in his blindness, bows down to wood and stone, which, as everybody knows, are powerless to affect the lives of men, unlike copper bracelets and lengths of steel chain.

It amounted to a search for certainty, for reassurance. All ages have searched for such things, but never has there been such an age as this for dismissing as false conclusions the certainties and reassurances found in previous times. Orthodox religion would not do; authority – political, moral, parental, pedagogical – would not do; Significant Form would not do; materialism would not do. What would do? The market-place resounded with rival claims, the interesting difference in the case of the Sixties, as opposed to the market-place of earlier times, being that now it was the buyers, rather than the sellers, who were shouting the wares.

It happened in small things as well as large. A tiny clue was provided by the sudden rush, during the decade, to buy foods believed to be more wholesome, because more 'natural', than the buyer's customary fare. From being the province of a small and dedicated band, the shops selling natural foods, or 'health' foods as they were called, began to be patronized by ever-growing numbers of people, and the numbers of the shops themselves began in consequence to multiply, eventually springing up in almost every neighbourhood, and even, in some cases, being run by the same proprietors as the chains of food-stores which had done so much to turn people away from the processed food they sold in the direction of the natural.

In the big things, of course, it happened even more. Much faith was placed in gurus of all kinds, though the turnover was rapid, as the certainties they offered proved to be temporary, and the conviction they carried, brief. A Canadian professor, Marshall McLuhan, offered a new world-view, declaring in a succession of books that the printed word was finished. Enthusiastically taken up, on both sides of the Atlantic, by those whose business it was to spot new trends, and, when unable to spot any, to create them, McLuhan became a party game, as, a decade or so earlier, had the U and Non-U categories of Professor Ross and Miss Nancy Mitford. Soon, many were to be heard decrying linear thinking, speaking of tactile values, and dividing media into cool and hot. Beneath it all there could be clearly sensed the desire of the customers to be told that there was a clue to the world and that McLuhan had found it.

Soon, however, new fashions in clues, and gurus, had overtaken Marshall McLuhan, and he fell from public notice with an abruptness that surprised only those who had never studied the history of primitive religion. He was said to have taken a job with an American University; then to be suffering from a brain tumour; then little more was heard of him, though his name echoed occasionally through the words of those who did not realize that the idol-smashers had been busy even with the idols they had themselves created, and who still thought McLuhan's a name to conjure with. His place did not long remain empty, being filled by a hairy Indian mystic who called himself the Maharishi, and filled the lobby of the Waldorf Hotel (where, in pleasant contrast to the previously accepted standards of Indian mystics, he held comfortable court) with an enchanting giggle. From the Waldorf he moved to television, taking his giggle with him, and appeared on several programmes, gathering around him a band of disciples all on the look-out for they knew not what.

Among these last were the Beatles, M.B.E., four pleasant young men who had grown up in a hard school, convinced that their problems would be solved when, and perhaps only when, they had a million pounds. Many believe as much, but it is given to few to test the belief; to the Beatles, however, it was given: heaped up, pressed down and running over. Not merely one million pounds, but several, came their way; to their dismay, they found that their problems were still not solved.

Could it be true, after all, that money did not bring happiness? There was certainly other evidence; over the decade, though happily only in one corner of it, there brooded the awful figure of Paul Getty, richest man in the world, a living proof, if his miserable, suspicious face was anything to go by, of the old saw. Getty lived in constant terror that somebody might come and take some of his money away. For years a story had circulated to the effect that he had installed in his home a coin-box telephone for the use of his house-guests; to the amazement of all who would think well of their fellow-men it turned out that the story was perfectly true.

Few decades could compare with the Sixties for the number of nouveaux riches who appeared, the entertainment business being the chief supplier of wealth beyond the dreams of those to whom it suddenly came. The confusion it spread among the more thoughtful of them was painful to behold, as they discovered that everything they had persuaded themselves since their (generally poor) childhoods, to the effect that as soon as they had amassed enough money they would live in a Nirvana of perpetual happiness, was untrue. They should have looked upon Paul Getty, who had always been vastly, immeasurably[1] wealthy, and yet went about looking like a man who cannot quite remember whether he remembered to turn the gas off before leaving home. In a sense it is a lesson that every generation has to learn, and in a sense it is implicit in the parable of the talents: that only he who brings human qualities to his money will receive more qualities from it. And if the richest man in the entire world, perhaps the richest man who had ever lived, had not learned the lesson, what hope was there for those who might suddenly find themselves possessed of wealth for the first time?

They had, these four young Beatles, set the fashion for a generation, changed for ever the idiom of popular music, attuned themselves to the spirit of the age. And yet they could not be at rest with the world or with their own spirits. More and more frantic grew the Beatles' search for this elusive inner peace, at times taking some of them across the very bounds of the law, into the forbidden and exciting regions of smoking that which they were not permitted to smoke. Alas, the forbidden and exciting region visited, it turned out to be more forbidden than exciting, and the search for certainty was on again.

And so they came to the Maharishi, plums ripe on the tree and to be collected for the shaking. The Maharishi shook, and when he went back to India he was followed by the Beatles and their ladies, and presently joined by other notabilities in search of certainty. These included Miss Mia Farrow, who had even briefly sought it in marriage to Mr Frank Sinatra and who later, in a court action at which it was given in evidence that she had used the word 'fuck' in a public place, declared that to urge upon another that he or she should get fucked, so far from being

[1] Literally; he once said he did not know how many millions he possessed, and that any man who did could not count himself as really rich.

Conduct Whereby a Breach of the Peace Might be Occasioned, was in fact the nicest thing she could wish on anybody, and in that sense she had urged it. (She was acquitted.)

The idyll in the Maharishi's close-carpeted eyrie did not last long. Soon Beatles and ladies, Farrow and other notabilities, had returned, some of them expressing grave disillusionment. It was never made quite clear what had upset them so, but there were hints that the Maharishi's courteous request, as payment for his spiritual ministrations, for ten per cent of a week's earnings, which in the case of the Beatles and a good week could amount to several hundred thousand pounds, might have had something to do with it; in any case the search was on once more.

Yet there was too much evidence of a new spirit, a new restlessness, in the age, for even its most extravagant manifestations to be dismissed as without portent.

> He keeps himself in superb physical trim ... He does not smoke or drink or take stimulants of any kind. He is a vegetarian and fasts for a whole day every week, usually on Thursdays ... He concluded sombrely that 'it is better to forgo all fantasies' and went off to brew up a couple of cups of clear tea and honey ... 'The best part of the flower becomes honey,' he said, 'and when I eat honey that flower becomes part of me' ... He recently sent back his rented television set and sold his Rolls-Royce.[1]

The Sixties must have been the first decade in which that could have been an account of a meeting with a young and very popular film actor, yet Terence Stamp, the subject of it, was disquietingly close to being representative of his generation among the successful. They ate strange food, calling it macrobiotic, and seemed to thrive on it; they dabbled in strange religion, calling it Zen Buddhism, and seemed to grow calm on it; they wore strange clothes, calling them fashionable, and lo! the clothes became fashionable among many who had noticed that their exemplars were famous, and perhaps thought that if they imi-

[1] Herbert Kretzmer, *Daily Express*.

tated them exactly enough they would discover the secret, and that they too would thus become famous, and perhaps not only famous but rich. Few did, and most after a time drifted back into more conventionally acceptable modes of life, though some never did recover their original equilibrium and, failing also to gain inner harmony on the one hand or riches on the other, lent some strength to the complaint that the successful were leading astray many of weak will and foolish judgment. Most celebrated of all the experimenters in other-worldly ways of life were some of those very Beatles, one of whom, towards the end of the decade, caused great offence to many by going to bed in public with his new bride, a Japanese lady who was variously described as a sculptress and a film-maker, though none could remember seeing any sculpture by her, and the only film she was known to have made consisted entirely of shots of naked buttocks moving, with more or less grace, away from the camera. Mr and Mrs John Lennon, then, having been married, elected to spend their honeymoon entirely in bed, a custom which was, after all, not entirely original. What made their honeymoon different from most is that it was spent in conditions of extreme public exposure, in a suite at the Hilton Hotel, Amsterdam, to which reporters, interviewers, newspaper and television photographers and other interested parties were free to come, and in suitable cases invited to join them in the bed, and there celebrate with the loving couple what was supposed to be the point of the entire proceedings, to wit a demonstration on behalf of personal and international peace. To this end, the walls of the bedroom were decorated with signs reading 'Bed Peace', 'Hair Peace', 'Stay in Bed', and 'Grow Your Hair', and the peaceful two argued, reasonably enough, that if everyone stayed in bed, occupying themselves in growing their hair, there would be no wars. To the question, what would happen if most stayed in bed and grew their hair but a few of the more ruthless declined to do so, they had clearly not addressed themselves, for the philosophy behind the performance was summed up by Mr Lennon, who said that all would be well if the Vietnamese, both North and South, would only take their trousers off, followed by the Arabs, the Israelis, the Russians and the Americans, while Mrs Lennon unwittingly touched upon the fallacy in the argument by proclaiming that their mood could be summed up in the words: 'Remove your pants before resorting to violence.' It might, of course, be objected that this is the spirit which in practice presumably guides every rapist, but granting that Mrs Lennon meant to say that he who removes his pants will be unable to resort to violence, it still left unresolved the problem of what to do about those whose pants stayed resolutely on, and still more the problem of how to deal with those who had learnt to do violence while naked from the waist down, or up, or even both.

All this confusion in the minds of the young people concerned, together with more or less unconscious feelings of envy, made it certain that they would in time become the recipients of much criticism, some of it almost alarmingly violent, and when it was revealed that the Lennons' honeymoon was being filmed throughout, apparently with commercial ends in view, great fury did indeed break out. Some, observing it, concluded that those who are created by publicity will inevitably be destroyed by it, and instanced the many popular stars who had waxed and waned in the past, waxing when, either by design, or by accident, they caught a popular mood, and waning when a new mood demanded a new fashion and a new idol.[1] Where, these sceptics asked of those who insisted that the Beatles were the harbingers of a new style of living, is Larry Page, once known euphonically as 'the teenage rage'? Where is Terry Dene? Where is Johnny Ray, before whom young girls would faint in ecstasy, not all of them paid to do so by public relations officers?

It cannot be denied that much of the nonsense talked by the young idols, in particular Mr and Mrs Lennon, invited much of the criticism, though as against that one might reflect that the

[1] No method of predicting when, and to whom, this will happen has yet been devised; presumably, if one were, no impresario would ever be unsuccessful. And compare the unpredictable and inexplicable way in which, throughout the Sixties, restaurants went violently in and out of fashion, the food and wine and service remaining exactly the same throughout.

intimate conversation of the newly married is not usually expected to be either coherent or profound, though as against *that* one might reflect that the intimate conversation of the newly married is not usually expected to be filmed, recorded and made public. Nor can it be denied that much of the nonsense, even when it was not so extreme or so obtrusive as to invite the more extreme or obtrusive criticism, was still nonsense. Nevertheless it differed from most of the nonsense talked, under the guise of philosophy, by those who were in the business of making money out of popular entertainment[1] in two crucial particulars. First, there was nothing either proselytizing or pernicious about it; second, it was gentle, introspective, and pacific. A deep sense of unease afflicted many of those who studied this phenomenon, so much so that their unease took the form of extreme hostility to it; it seemed as though they feared for their ordered, aggressive and interfering world, though in truth there was little danger to it from the young people who sat cross-legged on the floor in caftans and believed that, as Mr Stamp put it, 'We are, literally, what we eat.' At the back of much of the more savage criticisms could be detected a fear of the rejection by those criticized not merely of the values of adult and organized society, but of the forms and processes of its organization. It was not possible to imagine Mr Stamp voting in an election, Mr and Mrs Lennon becoming active participants in the work of the Blackheath Society, or Mr Paul McCartney joining the Civil Defence organization in a voluntary capacity. At the back of the hostility, therefore, there was after all some cause for concern, for if enough people decline to vote in elections, to join the Blackheath Society or to learn in their spare time how to handle the stirrup-pump and recognize the symptoms of radiation-sickness, the country will be in a bad way. All healthy societies can tolerate dissent, even vigorous dissent, and the amount they can tolerate is often a good

[1] E.g., the 'philosophy' of Mr Hugh Hefner, proprietor-editor of *Playboy* and impresario of the 'Bunny Clubs', of which it has been pertinently said that it would not impress anyone with as much knowledge of the subject as can be gained by catching sight of a copy of a popular philosophical digest in a bookcase on the other side of a fairly large room.

guide to the health of the society; but few can tolerate more than a minimal quantity of total rejection without becoming distinctly uneasy at what might happen if the rejection spread. 'Tune in, turn on, drop out' was a slogan popular among many of the youth in the United States, and to some extent in Britain, and it may be that the danger in it, unrecognized by those who used it (for whom in many, if not most, cases it was entirely a personal guide to behaviour and not a recommendation to others to emulate their example), had been sensed by those whose lives, to a larger extent than those of most people, depended upon the participation of the whole community; this might, therefore, explain the high incidence of hostility in middle-class circles, whose inhabitants stood to lose most from the rejection by any sizeable number of the society by which (and, it sometimes seemed, for which) they lived.

Not surprisingly, given the strange things that were floating in the air of the times, astrology flourished as never before. In a single week, it was possible for one born in May to be told that he was the soul-mate of all the September-born and for one born in September to be assured that no alliance with one born in May could possibly succeed, and for both to believe.

For there was no amount of manifest absurdity that could deter those who wanted to believe from believing. Many of those in the trade consequently waxed successful, even enormously rich as, by public demonstration and private consultation, they exhibited their supposedly occult powers. Every now and again, some public figure would admit, more or less shamefacedly (but it could be observed that the shame lessened as the shadows of the decade grew longer), to visiting, regularly or occasionally, an astrologer, whereupon the astrologer in question took larger consulting-rooms and hired an extra receptionist.

One of the most notable was Maurice Woodruff, who had been at it for as long as anyone could remember. At the very beginning of the decade he had been hired to ply his curious trade in the *Sunday Dispatch*, and his engagement drew a letter of fierce protest to that newspaper by a number of distinguished writers who had themselves contributed to its pages. The dog, not the flea, died; the *Sunday Dispatch* is no more, but Woodruff to this day waxes ever more famous and wealthy.

A march was stolen on Woodruff, towards the end of the Sixties, by rivals who, more brazen or more enterprising, began to claim that their horoscopes were prepared by computer, and to invite customers to send their names and birthdates, accompanied by a sizable sum (a reduction for quantity being offered in the case of multiple applications), when they would receive in return individually and electronically prepared charts of their lives and fortunes. Woodruff himself departed for newer and lusher, not to say greener, pastures in the United States, and there flourished more than ever, amid the astonishing boom in his trade that the decade had there produced, one of its most significant aspects being the extent of its attraction for young people.

In the circumstances it is hardly surprising that the Sixties also turned out to be the great age of flying saucers; these craft, supposedly from outer space, had had a brief vogue in the previous decade, when many people had been convinced that they had seen Unidentified Flying Objects (as they came to be called officially) moving across the sky at great speed. But it was in the Sixties that the things became most popular, and many more books were published the authors of which actually claimed to have observed extra-terrestrial craft landing, and to have met and talked with the occupants. As, throughout the Sixties, man's first voyage to other worlds came closer, and finally took place when the decade had only a twentieth of its course to run, so it seemed more and more likely that the traffic must also be going the other way, and since the evidence of extra-terrestrial visitors was slim, and much of it, including the photographs, so obviously and pathetically faked that it must have put off even some of the most gullible, there could be only one conclusion, to wit, that conclusive evidence existed, but was being suppressed. 'Thousands of people', said the *Sunday Express*, 'have seen "things in the sky" ':

> The official attitude is usually one of ridicule. But sometimes there is a mystifying reticence. Why? Could it be that the Government knows more about 'flying saucers' than it is willing to tell the public?

* * *

It was by no means only a matter of astrology and flying saucers; the psychopathology of gullibility was explored in some detail during the 1960s. Not long after President John Kennedy was assassinated by Lee Harvey Oswald an entire industry arose, the product of which was a variety of theories about the assassination, which theories had nothing in common but their agreement that, whoever had assassinated the President, it was not Oswald, or at any rate not he alone. The industry originated in the United States, its leading industrialists including the enchantingly palindromic Revilo P. Oliver, who declared that the President was a Communist agent who had been assassinated because he had begun to jib at carrying out the orders of his masters, and another called Popkin, who insisted that it had all been done with doubles, much as, during the Second World War, some had believed that Hitler had been dead for many years and his place supplied by a man, manipulated as a puppet by the remaining Nazi leaders, who happened miraculously to bear an exact resemblance to the dead Führer.

Presently, as was inevitable, the industry put down roots in Britain. An organization called the 'Who Killed Kennedy? Committee' was set up, attracting to itself such thinkers as Caroline Wedgwood Benn and Kenneth Tynan, and it was presently to be seen and heard casting doubt on the official conclusion on the assassination that had been come to by the commission appointed to investigate it, who had published their conclusions in one fat volume of a report and twenty-six attendant volumes of evidence.

The industry received a serious setback when a branch factory was set up under the managership of Hugh Trevor-Roper,

Regius Professor of History in the University of Oxford. The acquisition of so outstanding a figure was greeted with joy throughout the industry, but the joy proved short-lived, and died when the professor's major contribution to the subject was published, which followed the general line of the American head of the industry, Mr Mark Lane, a man who had been quicker than any to see the possible fruits of investment in the business. The professor's contribution made a great stir, until it was pointed out that his facts were in large measure wrong and his conclusions in even larger measure untenable, and critics more extreme than some went so far as to suggest that he can hardly have read the report he had so savagely denounced. Certainly he can hardly have read it with much care; but even such a dereliction of scholarly duty was nothing compared to the one perpetuated by Bertrand Russell, who put out a statement denouncing the commission's conclusions on the very day they appeared, subsequently admitting, in an unguarded moment (and in print, which made attempts to explain his admission away less than wholly convincing), that he had not read the report. Slowly, the industry declined, and its members took up other activities, though one British publishing house, Peter Dawnay, went into the industry so enthusiastically that after a time it seemed that their entire output was devoted to its products, one Joesten producing, at regular and ever-shortening intervals, books demonstrating the falsity of all theories about the assassination but his own, which were of a quality to make Messrs Lane, Oliver, Popkin, Tynan and Trevor-Roper appear particularly hard-headed sceptics.

There were subsequent attempts to encourage the growth of cuttings taken from this insane root that had taken so many reasons prisoner. When the Secretary-General of the United Nations, Dag Hammarskjöld, was killed in an aeroplane crash during the troubles in the Congo, stories were quickly available to the effect that his plane had been the subject of sabotage, and after a time the story was embellished to include a sub-story suggesting that Hammarskjold, shortly before his death, had himself arranged the death of Patrice Lumumba, the African leader whose murder by a rival group in the Congo was probably the only wholly beneficial thing that had happened to that unhappy country since the exposure by Roger Casement in 1903 of the atrocities committed there by the Belgians.

Towards the end of the decade a play was written about the death of Hammarskjold by Dr Conor Cruise O'Brien, the confusion in whose mind had been amply demonstrated in a celebrated magazine-article he had written to show that the freedom and influence accorded to writers in the Soviet Union compared favourably with that achieved by writers in countries such as Britain and the United States. O'Brien's play was largely constructed out of conspiracy-theories, but so far from its being taken with the seriousness it deserved, managements struggled energetically for the right to put it on a stage, that same Kenneth Tynan who had worked so hard in the Who Killed Kennedy? industry, and was now *Dramaturg* at the National Theatre, being narrowly defeated in his efforts to gain the privilege.

Tynan therefore had to rest on the laurels he had acquired shortly before, from his part in the staging of *Soldiers*, a play by Rolf Hochhuth which in part suggests not only that the death of the Polish leader General Sikorski, in 1943, was the result of planned sabotage, but that the sabotage in question had been arranged by Lord Cherwell, chief scientific adviser to Winston Churchill, with Churchill's passive connivance. It now seemed possible to believe that no public man in modern times had ever met his death except as the result of a conspiracy, and several, including Tynan, apparently did believe just that. There was, alas, no shortage of assassinations to feed the theory. When President Kennedy's brother Robert was shot dead during the campaign for the Democratic Presidential nomination of 1968 it was not long before the original industry was revived and factories long since silent and deserted sprang to life again, the Joesten-Dawnay branch being the first on the market with a product linking the two assassinations, with admirable economy, as the work of a single conspiracy. And when James Earl Ray, charged with the assassination of the American Negro leader Martin Luther King, pleaded guilty and was sentenced to ninety-nine years' imprisonment, it was not long before voices could be heard insisting that he too had been the agent of a conspiracy, and his victim marked down by sinister forces who had chosen as their instrument (as had those responsible for the deaths of the Kennedy brothers) a man with a record of instability so great that he would have been most unlikely to be selected by any self-respecting conspirator to run an errand to a shop round the corner.

The public controversy caused by *Soldiers* concentrated mainly on the affront to Churchill's memory, most spiritedly defended first by his son Randolph and then, after Randolph's death, by his grandson, Winston Churchill Junior; but in the course of it accusations and counter-accusations were made as to the good faith of many involved in it, and eventually the writs began to fly, and legal action even threatened to come between Tynan and Professor Trevor-Roper, who had laboured so happily together in the Kennedy vineyard but now fell out most grievously. Meanwhile Hochhuth insisted that he had evidence which proved his theory, but that it was locked up in a Swiss bank and would thus remain for fifty years, though no entirely satisfactory reason for this arrangement was ever forthcoming.

Still the frantic hunt for certainty went on. What else, after all, was the belief that mad or half-mad individuals could not, by killing public men, affect the course of history? For such a belief requires that only broad currents are allowed to do so, and the killing of public men must therefore be the result of plots, which can, in proper circumstances, be fitted neatly into the definition of a broad current.

Wherever one looked there were lost souls crying out to be found. At the age of fifty-one an aircraft designer of repute, a Mr Petter, declared that industrial civilization is built on false foundations, the false foundations in question being money and power, and left for a life devoted entirely to contemplation in

Switzerland, a land not widely known for the practice of asceticism, or for that matter the theory of it. Most astonishing of all, perhaps, was the action of a fashionable hairdresser. (The Sixties were the age in which a number of trades, previously thought of as lowly ones and their practitioners of little account, had come into their own, and even into other people's. Barbers, photographers, models, singers – all jostled not only for money and fame, like other men, but for glory itself, and were not disappointed, their slightest activity being faithfully described in newspapers and magazines, several of the latter existing, on glossy paper, solely for this purpose, and their slightest word being no less faithfully recorded, the words of some of them being slight indeed.) The hairdresser, nicknamed Mr Teasy-Weasy, suddenly announced, at the height of his fashion, that his life was empty and meaningless, and departed abruptly for North Africa, there to seek a holy man in the Atlas Mountains who would fill his life with meaning once again. He returned shortly afterwards, his quest having proved fruitless; but the significant thing, after all, was that he had gone on it. If the very hairdressers found life empty, it was clear that the foundations might subside at any moment beneath us all.

No field was safe from the seekers, nor was their seeking safe from the conclusion that green wickerwork men were cycling round their hats. Dr Leslie Hotson announced to an understandably excited literary world that he had at last solved the mystery of the dedication of Shakespeare's Sonnets, and revealed that Mr W. H. was one William Hatcliffe. To the reasonable objection that there was no evidence that Shakespeare had ever had anything to do with this Hatcliffe, Hotson replied triumphantly that their connection was demonstrated, to his satisfaction at least, by a cipher cunningly concealed among the lines, and revealed only and at last by him, giving as example this:

W*hat* merit *live*d in me, that you should love

from Sonnet 72, suggesting that he had devised a system so

admirably flexible in its scope that it could be used to demonstrate the dedication of the Sonnets not only to all the familiar candidates, but to anybody at all, including King George III and Bernard Shaw.

Perhaps the most pathetic of all the gropings in the dark backward and abysm of time was the cautionary tale (but the Sixties were in no mood for caution where their myths were concerned) of Major Eatherly. By the beginning of the decade he was as firmly part of the received belief of millions as was the roundness of the earth, the fidelity of dogs, and the chivalry of King Arthur. Eatherly was the pilot of the aeroplane from which had been dropped the atomic bomb on Hiroshima. Shortly after the deed, he had repented of his part in it, and for the rest of his life sought expiation by demanding, and getting, punishment. This he had achieved by taking to a life of petty crime and mental breakdown; in and out of prison and hospital, he wandered through the world, a self-created Ishmael, taking the burdens of man's terrible sin on his own shoulders.

The perfect paradigm of our times, Eatherly narrowly escaped being compared to Jesus Christ, who also suffered on behalf of others. Millions shook their heads in admiration of the tidiness of it all; orthodox psychiatric opinion basked in the warmth of public approval, just at a time when many were beginning to mutter behind their hands at its claims and to suggest that its long reign was over, so that the certainties it provided would now have to be sought elsewhere. The whole orientation of the Left clasped Eatherly to its bosom, as the man who demonstrated that even the god of the godless was not mocked, and that he who takes the sword must perish by self-inflicted wounds.

The story grew, huge and solid; it could not be denied; nuclear weapons were the ultimate evil, and poor Major Eatherly, who pilfered from supermarkets under the very noses of the store detectives in order that he might be arrested and punished, had lived to prove it so. Eventually, as was inevitable, he was enshrined in a book[1] by Gunter Anders. Anders told the story

[1] *Burning Conscience* (Weidenfeld and Nicolson, London, 1962).

beautifully, touchingly, lingering on the moral to be drawn from the stark and inescapable facts.

Unfortunately it subsequently transpired that there was not a word of truth in any of it. With a crash that shook the decade, the whole elaborate structure was pushed over by a lamentably hard-headed American, William Bradford Huie,[1] who discovered, what had been open to all (including Anders) to discover, that Eatherly had never set foot in the aeroplane which bombed Hiroshima and therefore that whatever his undoubted defects of personality and his undoubted criminal record, they had, and could have had, nothing to do with feelings of guilt for committing the most awful military act of modern times. (Anders, at that point, vanished from the public eye, re-emerging some time later as one of the 'judges' of a bizarre court which was to put the United States on trial for its actions in Vietnam, and which differed from the great majority of judicial tribunals by announcing its verdict, which was one of guilty, before it had formally convened, let alone heard the evidence.) But Huie's version of the Eatherly myth, though it disposed of it, was not thought, in the circles in which Anders's version had had the force of scripture, quite *comme il faut*; some journals that had been keenest on the earlier version thought it best not to discuss the later, and to this day there are certainly many thousands, and possibly millions, who remain convinced that Major Claude Eatherly bombed Hiroshima and thereafter regretted having done so; so difficult was it to prise the decade away from such few certainties as it possessed, merely by demonstrating that they were built upon sand.

By the time the Seventies approached the thing had got right out of hand. Though disillusionment with the Maharishi had set in, it was felt that the potentialities of India as a provider of mental security were not exhausted, and the death during the decade of another and even odder mystic, Meher Baba, gave fresh strength to those who considered him the answer to whatever questions were troubling them. As long ago as 1931, on a visit

[1] *The Hiroshima Pilot* (Heinemann, London, 1964).

to London, he had been taken by some of his disciples to see a performance of *White Horse Inn* at the Coliseum Theatre, and had apparently been so struck by what he saw that he determined to remain silent for the rest of his life. From that time forth he never did speak word, communicating at first by means of a board covered with the letters of the alphabet, on which he spelt out what he wanted to say, and later, the board abandoned, entirely by signs. Meher Baba's career, and his strange powers, were documented by Mr Lionel Birch (himself no mean seeker after something or other, if the fact that he had been married seven times was anything to go by), who hinted strongly that Meher Baba might have been God, and certainly that many thought him so, supporting this thesis with the powerful, though imperfectly logical, argument that millions believed Jesus Christ to have been God, though had they been living at the time of his death they well might not have done so. Not long after that it was announced that a Worcestershire schoolgirl was studying, as one of the subjects for her 'A' levels, Black Magic and, the supply of instructors in this recondite area of learning being limited, was going for tuition to her local vicar, who said that he had no objection provided that she did not include first-hand fieldwork in her curriculum.

And yet, even in years so copiously provided with material on which madness could feed fat, there was one episode which stood out from the decade, and still stands out, as a monument to the willingness of man to suspend the operation of reason, on a scale about as great as the dancing manias of the Middle Ages, or the witch-hunts of a later era, both of which it may be said to have resembled in more than its scale. In July 1963 one of Britain's principal judges, Lord Denning (the Master of the Rolls), selected a leading Harley Street medical consultant and solemnly commanded him to examine the genitals of a distinguished Cabinet Minister, the examination being not to determine whether the Minister was suffering from disease, which is no business of the law, but solely so that the judge could be satisfied whether or no the genitals in question were the same as those to be found in a photograph that had figured as part of the evidence in a sensational divorce case among the nobility – the point being that the photograph had been so cropped that the head of the man in it was excluded, and his identity therefore unascertainable, or at any rate unascertained. The Harley Street consultant, whether for his usual fee was not disclosed, examined the genitals of the Cabinet Minister in question (who had readily agreed to the examination in order that his name, and presumably not only his name, might be cleared), and came to the conclusion that they were not, and could not be, the same as those in the photograph, and that their owner was therefore wholly free from blame in the matter of the divorce. This conclusion was later published by Lord Denning, along with other conclusions, many of them almost as remarkable. But how it came about, almost exactly two-thirds of the way through the twentieth century, and in a country as advanced as Britain, that a judge should have been obliged to ask a doctor to examine the penis of a politician, is something so extraordinary, and in many ways so significant, that it deserves examination as detailed as that which the Minister underwent.

# 2

## O say, have you heard?

In the late spring of 1963 men and women all over Britain were telling, and others were believing, embellishing and repeating, such stories as that nine High Court judges had been engaging in sexual orgies, that a member of the Cabinet had served dinner at a private party while naked except for a mask, a small lace apron and a card round his neck reading 'If my services don't please you, whip me', that another member of the Cabinet had been discovered by police beneath a bush in Richmond Park where he and a prostitute had been engaging in oral-genital activities and that the police had hushed the matter up, that the Prime Minister, Harold Macmillan, had known about some, or all, of these matters but had taken no action, and that a principal member of the royal family had been having sexual relations with one, if not two, prostitutes in circumstances that would have made exposure sooner or later inevitable. These rumours,[1] and more like them, passed with ever-increasing rapidity among ever-widening circles of the population, and though it is true that at the point when the madness came to an end they had still not passed beyond a group comprising a fairly small minority of the whole nation, yet that minority before the end must have numbered many thousands.

It all began on Saturday, July 8th, 1961, in the grounds of Cliveden, home of Lord Astor and famous (or, according to the view taken of the matter, infamous) as the meeting-place, in the Thirties, of the 'Cliveden Set', which had been influential, or at any rate active, in encouraging the policy of appeasement towards

[1] The author heard all of these stories at the time, most of them more than once, and all of them from people who believed, or professed to believe, that they were true.

Hitler. In July 1961 no thoughts of appeasement troubled the members of the house-party at Cliveden, who included Mr and Mrs John Profumo, he being at that time Secretary of State for War and she better known as the actress Valerie Hobson. Strolling in the gardens with other guests, Mr Profumo eventually came to the handsome swimming-pool, in and around which were found members of another house-party, the house in question being a cottage in the grounds of the Cliveden estate let by Lord Astor to an osteopath named Stephen Ward. Among those in Ward's party was a young woman named Christine Keeler, and at the time Mr Profumo came upon the scene she was engaged in some horseplay involving the hiding of her swimming-costume, which she had removed in order to swim naked but left upon the bank. Good humour apparently prevailed on the part of all those present; but Mr Profumo's eye had been caught by the nymph, and shortly afterwards were sown the seeds of what was to grow, nearly two years later, into a flower of monstrous proportions and lurid colours. From a Minister laughing innocently beside a swimming-pool to other Ministers being accused quite falsely of the most elaborately licentious behaviour is a long step; *facilis descensus Averni*.

Shortly after the fateful week-end Mr Profumo sought the telephone number of Miss Keeler from Stephen Ward, made an assignation with her, and began a brief and extremely indiscreet affair with her, in the course of which he visited her several times at Stephen Ward's flat (where she was living), took her for a drive in the car of a fellow-member of the Government borrowed for the purpose, and on one occasion received her (during his wife's absence) at his own house.

The affair came to an end after a short time when the Secretary of the Cabinet, Sir Norman Brook, was approached by the Head of the Security Service, who by a happy accident was not working for the Russians, and asked to mention to Mr Profumo that his acquaintance with Stephen Ward might be unfortunate, as Ward was also closely acquainted with the assistant Russian naval attaché in London, Captain Eugene Ivanov, who was, of course, like all such Soviet Embassy staff, principally a spy. Mr Profumo took this warning seriously; indeed, he took it even more seriously than it was intended to be taken, for he assumed that the security services had discovered his liaison with Miss Keeler and were using this opportunity to let him know about it. In this he was greatly over-estimating the ability of the security services, as, alas, others frequently have, to the great peril of the realm, for in fact the security services knew nothing of the affair. However, Mr Profumo took to heart what he thought was the warning he was being given, and shortly afterwards brought his relationship with Miss Keeler to an end.

His first step in this direction was to cancel an assignation he had made with her for the following day. It has often been said that there are no limits to human folly, and certainly no limits have yet been discovered, for as often as it is thought they have been reached, someone goes beyond them. On this occasion the someone was Mr Profumo, who let Miss Keeler know of his supposed inability to meet her by writing her a letter. The letter began by addressing her as 'Darling' and went on in affectionate terms. There is a school of psychiatric thought which argues that there is no such thing as an accident where human beings are concerned, a theory which in its most extreme form argues that even those who are knocked down by motor-cars are really willing themselves to be, and forget to take due precautions because their subconscious deliberately makes them fail to do so. Be this as it may, it is difficult to believe that Mr Profumo was not, when he wrote that letter, inviting his own destruction, urged on by some subconscious desire to punish himself for his real or imagined sins. In this, if so, he was far from being alone, even among the famous, let alone among humanity in general, for the earth is littered with pieces of paper on which men have written things that they must have known as they wrote them would destroy them, figuratively if not literally, if they ever came to public knowledge.

Even so, there was still a chance that all would have been well, had it not been for the fact that Mr Profumo was far from being the only man with whom Miss Keeler had had sexual relations. No precise and generally accepted definition of a prostitute exists, and by some definitions she was not one; but there was no doubt that she was sexually promiscuous and that on some occasions at least she took money in return for her favours, even though it appeared that they were at first usually granted in furtherance of her own pleasures.[1] She was, at any rate, involved with two West Indians, between whom there was a struggle for exclusive rights in her. There was at least one affray between them, and then, at the end of 1962, a shooting incident, in which one of them fired several shots at the flat of Stephen Ward, where Miss Keeler was visiting her friend Marilyn Rice-Davies, at that time living with Ward. Shortly after the shooting the man who had done it, John Edgecombe, was arrested, charged and, following proceedings in a magistrate's court, committed for trial at the Old Bailey. By the time his trial began Miss Keeler, obviously a vital witness, had gone to Spain, leaving no forwarding address. By that time she had also told in several quarters of her earlier affair with Mr Profumo; to a policeman, to a former Member of Parliament (who in turn passed the information on to Mr George Wigg, M.P.), and to two newspapers (the *Sunday Pictorial* and the *News of the World*, between which she had unsuccessfully tried to arrange an auction for her story); moreover, the security service by now had discovered what had been known to at least some hundreds of people for several months. In addition, she had handed over the fatal 'Darling' letter from Mr Profumo to the *Sunday Pictorial*.

Before the trial of John Edgecombe took place, the first of the rumours had started its snowball-like progress down the hill, gathering size and speed as it went. After it had gone only a short distance, a bit of it broke off and rolled in at the door of the Attorney-General, Sir John Hobson, who summoned Mr Profumo to him, told him that rumours about his relations with Miss Keeler were circulating, and believed his denial of any

[1] Compare the well-known story, attributed to Ferenc Molnar, of his motives for writing plays: 'It's like a prostitute; first, she does it to please herself; then she does it to please her friends; finally, she does it for money.'

impropriety. Shortly afterwards the Prime Minister got to hear of the rumours, and asked his private secretary to question Mr Profumo on the subject; on this occasion there were further denials, and further acceptance of them. Finally the Government Chief Whip became involved, and to him too Mr Profumo repeated his denials, being by him too believed.

Meanwhile Mr Wigg, who had been pursuing his own inquiries, came, or thought he had come, to the conclusion that there was, or might have been, a risk to the national security stemming from the fact of Mr Profumo's relations with the Ward-Keeler-Ivanov circle. Besides, as he later explained, there was still in his mind the notable defeat inflicted on him some time previously when, according to Mr Wigg, Mr Profumo had prevented him from exposing serious military deficiencies, by the use, also according to Mr Wigg, of questionable political methods. Not wanting to accuse Mr Profumo on the basis of what he had so far discovered, Mr Wigg contemplated for a moment taxing the Minister with the information and asking him what he had to say on the subject. To help him make up his mind, Mr Wigg said, he took legal advice.

One of the more interesting things to emerge from this case, though perhaps not widely enough, is the extraordinary naivety of the legal profession, and the even more extraordinary naivety of other people *towards* that profession. The first example of this was the ready acceptance by the Attorney-General of Mr Profumo's denials; the second came now, when Mr Wigg's 'old and wise and valued legal friend' advised him not to tax Mr Profumo with the information, on the bizarre grounds that 'In the circumstances he will not thank you; if he did not tell you the truth about Kuwait, he will not do anything different on this occasion.' Mr Wigg therefore decided to tax Mr Profumo not privately, but as publicly as possible, in the House of Commons, perhaps concluding that, whereas Mr Profumo would not tell him the truth privately, as man to man, when it might do him no harm, he would do so publicly, with every organ of publicity alerted, when it would undoubtedly ruin him.

A few days later Mr Wigg, under the absolute protection against action for libel of his Parliamentary privilege – 'That', he said, 'is what it is given me for' – raised the subject of the rumours – which by now included the suggestion that Mr Profumo had been instrumental in getting Miss Keeler out of the country – during a debate on, of all things, rumours. The Minister to whom he addressed his request for an explanation of the rumours about a Minister whom he did not venture to name (after criticizing newspapers for being afraid to publish information they possessed) was the Home Secretary, Mr Henry Brooke, who refused to oblige with a comment and went home to bed. In the subsequent dramatic events of that night nobody thought to wake him up and get him to return, though as Home Secretary he was nominally responsible, under the Prime Minister, for all matters relating to security. Perhaps his colleagues had simply forgotten about him; perhaps it never occurred to them that he could be of any use. But the Attorney-General, who had not gone home to bed, and was not to do so until dawn was breaking, telephoned to Mr Profumo and asked him to come at once to the House of Commons to discuss matters of considerable importance. Mr Profumo did so, pausing only to collect his solicitor, Mr Clogg, on the way, and thus precipitating yet another example of the peculiar standing and attitude of the legal profession. As Sir Lionel Heald – *another* lawyer – was to say later: 'If one wished to choose anyone to whom to tell, as one's solicitor, an untrue story, Mr Derek Clogg is about the last man in the world one would choose'; going on to add that when Mr Profumo was faced, in the middle of the fateful night, with what had been said about him, he was urged to have Mr Clogg present to see 'that there is no question of your saying anything which you ought not to say'. (Sir Henry d'Avigdor-Goldsmid – not a lawyer, and therefore apparently a man of some common sense – was to say in answer to *that* point that 'In my experience litigants nearly always deceive their solicitors, and very often there are cases where they specially select solicitors who will believe their lies'; and might have added, with nothing but good resulting, that since the first duty of a solicitor is, in fact though not in strict legal theory, to believe his client, the spectacle of a solicitor savagely cross-examining a senior Minister of the Crown and telling him that he would have to have proof of the truth of his words before acting for him, is so bizarre that one would have thought it would scarcely commend itself even to other lawyers, or even a judge.)

Mr Profumo arrived at the House of Commons, drowsy from the effects of a sleeping-pill he had taken, to be questioned by five of his senior Ministerial colleagues, including both the Attorney-General *and* the Solicitor-General, this double-banking presumably being organized to ensure that the maximum possible quantity of legal naivety was achieved. Anyway, it certainly was, for Mr Profumo's denials were once more believed, and he, his solicitor and the five Ministers then worked together to construct a statement which he might make on the morrow in the House and thus silence the rumours for ever. This, after a time, they succeeded in doing, but alas, included eleven words in the statement which were to prove the undoing of everything and everyone concerned.

It is perhaps worth pausing to consider those eleven words and what might have happened if they had not been included. Mr Profumo's statement said – as was perfectly true – that he had had no hand in the disappearance of Miss Keeler while she was waiting to give evidence in the Edgecombe trial; it gave the dates of his acquaintance with Miss Keeler – quite correctly; and it said – with complete truth – that he had not seen her since December 1961. But it included – what was not at all true – the sentence: 'There was no impropriety whatsoever in my acquaintanceship with Miss Keeler.'

It is often said by Members of Parliament that the House of Commons is a noble, forgiving, generous body. Anyone who has attended upon its proceedings for any length of time, without actually gaining a vested interest in disseminating the House's own good opinion of itself by becoming a member, knows that this picture is false; the House is in fact, collectively speaking, a mean-spirited body, and the frequency with which members find it necessary to tell each other, and the outside world, the contrary suggests that some of them, at any rate, know this to be true. Yet the claim has been seriously advanced that if Mr Profumo had left out those eleven words and declared that he had had a liaison with Miss Keeler but that that was nobody's business but his own and his wife's, the House would have accepted it and passed on for ever to other matters. In fact the House would have fallen on him and rent him asunder then and there. Public admission of such a liaison by a leading member of the Government, apart from anything else, would have provided a most serviceable tar-brush, which would have given the Opposition an excellent opportunity to paint the entire Government black, together with an overwhelming temptation to stifle their scruples and use it.

So, doubtless reflecting that if he admitted the truth he was ruined, whereas if he denied it there was just a chance of escape, and that in any case a man can only be ruined once, Mr Profumo accepted the wording urged upon him by his colleagues and approved by his solicitor, and next day made the statement, including the eleven fateful – and fatal – words, to a crowded and attentive House. Many men – all, perhaps – have said words that they have afterwards wished taken back unsaid. Mr Profumo, without doubt; for so far from his statement stilling doubts and silencing rumours, it served only to increase the former and amplify the latter, so that within a matter of days and despite his legal actions against the British distributors of two Continental magazines which had hinted that all had not yet been heard on the subject, the fact that there would be further instalments was clear to everybody, except perhaps the lawyers.

The explosion was precipitated by the start of police inquiries into the activities of Stephen Ward. Though, after Mr Profumo's statement in the House of Commons, Ward had publicly confirmed its truth, he knew, of course, that it was in one material particular false, and although it seems that he would have been content to continue in this attitude indefinitely, when the police began to interview him, his patients, his women and anyone else from whom it was thought possible to get information on which to convict him (of *what*, it was clear, was comparatively unimportant), his nerve, understandably, began to crack.

Believing that his pursuit was politically motivated, he believed also that it would be possible to motivate its abandonment. To this end he began to hint that he knew more of Mr Profumo's statement than he had hitherto told, and from hints he proceeded to unambiguous statements, writing to the Prime Minister, the Leader of the Opposition and the newspapers to declare that he did not see why he should be persecuted by the authorities when he had loyally backed up one of their number in his false statement to the House of Commons.

In this no doubt he showed political naivety, for although to suppose that police investigations may be started or stopped on political grounds is a not *very* unreasonable supposition, the picture that by now Ward was painting, and that was to be painted later by others in even brighter tones – that is, a picture of him as the Suffering Servant being obliged to carry the sins of his betters – was on the face of it absurd; if his betters wanted their behaviour concealed, the prosecution of a man like Ward was hardly the way to go about it. In any case, when he had written enough letters, and when a dossier compiled by Mr Wigg after a meeting with him had been passed to the Prime Minister, and when Ward had seen the Prime Minister's private secretary and repeated, vis-à-vis, his claim that Profumo's statement was false and that he could prove it so, there was really nothing left for the parties concerned to do except take such cover as was available, cover their ears, and wait for the bang. Mr Wilson (who had then been Leader of the Opposition for four months), Mr Ward and Mr Wigg waited for it in London, Mr Macmillan on a golf-course in Scotland, and Mr Profumo, with his wife, in Venice, where they had gone for a short holiday. In the middle of it he told her the full truth, whereupon they flew back to London together, he submitted his resignation, together with an admission of his guilt, to the Prime Minister, and the bang was heard far and wide.

It was at that point that the collective insanity which seized

Britain during this affair took its first firm hold. Until now the rumours that had been circulating were exaggerated versions of the truth; the truth being that Mr Profumo had, contrary to his denial, had an affair with Christine Keeler. To this was added, as the rumour went about, the story that he had had some hand in getting her out of the country to prevent her going into the witness-box at the Edgecombe trial, and although this story was false, there was nothing surprising about its being added to the original rumour and being believed. But although it is a short way from believing correctly that Mr Profumo had had sexual relations with Miss Keeler to believing incorrectly that he had, as the law calls it, conspired to pervert the ends of justice, it is a very long way from believing *that* to believing that nine High Court Judges had been engaging in sexual orgies, that a member of the Cabinet had waited table in a rather daring form of *déshabille*, and that yet another member of the Cabinet had been found under a bush in Richmond Park indulging in a somewhat unconventional form of sexual activity.

Even to be in a position to seek an explanation for this extraordinary state of affairs, it is necessary to go back in time a little and examine an episode which took place in the autumn of 1962, and in which one clue to the madness of the spring of 1963 may be found. This was what came to be known as 'the Vassall affair'.

# 3

# A moral issue [*sic*]

Sometimes the press went too far, and suffered accordingly, though its resilience was such that it speedily recovered, and there is no evidence that it has ever, at any rate in modern times, learnt any lesson from its experiences other than that it should be more careful in future. Just such an episode, the most spectacular of the decade, occurred in relation to one of the spy-cases that studded the Sixties, this one being the case of William Vassall, who was convicted of spying for Russia and sentenced to eighteen years' imprisonment in 1962. There followed a huge press outcry, the substance of which was that Vassall's superiors, and the intelligence services, should have suspected him earlier; he was a homosexual, and it was alleged that this (with its danger of blackmail in security work) should have been apparent. In some places the outcry went further and it was alleged that Vassall's superiors did know that there was a spy in the Admiralty (though they did not know it was he), and had known for eighteen months, ever since the break-up of the Portland spy-ring (the first such case of the decade). Finally it was alleged that the Minister for whom Vassall had occasionally run official errands in the course of his work, Mr Thomas Galbraith, had been on terms far too familiar with him. The implication was obvious; it was also wholly unfounded, as indeed were all these charges.[1]

The Prime Minister, Harold Macmillan, who had committed an appalling error of judgment in accepting the proffered resignation from office of the Minister concerned when the storm broke, was presumably feeling guilty. The more guilty he felt, the more he

[1] Mr Galbraith subsequently received complete apologies and would have been entitled to damages too, had he not generously waived his right.

sought a suitable recipient for the blame. Since the press had, in its retailing and manufacturing of baseless gossip, innuendo and unjustified deduction, behaved very badly indeed, a Tribunal of Inquiry was set up to establish the truth or falsehood of the various rumours and reports, and if possible to indict the press for its conduct.

The press witnesses cut, almost without exception, a poor figure as, one after the other, they turned out to have got most of what they printed by taking previously printed articles from other papers and repeating them with embellishments. Despite the presentation of the case by the Attorney-General, who displayed an almost wilful ignorance of the way in which newspapers operate, the press was coming out of the affair very badly indeed until, providentially, two journalists refused to give the sources they claimed they had for statements they had printed and, maintaining that refusal, were sent to prison (for three and six months respectively) in consequence.

There followed a great flood of indignation in the newspapers, though when the tribunal finally reported, clearing all the people who had been accused, and drily declaring that, in the case of one of the imprisoned journalists, what he had written had been 'in all essentials a piece of fiction', there were hasty apologies, under the shadow of legal actions which would have cost the offending papers many thousands of pounds, and both the martyred journalists, though greeted as returning heroes on their return from prison, not long afterwards quietly disappeared from their respective newspapers.

Behind the dam of truth a head of disappointment had built up; for a moment it had seemed that the natural tendency to believe the worst of our betters was to be given limitless quantities of carrion to feed upon, since by the time the Vassall Tribunal had been established to ascertain the truth of the rumours and allegations there was almost certainly a widespread belief that the newspapers had been right in their suggestions that a scandalous liaison between Vassall and the Minister had existed, and that both it, and later events, had indicated a massive defect (or, more correctly, yet another massive defect) in Britain's security arrangements. Some of the savage resentment of the newspapers' part in the Vassall business may have been caused by the disappointment suffered by those who had most looked forward to a winter of relish; nothing untoward had happened, Mr Galbraith's behaviour had been blameless, our security services were no worse than they had previously been known to be, and where many had crowded round the pot as the lid was lifted, hoping eagerly for the sweet savour of corruption, there was now only a ring of fallen faces at the sight and smell of wholesome but unexciting bread-and-butter pudding. Naturally enough the disappointed turned first on those who had promised them more interesting fare; and they turned with considerable vehemence.

The pent-up lake of disappointment sought an outlet; deprived of scandal once by the fact that there was no scandal, it seethed and bubbled and waited. When the dam went the second time, with the announcement of Mr Profumo's resignation, the flood-waters poured, unchecked, into the valleys of public life, sweeping everything before them in a great release of joy in the depravity of others. Mr Profumo had been to bed, not once but several times, with a girl who, whatever else she was, was undeniably attractive, at any rate to judge from the newspaper photographs;[1] sexual envy, if nothing else, demanded that he and the whole world he moved in be accused of corruption. When the rumours were first spoken aloud in Parliament, Mr Reginald Paget, unfolding his giant frame, rose to ask: 'What do these rumours amount to? They amount to the fact that a Minister is said to be acquainted with an extremely pretty girl. As far as I am concerned, I should have thought that was a matter for congratulation rather than inquiry.' As far as Mr Paget was concerned, acquaintance with a pretty girl no doubt *was* a matter for

[1] Compare the remark of Lord Denning, in his report into the whole affair, to the effect that anybody who had seen photographs of Miss Keeler in a bathing-costume 'could readily infer her calling'—a remark which presumably means, if it means anything at all, that any girl who poses for photographs in such dress reveals herself, *ipso facto*, to be a prostitute. The remark was perhaps the most outstandingly naïve of all the legal contributions to the entire business.

congratulation; but for many people, for men whose female acquaintances were now all too plain, and for women who had never been anything else, this was no matter for congratulation, but rather a matter for vengeance, for defilement, for the ruining of her beauty and the destruction of his maleness. With a roar of unholy joy, the deprived flung themselves on the sated. 'Censure', said Swift, 'is the Tax a Man pays to the Public for being eminent'; the tax is levied at a higher rate when the eminent are also incontinent, and that tax Mr Profumo was to pay in full.

But the Vassall affair had left another legacy behind it. The public inquiry, and the report of his findings by Lord Radcliffe, who had presided over it, had left most of the press resentful at the way in which its less reputable methods, of building a tower of innuendo upon a foundation of rumour and labelling the result a house of fact, had been exposed. There could now be little doubt that the man at the head of the Government which had put them on such public trial would, if he was ever caught in their trap, be shown no mercy.

The public was ready to be scandalized; the press was eager to provide the material. Using the public's avidity as its fulcrum, and the undoubted disgrace of Mr Profumo as its lever, it prepared to move the world. 'By applying corrupt standards', said the *Guardian*, which alone had stood out against the hunting of Galbraith, writing about the papers which had done the hunting, 'they undermine their own influence. Will they be believed next time they uncover a scandal?' Alas for virtue; the answer was to be a resounding yes, and the stage was now set for a massive exercise in hypocrisy, perhaps the most staining episode of the entire decade but one which, seen now in the context of hindsight, was perhaps inevitable; if, in the Sixties, the past was letting go of Britain, its grip was not to be prised loose without a struggle, and the Profumo affair can therefore be seen as the last struggle of the old, false standards (or, as some would have said and some would still say, the old, true standards) before a new attitude emerged. When, perhaps tomorrow and perhaps next year, another public man is found to have private standards that do not accord with the nation's unspoken assumptions about public life, he may well admit to the House of Commons that his sexual relations are not what the House of Commons would like them to be, and trust successfully to public opinion, purged of guilt by its excess of righteousness in the Sixties, to defend him against the House's reaction.

* * *

Now in every such case there must be a Pharisee, holding his gold coin of probity high above his head before contributing it to the temple, while the widow shuffles away after depositing her mite of humanity. In this case the issues could scarcely be seen for the armies of Pharisees marching in their holy wrath; and of these the commander-in-chief, beyond a doubt, was Lord Hailsham. Eight days after Profumo's fall, and four days before the House of Commons was due to debate the matter, Lord Hailsham appeared on the B.B.C. television programme 'Gallery' to discuss it. His behaviour was, to many, so extraordinary that a rumour was rapidly put about to the effect that he had been drunk. The charge was not only false, since Hailsham had arrived at the television studio perfectly sober and declined all refreshments thereafter, but absurd, since he is both an abstemious man and one who heartily despises all sins of the flesh and weaknesses of the spirit, as indeed he was to show before the night was out. A count of the text shows that in one passage alone he called Mr Profumo a liar seven times in ninety words, and the force with which he pronounced the word was such that it seemed, by some strange phonetic mutation, to be composed entirely of sibilants, so that it would not be fanciful to say that he *hissed* it at his interlocutor and the unseen audience. Nor was it his pronunciation only that gave him the air of a man who had entirely lost control of himself; his tie was awry, and his very face seemed to have changed into a mask of hatred and self-righteousness. The final 'liar', which occurred at the end of a sentence in which he was in fact putting a very reasonable point—'A great party is not to be brought down because of a scandal by a woman of easy virtue and a proved liar'

—was pronounced with such manic violence that those watching might have thought that he was about to go completely berserk.

Instead, however, he went on to propound one of the most curiously eccentric views of the British party system and its workings that can ever have been heard from the lips of any politician—certainly any politician as distinguished as Hailsham. Having denied that the forthcoming debate, and the scandal it concerned, would or should be a matter of party politics, he was asked why, in that case, the Conservatives had for the debate issued a three-line whip—that is, the most severe, peremptory and formal demand for their members' allegiance in the division lobby. (The demand is not, of course, constitutionally binding, and many M.P.s of all parties, faced with a demand for their loyalty which they cannot reconcile with the demands of their consciences, have defied the instruction and abstained, and even, in exceptional circumstances, voted against their own party; Lord Hailsham himself, when in the House of Commons, had done precisely that, in the most honourable circumstances, and lived to thrive politically, as have many erstwhile party rebels.) Hailsham denied point-blank that the whip was a summons to vote, insisting that it was nothing but a summons to *attend*, though he did not, wisely, attempt to explain of what interest to the whips a member's attendance at a debate could be if it were not followed by his vote at the end of it.

In the days which followed there were some desultory attempts to defend Lord Hailsham's novel view, but they were hardly convincing, and, interestingly enough, Mr Edward Heath, the future leader of the Conservative Party, had three years earlier put the case for the more generally accepted attitude, in a speech to the Conservative Political Centre which must have slipped Lord Hailsham's memory. 'The free vote', said Mr Heath on that occasion

> offers a superficial attraction to those who dislike party government ... if it were possible for members to be present all the time and to vote upon each issue without whipping,

> it might be possible to argue that the result would be the most representative available ... to say that the whips should be off for minor issues begs the question – what is a minor issue? ... all too quickly, defeats on the minor issues lead to lack of confidence in the larger ones ... on the whole, the electorate has demonstrated that it prefers firm Government.

Having thus made a double contribution to the business, Lord Hailsham went home, no doubt satisfied that he had done well. It has often seemed to those who have examined the career and conduct of this brilliant, passionate and in many ways likable man that beneath the seemingly impenetrable hide there is a final layer of self-awareness; if so, it may be that he later realized quite how completely he had undone himself.

In any case he was to be rebuked promptly, nobly and unforgettably by Mr Profumo's brother-in-law, Lord Balfour of Inchrye, who said, in a letter to *The Times*, that

> when sin and failing are weighed in the scales of human justice it is only right that each who sits in judgment shall take the man's life as a whole into account before passing sentence ... Lord Hailsham had no mercy. 'Why should he?' can well be asked. Yet surely such a proud and powerful Christian could have shown some element of Christian charity in his denunciation of a man with a shattered life.[1]

Looking back on the *affaire* from the end of the decade, where the waters, though more turbulent than ever, are disturbed by forces of rather more significance, Hailsham's performance seems more extraordinary even than it did at the time. And yet in the context of that time, one-third of the way through that unbearably strained decade, and at the moment when the strain, unknown to almost everyone, was at its greatest, it made some kind of macabre sense, or at any rate fitted into the lunatic atmosphere, in which anything, however preposterous, could be

[1] *The Times*, June 17th, 1963.

said and believed, and any public attitude, however grotesque, struck, without anyone finding it particularly odd.

For some of the moral conclusions drawn, for instance, those who drew them had not Lord Hailsham's excuse, that he was labouring under the strain of a political crisis which had imperilled the future of the party he had loyally served for many years. One outraged Anglican wrote to the *Church Times* to suggest that the corruption of moral standards that had resulted in the *affaire* could be traced to the influence of the Cambridge and Southwark theologians, and in particular to the publication of *Honest to God*, and from as far away as Belfast a voice cured in old-fashioned brimstone thundered the question:

> As a nation, can we afford to trust our destinies in the hands of a Prime Minister who is so easily deceived? ... He has forfeited the right to be the leader of the nation ... our nation will take a very long time to recover from this shock.

It was a voice that was to be heard at the end of the decade, shouting No Popery on the steps of St Paul's while the supporters of its owner brawled in the aisles inside, for this was the first recorded intervention in the public life of the United Kingdom as a whole of the Moderator of the Free Presbyterian Church of Ulster, the Reverend Ian Paisley.

But these ancestral voices were not the only ones, nor were they the most remarkable. For the outstanding generalization from the particular neither the politicians nor the churches could compete with *The Times*, which, in one of the most extraordinary editorials it has ever printed, denounced the Profumo *affaire* as the fruits, the inevitable fruits, of the years of Conservative rule. Rot was setting in, all standards were suffering, the British were making themselves out to be an immoral nation, and the reason, to be precise the *overriding* reason, was that 'eleven years of Conservative rule have brought the nation psychologically and spiritually to a low ebb'. The bringing had been done, *The Times* insisted, in the familiar tones of the comfortably housed, well fed, warmly dressed metropolitan citizen calling other people to endure apostolic poverty for the nation's sake, by the Conservatives' insistence that 'Nothing else ... mattered, compared with the assertion that the nation had never had it so good'. With a most judicious reservation, the editor ruled that 'In all truth the British people deserved some easement after their historic and heroic exertions', though expectations that he would indicate the precise limits of the easement which the British people deserved were dashed when he added a qualification to his reservation, sternly pointing out that, whatever the degree of easement earned by no matter how historic and heroic exertions, 'History is never a nicely balanced business of rewards and penalties.'

Sir William Haley, then Editor of *The Times*, has been much criticized for these words,[1] and from much of the criticism it would be difficult to defend him, nor would such a defence be of any great value now that the decade has ended in a decisive rejection by so many people of the standards by which he judged the nation and found it wanting. But in fact Sir William was only echoing two very substantial themes that ran through the Sixties, though one was heard more clearly than the other, and, whether he realized it or not, his intervention was made at the last moment at which such sentiments would be taken seriously. The politicians of course (this was the minor theme) were in the habit of exhorting the people to work harder, to forego present pleasures and present comforts for the sake of their own future, not to say that of generations yet unborn, and the people, who were not impressed by the politicians' own contribution to present economic and cultural stability, let alone to future prosperity, were apt to respond increasingly with some version of Harold Laski's gloomy question: 'What has posterity ever done for me?'

'If everyone were to work just five per cent harder,' the leaders of the people would say, 'our troubles would be over,' forgetting that on the record of leadership from which the British had suffered since at least the mid-Fifties, the chances of that five per cent increase in prosperity being squandered (together with a further five or ten per cent earned earlier) by Government were so high,

[1] Notably by the late Randolph Churchill, in *The Fight for the Tory Leadership*.

and the people's wariness on that score so great, that such exhortations had little chance of meeting with a positive response.

* * *

But the other, major, theme in the song of *The Times*, which was less frequently put into words, was the more important, and ultimately provided the crux on which the decade had to decide which way it would turn. There were many, both before and after the *affaire*, who saw Britain in the kind of light that shone on the later Roman Empire, hurling herself headlong to destruction amid gurglings of degenerate glee. To such people the signs were all too numerous, all too clear, and inferences were drawn from the widest imaginable variety of aspects of society. For them the new theology was demolishing the simple faiths by which simple people had lived for so long; the abolition of judicial hanging and flogging was withdrawing the only weapons with which society could hope to stem lawlessness and inculcate a proper fear of retribution into the lawless; the rising tide of equality in social life, and the increasing pressure from those who wanted it to rise still higher, was destroying the leadership, aristocratic in nature if not in name, which alone could steer the country through the perils of a hostile world; the modern methods of education were either leaving the masses virtually illiterate or educating them far above any station they could ever hope to reach, and often, it was argued with more passion than logic, both;[1] honest labour was now no more than a means of earning money rather than a conscious contribution to the general welfare, with the result that as soon as enough money was earned tools were downed, whether this made it impossible for firms to work on Saturdays or not; trade unions had become giant conspiracies to defraud manage-

[1] Even education in fiction was in the same plight: not many years before, the censor of films had refused a certificate to an honest and reputable study of conditions in a school in a rough, poor neighbourhood (*Spare the Rod*), on the grounds that it might, with its implicit criticism of corporal punishment, tend to undermine authority. By the end of the Sixties, however, he had licensed a film (*If*) which portrayed a boys' public school and ended with the scholars machine-gunning staff and visitors.

ment of the proper fruits of its knowledge, experience and investment capital; management was feeble and cowardly, so that no resistance was made to unjustified claims on the part of the workers; respect for the qualities of position and birth, education and social grace, was disappearing, leaving Jack claiming to be not only as good as his master but better; parental control and parental responsibility had been withdrawn from children, who now grew wild and ensured that the next generation would only accentuate the general decline; adolescence now, by virtue of its new-found economic power, dictated fashions in popular art, design and clothing; all the great bastions had been taken or, worse, corrupted from within, so that the B.B.C., for instance, once an impregnable repository of national virtue, was now a dark Satanic mill, taking in raw corruption at one end and grinding it out dangerously refined at the other; above all, worse than everything else and the unmistakable sign of approaching doom, uncontrolled and apparently uncontrollable sexual licence reigned supreme.

Even the erotic impulses that might be stirred simply by walking about the streets were feared by many, and to do them justice there was certainly no lack of stimulants for them in the Sixties. The extraordinary increase in 'strip clubs' which began almost simultaneously with the start of the decade, and within a few years had gone so far that there were whole streets in London and other large cities a majority of the buildings in which housed such establishments, ensured that the eye of even the most innocent passer-by would be caught by the photographs lavishly displayed outside, of the ladies to be seen even more lavishly displayed within, and within the doorways of each there stood men whose job was to invite the passer-by to enter, taste and see.[1]

[1] This gave rise to a strange action at law, in which the host of such a place, together with two of the ladies who worked there, were prosecuted for obtaining money by false pretences, the substance of the charge being that they had clearly implied that a customer would receive more than food, drink and public entertainment inside; on this understanding he entered, but was cheated of his hoped-for consummation and complained to the authorities, who prosecuted, and obtained convictions for all those charged.

At the same time cinemas appeared, the sole function of which was to show films that had been refused a licence for public exhibition (though in truth, the standards of censorship had changed so completely that these were hard put to it to bring in sufficient customers to keep them in business, since the ordinary cinemas were able to show almost anything they wished). The proprietors of these cinemas evaded the law in this field by forming clubs, membership of which was compulsory to would-be patrons, though since the conditions of entry were not particularly onerous, this was a trifling formality. The same rule, of prior membership, applied also to the strip clubs, and was treated in the same light spirit, so much so that it became their almost invariable practice to allow immediate entry on payment of a small fee and a signature in a book kept for the roll of members. Into this arrangement the customers entered with such enthusiasm that it became a common habit for those of them who did not wish to sign their own names to give instead those of bishops, newspaper editors and other morally upright folk, who were in consequence recorded as being members in good standing of a vast variety of strip clubs, and as having over a period of years paid them a total of many thousands, if not millions, of visits.

Poster advertising had, of course, long had an erotic content, which disturbed many people (some of them already considerably disturbed), and many of them found relief from the impulses thus stirred by writing or drawing on the advertisements in an obscene manner, and perhaps finding relief in this literary-pictorial masturbation from the desires which tormented them; the posters beside the escalators at London Underground stations always included a high proportion of advertisements for underwear, swimming-costumes, nightdresses and other products which necessitated illustration by photographs of the most desirable-looking young women. This display was almost a definition of the torments of Tantalus, for the ever-moving staircase ensured that those who wished to look upon the charms revealed beside it were unable to linger, being carried past them, driftwood on the tide, and those who wanted to add their own comments in crayon were in an even worse plight, though the more desperate among them were occasionally to be seen scribbling frantically as they went by and leaning over, in order to do so, at an angle which meant that they were in imminent danger of falling to the bottom of the escalator and thus being seriously injured if not killed.

* * *

It was against this backcloth that the drama of the *affaire* Profumo was now to be played out, and across the stage in front of it that there was to wash the tide of rumour that at one point threatened to engulf the entire nation, so that Lord Poole was moved to say that if the tide was not checked it would 'destroy us all', and was hardly exaggerating. 'I never remember a time', he said, 'when so many or so varied a number of rumours were circulating in Fleet Street or Whitehall. These rumours are disgusting in detail and probably disreputable in origin. There are certain curious aspects about them, and certainly most of them are untrue. But rumour and doubt and suspicion are horrible things – where and when possible they should be cleared up.' These were sentiments which were widely shared (or at any rate widely expressed, though there were also many 'in Fleet Street or Whitehall', and many more elsewhere, who were enjoying the rumours immensely, and wished they might never be cleared up); but the question which now had to be answered was: *how* were the rumours to be cleared up?

Three methods, as it turned out, were to be used. Three days after Mr Profumo confessed and resigned Stephen Ward was arrested and charged with a variety of offences, such as conspiring to procure abortions and living off the earnings of prostitutes; one week later the House of Commons debated the entire business; and four days later than that the Master of the Rolls, Lord Denning, was appointed to conduct a judicial inquiry into the circumstances surrounding the resignation of Mr Profumo and the possibility of a security leak arising out of those circumstances. Each of these shed its own particular share of light, and of darkness, on the business, and each must be considered if a full picture is to be drawn of what the Profumo case, its background, its surroundings and its consequences, meant to Britain in the Sixties.

# 4

# Standing room only

The debate took place amid a mood of growing political hysteria. Speculation about the fate of the Prime Minister was unrestrained, not only in the press and the ranks of the Opposition but also in his own party, and it was this that virtually dictated the respective tactics of the Labour Party and of the Prime Minister.

The first had to maintain that they were only interested in the security aspects of the matter (which, it was clear, had hardly stirred the interest of the nation) while actually trying to suggest that the air of moral corruption which now surrounded the Government could only be cleared by the Prime Minister's resignation. Macmillan, for his part, had to pretend that the moral question was the only important one, because on that score he was blameless, so that he could shuffle the security question off the stage while his integrity was down at the footlights striking poses. In a curious way, therefore, the interests of the opposing forces more or less coincided, and the outcome of the debate and of the crucial days which followed it therefore depended less on the merits of the issues involved than on the respective performances of the chief actors, and since the acting abilities of both Mr Wilson and Mr Macmillan were such that either could have earned a substantial living and a devoted following on the stage of the theatre had he not been called instead to the drama of politics, it followed that to keen students of the political drama the play was one the memories of which they would rightly treasure.

The play-like quality of the proceedings was emphasized by the fact that outside the House of Commons before the debate started was a queue of people hopeful of obtaining the few seats available to the public. Since all seats in the Public Gallery are

c*

allotted in advance by ticket, the only ones available for those who arrive ticketless being ones vacated during the course of the day by ticket-holders, and since it was extremely unlikely that anyone who had given his pin to see the peepshow would leave before he had had his pin's-worth, it was obvious to those who knew the procedure that the waiting hundreds had waited in vain – a fact which was repeatedly explained to them without having the smallest effect. This was the more understandable when it was realized that some of them had waited three days and nights for this opportunity, for all the world as if they were opera-lovers with a chance to hear Madame Callas.

In fact the situation was even worse than was supposed, as even those who had applied for tickets through their Members of Parliament (the proper procedure) well in advance – indeed, as soon as the date of the debate had been announced – found that no tickets were available for them either, the mystery being explained only on the day of the performance, when the Public Gallery was seen to be crowded with ladies, many wearing their best and most colourful hats, as though they were at a garden party, a wedding or a fashionable race-meeting, and it transpired that these were, almost without exception, the wives and friends of Members of Parliament, who had been provided with all the tickets allocated to Members for the use of their constituents.

Mr Wilson had decided that his best style would be the coldly analytical, and his speech may be studied in vain for any of those carefully prepared spontaneities with which he had so often been known to set the House on a roar. Having paid his tribute to hypocrisy in his second sentence, in which he said that the debate 'arises from disclosures which have shocked the moral conscience of the nation', he warmed to the main theme of his charge, which was an accusation against the Prime Minister of 'indolent nonchalance' in failing to detect the deception of his War Minister or to take proper steps to ensure that the security of the country was not endangered.

This case Mr Wilson deployed at great length, with great force and with great forensic skill. When the Prime Minister rose to reply it was immediately clear that, since he must have realized that his case in reply to Mr Wilson's charges would never convince a jury, he had to rely less on reason than on the rousing of emotion, the particular emotion suitable for his purpose being sympathy, much as some of the older generation of advocates, faced with the difficult task of pleading for a defendant who was obviously guilty, would rely on making the jury cry by a recital of their client's childhood hardships. To this end he assumed that air of a stag at bay with which students of his style had long been familiar, and which indeed seemed in him at times to bear an uncanny physical, or at any rate psychic, resemblance to Landseer's famous painting of the subject, carrying his assumption of the part so far that at one point this most meticulously efficient of Parliamentarians actually pretended to have lost his place in his notes. But his line was as clear as his opponent's. 'I know', he said, 'that I have acted honourably; I believe that I have acted justly; and I hope that when it has heard my account the House will consider that I have acted with proper diligence and prudence.'[1] Each of this sonorous triad of pleas was meant to be taken as of equal weight, for since there could be no doubt that he had acted honourably, and little doubt in any reasonable mind that he had acted justly, he clearly hoped that the impetus obtained by the acceptance of these two parts of his case would carry him safely across the treacherous ice of the third, and that the House, or at least his own uneasy party, would be no less convinced that he had acted prudently and diligently.

The rest of the debate was, except for two most pointed interventions, something of an anti-climax. The House of Commons contains a number of very parfit gentil knights, of whom Mr Reginald Paget is perhaps the most notable. Mr Paget had seen the performance on television of Lord Hailsham, and had not at all liked what he saw; moreover, he was a friend of Mr Profumo's, and one of those (there were, alas, some in the other category) who did not desert him in his dark hours. Mr Paget, therefore, contributed to the debate a speech lasting only five minutes, but

[1] *Hansard*, June 17th, 1963.

of an effect far greater than its length, for in it he produced, the better to punish Lord Hailsham for his unfortunate remarks, a phrase of such deadly and elegant cruelty that its like had not been fashioned in England since the death of Pope. Probably Lord Hailsham was already regretting the uncharitable nature of his references to Mr Profumo; he was now to be made to pay dearly for his lapse. Mr Paget – unfairly, to be sure – numbered Lord Hailsham among those who 'compound for sins they are inclined to by damning those they have no mind to'; then he added that 'When self-indulgence has reduced a man to the shape of Lord Hailsham, sexual continence involves no more than a sense of the ridiculous.'[1]

This was a style to which Mr Wigg could not hope to aspire; but if he could not handle the rapier he could wield a bludgeon with the best, and his unlovely pursuit of Mr Profumo could be to some extent pardoned, in view of the blows he dealt during his speech to Lord Hailsham. He too was unfair to Hailsham in saying of his now-notorious television broadcast that 'He is a great actor', thus implying, what was clearly not the case, that Lord Hailsham's emotion on that occasion had been spurious. Wigg went on:

> He claims this to be a non-party matter – the object being to try to make out that we on this side of the House have played party politics. Then suddenly he is in a jam. For a split second he finds himself in exactly the same jam as John Profumo found himself. Someone asked him, 'What about the three-line Whip?' He could have said, 'You have caught me', but he did exactly the same as John Profumo did. He lied. There is not a right honourable or honourable Gentleman on either side of the House who accepts Lord Hailsham's interpretation of what a three-line Whip means. The three-line Whip is the final appeal to loyalty on party lines, and Lord Hailsham knows it. Whether I am in order or not, I call Lord Hailsham a lying humbug.[2]

[1] *Hansard*, June 17th, 1963.
[2] Ibid.

Now there can be, and could be, no doubt whatever that Mr Wigg, in calling Lord Hailsham a 'lying humbug', was out of order. The rules of Parliamentary debate are quite unambiguous in these matters; whatever words are out of order when used by a member of the House of Commons about a fellow-member are equally out of order when used by a member of the House of Commons about a member of the House of Lords, and for a member to say in so many words that another has lied is an expression that the Chair will not tolerate, but will call immediately upon the offender to withdraw. To the astonishment of the House, however, and not least that of Mr Wigg, the Chair remained silent, and neither rebuked Mr Wigg nor called on him to withdraw, a state of affairs which could have been, and by some present probably was, read as a rebuke for Lord Hailsham on the part of the Chair more deadly in its silence than those of Mr Wigg and Mr Paget in speech. After this the debate wound unmemorably to its end, with its barely sufficient majority for the Government; though collectors of the more trivially unforgettable memorabilia may care to note that, after the excitement of the afternoon and evening, the House continued for another half-hour with a discussion of the regulations imposing standards of quality on publicly sold non-alcoholic drinks, introduced, it seems just worth recording, by a member named Darling.

* * *

Looking back on the political side of this episode from, once again, the safe haven of the decade's end, the strange dream-like quality of the Sixties emerges with renewed force. That men profoundly experienced over periods of up to thirty or forty years in every aspect of political life should behave as they did – which is to say as though they had never before heard of a man going to bed with a woman in circumstances which must lead inevitably to his ruin – has been explained in many ways; everything, from the low spiritual ebb to which Conservative rule and material prosperity had brought the nation, to the genuine belief on the part of many that there were revelations yet to come which would topple many more prominent public figures, has been put forward as a clue to the mystery, or even its solution. But, however plausible they looked at the time, none of these explanations holds water today, and we are left with the conviction that there was something in the air of the decade that had virtually unhinged the minds of otherwise calm and level-headed men. Nor is it more than a step from this surely incontrovertible fact to the explanation of it, which may be that the tensions of the decade, which were never more dramatically illustrated than in this business, and which had their common origin in the fact that the Sixties saw an old world die and a new one come to birth, contributed to the absurd and amazing state of affairs described.

It might be difficult to convince Mr Profumo that this was the case, yet it is a fact of history that in every age of transition men are never so firmly bound to one way of life as when they are about to abandon it, so that fanaticism and intolerance reach their most intense forms just before tolerance and mutual acceptance come to be the natural order of things. If this is what was happening in the Sixties, then Mr Profumo was the last victim of the old, unpermissive standards, and after he had been sacrificed on their altar in the most public, brutal and bloody fashion imaginable, the decade was ready to come to its senses and accept the new code, the new attitudes, that had been pushing their way through the soil unnoticed even while the crisis was at its height.

This, however, would not have been easily deduced from the words of John Cordle, Member of Parliament for the Christchurch division of Bournemouth. Mr Profumo having been a Secretary of State, he had seals of office which must be returned by a retiring or resigning Minister to the monarch. Traditionally this symbolic act is performed by the ex-Minister in person, and it was announced that this tradition would be followed in the case of Mr Profumo. Whereupon Mr Cordle, as if feeling bound to remind the nation that the full, rich, oily tones of Pecksniff had not yet been heard in the affair, said:

> I was appalled to hear that our beloved Queen should be so wrongly advised as to give an audience on Tuesday next to the former Minister of the Crown, who has proved himself so untrustworthy and at last made public admission of his guilt. It seems to me surely an affront to the Christian conscience of the nation at a time when standards in public life need to be maintained at the highest level. I am absolutely staggered.

When Mr Cordle had made his point, and the matter had been taken up by a section of the press, it had obviously become sufficiently controversial for the rule which forbids the monarch to become embroiled in controversial questions to come into force. It was therefore announced that Mr Profumo had asked to be excused the traditional audience, that his request had been granted, and that his seal of office would be returned by messenger. But the Queen, being wiser than many of her subjects, staggering less readily than Mr Cordle, and happily lacking an exaggerated idea of the Christian conscience of the nation, was graciously pleased (the formal phrase for once being a literal account of what happened) to write to Mr Profumo, to thank him for all the work he had done as a Minister in her Governments, and to express her sorrow at the unhappy way in which his career had ended.[1]

[1] The author feels bound to make it clear that the information on which this is based did *not* come to him from Mr Profumo.

5

# Thoroughly filthy fellow

Two further examples of the way in which the old world was giving way to the new, though not without putting up a vigorous fight, were the inquiry conducted into the whole affair by Lord Denning and the trial of Stephen Ward. Of the former little can be said without the evidence given before Lord Denning, which was never published, for his report (it is safe to say that it is the only blue-book for which both Her Majesty's Stationery Office and the largest bookshop in London opened their doors, outside which long queues had formed, at midnight, so as to be able to sell copies of it at the first moment allowed by Parliament) is no more than the unravelling by a distinguished legal mind of a subject that was, in its psychological and social complexity, far beyond him.

Considered in retrospect, the report into the affair is not an attractive document. The very title—*Lord Denning's Report*—should have been a hint as to the kind of thing to be found inside it, for only a man conscious of the fact that he was shortly to be alone in the centre of a stage that had been crowded to danger-point for months past would have given it so personal a flavour, the titles of Government blue-books generally being of the most severely detached nature, such as *Report of the Nyasaland Commission of Inquiry* or *Report of the Committee on Housing in Greater London.* Popular usage promptly dubs most of them with a more convenient name, such as—in the case of the two cited—the Devlin Report and the Milner-Holland Report, and their chairmen are thus immortalized; but Lord Denning was clearly taking no chances.

Inside, it was worse. The section headings read like those of some old-fashioned crime-novel: 'Christine tells her Story', 'The Lawyers are Called In', 'The Meeting of the Five Ministers', 'The Slashing and Shooting'. The sub-headings manage to reach an even more grotesque level: 'Those Who Knew', 'A Meeting Is Arranged', 'Critical Conversations', 'Christine Goes Back to the Newspapers', 'Mr Profumo's Disarming Answer', 'Paul Mann Takes a Holiday', 'The *Daily Express* has a striking First Page', 'Mr and Mrs Profumo Go Home', ' "He's a Liar" ', 'Mr Profumo is Warned', 'The "Appalling Allegation" ', 'Negotiations for a Cottage', 'The Borrowed Car', 'The Cup of Tea', 'The Spaniard's Photograph', ' "The Man in the Mask" ', ' "The Man Without a Head" '. And the text is actually worse still.

> Mr and Mrs Profumo left for a short holiday in Venice ... He decided to tell his wife. But they had a quiet dinner together first. After dinner Mr Profumo told his wife the truth – for the first time – that he had had an illicit association with Christine Keeler ... Mrs Profumo said 'Oh darling, we must go home now just as soon as we can and face up to it.'

* * *

There remains, before any conclusion may be attempted, the third strand in the rope with which the Profumo affair was carefully tied before being stored away as a curiosity to excite the wonder of future ages; the trial, suicide and conviction (in that order) of Stephen Ward. About this too the most lurid rumours were current, most of them based on some form of the supposition that Ward was the victim of a plot by the Establishment, which was determined to shut his mouth lest he open it and emit the names of other prominent people who had been scandalously compromised. It was never satisfactorily explained how his mouth could be effectively shut if he were to be ushered into the witness-box at his own trial and there given, as are all witnesses in the English courts, a virtually absolute protection against actions for libel arising out of his evidence; unless, of course, it were to be postulated that his suicide was no suicide at all, but a murder disguised to look like one, and the fourteen letters Ward left, before, on the eve of his conviction, he took his own life, so many forgeries. But not even the members of the Who Killed Kennedy? Committee have so far ventured to express this view, though there were a number of people who subscribed to send fifty dozen white roses to Ward's funeral, with a card reading 'in memory of a victim of British hypocrisy'.

Of the trial of Stephen Ward the only thing that can now be said with any certainty is that he was not guilty as charged, and that apart from the judge and, presumably, the prosecuting counsel – that same Mervyn Griffith-Jones whose concern for the morals of other people's wives and servants played so notable a part in another celebrated trial of the Sixties – few could seriously have believed that he was. What he was much more widely believed to be was what prosecuting counsel called him: 'a thoroughly filthy fellow'; and the phrase (which seemed to come most naturally from Mr Griffith-Jones's disdainful mouth, and can be marked down to him for such credit as is fitting, along with his subsequent definition in the same case of a respectable girl as one who doesn't want to go to bed with anyone) may stand as the epitaph on at any rate one side of Ward's gravestone, the one carved there by the disapproval of society.

The conduct of the case, the obvious inadequacy, to put it inadequately, of by far the greater part of the prosecution's evidence, the zeal with which Mr Griffith-Jones hunted his prey – these and other aspects of a miserable miscarriage of justice may stand as a monument to an episode of which the British legal system has no reason to be proud, and may even, if such a feeling can ever penetrate the self-protection in which the practitioners of that system are wrapped (the judge did not fail to say at one point: 'We of the Bar are men of the world'), be by now ashamed. Yet one single episode of the case must be recounted again, for it epitomizes those aspects of it that, with the Sixties left behind, now seem almost unbelievable, so impossible is it that they could occur, at any rate in the same form, today. It is impossible, for instance, that evidence as *obviously* perjured as was much of that given by most of the girls in the case could be treated seriously now, if only because in the different atmosphere now prevailing a rather more sophisticated approach to prosecution witnesses would be almost bound to exist on the part of the jury, and even police evidence is often now treated in a rather more robust way than was apparently the case at the time.

Most important of all, however, is the fact, surely not to be denied, that far fewer people now are willing to condemn a man – either literally or metaphorically – for being a thoroughly filthy fellow if he has not in fact done the particular acts alleged in the indictment. To speak of Ward as a victim of British hypocrisy, as some did, is to strain language; to speak of him as a marked-down victim of the Establishment, as others did, is absurd; to speak of him as a scapegoat for all the prominent people who should have been in the dock at his side, or at the very least in the witness-box opposite, as did still others, is to betray a misunderstanding of the law and its function; but to say that he was convicted of being a thoroughly filthy fellow is true, and indicates the gulf that has opened, without – as is commonly the way in history – anybody being conscious of the opening until it was complete, between those days and these.

The moment at which the lost atmosphere of the Sixties – the years in which things could happen that could not happen now – was shown at its clearest was during the last day but one of the trial. Not far away, while the Ward trial was proceeding at the Old Bailey, the Court of Criminal Appeal was hearing submissions on behalf of Aloysius Gordon. He was one of the men with whom Christine Keeler had been involved, and whose success with her had resulted in the affray between him and John Edgecombe, and ultimately in the Sarajevo-like shots which Edgecombe fired. Gordon had been charged with assaulting her; he was found guilty, and sentenced to three years' imprisonment. But after his conviction inquiries had continued, the strands in the Profumo affair and the Ward case having become entangled with others not strictly relevant to them, and as a result of these inquiries Gordon's appeal was allowed, on the grounds that, had the new information, together with the witnesses who could have supported it, been available at his trial, it would not have been right to convict him. The statements that the Court of Criminal Appeal had before it were such as to cast reasonable doubt, to put it mildly (which is the way the court was careful to put it), on the evidence given by Christine Keeler at Gordon's trial. (In fact she was subsequently charged with perjury and sentenced to nine months' imprisonment, though it was doubtless thought by those who decide such things that it would have verged upon bad taste to engage Mr Mervyn Griffith-Jones to lead for the prosecution.)

Now it is inconceivable that the Court of Criminal Appeal, which on this occasion was sitting under the Lord Chief Justice, did not know that while they were quashing Gordon's conviction the trial of Stephen Ward, which depended to at least as great an extent as that of Gordon on the evidence of Miss Keeler, was proceeding. And before the Ward trial had proceeded for many more hours what had been said in the appeal court was known at the Old Bailey and indeed referred to by Mr Griffith-Jones in his closing speech, when he blandly dismissed it as irrelevant, on the grounds that the appeal judges had not ruled that Christine Keeler's evidence in the Gordon case was perjured, only that the absence of the witnesses who would have sworn that it *was* perjured provided the 'reasonable doubt' the existence of which in a jury's mind must prevent conviction.

Many arguments have been deployed over this matter, and the law was subsequently amended to enable the Court of Criminal Appeal to order a fresh trial in such cases. The conduct of the appeal judges has been defended on the grounds that they were unable to produce (because no evidence is given in an appeal court, only arguments on law) the statements they had before them, and which cast not merely reasonable but overwhelming doubt on Christine Keeler's veracity. The defence is absurd; nothing inhibited the Court of Criminal Appeal from saying whatever they wished on the subject, from quoting the statements directly or in their own paraphrase, or indeed from simply making known the dangers of relying on Christine Keeler's evidence.

Nothing can stop a judge from saying what he wants to, least of all Lord Parker, who is not noticeably reticent, let alone taciturn, when it comes to expressing his views. Moreover, knowing as they did what was happening at the Old Bailey, it was their clear *duty* to make the strongest possible indication of the reasonable doubts now surrounding Christine Keeler as a witness, for the appalling truth is that not only had she been lying in the Gordon case, as her subsequent trial for perjury established, *but she had repeated some of the very same lies in her evidence against Ward.* Nobody has ever explained why the judge in the Ward trial did not immediately adjourn it, when he heard the news from the Court of Criminal Appeal, until this crucial matter could be cleared up one way or the other, for to shelter behind the appeal court's statement that their own decision did not establish that Christine Keeler had been lying, only that a reasonable doubt now entered where it had not been before, is clearly inadequate; a reasonable doubt in one court is a reasonable doubt in another, especially when it refers not only to the same witness but to the same evidence. Shortly afterwards those reasonable doubts were brought into the light, at Miss Keeler's own trial, and there seen to be very reasonable indeed, so reasonable, in fact, that she was sent to prison on the strength of them. But by that time Ward had been convicted and was dead by his own hand, and Mr Griffith-Jones was a year closer to the judgeship to which he was appointed in 1967. (There was perhaps some tiny element of consolation in the fact that so fastidious a man should have become the Common Serjeant.)

At the end of the trial a distinguished and well-known High Court judge remarked privately, after reading the reports of the case, that, had it been tried before him, he would never have allowed it to go to the jury, and would have had some pertinent observations to make about the bringing of it. And that, presumably, will have to stand as the epitaph on the other side of Stephen Ward's tombstone.

* * *

A few tentative conclusions may be drawn; certainly there was no lack of them being drawn at the time.

'I do not', said Mr Macmillan in the crucial debate, explaining why he had thought it not too surprising that Mr Profumo should have begun his fatal letter 'Darling', 'I do not live among young people fairly widely.' (*Hansard* was kind, and rewrote this, or allowed him to rewrite it, so that it read: 'I do not live among young people much myself.') This claim was indeed true, and even understated, and serves now as a signpost to the most important lesson of all those that the business taught Britain.

For the Profumo scandal marked, though it did not, of course, exhaust all the aspects of, a change in society's attitudes. On that side stood a society which still felt obliged to maintain Puritan attitudes in public; on this side stands a society which no longer feels it necessary. On whether the move from one side to another is a good thing or a bad, opinions may, and clearly do, differ; but most people are not obliged to declare in public their attitudes to such matters, and many will insist on waiting a little longer to see whether there is not more evidence produced on which they can make up their minds with greater confidence. That a decisive and radical shift in public opinion has occurred, however, and that the Profumo affair played a large part, not in bringing that shift of opinion about, but in forcing people to realize that it was taking place and in persuading many who realized that it was taking place to behave as though it was, cannot seriously be doubted.

At all times, and in all societies, the closer the truth approximates to that which people believe is the truth, the better. Moreover, the closer the truth approximates to what people feel obliged to *say* is the truth, the better also. That men have lusts, that they sometimes go to extraordinary lengths to satisfy those lusts, that this applies to men in positions of responsibility and power as well as to men in positions of obscurity and unimportance, that whatever a man's tastes there is always somebody willing to supply his indulgence of them at the appropriate price, that greed and selfishness, pride and vanity, revenge and self-seeking, true righteousness and false righteousness run through all sections of society, that all human actions are determined by a complex play of motives and forces because all human beings are subject to many springs of action, that few are proof against all temptations though most are proof against some, and that men should therefore be chary of condemning those who have succumbed to the temptations to which those impelled to condemn them are immune, that life in a country as pluralist, multifarious and complex as Britain goes on very much as before when something that looked as though it might entirely change the nature of the country and its people comes to an end,[1] that witnesses sometimes lie on oath, that the men who own and edit newspapers are neither better nor worse than the men and women who read them and that if they were they would find it more difficult to attract readers, that deep within all men, and not so deep within most, there lurks a response of fierce joy to the shame and pain of others – that all these things are so is true; what is not true is that all these things are recognized as being so. Sometimes something happens to bring people face to face with these truths, and with the recognition that they have been concealing them from themselves. Only in such recognition will they find full psychic health; for the suppression of unwelcome facts, and their replacement by comforting fictions, can only increase the danger of breakdown when the full truth becomes known.

The personalization of the problems that beset countries is a dangerous technique which invites the drawing of false parallels and dubious conclusions. Nevertheless Britain in the Sixties can fairly, though cautiously, be compared to a patient undergoing psycho-analysis, and reaching the stage of being brought by the therapist to face the truth about the blocks with which he had protected himself from self-knowledge. The self-knowledge that Britain had been hiding from implied that she had lost her once commanding position in the world, that the days of her glory were no more, that she was no longer in a position to command obedience, admiration or danegeld from the rest of the world.

In order to enable herself to continue to hide from these truths

[1] Cf. the Abdication crisis of 1937, or even the Blitz of 1940.

it was necessary for Britain to erect barriers around them. These barriers were the traditional psychic defences: the investment of others with superhuman powers and qualities, the making of impossible demands on them for standards of conduct they were unable to meet; the obsession with a love-object or hate-object which in neither case merited the intensity of the passion. Suddenly the patient is over the divide; maturity is attained, and the barriers and props can be dispensed with. But crossing the divide is the most dangerous moment of the treatment, and the fever of wild rumour into which Britain fell during the months of the Profumo affair is eloquent testimony to the danger. Mr Profumo was not as good as the impossible and imaginary figure of the 'public man' who had for so long been invested with qualities no man could possess or at least maintain for long, and who had then been put under half-fearful, half-gleeful watch by a public which was waiting for him to fall. Nor was he as bad as, once he fell, he was made out to be. Nor were those with whom rumour had its way, while reason hid her face, guilty of the impossible sins attributed to them. But when a boil is lanced it emits pus; that is no less true of a nation than of an individual, and no less true of a psychological than of a physical boil.

Yet healing is impossible without the lancing of the boil. The Profumo case was that traumatic moment; when the boil burst, the truth about public men (which is only, after all, that they are the same men as private ones) became known, and with it the recognition that the whole argument was spurious, a screen thrown up to hide the real argument behind. From that moment we may date Britain's start on the road back to full national health, which is to say full national self-recognition. The road is a long one and its end is still not in sight, nor can anyone say with any certainty that all will be well when Britain arrives there.

All the same, it is not too early to be sure that the cleansing properties of the affair were in the end greater than their staining properties. In that sense Mr Profumo did the State some service; it is to be hoped that, in his lonely exile, *in* but not *of* our society, he knows it.

# 6

## Mugg's game

The Sixties had a number of patron saints: Dionysus, Baal, Pelagius and Aphrodite according to one school of thought; Amos, Calvin, Savonarola and Joanna Southcott according to another. One group urged on their followers to live for themselves, for the moment; either because the end of all things was at hand and they might as well enjoy the last days, or because the end of all things was at hand and only by doing so would they, and the world, be saved. Their rivals also declared that the end of the world was nigh, or that it would be if people did not pull themselves together, but offered an altogether different, and far more rigorous, set of rules for conduct to meet the coming emergency. Both appeals were made without, strictly speaking, the permission of the impressive authorities cited, but one man combined the roles of priest and acolyte as, indeed, he combined the roles of the voice crying in the wilderness and the voice full of the most worldly relish.

He was Malcolm Muggeridge, who in some ways epitomized the riven nature of the decade, for as much as he was sinner when it started he was saint at its end, and although his formal canonization was expected to be somewhat further delayed, many lived in the immediate expectation of his assumption into heaven as the Blessed Malcolm, while some claimed that the process had already started, and swore they could see light under his boots.

On almost the last day of the previous decade Mr Muggeridge, appearing on an American television programme, had so conducted himself as to be charged by Han Suyin with the worst sin possible between the sexes: her accusation was 'of trying to brainwash us into thinking that our greatest aim in life is to be sexually attractive to men'. That was in the dying hours of the Fifties, but as late as March 1963 Mr Muggeridge was being denounced in Britain as a mocker of religion, the scorner of sacred things, the destroyer of all that was pure and holy. 'Is Mr Muggeridge,' asked one such critic, 'who has never disguised his attitude to religion, the explanation of why the B.B.C. has so often flown in the face of Christianity and the Churches recently?'

Such charges may have been justified, at any rate in the most general terms (for nobody could believe that the B.B.C. had abandoned its Christian stance on the mere say-so of Mr Muggeridge, however forcefully he might have demanded that it should); but long before the decade was half over Mr Muggeridge had experienced a conversion and put aside worldly things, and has spent his time since then urging others to do likewise, including many who had no worldly things to put aside.

St Mugg has declared that he experienced no dramatic Damascus-road revelation, that his new outlook on life had come upon him gradually; there is no reason to disbelieve him. But the cause of it, whether sudden or drawn out, and whether or not he recognized it, and whether or not he would admit it if he did, was the distaste he developed for the things of the flesh. This distaste, the growing power of which over him can be charted from his utterances on the subject, grew into a disgust, thence to a loathing, thence to an obsession, which eventually brought him to the edge of a cliff on the other side of which were only those poor folk who throughout history have scourged and mutilated themselves for the sins of their fathers. Mr Muggeridge, who had once been described as 'a religious maniac in search of a religion', had clearly found it in a creed which started with the extirpation of sex, from which all else followed. 'After sixty', he said, 'a man must decide either to curb his appetites or surrender to them. I have conquered mine.' Sex, and its handmaid, affluence, were now to be the cause of every evil, the worm in every wood, the cancer rotting beneath the apparently healthy flesh of every body. Sex leered at him from advertisement hoardings, from the television screen, from books and newspapers and magazines. In the streets he was not free of it; asleep, assuredly, his dreams did not let him forget its hideous existence; the very air whispered its loathsome message in his protesting ears. 'Sex', he said, in a dreadful unconscious revelation, 'has come to be funny, and as I get older it seems to be funnier and funnier.'

The material comforts of life, which he came to regard as interchangeable with sex and every bit as objectionable (though he was not so eager to give these up), he denounced no less. The colour supplements of the Sunday newspapers excited his particular wrath, and to keep his thesis intact he affected to believe that the whole country, from Warrington to Dover and from Mousehole to Whitby, lived in a haze of Drambuie, After Eight chocolates, Kosset carpets, Jaguar motor-cars, Swedish glass, Viyella blankets, Lanvin perfume and king-size cigarettes.

Nor was help anywhere to be found, at any rate in the traditional quarters. The Church had long since ceased to offer salvation. 'Words', St Mugg wrote, 'cannot convey the doctrinal confusion, ineptitude and sheer chicanery of the run-of-the-mill incumbent, with his Thirty-Nine Articles in which he does not even purport to believe, with his listless exhortations, mumbled prayers and half-baked confusion of the Christian faith with better housing, shorter hours of work and the United Nations.' As for progress, it was not only an illusion but a devil's snare: 'The world has come to a full stop in its efforts to achieve Utopia,' he keened, adding: 'The joke is that man has created an utterly diabolical situation and then called it perfection.'

Sometimes it seemed as though nothing would ever please Mr Muggeridge again. He was, however, destined to receive from Heaven one precious gift, surely brought by an angel especially for him, and, it is to be hoped, duly acknowledged in his nightly prayers. At Emley Moor, in Yorkshire, the mast from which was transmitted the electrical impulses that became pictures on television screens tuned to commercial television throughout the area suddenly fell down, and at one blow rendered dark the television sets of four million people, and joyless their lives. This would in itself have been enough to cause Mr Muggeridge to fall upon his knees and praise God by measure, for he had long been of the opinion, and repeatedly declared, that television was a sin, a disgrace, an evil and a national disaster, and he was heard, it is said, to emit heartbroken sighs as he pocketed the substantial fees he was very properly paid whenever he appeared on it, which he did frequently. But there was more satisfaction still for Mr Muggeridge in the fall of the television mast, for it fell squarely athwart a Methodist chapel and smashed it to fragments, two men in the building at the time only narrowly escaping death or injury by diving beneath a pew.

O perfect symbolism! O awful warning! O if the things which were done in thee had been done in Sodom and Gomorrah, they would long since have repented in sackcloth and in ashes! For too long, Mr Muggeridge had argued, the Churches had gone a-whoring after strange gods, gods which flickered and squeaked in darkened rooms, and which were propitiated with burnt offerings consisting of pre-frozen television dinners served on special trays that clamped to the arm of a chair, so that the eater need not cease for a moment to be a viewer also. Clergymen, as well as Mr Muggeridge, had appeared on those screens, some trying to appear bonhomous and ordinary, some speaking of anything except religion and reacting with embarrassment, if not active distaste, whenever any of the lay performers raised the subject, some anxiously inquiring of those who would in an earlier day have looked to them for guidance what they might do to be saved. Now they were punished for their heresy, now they would suffer for their idolatry. From the sky the idol had been flung upon the temple, and those within had been hard put to it to get quickly enough beneath a pew. The casting out of modernism with Beelzebub could not be ignored, the great darkness that had come upon four million people, so that some thought themselves, when it happened, struck blind, must not be forgotten. Mr Muggeridge, it seemed for a moment, was right; those who live by the media will perish by the media, and men looked anxiously upward in case a bale of colour supplements should be hurtling downwards from a passing aeroplane.

* * *

But not all churches were falling; one at least was rising, and it is strange that Mr Muggeridge has still not been observed trying to fit it into his scheme of things, the more so since it was an extraordinary attempt to go against the grain of the times. This was the building of Coventry Cathedral.

The third cathedral to stand on the site, it replaced the one destroyed by bombing in 1940, and was designed and carried through by Basil Spence who, in his illuminating book on the subject,[1] says that he conceived the ambition to build a cathedral when he was dug in on the beaches of Normandy two days after the invasion of Europe by the Allies in 1944, and presumably had very little certainty of ever again building so much as a sandcastle, let alone a cathedral. However, he survived, and like some latter-day Jephtha remained determined to carry out his rash vow, so that when, after a series of bitter and hilarious disputes over the design for the new cathedral (first it was entrusted to Sir Giles Gilbert Scott, but his design was rejected by the Royal Fine Arts Commission, then the authorities decided to open it to competition, stipulating, however, that only designs in the 'Gothic style' would be acceptable, and finally the condition was stood on its head, and it was decided that anything *except* the 'Gothic style' would be considered), he had the opportunity of submitting a design for the new building, he seized the chance with such vigour and self-confidence that, of the two hundred and nineteen submissions, his was the clear and unanimous choice of the committee charged with the examination of the designs and the selection of the one to which Coventry Cathedral would be rebuilt, to the greater glory of God. Apart from anything else, Spence's Coventry was one of the last major buildings in Britain to be conceived entirely by a single mind; from then on, more and

[1] *Phoenix at Coventry* (Bles, London, 1962).

more buildings were the work of groups or partnerships of architects, and this seems likely to remain the pattern for the foreseeable future.

The tribulations that Spence went through in the building of his masterpiece at times recalled the ordeal undergone by Wren in the building of St Paul's, and a lesser spirit would have found not only his resolution, but his mind, giving way under the strain. Spence, however, survived, though by a curious turn of fate he was very nearly ruined in the process, since whenever his name fell to be considered by those in a position to commission architectural work from him, it was regretfully put aside, on the grounds that, since he was busy with the cathedral, he would obviously be unable to take on other work. After all this, and much more, including a substantial number of quarrels between various of the people involved (though rarely including Spence, a man of surprisingly mild temper for an artist who, by the nature of his art, must work in the real world as well as the world of the imagination), the building was finished, and consecrated in 1962 before a congregation consisting of the Queen and the Duke of Edinburgh, together with upwards of two thousand carefully chosen notabilities and other guests; at this point yet another fuss broke out, over the fact that the Communion at the consecration service was restricted to the royal family and their immediate entourage.

Spence had gathered around him a team of artists, to each of whom was entrusted some particular feature of the building, within his overall conception. Thus the mighty tapestry of Christ in Glory over the altar was the responsibility of Graham Sutherland; the baptistry window, ablaze with colour not seen in church glass for several centuries, the most notable feature of which is the central portion which burns bright gold when the sun strikes through it, was by John Piper; the nave windows, by a stroke of considerable daring, were entrusted to two young students of the Royal College of Art, Geoffrey Clarke and Keith New;[1] the sculpture of St Michael and the Devil (St Michael is

[1] They worked on the windows with their teacher, Laurence Lee.

the patron saint of the cathedral; the Devil needs no introduction) is the work of Jacob Epstein (it was his last major sculpture); the lectern is by Elizabeth Frink; the font consists of an unshaped boulder from Bethlehem, with a scallop design scooped out of the top by Ralph Beyer; the whole is enclosed in the now famous 'zigzag' walls in soft pink stone, and constitutes a supreme affirmation of a dying faith which, almost before the building was completed, was under radical attack from within as well as without.

Had the building of the cathedral been delayed another ten years, it seems hardly possible that it would have taken anything like the shape which Spence gave it, and even unlikely that it would have been built at all, since it came at what must have been the very last moment at which the affirmation of faith could be made, with general acceptance, in such a form. Coventry Cathedral therefore seems likely to be the last building of its kind to be built on such a scale in Britain, and to stand for future ages like a boundary-stone that marks the divide between one age and another. If, that is, it stands at all, for ever since the building was completed there have been rumours that the ground on which it is built suffers from subsidence, and that long before it has lasted as long as either of its predecessors (five hundred years in each case, the first being destroyed by Henry VIII and the second by Hitler) it will have collapsed more or less gracefully into a hole in the ground, though whether this catastrophe, if it happens, will be taken as a dreadful symbol of the collapse of the Anglican Church is another matter. Certainly if Mr Muggeridge is still about it will be.

* * *

Lenin and the Jesuits are both said to have believed, in the days of their greatest power, that if they were only enabled to teach the children their doctrines they would have believers for ever. (Both, to judge by what has happened since to the institutions they founded, were wrong.) St Mugg certainly seemed to share their view, but held it upside-down, for he came in the Sixties to regard education, particularly higher education, as the royal road to hell, and scarcely to be distinguished, in its vileness, from sex. Elected by the students of Edinburgh University as their rector, he took the opportunity of his rectorial address to denounce education in general, and the things he believed it led to in particular.

> There is no doubt that we shall go on raising the school age, multiplying and enlarging our universities, increasing public expenditure on education until juvenile delinquency, beats and drug-addicts and general intimations of illiteracy multiply so alarmingly that, at last, the whole process is called in question.
>
> In the same sort of way, the so-called 'permissive' morality of our time will, I am sure, reach its apogee. When birth pills are handed out with free orange juice, and consenting adults wear special ties and blazers, and abortion and divorce – those two contemporary panaceas for all matrimonial ills – are freely available on the public health, then at last, with the suicide rate up to Scandinavian proportions[1] and the psychiatric wards bursting at the seams, it will be realized that this path, even from the shallow point of view of the pursuit of happiness, is a disastrous cul-de-sac.
>
> The curtain, indeed, is falling if it has not already fallen on all the Utopian hopes which have prevailed so strongly for a century or more. I personally rejoice that it should be so because I know that then, looking desperately into the mystery of things, we shall once again understand that fulfilment must be sought through the spirit, not the body or the mind, and will be realized, if at all, elsewhere than in this world of time and space.[2]

[1] Mr Muggeridge's way with a fact has always been cavalier; but it would be a pity to let so handy an inaccuracy stand uncorrected. The belief that in Scandinavia, especially Sweden, the suicide rate is exceptionally high – a belief which has sustained several generations of opponents of the Welfare State – is a myth.

[2] *The Times*, February 17th, 1967.

Not long after his installation as rector at Edinburgh, the council of the student body decided to ask that contraceptive pills should be available from the university's health centre. This request, which took account of the fact that many undergraduates did in fact go to bed together, whether Mr Muggeridge would or no, and preferred advertising this fact to increasing the numbers of unwanted pregnancies that resulted from the still surprisingly high level of ignorance and inhibition about such matters in the young, Mr Muggeridge deplored. He, after all, had summed up his view of the matter with the words: 'Human love only shines in all its splendour when the last tiny glimmer of desire has been extinguished' – and did not see why those in whom that last tiny glimmer had *not* been extinguished should follow the road he had at last forsaken.

He therefore took the opportunity to resign from the post of rector, announcing his decision from the pulpit of St Giles Cathedral, the High Kirk of Edinburgh. The core of his sermon was as follows:

> The students in this university are the ultimate beneficiaries in our welfare system. They are supposed to be the spearhead of progress, flattered and paid for by their admiring seniors, an elite who will happily and audaciously carry the torch of progress into the glorious future opening before them.
>
> There is practically nothing they can do, in a mood of rebelliousness or refusal to accept the ways and values of our run-down, spiritually impoverished way of life, for which I should not feel some degree of sympathy or at least understanding, up to and including blowing up this magnificent edifice in which we now sit.
>
> How sad, how macabre and funny it is that all they put forward should be a demand for pot and pills. It is the most tenth-rate form of indulgence ever known. It is the resort of any old slobbering debauchee anywhere in the world at any time – 'dope and bed'. The feeling raised in me is not so much disapproval as contempt. This, as you may imagine,

> makes it difficult, indeed impossible, for me as rector to fulfil my function.[1]

In fairness to the students, it should be pointed out that at no time had they put forward any demand for 'pot'; the belief that they had stemmed from the alarming fantasies which welled up from Mr Muggeridge's by now deeply disturbed psyche. But he left the post and the pulpit simultaneously, and left the rectorship neatly booby-trapped by saying that the ensuing election to fill his vacated post 'would show what calibre of candidate would come forward who would accept these views of the Students' Representative Council, and would also show what were the opinions of most of the students'. (At the subsequent election the victor was Mr Kenneth Allsop.)

From then on St Mugg became a well-known 'turn', much in demand from organizations that wanted a neatly packaged denunciation of other people's immorality. He denounced the practice of heart transplants, he visited Westminster Abbey and, finding it a-clatter with transient visitors, declared: 'If I were dean I would bar tourists' ('But I *am* dean,' said the dean, and continued to allow them in), and wrote the epitaph on his own decline in these scarcely credible words:

> My greatest, indeed, as I grow older, my only earthly dread is that our present way of life should prove viable. I find in the bomb a welcome assurance that such fears are groundless ... If there had been no cliff the Gadarene Swine would have had nowhere to hurl themselves. The bomb constitutes a cliff, and we should be duly grateful for it.[2]

How sad was that decline, how sad that one of the bravest and most astringent minds of the time should now cower so cravenly in a corner, begging the world to stop trying to inflame his withered desires, lest the attempt should prove successful! Yet the realization of what lay at the bottom of his revulsion from

[1] *The Times*, January 15th, 1968.
[2] *Sunday Times*, August 1st, 1965.

the world and all that therein dwelt did not diminish, for those who admired him, the sadness at the spectacle of Mr Muggeridge, without even realizing it, basing his entire new-found philosophy on the vain plea of Sir Thomas Browne in 1642:

> I could be content that we might procreate like trees, without conjunction, or that there were any way to perpetuate the World without this trivial and vulgar way of Coition; it is the foolishest act a wise man commits in all his life; nor is there any thing that will more deject his cool'd imagination, when he shall consider what an odd and unworthy piece of folly he hath committed.

In the Sixties, Malcolm Muggeridge's imagination was cool'd indeed.

7

# Odium theologicum

And yet Mr Muggeridge was not, even at his most extreme, speaking in a moral vacuum, nor was he addressing himself to matters in which other men professed no interest. On the contrary he was involved in one of the most important debates of the entire decade, and one which stressed yet again its two-headed nature, standing at the crossroads which lay at the heart of the territory the Sixties had to traverse.

A theological storm of huge proportions broke during the decade, and happily to hand came, to start with, a lightning-conductor in the form of a new translation of the New Testament, planned and directed, said the editors, 'with the object of providing English readers, whether familiar with the Bible or not, with a faithful rendering ... into the current speech of our own time'. To embark upon a new translation of the Bible with a misconception as gigantic as that, which supposes that the current speech of our or any time may be stopped in its ever-developing course to enable those who use it to be reached in their own tongue, as if the translators who created the Authorized Version used the current speech of *their* own time and succeeded because of it, augured ill for the enterprise. Sure enough, the result was a language dead to the eyes, the ears and the mind, and which neither the people of King James's day nor those of Queen Elizabeth the Second's – nor, indeed, those of any day in between – would have recognized as part of their current speech. Its critics ranged from those who regarded a new translation of the Bible from an aesthetic point of view to those who saw it solely as a theological problem, with those who insisted that it was only a linguistic one somewhere in the middle. On the whole criticism was muted; ominously, enthusiasm was even more muted, and those who lacked it could hardly be blamed for not responding to a translation which tottered between 'And they went each to his home' and 'He saw how crafty their question was, and said, "Why are you trying to catch me out?"'

Then the storm broke. 'It is not every day', said the *Church Times* in an editorial, 'that a bishop goes on public record as apparently denying almost every Christian doctrine of the Church in which he holds office.' Nowadays, of course, it is, or at least it seems as though it is, but when John Robinson, then Bishop of Woolwich, published *Honest to God*[1] in 1963, it was more of a novelty.

In a decade as embattled as the Sixties it was hardly likely that religion would remain off the battlefield, that it would not experience, as every other aspect of personal and public life experienced, the strains caused by the certain past letting go and the uncertain future taking hold. Nor can it be argued that the signs of the Rough Beast's coming had not been visible for some time, that portents had not been plentiful enough. Everywhere the churches stood empty, men quarrelled at the very doors of the synagogues, the muezzin from the tower called in vain. 'He put his arm around the heart of the world,' wrote Cassandra in the *Daily Mirror* about Pope John, an ominously sugary phrase that summed up the extraordinary effect this extraordinary man had had, an effect much commented upon, often without the commentators noticing that Pope John's appeal had been overwhelmingly to unbelievers, who had sadly misunderstood his purpose and translated it, for their better comfort, into a vague apple-cheeked goodwill. God had clearly failed; perhaps Man would do better?

The problems were two, one more modern than the other. Belief had always been difficult, evil a hard bone to gnaw, dogma and liturgy remote and incomprehensible, the creeds easier to repeat than to understand and easier to understand than to live by.

[1] S.C.M. Press, London.

But now there was worse. 'There is a large part of the community quite indifferent to religion,' said the Archbishop of Canterbury in 1969, in an understatement of sublime dimensions. By the Sixties it was easier to get a camel to pass through the eye of a needle than to get men, rich or poor, into the churches. Half of them were still married in church, many brought their children for baptism (though few for confirmation), many sought to be buried, or to bury their relatives, in the bosom of the church. At Easter attendances rose, though it was noted with sadness that the Easter Offering, traditionally devoted to the upkeep of the pastor, had not risen by a proportion commensurate with the fall in the value of money; at Christmas, too, many a church was filled, if not with the devout, then at any rate with the musical. But for the rest of the year those indignant writers of letters to the newspapers who, outraged by some deplorable act of immorality or selfishness (or what they saw as immorality or selfishness, which was not necessarily the same thing), were accustomed to ask whether Britain was or was not a Christian country, had long since been answered in the negative.

What was to be done? All around, the prophets, false and true (though the confusion was made worse by the fact that none could tell which was which), thundered their answers, which were as mutually contradictory as ever in history. Some said that there was no sin, others that there was nothing else, still others that there might be, but if so it was not what had for so long been thought of as sin. Everywhere men longed for a scientific form of myth, a non-compulsory set of commandments, an undivine God. Such demands were not new; they had been made afresh in every age, and always sternly refused. The refusals had, in the past, been met in a variety of ways: some of those refused had run mad, or heretical, or launched Reformations, or communed secretly with the Devil, or accepted the refusal as best they might. Now, however, and indeed for a long time, men had met refusal with indifference, so that instead of running their heads against the stone front of the Church they had turned away and found better things to do.

At which point influential voices had begun to ask whether the Churches were right to refuse man's demands, or whether perhaps they had themselves been mistaken all along. Not many years previously such doubts had existed only on the periphery of the Churches and their activities. When in 1948 the Bishop of Birmingham, in his *Rise of Christianity*,[1] had cast subtle doubt on some of the traditional beliefs of orthodox Christianity, the Archbishop of Canterbury, it is true, had said: 'If I held his views I would feel compelled to resign'; but the subjunctive came to the bishop's rescue; *he* felt no compulsion to resign, and if he should have done, what then should the action of Canon Stanley Evans have been, who wrote five years later in an obituary of Stalin that

> Working people who have seen in him the leader of their historic struggle for emancipation; Asiatic people who have seen in him their greatest and most powerful friend; colonial peoples who have seen in him the lode-star of their liberation; honest men and women of every class and every philosophy who have seen in him an outstanding leader in the struggle for world peace in which we are now engaged – these too have mourned.[2]

In those days the bosom of the Church was broad enough to accommodate everything, from doubt to Stalin-worship, because the Church was confident that, in the last resort, the people would rally to her support. The Church was right, too. Two years later than Canon Evans's heartfelt grief for the world's most outstanding practitioner of mass-murder, poor Mrs Margaret Knight, who had never murdered anybody, ran into a terrible storm for saying on the sacred airwaves of the B.B.C. that Christianity was not literally true and that people could be good without believing in God; she was denounced by a thousand voices, the loudest being that of the *Daily Sketch*, a paper not usually noted for the intensity of its religious fervour, which

[1] Longman's, London, 1947.
[2] Society of Socialist Clergy and Ministers, 1953.

called the good lady 'The UnGodly Mrs Knight'. In those days her defenders were few and their voices low; happily, she lived to see the boot laced firmly up on the other foot. When the Bishop of Woolwich published *Honest to God* it was the voices of his opponents and critics that gave off a timid and querulous sound.

Over his arguments, what they were and what they signified, there has been much dispute, and it is certainly not yet settled, though amid the dispute there is at any rate one fact that no party to it will deny, namely that at least three-quarters of a million copies of his book have so far been sold (the original print-order by the Student Christian Movement Press was for six thousand, and when this was sold out on the day of publication a further three thousand were ordered, and then – as the publishers came to realize that they were dealing with something rather far out of the ordinary – another twenty thousand, since when the presses have scarcely stopped turning), a total reached by few theological works of the past other than the Bible. So whatever the bishop had written, and whatever he had intended to write, and whatever others might claim that he had written, there could and can be no doubt that a very large number of people wanted to read it.

To start with, of course, he had one advantage over most other Anglican bishops: large numbers of people had heard of him. It is true that the reason for their knowledge of this particular bishop was somewhat adventitious, stemming from the fact that he had given evidence for the defence in the *Lady Chatterley* case, on that occasion going so far as to say that *Lady Chatterley's Lover* was a book that all Christians might read with profit, and also using, perhaps in an unguarded moment, a phrase that he was almost certainly to regret later, and which has been used as a stick to beat him with, especially by Mr Quintin Hogg, who has ever since gone up and down the land saying that the bishop compared Lawrence's book to Holy Communion. In fact all the bishop had done was to quote the admirable words of Archbishop Temple, who had said that Christians do not make jokes about sex for the same reason that they do not make jokes about Communion – not because it is too sordid, but because it is too sacred, adding that in this sense the Christian view of sex was that it was indeed a form of holy communion. (He even went so far, lest anybody should miss the point accidentally, to add here, 'lower case, of course', thus indicating that he meant the words to be spelled without capital letters, because he was using them not in their theological sense, as the name given to the Sacrament, but in their literal or colloquial sense, which was excellently said, for whatever view is taken of the sexual act, those who believe, as presumably Christians do, that all the things of man are given to man by God must accept that sex too is holy, and that it is an act of communion they would be hard put to it to deny.)

From that day forth the bishop was a marked man, and he was marked not only by his enemies, but by the general public, who, more tolerant than they are often given credit for being, may have felt, as they bought *Lady Chatterley's Lover* to the tune of four million copies, that if they could read and enjoy it, it was not for them to criticize the bishop for doing so. When, therefore, he published his book, the numbers sold suggest that many who would not otherwise have ventured to tread upon the thin ice of theology may have bought it to find out what he was up to now, and perhaps in a few cases because they were sufficiently confused to believe that he was the author of *Lady Chatterley's Lover* and that this might be a sequel.

If so, these purchasers must have been disappointed, even with the notorious Chapter Six; this introduced a phrase – indeed, it is the title of the chapter – which, although the bishop did not coin it, and puts it into quotation-marks to show that he did not, has been tied ever since not only to him but to all those who seek to increase the charity-content in human relations and in the Churches' view thereof. The phrase was 'The New Morality', and as a matter of historical interest it should be said that it was coined by the Holy Office in the Roman Catholic Church, with no kindly intent. The New Morality to Bishop Robinson was not new at all, of course, but he would have had to be very naive (in some ways, it is clear, he is) not to realize that a remark like 'Nothing can of itself always be labelled as "wrong"' would cause great scandal, especially since he promptly illustrates its meaning by examples in the field of extra-marital sexual relations. Great scandal is what the chapter did indeed cause, especially among many who had not read it, just as the tougher parts of the book – his theological arguments for a demythologized Christianity, a depersonalized, or at any rate unlocated, God, and ultimately an unreligious religion – caused great outcry among many of those who could not bear, or thought they could not bear, to see such massive dogmas challenged.

'What should happen to an Anglican bishop who does not believe in God?' asked T. E. Utley in the *Sunday Telegraph*, adding that his question was one of 'Church discipline which cannot be shirked without the gravest repercussions on the whole Anglican Communion', and going on to make it clear that, in his view, the bishop should be driven from his see, and lamenting only that the procedures of the Anglican Church were too cumbersome to enable this to be done easily.

Others were even more direct. A colonel wrote to the bishop to say that he had done nothing to cure the widespread lack of faith and moral fibre, but on the contrary had gone 'out of his way to offend so many by such objectionable publications', which did 'little more than to quote from the heretical out-pourings of Bonhoeffer, Tillich and other alien agnostics'. A clergyman, who criticized Bishop Robinson in rather more charitable terms, ended by begging him

> not to publish these sensational advanced ideas in the public press; for you are not there speaking to trained minds, but to people who need – not the strong meat of the advanced theologian, but the simple milk of the Gospel.

Another critic, Canon Fenton Morley, illustrated the common inability of many of the critics to make up their minds whether the bishop was to be condemned because he had led the faithful astray or because he had entirely failed to reach them; at one point the canon said the bishop's book 'represents a tendency to please the senior common-room agnostic', and at another declared that it 'seems to have failed to get through to the man in the cloth cap', a dualism of attitude that ran parallel to the twin claims, also heard at the time the book was published, that the bishop's attack on the concept of a God 'out there' was both a cruel theft of a comforting image from those who had held it all their lives, and a laughable work of supererogation, since nobody had believed anything of the kind for many years.

The temperature mounted rapidly. An energetic Scottish lady cried out that 'A bishop who writes a book like this should be stripped to his socks', and inked in the enchanting picture she thus conjured up by adding: 'If the Archbishop of Canterbury doesn't unfrock him, I and the women of England will'; alas, she never made good her threat, so the public debagging of a bishop, a spectacle which would surely have attracted spectators of all shades of religious opinion and of none, never took place.

As far away as Belgium a newspaper said that the bishop's 'extremely confused definition of divinity will only please supporters of German metaphysics', and harked back to the priest who had warned the bishop against feeding strong meat to simple milk-drinkers with 'What is disturbing is that his book has such readership.' *The Times* took an even narrower view of the bishop's inopportune publication: 'It seems', said that newspaper, 'cruelly discouraging to many Christians'; and went on: 'Is it for one of our fathers in God, they might ask, to wash our dirty linen in public?'

Mr Ivor Bulmer-Thomas, who had once been a Labour Member of Parliament (of, it must be said, a singularly conservative stripe), when he had been plain Mr Thomas, but had subsequently left Parliament, taken to himself a hyphen, and risen far in the lay work of the Church of England, declared to the Church Assembly that 'If a questionnaire had been taken as to who had done the most harm to the Church of England since Bishop Barnes, ninety-nine per cent would put the Bishop of

Woolwich at the head of their list', a statement sufficiently dogmatic to distract attention from the fact that that would not in itself prove the bishop wrong, and also from the fact that Mr Bulmer-Thomas had provided no evidence for his suspiciously all-embracing statistic.

Eventually even the Archbishop of Canterbury's sixteen stone toppled slowly but inexorably off the fence, like a man falling in a dream. He wrote a pamphlet called *Image Old and New*,[1] which did not sell nearly so many copies as the bishop's book, but in which the archbishop began by saying that 'It should be the mark of Christian faith to learn from the shock of new ideas, but it is also necessary to see where such ideas may be misleading' – an unpromising start, which was eventually followed by the nearest approach he seemed willing to make to a conclusion, with the words: 'There is ever an urgent place for *withdrawal* in the Christian life, far beyond what the new school of thought realizes or allows. It is demanded by the relation of man and the world to the Creator; and this is a doctrine which (so far) comes but little, if at all, into the Christianity of the New Image ...'

But the crash of a million and a half half-crowns on the bookshop counters made more noise than the bishop's critics. *Something* in what he was saying must have captured the imagination of the Sixties to produce that effect. Perhaps he had not quite

> ... cried to the lifted thunder
> Of thronging hammer and hod
> 'Throw open the third window
> In the third name of God',

but he had started a theological discussion, in a profoundly untheological time, on a scale that had certainly not been seen since the Tractarians, perhaps not since the days when the Anglican Church was being founded on the rock of Henry VIII's divorce. For the bishop's defenders were not merely the mute hundreds of thousands who had bought his book, nor the less mute thousands who had written to him (they far outnumbered

[1] S.P.C.K., London, 1963.

the critics) to thank him for it; they also numbered some powerful and eminent thinkers in their ranks. If the Bishop of Bristol felt moved to say that the Bishop of Woolwich 'could perhaps be accused of irresponsibility in publishing his book', there was the Dean of Trinity College, Cambridge, to reply: 'One cannot but admire the sense of responsibility shown by the episcopal bench as a whole. It is so profound that it has prevented them from saying anything of theological importance for at least the past two decades.' If the Bishop of Pontefract could declare that *Honest to God* was a 'dangerous book likely to disturb the faith of more people than it will stimulate', there did not lack a Bishop of Llandaff to say that 'We find ourselves obliged to ask questions about things which we have thought and said and accepted for years, and when we try to answer them we find the bishop's answers so often ring more true than our own', and to add, of the chapter called 'Worldly Holiness', that 'No Christian can read it without profit', which was almost what the Bishop of Woolwich had said about *Lady Chatterley's Lover*, though not quite.

* * *

Books like *Honest to God* do not spring, complete to the last quotation from Tillich and Bonhoeffer, from the head of a bishop without having first got into the head in question. St Simeon Stylites could not have written such a book, and perhaps the Bishop of Woolwich could not have written it either until the air of the Sixties became so thick with the tensions between new worlds and old ones that it infected his mind. All such works are to some extent the product of their time and of the spirit of their age, and although it is profitless to discuss to precisely *what* extent this is true, it is useful to remember, in the present case, that the Sixties were a time of theological ferment, not only in the Church of England but in other Churches, and not only in Britain but elsewhere. The upheavals of the Vatican Council, where the Jews were relieved, not without some opposition, of the charge of deicide, and ecumenicism and reunion were the order of the day, where the ancient condemnation of Anglican orders was softened, as Lord Acton stared amazed from his grave at the difference between Pope and Pope—these things too were part of the decade, and mirrored in their way what was happening to the Church of England. Nay, in Britain the Jews themselves, who had not had a theological dispute for several centuries, were riven asunder by an argument over the questioned orthodoxy of Rabbi Louis Jacobs, who found himself labelled at one point 'the Jewish Bishop of Woolwich', a description which may well have pleased neither the rabbi nor the bishop. Rabbi Jacobs was widely expected to become Chief Rabbi of Britain, but fell into disfavour with his ecclesiastical superiors, and schismatized. Then a new potential Chief Rabbi arrived, from the United States, cautiously refraining from committing himself until he had seen how the land lay, and seeing how it lay with such appalling clarity that he promptly had a heart attack and returned to the United States as soon as he was well enough to travel. Finally another rabbi, Dr Jakobowits, plunged bravely into the battle, to such effect that on the surface at any rate things rapidly became calm, though beneath it the argument rumbled on.

All these things were happening in the world of religion in the turbulent Sixties, and the Bishop of Woolwich was by no means the only author to challenge orthodox belief. Before his book was written, a significant volume of essays called *Soundings*[1] had appeared, with names that were already causing stirrings among the faithful, names like Vidler and Williams and Montefiore. The first sentence of the introduction to *Soundings* says that 'The authors of this volume of essays cannot persuade themselves that the time is ripe for major works of theological construction or reconstruction', and looks forward to others doing what they recognize they cannot themselves do 'in a future generation'. Little did they know, unless, as is possible, Dr Vidler (author of the Introduction) had his tongue in his cheek, and suspected very well the explosion that was shortly to take place, how soon future generations would be knocking on the door, on all doors,

[1] Ed. Rev. A. Vidler (Cambridge University Press, Cambridge, 1962).

of churches, cathedrals, theological seminaries and the houses of plain men. Less than a year after *Soundings* the *Daily Herald* streamed across many columns the headline 'GOD IS NOT A DADDY IN THE SKY'—words which not many years before would have killed the paper's circulation overnight—and the *Observer* a month or two later, in fittingly smarter tones, was giving a kind of guide to swinging theologians ('At Glasgow, Professor Gregor Smith was actually married by Barth; at Edinburgh, Tom Torrance was one in his household ... The Chadwick brothers, one at Oxford and one at Cambridge; Cross; the fragile, profound, wayward Warden of Keble, Austin Farrer ... '). Then there was the bishop himself, and soon the works of those 'alien agnostics'—Bonhoeffer, Tillich and Bultmann—whom he had quoted so pertinently in his book (Bultmann surprised everybody by being alive, and actually writing a review of *Honest to God* in a German newspaper) were being published in English. Anon came a volume of lectures called *Objections to Christian Belief*,[1] which was not what it sounded, for the contributors were all concerned to *answer* the objections to Christian belief in their own field. After that there was Canon Douglas Rhymes with a book called *No New Morality*,[2] which was devoted entirely to finding a new basis for sexual morality, and caused scandal even more painful among that rapidly diminishing band who were capable of being scandalized, for in it he denounced almost the whole of traditional Church teaching on the subject, and concluded that 'sex is good and enjoyable if it serves the fulfilment of man as a total being.' A former Cabinet Minister, Lord Eccles, joined the throng (he must have been the first since Gladstone to publish a work of theology) with a book the title of which—*Half-Way to Faith*[3]—indicated the nature of his own dilemma and that of many more whom the Bishop of Woolwich had tried to reach, though Eccles made it coldly clear that the bishop had failed in

[1] Constable, London, 1963.
[2] Constable, London, 1964.
[3] Bles, London, 1966.

his case; Monica Furlong hurled *With Love to the Church*[1] at the Church's head, and raised bruises; James Mitchell edited a volume of essays under the appealingly impertinent title *The God I Want*;[2] an entire book was published on the reception and impact of *Honest to God*, called *The Honest to God Debate*[3] (in the climate of the times the publishers might have been tempted to go further and call it *Son of Honest to God*); the bishop, emboldened, agreed to write a series of articles for the *Sunday Pictorial*, in which he briskly disposed of Adam and Eve, the Virgin Birth, Life after Death, the Resurrection ('Next Sunday: Did Christ really rise from the tomb?') and the Miracles; further emboldened, he declared that 'Regarded as a code of conduct, the Sermon on the Mount is quite impracticable', on the grounds that it 'tears the individual loose from any horizontal nexus'; further emboldened still, he declared, in answer to those of his critics who still had breath left (the M.R.A. spokesman had declared, in the weirdest of all the attacks the bishop had to suffer, that he approved of 'concubines and teenage contraceptives') that 'What is dissolving is the *casing* of the Church, and ... this process could be one of release and liberation', spoke of 'pulpits six feet above contradiction', added that 'The pains of disintegration are salutary', and summed up by saying that 'The next five years, I suspect, will tell which way the Church will die.'

It was all very exciting, and many a theologian must have concluded that bliss was it in that dawn to be alive, but to have a good publisher was very Heaven. Yet there was a real argument going on. 'People today', said Bishop Robinson some years after the publication of his book, 'are looking for points of meeting and commitment that will not take them out of the world – and will bring them together face to face, not face to back as in the traditional pew.' And in *Honest to God* itself he had said, in the Preface: 'I believe we are being called, over the years ahead, to far more than a restating of traditional orthodoxy in modern terms. Indeed,

[1] Hodder and Stoughton, London, 1965.

[2] Constable, London, 1967.

[3] Ed. Rev. David Edwards (S.C.M. Press, London, 1963).

if our defence of the Faith is limited to this, we shall find in all likelihood that we have lost out to all but a tiny religious remnant.' (Only St Mugg believed it to be the Church's *duty* to 'lose out to all but a tiny religious remnant'.)

It was not simply, of course, that the new theology and the new morality were designed to make it easier for men to practise what they pleased without feeling guilty about it, though that is what many of the opponents of the bishop and his associates declared. They had gone deeper, and searched out, with the aid of depth-psychology, anthropology, sociology and many another science, the springs of traditional Christian belief, and sometimes what they found at the end of their search was by no means comforting, as the famous dream recounted by Mr Harry Williams of Cambridge made terribly clear. Indeed, the episode of 'Williams's Dream', as we may call it, deserves recounting at length, for the lesson it teaches can be considered the crux of the whole argument, so that those who accept the lesson have overthrown the old gods and those who reject it stand by the old gods, and eventually it will be determined whether the accepters or rejecters have carried the day. Said Mr Williams:

> I know a man – he was a person of some academic intelligence – who was loyally practising his religion as a devout and rather high church Anglican. One night he had a nightmare which proved to be a turning point in his life. In his dream he was sitting in a theatre watching a play. He turned round and looked behind him. At the back of the theatre there was a monster in human form who was savagely hypnotizing the actors on the stage, reducing them to puppets. The spectacle of this harsh inhuman puppeteer exercising his hypnotic powers so that the people on the stage were completely under his spell and the slaves of his will – this spectacle was so terrifying the man awoke trembling and in a cold sweat. After several months he gradually realized that the monster of the nightmare was the god he was really worshipping ... And to this god he had painfully to die. He had

to accept the terrible truth that the practice of his religion had been a desperate attempt to keep his eyes averted from the monster of the nightmare ... His dream showed him that he was a devil's slave—his devotion and his goodness being a compulsive response to a deeply embedded feeling of guilt ... But ... life and behaviour based on feelings of guilt exclude charity. To be bullied, compelled, by subtle inner unidentifiable fear to apparent worship and goodness is to destroy the self. And without a self one cannot give. There can be no charity, no love for God or man. The dreamer ... was seen, about two years after his nightmare, drunk among the bars and brothels of Tangier.[1] He was learning that for him evil was not what the priests had told him it was, but rather that evil was the disguised slavery to his own hidden corruption ... Now I am not suggesting that it is a good or morally desirable thing to spend one's time drunk among the bars and brothels of any city. What I am suggesting ... is that there are worse, much worse, evils than that ... If ... you are the slave of guilt-feelings, you can deceive yourself and call it the service of God or even free response to God's love. That is why a congregation of 'good' people in church can be much further from the heart of God than those who have strayed from the path of conventional behaviour.[2]

With that it may be seen how far, in the Sixties, the shaking of the foundations had progressed, for from that point there could be no turning back, and those with an interest in theology, deep or superficial, had to choose between a received authority which declared that there was nothing, or not many things, worse than to be drunk among the bars and brothels of Tangier, and a new understanding that announced that there were many much worse things, and among them could be the practice of the Christian religion.

* * *

[1] It should be stressed that Mr Williams's friend recovered his stability, found a new, surer basis for his Christian faith, and rose to ecclesiastical preferment.

[2] *Objections to Christian Belief.*

As with so much in the Sixties, it was Authority that was challenged, and challenged by men who had seen it from the inside, so that if the foundations were shaking they were doing so because they were being sapped from beneath rather than battered from without. Now it is a mark of Authority, indeed almost a definition, that it must be either accepted or rejected, and so, once it has been rejected, new reasons for following the precepts it has taught must be found, if they are to be followed at all. Finding these new reasons was the chief work of the new theology, and that work could therefore be seen as an attempt to provide foundations that would be more secure than the old ones, because founded in greater knowledge of man and his nature. Such an argument could hardly be expected to appeal to Authority, which was caught in a cruel dilemma, since it could hardly claim much success in modern times for its own way of going about things, yet could not, equally, admit that it had gone about them the wrong way for years, if not centuries. Nor was there anywhere a representative of Authority to speak with the confidence of Dostoievsky's Grand Inquisitor, who denounced Christ himself for bringing to men by his example a freedom that could only destroy them, as they were incapable of exercising it. Even the Pope had left the Grand Inquisitor in the lurch, and his attempts to get back to his old ally only emphasized the more cruelly how complete had been his abandonment.

Nevertheless the attempt was made. One of the first acts of Pope Paul's papacy was the appointment of a commission to advise him on a subject the Roman Catholic Church had long been nerving herself to face: contraception, and the Church's traditional teaching on it. The development of new methods of preventing conception, in particular by means of a pill taken orally, had raised the question whether the Church should now relax her teaching on this matter, which was that all forms of artificial contraception were contrary to God's Law, and therefore sinful. The commission deliberated long and came to the conclusion, by a large majority, that the Church should indeed speak on the matter with a different voice. The Pope, however, deliberated longer, and in spite of many appeals to him by a number of authoritative voices in his own Church, including a dramatic flight to his side by Cardinal Alfrink of Holland, where the Roman Catholic hierarchy had long since entirely abandoned the traditional prohibition and much else of the Church's teaching, finally came to the conclusion that God called upon him to uphold the doctrine and to forbid those who accepted his teaching to practise any form of artificial contraception whatever.

It might have been thought that this was a matter concerning only those who accepted the Pope's authority, since those who did not could hardly be expected to obey it; but although the encyclical *Humanae vitae* aroused a storm that shook the foundations of the Roman Catholic communion quite as much as the new theology was shaking those of the Anglican, a surprisingly high proportion of the protests and criticisms came from those who were not of the Roman Catholic persuasion, and in many cases from those who were not very noticeably of any. The Bishop of Woolwich, for instance, said tersely that 'Few will now bother to ask whether the Pope is infallible; they are more concerned with whether the Pill is infallible';[1] the Planned Parenthood Federation said that the Pope's decision would 'encourage those who have a vested interest in carrying out unskilled and illegal abortions'; and the *Daily Mirror* said editorially that the Pope was 'mistaken in his decision'.

Among Roman Catholics, however, the volume of disagreement and disaffection was no less considerable, and clearly astonished and dismayed the Pope and the Roman hierarchy. To the claim made by Cardinal Ottaviani that 'The Church cannot have erred for centuries' a large number of voices were raised to say that the Church had certainly erred now. The most extreme view among Catholics in Britain was that of Dr Anne Biezanek, who had for some time been refused the sacrament because she ran a clinic at which advice on birth-control was dispensed; she said simply that 'The Pope's stand is evil.' This was putting it strongly, but Paul Johnson, a Roman Catholic and editor of the

[1] Medical evidence has shown that it is not. Score one for the Pope.

*New Statesman*, put it scarcely less strongly in his own way when, ever on the alert for a conspiracy, he declared of the Pope's decision that it had been 'shaped more by the need to appease powerful reactionaries in the Church than by the real merits of the argument', and added that 'Most Catholic parents feel that they know more about the practical problems of married life than an elderly bachelor in Rome' – which, though doubtless true, did not advance the argument, which was one about God's law rather than the practical problems of married life, and on which it was at least possible that the elderly bachelor might be as well informed as most Catholic parents. One such Catholic parent was Lady Antonia Fraser, who said sharply of the Pope that 'He could have spared a paragraph in his long encyclical to assist the people who will be left holding the baby.' Another Catholic layman who had never been averse to giving advice to the Pope or indeed anybody else who he thought might be in need of it was Norman St John Stevas, M.P., who described the encyclical as 'partial, inadequate, and propaganda rather than rational theological argument', and argued this view at greater length in an essay called *The Pope, the Pill and the People*.[1]

But it was not only among the Catholic laity that the encyclical had caused disturbance. In Britain the first official statement on the subject was by Cardinal Heenan, who said: 'The encyclical is clear enough; this was no snap decision' – a statement which, though undeniable, did not advance matters very far. A number of priests advanced them a good deal further, so much further, in fact, that they were suspended from their duties, whereupon a fund was set up by their parishioners to maintain them, and fifty-five priests joined in the writing of a letter to *The Times* making it clear that they were unable to accept the teaching, presently being joined by seventy-six leading laymen.

Eventually the English and Welsh bishops met, discussed the matter, and put forth their conclusions, which were, according to Cardinal Heenan's gloss on it, that 'The priest has to say: "This is the teaching of the Vicar of Christ in the encyclical"; he can then

[1] Paul Hamlyn, London, 1968.

say: "For my part, personally, I do not agree" '–though it was promptly pointed out that even this did not solve the problem, since it did not actually indicate what the laity ought to *do*. In any case, the ambiguities in the statement were sufficient to persuade the Right Reverend Anselm Thatcher to withdraw from his priestly duties on the grounds that the bishops had failed to support the Pope's ruling without equivocation; he would have found comfort, and perhaps a cure of souls, in Scotland, where the bishops made it clear that they accepted the Pope's encyclical without reservation.

It seemed probable that the encyclical was, up and down the land, setting brother against brother and husband against wife; certainly there was irrefutable proof that it was setting nephew against uncle, indeed against uncles, for Father John Harriott severely criticized both of his (they were also priests) for their action in forbidding the sale, at the doors of their churches, of the *Catholic Herald*, which had taken editorially a critical view of the Pope's ruling. At Leatherhead matters went further still, when a prominent lay member of the Church announced that, to signal his disapproval of the Pope's encyclical, he would until it was rescinded put in the collection plate not money, nor money's worth, but a written protest, and invited others to follow his example.

The clerical opposition to the Pope's teaching was summarized succinctly and pointedly by Father Peter da Rosa, a young priest whose outstanding intellectual ability had been recognized early and who had been appointed to a most responsible teaching post in consequence, while his striking good looks and charm of manner had at the same time made him much in demand for putting the Roman Catholic point of view on television. He was among the fifty-five priests who had signed the letter of protest, and later wrote publicly that he saw 'bishops everywhere, not least in England, realizing, with due love and respect for the Holy Father and his office, that they too are true shepherds of their flocks and not just Vatican sheepdogs obedient to every whistle, and snarling and snapping at the heels of wayward sheep'.

Yet the Pope's view was unmistakable, and, to those who accepted his authority, presumably undeniable. 'One cannot', said Father Geoffrey Smith of St Ethelreda's, Holborn, 'subordinate moral principles for expediency', and thus revealed the nature of the argument, for if it was true that God forbade, through the voice of his Vicar, the use of, as the Pope put it, 'every action which, either in anticipation of the conjugal act, or in its accomplishment, or in the development of its natural consequences, proposes, whether as an end or as a means, to render procreation impossible', no plea that this would cause great hardship and suffering could be accepted, and only two courses of action were open to those unable to accept the ruling, these being either to insist that the Pope had misunderstood his divine instructions or, accepting that he had heard aright, reject the instructions themselves, and his God with them.

The Pope's encyclical, said Douglas Woodruff, a prominent Catholic layman, was 'a reminder that the mission of the Catholic Church is with the eternal destiny of the human soul'—a view which, whether right or wrong, could hardly have been contrasted more strongly with the view of the Bishop of Woolwich that 'Persons matter, and the deepest welfare of the particular persons in this particular situation matters, more than anything else in the world', and it began to be clear that, *mutatis mutandis*, one view or the other would have to be accepted in the Church of England as much as in the Church of Rome. (Of the Church of England's attitude to the encyclical there could be no doubt, the Archbishop of Canterbury, as soon as it was promulgated, restating the Anglican view that 'The means adopted to limit the number of children in a family are a matter for the consciences of each husband and wife.')

In Rome the Pope's distress continued to grow, as further evidence appeared almost daily of the extent to which his authority was no longer accepted by his flock, and he whose election had been hailed as a triumph for those forces, set in motion by Pope John, which would blow a new wind through the halls of Catholicism, was now not only denounced by large sections of the more articulate of the faithful, but began to respond to the denunciations in a manner that could only increase them.

He demanded obedience; it was not offered. He called for silence; the noise redoubled. He thundered against 'corrosive criticism', 'excessive ecumenism', against the opposition to his encyclical, finally against 'anarchy' which he insisted was tearing the Church apart, nay, was 'crucifying it anew'. A newspaper plot was discovered by the Vatican authorities, and a Jesuit theologian, a Father Greco, wrote in the Vatican newspaper that 'A well-financed, massive pro-pill lobby has for years been at work in the Roman Catholic world, trying to force the Church to accept contraception.' All in vain; though Malcolm Muggeridge spurred to the Pope's rescue, declaring that, although he was not a Catholic, and indeed only a dubious kind of Christian, he welcomed the encyclical, it was clear that the affair had breached a dam for the Catholics, as John Robinson's book had for Anglicans, that would never be repaired. And sales of the oral contraceptive pill, medical researchers presently reported, not only continued to rise but, since the controversy began, rose even faster, the only rational explanation for which curious (and, for the faithful, presumably disheartening) fact being that many who had not, before the Pope's ruling and the attendant publicity, heard of such things at all, now had.

On the other hand the Pope, doubtless reflecting that *he* was not mocked, even if God was, had the last laugh as far as the Sixties and the pill were alike concerned. For the decade ended in a huge reaction against the pill, on strictly medical grounds, and the last days of the Sixties echoed to warning after warning from the most eminent scientific quarters; brand after brand was withdrawn from sale, new research was urgently undertaken, and those who had so often and so vociferously declared that the pill had no harmful side-effects fell silent. Eventually the argument from science quite drowned the argument from theology; certainly it seemed as the decade ended that it would go on longer.

# 8

# Run it down the flagpole

There were more traditional, more conventional crossroads too, with more familiar guides stationed at them, pointing the nation down familiar paths. Politics still existed in the Sixties, and although by the end of the decade there had been a widespread rejection, active or passive, of many of the traditional processes of political participation, and an even more widespread growth of cynicism about its practitioners, nevertheless the Sixties were dominated, even if only formally, by politics. Nor was this surprising, for political events exemplified again and again the dilemma of Britain, her two-headed stance, her agony as the opposite forces in the decade, in trying to pull her one way and the other, seemed likely to pull her apart, and by the end of the decade almost had.

Politics in turn was dominated by economics; there was hardly a moment during the decade when some Government or other was not exhorting the nation to work harder, to save more, to be more efficient, to export more vigorously, to import more selectively, to defend the health and strength of the pound sterling.

The purpose of all this, it was explained, was to enable Britain to survive with her greatness intact. But wherein lay her greatness? And how might it be saved? On these grave questions no two could agree; but in time, from the whirling mass of advice and argument, action and reaction, three planets coalesced from the spinning fragments and came to dominate the heavens over Britain in the Sixties. The end, the means, and the men who would provide the latter to bring about the former – these were the three themes of politics and economics in the Sixties, and in each of them could be discerned the temper of the times and its effect on Britain.

Economic efficiency was needed in order to establish, or re-establish, Britain's place in the world; what that place was, or should be, had to be decided; the politicians would announce what Britain's place was and organize the efficiency that could bring her into it.

But what was it? For some there could be no doubt. Britain's place in the world was what it always had been. For these the lion still kicked, though every time it did so another tuft of fur came out. And in no field did it kick more vigorously, or shed more fur, than in that of Britain's overseas responsibilities. Once the Royal Navy had commanded the seas, but those days had long since gone by. Now, throughout the decade, the debate reverberated: what place was there for a British presence beyond Britain's shores? As part of the multi-national forces deployed under the NATO treaty, the British Army of the Rhine had an unexceptionable role to play, but outside Europe the matter was by no means so simple. Presently a phrase with ominous echoes began to be heard, and soon the entire debate began to revolve around it. 'East of Suez'–a quotation from the supremely unfashionable Kipling, who had demanded to be shipped there–were the words; and many a further word was expended on discussing their implications. Britain had obligations–self-imposed for the most part–in the Middle East, where there was a permanent garrison in Aden and treaty commitments to the sheikdoms round about, and in the Far East, where Singapore and Malaysia looked to Britain, with fluctuating degrees of confidence, for military help in the last resort, and where Hong Kong kept up the brave pretence that she could or would be defended if China, having long since got out of bed ('Let China sleep,' said Napoleon; 'when she wakes, the world will be sorry'), should put her foot down on the rug beside it.

Britain was still a world power, ran one argument, and must show the flag in all the old familiar places. Britain was a small European power, ran the other, and must learn to itch where she could scratch. The Empire had vanished, other countries managed to obtain their oil supplies without having troops sitting on the wells, and it was time to go. That at any rate was the final decision, taken by the Labour Government, and it was followed, with only a little more reluctance, by a decision to 'liquidate our presence', as the phrase went, in the Far East also. Some rash promises were hastily made by the Conservative Opposition about reversing the policy if they were elected, but it soon became noticeable that the promises were made less and less frequently, and more and more vaguely, as time went by.

And yet the lion must needs adjust its dress before leaving. Just before the departure from Aden, fierce fighting broke out there, partly between rival groups seeking to fill the power vacuum that the departing British would leave, partly between some or several of the rival groups on the one hand and the British on the other. Such hours commonly produce appropriate men, and this hour was no exception, the man being Colonel Colin Campbell Mitchell, one of those men who, denied inches by a niggardly nature (though lavishly supplied with courage instead), have throughout history tried to make up for their lack of physical stature by imposing themselves on the situation around them. It worked for Colonel Mitchell, who, with such inspiring cries as 'One move out of them and we'll blow their bloody heads off,' forcibly occupied an area of Aden that higher policy had previously decided the British should keep out of. With a fantastic stroke of luck that he, and his more romantic supporters at home, energetically maintained was in fact the result of judgment, he got away with it, bloodshed being almost entirely averted.

Thus did the little colonel become a hero overnight, and his face began to stare out of newspapers and television screens more and more frequently, there being no particular reason to suppose that this was in any way unwelcome to him. Soon afterwards the continuing rationalization of the British armed forces brought about the merging of his regiment, the Argyll and Sutherland Highlanders, with another, and a campaign to 'Save the Argylls' was launched. The campaign having failed, Colonel Mitchell resigned his commission and began to be interested in a political career, like Napoleon before him. For some time he seemed unable to make up his mind whether he was a Scottish Nationalist or a Conservative, but he was presently offered a distinctly winnable seat by the Conservatives, and accepted; he won it.

But Britain neither saved the Argylls nor stayed in Aden. Soon there would be no military presence east of Suez, and not much of one east of the Rhine; nor were voices lacking in Britain to insist that she should have no troops east of Dover, or west of it for that matter. One of the most remarkable stories in the world's history was coming to an end; it was the story of a tiny island which had sent forth her sons to conquer the world, and seen them succeed to such an extent that those at home had come to believe that it must go on for ever, and ultimately that it not only *must* go on for ever, but *should*. But the flag that had once flown over so many lands was coming down now, as dusk fell; and – ultimate indignity – there was none to give it the ritual sundown salute. As late as the Fifties it was possible to hear regrets, or even complaints, about the Attlee Government for, as it was put, 'giving India away'; by the Sixties such voices were all stilled, and the shrinking dominions could no longer boast a Clive or a Rhodes, a Milner or a Lugard, an Elgin or a Curzon. Perhaps it was fitting, seeing in what haste and hugger-mugger it was happening, what bathos attended the last rites, that the last proconsul should be Colonel Mitchell, and that it should be he who helped, all unknowing, to destroy the last illusions of Empire as, amid a skirl of pipes and a flurry of sand, Britain's troops left the Middle East, where so many of her sons had laid their bones, for ever.

* * *

But fast as the illusions were falling, they were not falling fast enough. When, half-way through the decade, the Government of Rhodesia declared that country independent, in order to avoid having ultimately to hand over political power to men with unacceptably black faces, and for that matter black behinds, powerful words were expressed by the Government in Britain. To a considerable extent and for a considerable time these were echoed by the Conservative Opposition, until a skilfully organized campaign forced the leaders of the party, ostensibly as committed as Labour to the mystic principle of 'one man, one vote', to abandon their bipartisan support for the Government's policy of bringing the dissidents to heel by economic sanctions, and to accept the policy, more and more cheerfully expressed by such figures as Lord Salisbury and Mr Patrick Wall, of sympathy for the rebels.

All of which was greatly deplored; nevertheless it was not easy to see how anything could be done about it, except for those whose solution had from the start of the whole imbroglio been to put down the rebellion by force, heedless of the military logistics involved.

In the Sixties Britain had begun at last to cut her international coat according to her national cloth; but fiction in such matters dies hard, and there was no apparent disposition to recognize the grim facts of life about Rhodesia. Rather was there the continuous chanting of 'Sanctions are beginning to bite', followed by an increasing acceptance of the view that whatever was inevitable was also right, and therefore that the rule of the white minority in Rhodesia was in many ways quite admirable, and that its rulers fully intended to share power with the black majority in the not too distant future. Thus, as so often, the riven Sixties got the benefit neither of policy nor of principle.

Individuals, as well as whole peoples, felt the sting of Britain's inability to move the world to her ends, and the unwillingness of so many of her leaders even to try. As good an index of Britain's declining power as the annual counting of the number of capital ships possessed by the navy, or the number of square miles still marked red on the map, was provided by the fate of two British citizens who ventured into Communist lands and there suffered bitterly, while the Government, back home, wrung its hands and declared, like Lear, that it would do such things, that what they were as yet it knew not, but that they should be the terror of the earth.

Gerald Brooke was a young and idealistic lecturer at a London technical college who visited Russia as a tourist in 1964, his visit happening to coincide with an urgent wish on the part of the Russian authorities to effect an exchange for a pair of Russian spies serving long terms of imprisonment in Britain. There being no British spies at that time imprisoned in Russia, Brooke was arrested and charged with illegally bringing into Russia publications forbidden within her borders. These, it transpired, were leaflets that he had with him, some of which contained views indicative of a belief that free institutions were to be admired, and tyrannical ones deplored. Brooke was arrested, and subsequently sentenced to five years' imprisonment in a concentration camp. There, as reports which seeped out made clear, he was subjected to the harshest possible conditions, in the hope that the British Government would agree to the release of the Russian spies in order to save him further torment. The Government, apart from claiming from time to time that they had the situation under review, did nothing, the difficulty of thinking of anything to do being considerably enhanced by the fact that Mr Wilson had long nursed a desire to build, or even to be, a bridge between East and West, over which the warring factions would advance, meeting in the middle to exchange embraces, and perhaps glass beads as well.

Anyway, Brooke stayed in his camp until the Russians let it be known that on the expiry of his original sentence he would be charged with further offences and sentenced to an even longer term of imprisonment. At this, Wilson gave in and allowed the exchange for the Russian spies, who were sent off from London Airport with champagne and smiles.

There were those in Britain who defended the Russian treatment of Gerald Brooke, or who were willing to condemn him for what he had done, or at least to urge that nothing should be done to save him if it might upset his captors. This last argument was even to be heard in connection with the case of Anthony Grey, a British journalist acting as representative of Reuters in Peking. He was arrested in 1967, shortly after the trial and imprisonment of a number of Chinese rioters in Hong Kong; he was not put on trial but confined to one room of his house, where he was subjected to a variety of psychological torments, under the stress of which his mind began, inevitably, to suffer, so that nearly a year after his release he was still unable to meet old colleagues, or even relatives, without strain. But in Grey's case it might be counted as gain that, since Mao Tse-tung had never visited Britain, Mr Wilson was unable to tell him, as he had told Kosygin, that he was part of the British way of life, and since Mr Wilson had never visited China, he was unable to boast of his friendship with any of Mao's henchmen, as he did in the case of Mikoyan, whom he had met a few times many years earlier.

Mr Wilson was by no means the only appeaser. For some reason television organizations had, during the Sixties, an outstanding record in this respect. On the occasion, for instance, of the fiftieth anniversary of the Russian Revolution, both the B.B.C. and Granada Television mounted elaborate commemorative programmes of which the chief quality was their lack of any serious criticism of anything that had resulted from it. Even more extraordinary was the way in which the B.B.C. bent to Russian pressure over a programme they had devised dealing with the show-trial in Moscow of Andrei Sinyavsky and Yuri Daniel; a Russian representative visited the B.B.C. and threatened that Russian co-operation in B.B.C. enterprises would be ended unless the B.B.C. abandoned the programme. The B.B.C. for a time looked likely to accept the ultimatum, announcing that the programme had been postponed and refusing to give a date for its transmission, but it soon became apparent that a considerable outcry would result if the programme were cancelled, and it eventually went out, though it was postponed sufficiently for it not to interfere with the celebrations attendant on the anniversary of the Revolution.

Most remarkable, however, was the case of the unique film record that was destroyed after transmission by Rediffusion, then holders of the London weekday commercial television franchise. This concerned a programme on Russia in which John Morgan had held an interview at a secret rendezvous outside Moscow with three young opponents of their regime; what made the episode unique was that all three insisted on speaking directly to the camera, so that they could be, and undoubtedly were, identified when the programme was shown. Morgan warned them of the possible consequences to them – a warning that was, of course, quite unnecessary, as they would have known much better than he about what would follow – but they insisted on going the full length of their courage, and the interview was subsequently shown, and its text published, in Britain. Shortly afterwards, after Russian representations to Rediffusion, and in circumstances that were obscure, the film was destroyed (though there have been reports that the technicians, appalled by the order, surreptitiously made an extra copy; if so, its whereabouts remain unknown), and when the news leaked out Rediffusion claimed that they had destroyed the film because storage facilities for film that had already been shown were limited, much as the curator of the Louvre might excuse his burning of the Mona Lisa on the grounds that wall-space was in very short supply.

It was not easy to guess at the deeper national reasons for an attitude that had so worked itself into the country's bones that it was capable of producing examples like that. Britain's decline as a world power and as an industrial and economic force had been gradual but continuous; along with it, of course, went an even greater and more rapid increase in the number and vehemence of the voices drawing attention to this decline. It is a well-known psychological fact that if a man already conscious of a number of psychological deformities in himself has his attention repeatedly drawn to them by bystanders who exaggerate the extent and nature of these weaknesses, and even claim to have discovered further ones that he does not know about and that may be wholly imaginary, he will eventually begin to take on the characteristics attributed to him, and to behave in fact as he is told he behaves in imagination. It may be that Britain had declined so far, and had been told so often that she had declined even further, that she eagerly adopted the role for which she had been cast, and, convinced that she was a weak and spineless creature who would truckle to the powerful and ruthless, began to *be* such a creature, and to truckle to anybody who would pause long enough to be truckled to. Since it was in the interests of the Russians to be truckled to by Britain, their leaders were always willing to stop for a truckle, and since there seemed no likelihood that the due tribute of truckle would ever be denied, the process continued, and even increased, reaching its nadir at the time of the invasion of Czechoslovakia in 1968 by troops from Russia and her colonies, when Mr Wilson condemned the invasion in the most forthright terms but declined to take any action whatever, however diplomatic, possibly on the grounds that if Britain would not take action to save her own citizens from wrongful arrest and false imprisonment, she could hardly be expected to do so on behalf of a far-off country of which we knew nothing. It is true that no member of the Government attended the annual Revolution Day party at the Russian Embassy in 1968, but they were back the following year, and it is not even certain that the Russians had noticed their brief fit of the sulks.

9

# The pound in your pocket

Besides, suppose Britain had suddenly decided to enforce her will on the world, to make other nations, under pain of instant conquest, accept her as once they had? An unlikely enough thought, to be sure; but suppose Britain had, none the less, suddenly been seized by it? With what could she enforce her newly rediscovered will? The decade was littered with British missiles, for instance. Some of these were cancelled shortly before the prototypes were built, some shortly afterwards; some failed to work, some proved too expensive. They became a dreadful symbol of the country's erratic attempts to move into the future, a paradigm of national impotence as the thrusting rocket failed to take off, failed to achieve its intended climax, blew up in mid-course, or found itself being withdrawn for reasons outside anyone's control. Not all were made in Britain, but even the imported ones failed; they had various purposes too, some being military, some civil – these last concerned to get Britain (first alone, then in European concert) into the race for the stars – but all sooner or later fizzling out, as much literally as metaphorically. It seemed that the country simply could not get a rocket off the ground, and since 'to get off the ground' had become, in the Sixties, one of the most ubiquitous of clichés, the successive failures were as much apparent as real. Their titles – Blue Streak, Black Knight, Blue Steel, Skybolt, Black Arrow – were splendidly colourful, and if nomenclature alone could have made them succeed, Britain by the end of the decade would have been master of the world and of the planets as well. Nor was it lack of money that haunted the successive projects, for the sums expended before each was cancelled were as astronomical as the heights each failed to attain in flight. The consequent jeering, which was not entirely due to the extraordinary spirit of self-abnegation which had come over the country during the decade, was mixed with a good deal of genuine anger at the waste, each major political party denouncing the other for its extravagance and incompetence and offering to do better more cheaply, without any prospect of being able to fulfil its promises, and indeed without any serious belief on the part of the audience that it would or could do so, a scepticism which in the event proved abundantly justified. Missiles, in the Sixties, were not destined to carry Britain upward; still less forward.

Eventually the sums committed, spent and lost in weapons and missiles that were cancelled shortly after becoming operational, or even before, grew so huge, and the announcement that it had happened yet again so frequent, that the public's response to the news became numbed, and it was clear that no amount of wasted money would provoke a reaction serious enough to trouble those responsible, or even to compel serious inquiries as to who *was* responsible. In the circumstances it was not surprising that some of the firms responsible for carrying out Government contracts in the field of defence systems and equipment began to be infected with the same spirit, and to believe that nobody ever missed a slice off a cut loaf.

Two sets of mistakes, on a truly gigantic scale, were made in their own favour by two of the leading firms in those modern industries on which Governments depend for the means of the nation's defence. Early in 1964 startling rumours began to get about, suggesting that the supervision of a major Government contract with the Ferranti Company, for the production of the singularly ill-named Bloodhound missile, had been so lax that the company had got away with gigantically inflated profits, far in excess of anything envisaged by either side at the time the contract was being negotiated. The usual flurry of denials took place, but after a time Ferranti admitted that they had made rather more than the Government had bargained for, and offered to pay back about a million pounds of it by knocking it off the price of future work; in no circumstances, they added, would they actually pay back cash, and certainly not to the extent that the Government was suggesting, which was something in the region of twice what the firm had offered. Moreover, the firm would not allow any detailed inspection of their accounts.

At this the Government announced that they were setting up an inquiry into the affair, whereupon Ferranti hastily announced that they would, after all, permit the inspection of their books, a change of heart which may have had something to do with the fact that at the time the Government announced the inquiry they also announced that Ferranti seemed to have made a profit of 113 per cent on capital, 63 per cent on cost and 40 per cent on turnover – which even the Minister, Mr Julian Amery, one of the most devoted admirers of the fiercest and most unbridled form of the profit system, declared was 'by any standards excessive and unjustified'.

When a few months later the committee of inquiry reported to the Government on what it had found, it appeared that even Mr Amery's gloomy estimates were short of the reality by a substantial margin, the company, it appeared, having made a profit of 45 per cent on turnover, 82 per cent on costs, and God knows what on capital. The committee was very severe with both Ferranti and the officials in the Ministry of Aviation who were responsible. These, it declared, had placed reliance on their cost-estimating organization 'without the means of checking the accuracy of the estimates'; they lacked effective collaboration between branches of the Government service 'which should have been working together towards the common goal of fair and reasonable prices'; and the affair revealed 'a lack of direction and a lack of drive in making the best use of the Ministry's resources'.

As for Ferranti, the committee of inquiry concluded that 'They submitted quotations and agreed prices which they knew were very likely to yield profits that the Ministry would not regard as fair and reasonable, profits which can only be described as excessive'; that they quoted and agreed ostensibly fair and reasonable prices 'which they knew were much too high'; and that by saying nothing on the subject they 'misled the Ministry'.

The debate in the House of Commons on the affair was enlivened by a startling charge against the two Ferranti brothers (one of them a Conservative Member of Parliament) made by Mr George Wigg, to the effect that their firm had been virtually bankrupt before the war and had been built up to its present profitable condition because, while some people (e.g., undoubtedly, Colonel Wigg) went to the war, others stayed behind; it subsequently transpired that Ferranti senior had been seventy years old when the war broke out, and the Ferrantis junior nine and eleven respectively. Mr Wigg declared that he had been misunderstood, and after further discussions, and the generation of a good deal of heat, Ferranti agreed to pay the Government some four million pounds, and in cash. Amid the heat it was hardly noticed that the Bloodhound missile, about which all the fuss had occurred, had been cancelled, and of its total cost to the public Ferranti's excess profit accounted for a mere 6¼ per cent.

Reform and improvement in the costing and accounting departments of the Ministry of Aviation were promised, and may, for all anyone could tell to the contrary, have taken place. But exactly three years later it was revealed that, at the very time the Ferranti affair was going on, a far worse example of the same thing was happening behind the distinguished portals of Bristol-Siddeley Engines.

With an exactitude that must have made the Ministry's negotiators get that uncanny feeling of familiarity that is said to convince many people of the truth of reincarnation, Bristol-Siddeley, in the early stages of their negotiations with the Government, followed the unhappy precedents set by Ferranti, refusing to allow the Ministry officials to inspect their accounts, and offering to pay, *ex gratia* and without prejudice, first half a million pounds, then two million; their willingness to go as far as this may have been occasioned by the unwelcome publicity even then (at the start of the negotiations) being given to the Ferranti affair. Eventually yet another committee of inquiry was set up, this one headed by Sir Roy Wilson, whose report was so critical of Bristol-Siddeley that there was an immediate demand for prosecution of their senior management, and the possibility of such action was discussed between the Attorney-General and the Director of Public Prosecutions, though they decided against pressing charges.

Between 1959 and 1963, the report declared, the conduct of the firm had 'amounted to intentional misrepresentation, by which the department's representatives were deceived ... Bristol-Siddeley Engines budgeted for, and achieved, exorbitant profits on their overhaul contracts with the department.' Further, 'The approximate extent of the profitability of these contracts was, at the time, known to the company at all levels of management.' The report gave details of work charged for twice, of the gross inflation of numbers of hours worked, and of other, similar pranks, the extent and gravity of which may be judged by the fact that the firm, before the committee of inquiry reported, had paid back, like Ferranti, almost exactly four million pounds.

A further inquiry, for reasons which were never entirely made clear, was then undertaken by the House of Commons Public Accounts Committee, which, by a casting vote, determined that Sir Reginald Verdon-Smith, chairman of Bristol-Siddeley, and Mr Brian Davidson, its business director, had not lied to the Public Accounts Committee when it had first investigated the matter, though their evidence was 'inadequate and confusing' and the financial administration of the company 'even more deserving of stricture than it appeared'.

This compounding of confusion, it was generally agreed, would be a good place to leave the matter, and demands for the prosecution of leading figures in the company gradually died down, as did the even more alarming proposals, by some Labour Members of Parliament, to avoid future waste of public money in the aircraft and allied industries by nationalizing them.

Eels, we are told, get used to skinning, and though it is true that we are not told this by the eels, it does seem that taxpayers get used to being fleeced. By the end of the Sixties campaigners for various reforms thought nothing of saying that their idea would cost 'a paltry ten million pounds', or that the money already spent on some cause deemed worthy by the speaker 'amounted to a miserable seven million a year', and such language occasioned no surprise among a community which had for so long been subjected, at intervals of a year or two, and sometimes of only a few months, to announcements that some project in which anything up to a hundred million pounds of their money had been invested was to be abandoned forthwith, and the loss, in the happy phrase borrowed by Government from accountancy, 'written off'. Ritual demanded at such times that the party out of office should denounce the party in office for such reckless squandering of public funds, but they had to tread warily in doing so, for the gestation period of many of the cancelled projects was long enough for them to have been conceived during the tenure of office by those doing the denouncing, so that if they were not careful they would find themselves in the position of complaining at their own extravagance. But even without such pitfalls the ritual never took on any real substance, as both parties were in the position of the pot, and neither of the kettle. From time to time the Public Accounts Committee of the House of Commons, or the Auditor-General, would draw pained attention to some more than ordinarily shocking waste of money, and would be met with the promise of reform and amendment. The public, which no doubt made its own evaluation of the promises, also made no more than token protests, so that the proponents of the eel-theory seemed to have been proved right. Even they, however, never dared to claim that the eels actually *enjoyed* it.

* * *

Above the decade, symbol of Britain's economic ills as it had once been of her strength, there floated the battered, dog-eared pound, its handsomely unequivocal promise to pay the bearer on demand the sum of one pound, which had once been redeemable in gold, now serving only to remind those who stopped to read the small print that times had changed. From the beginning of the decade the health of the pound had dominated all political and economic thinking and argument, and its fluctuating fortunes had been watched and graphed as meticulously and anxiously as the fever-chart of an exceptionally frail but immensely wealthy patriarch who has to be kept alive for a little longer in order that his gifts to his relations *inter vivos* should not, by falling within the seven-year period, qualify for estate duty at the full rate.

But however closely the pound's graph was watched, its trend was perpetually, remorselessly, downwards. Sometimes the ominous words 'Pound hits new low' appeared daily for weeks or even months on end, and the formal devaluation of the currency undertaken three-quarters of the way through the decade by the Labour Government, after months of the ritual denials that any such move was contemplated, only made official what in practice had been happening for some time. The value of the pound was determined not by Government decree, let alone by what was printed on it, but by the degree of confidence displayed by those who traded in or with it, or who kept their balances in London in it. Throughout the Sixties, even in the early euphoric years when the Macmillan Government was so cheerfully urging the nation to eat the seed-corn, there was very little such confidence to be found.

'Productivity' became the magic password that would open the doors to prosperity, to those sunlit uplands of which chancellors of the exchequer had dreamed for twenty years and more, like Haig in the First World War insisting again and again that just one more big push would do the trick. Alas, push how they might, no chancellor managed to do the trick, and each in turn found himself treading more and more wildly first on the brake and then on the accelerator, and then on the brake again. Wage-policies and incomes-policies followed each other like the costumes of quick-change artists, and all fell at the same point; that point was the inescapable fact that, although if everybody brings an orange-box to view the procession none will see it, it is impossible to convince those who are first on the pavement with their orange-boxes of the truth of this. Those who had sufficient industrial bargaining strength to obtain benefits commensurate with, or greater than, the inexorable rise in the cost of living could not see what was wrong with the system, and as fast as chancellors prophesied that one more huge effort on the part of everybody would see us all out of the wood, so fast (and even faster) did the trees spring up to make the wood darker and more impenetrable than before.

Nothing contributed a greater supply of darkness than the chaotic and antique state of Britain's labour relations. Much effort and ingenuity was expended, from time to time, to prove that Britain did not lose in industrial action as many man-hours per worker-year as many other countries, notably the United States. But this was small consolation to those contemplating the anarchy on the labour front that, year after year, troubled Britain. Management and union leadership were chicken and egg in this situation; management failed to foresee trouble and had no means of settling it simply and quickly when it arose, and union leaders, official and unofficial, increasingly took advantage of this state of affairs to compel the meeting of greater and greater demands.

At times it seemed almost as though a contest had been arranged, and substantial prizes offered, for the most prolonged and fruitless industrial dispute any competitor could organize. The competition for the first prize was keen, and the balance swung this way and that throughout the decade, likely candidates including the dispute between two sets of workers over which of them should be allowed to bore the rivet-holes in the sides of ships, which went on for some four months; the strike at the Roberts-Arundel factory in Stockport, which went on for over nine months, and which was distinguished both by the fact that it produced the greatest violence seen in a British industrial dispute for more than a quarter of a century and also by the fact that long before the end the original reason for it (a question of trade union recognition) had been entirely forgotten by both sides, and their intransigence seemed to have become an end in itself; and the strikes – there were several of them during the Sixties – which broke out because a foreman swore at one of the workers, whose comrades, displaying all the qualities of modesty, sensitivity and revulsion from profanity that have always characterized the

British working-man, promptly came out *en masse*. But in the end there could be no doubt that the first prize was won, and most deservedly, by the strike of building workers at the Barbican site in the City. This was an immense project, which had been nearly twenty years in the planning, for a series of residential blocks which would comprise something like a complete township, and as a target for those whose task it was to disrupt industry whenever and wherever possible it became an irresistible attraction. On a pretext so trivial that nobody could remember what it was even the morning after the strike began, a small but brilliantly organized body of men, probably not more than eight in number, managed to persuade all two to three hundred workers on the site to down tools, organize picket lines and sit it out. This they did with such willingness that the strike went on for over a year before it was finally settled, while the unfinished building grew rusty and dilapidated within the strikers' lines. From time to time violence flared, police and pickets rolled over and over in the gutter, and the management blew now hot, now cold, now fierce, now conciliatory, and all to no avail. A court of inquiry having established that there were faults on both sides but that there were more on the side of the strike organizers (the strike was 'unofficial' throughout, and thus, according to the mythology of the Sixties, somehow more deplorable than one backed 'officially' by the unions), the 'official' union leadership took the unprecedented step of co-operating with the employers in publishing a full-page advertisement in several newspapers, denouncing those who were attempting to keep the strike going and calling for a return to work. Thus encouraged, the employers took on labour from other building enterprises and restarted the work, only to find that the intimidation practised throughout the months of picketing, and consisting of nothing much worse than the traditional methods of flying bricks and bottles, had now been put on a scientific basis: the unofficial leaders engaged photographers to take pictures of those reporting to work in defiance of instructions, one of the organizers explaining with an engaging frankness that this was being done so that those who were willing to work could be visited at their homes by strike organizers as soon as they had been identified, and there have the reasons for the strike explained to them and their participation in it earnestly sought.

Much dismay was expressed at these and other indications that the unions were behaving as though the law did not apply to them (as indeed, in many respects, it did not), but the old Adam died hard indeed during the Sixties, and no case brought home the truth of that as sharply as that of Douglas Rookes, whose story began in the middle of the Fifties, when he resigned from the trade union (the Association of Engineering and Shipbuilding Draughtsmen, subsequently renamed the Draughtsmen and Allied Trades Association) to which he belonged, and which indeed he represented in the office at B.O.A.C. where he worked. Coming to the conclusion that he did not approve of certain aspects of the union's policy, he resigned from it, and thus fell into the grip of a nightmare from which he was not to awake until almost exactly ten years had passed. For his union instructed B.O.A.C. to dismiss Mr Rookes from its employment for leaving their embrace, and B.O.A.C., the chairman of which was Sir Miles Thomas, obeyed the union's dictates (which had been supported by the threat to strike if the Corporation should prove recalcitrant) and dismissed him. At which he brought an action against the union officials who had insisted on his dismissal, charging that since the union had a contractual agreement with B.O.A.C., a threat to stage a strike (which, there was no doubt, would have been in breach of that agreement) was a threat to do something unlawful, and in the circumstances he could recover damages. So indeed he did, though not until he had experienced a decade of the law's delays, a decade during which he had been compelled to earn his living (being unable to follow his trade without a union card) chipping rust off bridges. He finally got a verdict and £4,000 in damages, news which was greeted by him with joy tinged with bitterness, by Sir Miles Thomas with a defence of his original action in sacking Mr Rookes ('We just could not afford a strike over a comparatively minor point of that kind') and by the T.U.C. with dismay, as they faced the possibility that unjust acts by unions might from now on be visited home on those doing them. 'Nobody at any time,' it had been said by union officials during the long-drawn action, 'for any reason whatsoever, has any right to resign from a trade union', and Mr George Woodcock, then general secretary of the T.U.C., put it with equally brutal frankness when he said: 'We must have a change in the law.' Such a change was effected as one of the first actions of the Labour Government after gaining office in 1964, and it meant that never again could such an action as Rookes v. Barnard have the same conclusion, though the amending legislation stopped short, surprisingly enough, of retrospectively depriving Mr Rookes of his verdict and his damages.

But now, after all, there was a Labour Government, claiming to be able to speak the worker's language, and drawn from a party financed by the unions for so long that they had forgotten who paid for what (or, as Lenin used to ask more economically, 'Who whom?'). A Prices and Incomes policy was boldly conceived and promulgated, and unions and managements alike were invited to sign a Declaration of Intent, the intent in question being that they would keep down respectively price rises and wage demands. 'Norms' were established for income rises anything above which would have to be 'earned' by higher productivity, with a Prices and Incomes Board appointed as the adjudicator in all such matters.

Alas for good Intents, no notice was taken of these fine phrases and finer promises, and prices continued to chase wages, and wages, prices. A great deal of goodwill had been generated by slowly rising public anger towards anyone who would put a toe in the hot water of union reform; such spectacular dramas as the seizure of the Electrical Trades Union, which was held as a Communist fief against the repeatedly expressed will of the members for thirteen years, and the campaign to force the closure of the Ford plant at Dagenham (a campaign which came very close indeed to success before the management nerved itself, armed with the report of an official inquiry into conditions at the plant, for resistance), together with such episodes as the attempt to ruin the

Barbican building project, had given the public, including very large numbers of union members, a keen desire to see the unions brought under the rule of law and made responsible in law for their actions, which in some respects they had not been since the Trades Disputes Act of 1906.

Thus, after a gigantic heaving and thrashing on the part of the Labour movement's whale, a somewhat battered Jonah emerged in the shape of the Industrial Relations Bill. This was a measure which offered the trade unions almost everything the most demanding of them had ever asked; including an employee's statutory right to join a union, the provision of unemployment pay for those out of work because of an unofficial strike, greatly strengthened contracts of employment, and many other beneficial proposals, in return for which they were asked to agree to a legally enforceable delay of twenty-eight days before an unofficial strike might take place, in order to see whether the time could not be used to settle the dispute in a more amicable way.

At this violent uproar broke out among the whole of the left wing of the Labour Party, the T.U.C., and union leaders, and as soon as the Conservative Party announced that it would not vote against the measure in Parliament (so that it was now safe for a minority of Labour M.P.s to do so, knowing that the great majority of them would turn out to save the Government), a group of dissidents announced that they were going to oppose the bill at all its Parliamentary stages, whereupon battle-lines were drawn and the contestants settled down.

Again and again Mr Wilson declared that the proposed bill was necessary, not only to the survival of the Labour Government, but to the economic survival of the country; in vain. When he was faced with a risk to his own political position, his frail nerve snapped, and he dropped the bill at the insistence of the T.U.C., who gave in return a 'solemn and binding' promise to do something about union reform themselves, though what it was that they were to do was never specified. Nor, in the event, did they do it, whatever it was.

* * *

It should not be supposed, however, that it was only the union leg of the national tripod of economic forces—labour, management, Government—that was worm-eaten. Apart from the share of general responsibility on the part of antiquated and inefficient management for the state of labour relations, particular blame for many of the most spectacular industrial debacles of the decade could be laid firmly at the door of the employers, and not a few at that of the Government, in some cases indeed both the one and the other actually finding themselves in the extraordinary position of resisting intelligent and constructive moves made by the unions in the name of efficiency.

One of the most characteristic industrial tragedies of the decade was that of the Fairfields shipyard. The shipbuilding industry on the Clyde had long been virtually bankrupt, and its methods, especially in the field of labour relations, made it impossible for anything to be done that might seriously affect the situation. The managements compared unfavourably with the pre-war coal-owners, and the unions were probably the most uncooperative and restrictive in industry. As the whole of the Clyde slowly, but less and less slowly, ran downhill, an attempt was made by a group of far-sighted people, headed by George Brown, to reverse the trend by creating a new shipyard group on the Clyde that would abandon the old methods and try new, modern ones. This, backed by industry and by the unions, was the Fairfields yard, and after a painful start (for old suspicions died hard) it suddenly began to work. Restrictive practices were swept aside as good reason was shown for their abandonment and confidence that they were unnecessary established, new organizational methods were introduced; gradually, in the middle of the most run-down and old-fashioned industry in the land there appeared an up-to-date shipyard, with a contented labour force, an imaginative management and even the possibility of profit.

But the dead weight of tradition, inertia and timidity was too great. As the Government lost its nerve, the old groups re-established control, the yard was merged with others, the men who had created Fairfields drifted away to other enterprises and, in the words of an embittered foreman, typical of those who had suddenly, for the first time in their working lives, seen the way forward, Fairfields was once again in the hands of those who 'thought critical-path analysis was a Greek shipowner'. The new group went by the name of Upper Clyde Shipbuilders; they built the *Queen Elizabeth 2* and shortly afterwards found themselves facing imminent insolvency and complaining that the nine million pounds provided by the Government to shore the group up was not enough. A door had been opened in an ancient wall of mutual suspicion, ignorance and inefficiency, and a way through to new and harmonious industrial relations shown. Then it was slammed shut. The Sixties' backward-looking face smiled upon Fairfields, while its forward-looking one wept to see the lost chance.

It was very fitting that the consortium which had succeeded Fairfields should have been the firm to build the new Cunarder, the building of which was itself a symbol of much that was wrong with British industry in the Sixties, or more precisely of what would never be put right until some fundamental re-thinking had taken place.

Cunard, having achieved the extraordinary feat of losing some fourteen million pounds in ten years, much of it because of the declining passenger-liner trade on the North Atlantic route, decided that it would build a new giant passenger liner to ply the North Atlantic route. This was to cost thirty million pounds, and the Government, somewhat dazed, found itself contributing a loan of seventeen millions towards it. The building was bedevilled by quarrels and delays (there was a bizarre sideshow when for a time it appeared that the chairman's wife might be going to take an active hand in the design of the interior), but eventually the liner was built, for not very much more than the original estimate, and named, with a striking lack of originality which ominously mirrored the thinking of the Cunard board, the *Queen Elizabeth 2*. On her acceptance trials, however, she was found to be very far from ready, much of the interior accommodation being only half-built, and a good deal of that which was built having been unbuilt by the enormous and—even for the Clyde—virtually unprecedented amount of stealing that had gone on during and after the building. Moreover, she had hardly put to sea when she broke down, the turbines of the engines being found to be seriously defective and their total replacement a matter of urgency, and in these unpropitious circumstances she limped home, while an acrimonious dispute broke out about the responsibility for the fiasco and for its remedying. Date after date for the maiden voyage was chosen and abandoned, and eventually the *Queen Elizabeth 2* put to sea in a flood of the most unfavourable publicity any such enterprise can ever have had. It was estimated that, in order for Cunard to recoup her building costs, repay the Government's loan and show profit, she would have to be full on every voyage for at least two years, and nearly full for more than twenty thereafter, but within a matter of weeks she was crossing the Atlantic with some cabins empty, and the likelihood of her getting Cunard's money back, let alone the taxpayers', began to recede rapidly. It was generally agreed on all hands, however, that when the repairs had been done she was a fine and beautiful ship, and she thus stood as a triple monument: to the ability and skill of British industry, as represented by her design and eventual performance; to the lamentable state of that industry in the Sixties, as typified by the fact that she had put to sea in an unready and defective condition; and to the quality of British management, as witnessed to by Cunard's insistence on building a liner that was unlikely ever to pay.

This kind of industrial madness was not confined to employers and employees, any more than was the seemingly implacable urge to economic self-destruction. When the Government took a hand directly, it showed that it could compete without fear of successful rival for the glittering prizes in the field of waste and inefficiency.

Throughout much of the decade a kind of mad lobster quadrille was danced between Britain and France. Having decided that they would build, as a joint enterprise, a supersonic civil airliner, eventually named the Concorde, both countries then found themselves, at different times and alternately, trying to get out of their obligations under the agreement and to cancel the entire project, as the costs inexorably mounted and the estimated total expenditure on research and development (before, that is, any production of the aeroplanes for service) rose from one hundred and eighty million pounds to two hundred and fifty million, and then to three hundred and fifty, and then to six hundred, and then to seven, and then to an estimate (even that certain to be exceeded) of one thousand million pounds. Long before this point was reached there had ceased to be any serious chance of the aircraft being commercially successful, if the amortization of the gigantic amounts of money spent on it should be attempted, though it is true that both companies (Sud-Aviation in France and the British Aircraft Corporation in Britain) had cheerfully refused to contemplate putting a penny of their own into the development costs. Before even the prototypes got off the ground horror-stories about the unsolved hazards of flying such aircraft at supersonic speeds, and about the uneconomic payload to which they would be restricted in the interests of safety, were circulating. Opposition to the project mounted, not only from those who objected to the never-ending increases in cost, but from those who did not believe the Government's assurances about the noise of the sonic boom, these being to the effect that it was acceptable, or, in the alternative, that if it was not then the aircraft would not be allowed to fly over land; sceptics pointed out that the noise would *not* be acceptable but that the aircraft *would* be allowed to fly over land.

The haste that was the undoing of the hasteners was evident in yet another of the technological marvels of the age, the new Underground railway line in, or rather beneath, London, and the first to be added to London's subterranean network since 1907. Called the Victoria Line because it began at Victoria, it extended far to the north and was ultimately to be extended to the south, passing beneath the Thames in its progress. The dislocation of traffic caused by the construction works was so immense that it may well have been that, however much time was subsequently saved by the new line, it could never make up for that lost while it was being built – a situation similar to that of the Knightsbridge Underpass, a traffic conduit which was similarly supposed to work marvels, but which had dislocated the even flow of vehicles for so long during its construction that it too had apparently built up a debt of delay that could never be repaid; this debt grew rapidly larger when, in the first months after its opening, it spent most of the time closed to all traffic while heroic efforts were made to stop the walls pouring water into the tunnel (thus making it difficult or even dangerous to enter) whenever it rained. The Victoria Line does not admit water; but on occasion, it seems, it does not admit passengers either, having begun its career of obstruction in fine style by refusing to accept the sixpence which the Queen herself, on the day of the new line's inauguration, thrust into the wholly automatic but unfortunately inoperative jaws of the machine that, at the entrance to the station, is supposed to issue and check the tickets and let duly accredited passengers through. This, it seemed, was a portent, since for some considerable time afterwards, while the trains ran below with admirable precision, comfort and safety, the machines up above jammed, broke down, rejected perfectly good coins and even, in a final spasm of bad temper, seized in a steel grip passengers who were slow to pass through or who were encumbered with parcels or suitcases, and showed every sign of holding them to automated ransom. (A few years previously, at the opening of a new and loudly fanfared hotel in Manchester, the Piccadilly – Manchester being a city in which the need of a new hotel, or even a tolerable old one, had long been pressing – a ceremonial banquet had been arranged, and was proceeding with efficiency and good humour, when a large part of the ceiling fell down on the banqueters. Order being restored, Lord Shawcross was called upon to declare the hotel open, and did so, referring in his speech to the unhappy accident that had taken place only a few minutes before as the kind of 'teething troubles' to which new buildings were always liable, while the plaster fell in flakes out of his listeners' hair and into their coffee.)

Nor did the Government seem able, even when it had a very good idea of what Britain needed to do to be saved, to carry through to success its own plans, its own proposals. Failure to do so bred a kind of panic, so that a bitter and sullen obstinacy arose (as in, for instance, the case of the Concorde) which prevented those responsible from being able to dispense with projects that had suddenly become (or suddenly been seen to be) unprofitable, or to have the flexibility and imagination necessary to adapt plans to changes in circumstances.

'This island', Aneurin Bevan once said, 'is made of coal and surrounded by fish; it would take an organizing genius to engineer a shortage of either.' His words were often quoted against the Labour Party, as shortly after he had uttered them, during the lifetime of the Attlee Government, an acute shortage of both had been felt. But much later, during the Sixties, coal was back in the middle of the industrial and political argument, and its fortunes, and the relations of the coal industry with the providers of other fuels and with the Government, were providing countless symbols of Britain's economic sickness and her hopes for a cure.

The coal industry had long been running down; it was the crudest as well as the most cruel of all ways of firing the homes and factories of Britain, and the decision had been taken at the beginning of the decade to reduce, and ultimately to end, the country's reliance on it. Oil was providing more and more of Britain's fuel needs, and whatever the instabilities of the Middle East, nobody seriously contemplated the possibility of supplies drying up, or even being seriously interrupted. Coal, on the other hand, was becoming increasingly expensive to provide, as more and more seams were worked out and the political dangers of pit-closing meant that more and more hopelessly uneconomic mines were kept in operation. At last the Wilson Government nerved itself to work out a future run-down for the coal industry that rested on the provision of increasing quantities of cheap power not only from oil, but from nuclear reactors and from natural gas,[1] discovered in large quantities beneath the North Sea just as the decade began.

Unfortunately, no sooner had the plans been drawn up than the planners found themselves with the bulky figure of Lord Robens, chairman of the Coal Board since 1962, adopting a most uncharacteristically tiger-like stance at their throats. Robens battled long and indomitably on behalf of his men, insisting that they should not be thrown on the discard pile merely because the economic patterns of providing power had changed (in one way a reasonable enough demand, in view of the lamentably inadequate plans for retraining and resettling those miners who would be deprived of their traditional livelihood before retiring age). Yet for all his struggles, and all his successes, he was fighting against history, and must have known it. As with the railways, so with coal; rationalization was the word for the Sixties, and if it was going to be cheaper, quicker and cleaner to produce fuel from nuclear reactors or the natural reservoirs of gas beneath the sea, then nuclear and gas power would come to dominate the last third of the century, as coal had dominated the first two-thirds and the whole of the previous one.

Robens and the other defenders of coal would have been on stronger ground if they had attacked the basis of the hopes that nuclear power and natural gas would in fact solve the country's fuel problems, as there was a good deal of evidence accumulating during the Sixties that they would not. Already, half-way through the decade, the advocates of nuclear power, who used to say, by way of a striking illustration, that they could make the *Queen Mary* sail right round the world without stopping on a piece of fuel the size of a walnut, had been compelled to trim their enthusiasm rather sharply, and not only because the *Queen Mary* had also proved uneconomic and had to be sold; even at the end of the Sixties, and in the most favourable circumstances, industrial nuclear power in Britain was more expensive than the

[1] i.e. gas found in its gaseous state, not derived by intermediate processes from solid fuels.

more traditional kinds, and by then nobody was guessing when it would cease to be.

In the field of natural gas the situation was even more suspect, as the immense teething troubles inherent in launching the new grid, particularly the massive conversion both of pipelines and of domestic equipment, were combined with sudden doubts about the quantity of gas in the reservoirs and the length of time it would last. The most pessimistic estimates reduced the latter to only some ten or fifteen years, at the end of which, enthusiasts began to realize, it might be necessary to convert the entire country *back* to coal gas, except that by then there might not be enough coal being mined to produce the required quantity; in the circumstances it was not surprising that the enterprise began to be nicknamed the North Sea Bubble.

The whole imbroglio was a perfect illustration of the erratic and dubious enthusiasm with which Britain was tumbling towards the future during the Sixties, the sudden wild bursts of vigour being alternated, and indeed combined, with the gravest suspicions about the whole enterprise, and a desperate longing for the comfortable and inefficient past. And the symbolism was deep, for coal was the perfect index to Britain's situation in more than one sense. It was the traditional rock on which her ancient prosperity had been built, and with which her Industrial Revolution had been powered, at a time when the human cost was not counted; further, supplies of it were dwindling, and would eventually disappear entirely, at any rate in any economically workable form; further still, the weight of inertia in coal's favour was colossal, and the pressure it exerted in the direction of 'feather-bedding' an increasingly uneconomic industry was typical of so much of the economic scene in the Sixties.

But if Government showed the way, how could people fail to follow? The cult of the amateur dies hard in Britain, and at no time did it die harder than in the Sixties. The 'English disease' can be defined in a dozen different ways, and has been, but they have in common that irreducible minimum of amateurism that seems to cling to matters British and to deflect the aim of the country, whether that might be to increase exports, improve education, or stop producing goods more likely to fall apart than not. Usually, no excuses were made for the amateur in a professional world; either his gentlemanly status was ignored entirely or his importance was minimized. Sometimes, however, he was actively defended; amateur directors on the boards of complex businesses, for instance, were supposed to bring to the firm's affairs a worldliness, a sophistication, a knowledge of their fellow-men, that the professionals, concerned only with the esoteric mysteries of balance-sheets and production schedules, must necessarily lack. 'Broad horizons' are said to be seen by such people and 'varied experience' employed; 'contacts' too are had, from a wider spectrum than the professional can know. And so it is generally believed, until something happens to disturb the complacency of those who believe it, and to expose their gullibility.

Just such an occurrence took place in the dying days of 1963, when the affair of the Norwich Union Insurance Society broke upon an astonished and delighted country. The Norwich Union was an old-established and reputable firm; its headquarters were, and always had been, in Norwich, and its Board of Directors were drawn almost entirely from the area and from the narrowest imaginable range of interests therein. The President was Sir Robert Bignold, formerly a Mayor of Norwich, the Vice-President was Sir Richard Barrett-Lennard, Chairman of the local savings bank; there was also the Notary-General of Norwich, the director of a Norwich shoe-firm, a director of a local brewery, a doctor from the local hospital and Lord Townshend, who was a descendant of the famous 'Turnip' Townshend, and who, for all the sense he displayed on this occasion, at any rate in public, might have had one of his ancestor's products for a head.

These distinguished folk were approached, as those in charge of many British firms had been, by officials of an organization called the Arab Boycott Office, which exists to put pressure on firms that do business with Israel, to persuade or compel them to end or reduce that business. The Norwich Union did do business with Israel, as it did with Arab countries and as any insurance company with an international trade did, though it was not suggested that the Norwich Union did a particularly large share of such business. As events soon showed, however, it was not insuring Israeli risks that concerned the Arab emissaries, but the presence on the Norwich Union board of Lord Mancroft, who was also a member of the board of Great Universal Stores, which is run by Sir Isaac Wolfson. And both of these gentlemen, as the Arab Boycott Office had noted with horror, were Jews.

On the whole, the Norwich Board was given to understand, it would be as well if Lord Mancroft were extruded from their business. The men of the world, with their sophistication, their broad horizons, their varied interests and their contacts, saw the force of this argument, and approached Lord Mancroft with a request to save them the trouble of sacking him; he, with an understandable fastidiousness, promptly resigned, and shortly afterwards it became known that one of the country's oldest and most reputable insurance companies had got rid of the Chairman of its London Board because he was a Jew and a group of Arabs had told them to do so. The Norwich Union Chairman, Sir Robert Bignold, came under a fire of criticism so intense and withering that within a matter of hours he retired to a sick-bed in a state of nervous exhaustion; firms and individuals began to cancel their business with the offending company; the Prime Minister publicly deplored the affair, and the Ambassadors of several Arab countries were called to the Foreign Office and rebuked; two other directors of the London Board of the Norwich Union resigned (one of them, Sir Hughe Knatchbull-Hugessen, was a man who could have been said to know amateurism from the inside, having been the British Ambassador to Turkey during the Second World War, and thus the man from whose safe the spy Cicero removed numbers of vital military secrets) on the ground that they had not been so much as informed, let alone consulted, when the decision to get rid of Lord Mancroft was taken; and Lord Mancroft stoutly declared that no anti-semitism existed among the Board of the Norwich

Union and added, in a charmingly unconscious echo of the old adage, that all its members were his good friends.

Eventually, the Norwich Union offered to re-instate Lord Mancroft on the Board, managing to devalue even that offer by letting the news be announced before telling him about it; he gracefully declined and shortly afterwards Sir Robert Bignold accepted the post of scapegoat and resigned the Chairmanship.

So the matter ended, though not before much heat and less light had been generated and some agreeable moments passed by all who were not directly concerned and even by some who were. But the pearl that remained when the oyster had been swallowed was the amazing truth that Sir Robert Bignold and the rest of the Board of the Norwich Union had been quite unconscious of the fact that they were doing anything, when they forced Lord Mancroft to resign, that anybody might consider wrong or even disgraceful, and that the storm, when it broke, took them entirely by surprise. Even in the Sixties, it seemed—perhaps *especially* in the Sixties, a decade which sometimes seemed to be composed almost entirely of unreality—it was possible to be at the head of a huge commercial concern and yet lack the smallest understanding of the nature of the real world, the attitudes of the people in it, and the possibility that others might find odd what one finds perfectly normal oneself.

* * *

Of all the figures who symbolized Britain's Sixties, none did so more strangely than Dr Richard Beeching, one of those people who produced during the decade magnificent plans for the reorganization or rebuilding of huge sections of British national and industrial life and flung them at the nation's head with a positively eighteenth-century conviction that the people needs must love the highest when they saw it, oblivious, as indeed was the eighteenth century, of the fact that the nation did not and would not do any such thing. (Professor Buchanan advocated the demolition and re-erection of all our cities; Sir Harry

Pilkington demanded the abolition and reconstruction of the entire commercial television network; Lord Fulton proposed the reformation of the whole of the Civil Service, Lord Franks the radical alteration of the principles and practices of Oxford University, the Monopolies Commission the unlimited reorganization of the licensing laws.) Dr Beeching, seconded at the suit of the Minister of Transport, Ernest Marples, to British Railways after an unseemly public squabble over his salary (as a director of I.C.I. he had been drawing £24,000 a year, and did not see why he should take less as chairman of British Railways simply because his predecessor in the post had done so), produced a plan for the thorough and relentless reshaping of the country's railway system, and of the principles on which it operated, that took account of Britain's national needs, of the railways' financial situation, of the pattern of demand for rail services that existed in the present and that might be predicted for the future, of the proper costing basis for all this, of the new kind of equipment, capitalization and fare-structure required, but omitted – since these things were no part of Beeching's brief – to take into account the extent to which people were used to having subsidized rail transport and their unwillingness to give it up, the force of the inertia imperceptibly exerted by an organization like British Railways, no matter who the essentially temporary chairman might be, the hostility to any kind of change displayed by the trade unions, together with their unrivalled skill at delaying and frustrating changes of which they disapproved, and the timidity of politicians faced with resolute opposition from all, or even any, of these forces.

The plan proposed by Dr Beeching (later, as a consolation prize, to become Lord Beeching) involved the closure of half the national network of railway lines, including, for instance, almost all of those in Wales; substantial increases in many fares, the aim being to make services like the suburban 'commuter' lines pay for their operation; the more productive use of rolling-stock; the introduction of new container-loaded 'liner' goods trains; the abolition, on many lines which were to be retained, of stopping services; and the reduction of the railway labour force by some 70,000 men out of some 470,000. The plan was for British Railways to become solvent, self-supporting without ruinous and economically debilitating subsidies, and above all efficient in terms of the role it would play in the general national economy, particularly as it developed through the remainder of the Sixties and into the Seventies. But the Beeching Plan spent the next five years being trimmed, weakened, modified and resisted, and when the Labour Party won office in 1964 and power in 1966 the modifications were sufficient to affect the very basis of the plan. Eventually Beeching went back to his job at I.C.I. after a last vain attempt to persuade the Government to let him plan and organize a genuinely integrated national transport structure, and was succeeded in the chairmanship of British Railways by Stanley Raymond, who accepted a salary rather more in line with those of Beeching's predecessors in the post, and was subsequently appointed, as we have seen, to be chairman of the Gaming Board set up after the reorganization of the system of licensing for gambling enterprises. But at any rate he got a knighthood, as Dr Beeching had got a peerage.

It did not pay, it seemed, to innovate, to suggest the abandonment of practices that many had for long found comfortable and profitable. The old traditions died hard, the old methods continued to be used long after they had proved uneconomic and even ruinous, and those who attempted to break into established markets by the use of new methods were apt to find themselves treated as though they had introduced bubonic plague into the situation rather than rational economics. That was the experience of those who conducted the Fairfields experiment to its inevitable doom, and it was also the fate of one who attracted considerably more publicity, who indeed became one of the most heavily publicized figures of the entire decade, and not only because of the spectacular way his rapid rise was followed by an even more rapid fall.

John Bloom, a young and brilliant businessman, entirely self-made and not so much self-taught as untaught, burst violently and cheerfully into the traditional washing-machine market. His direct-selling methods, backed by one of the biggest and most expensive advertising campaigns in history, were furiously resented by the established sections of the trade, largely because he compelled them to be more competitive by bringing down his prices to a level which substantially undercut his rivals while ensuring him a good profit. To the surprise of everyone except the cynical, the price of his rivals' machines began to fall rapidly under the pressure of his competition, though they did not use his methods, which suggested that they had been substantially overcharging before. But Bloom got no quarter from the competitors whom he had forced to be more efficient; when his empire proved unstable the ring of hawks around him closed in, and eventually he came down in one of the most spectacular financial crashes of the decade. Ultimately, criminal charges were laid against him, and his ensuing trial looked like being the longest since that of the Tichborne Claimant, and possibly longer. So great were the fears of a record trial, and so real the dangers of a juryman, or even the judge, dying in the course of the hearings (thus necessitating the whole thing having to start again from the beginning), that a deal was made between the prosecution and the defence by the terms of which most of the charges were dropped entirely while Bloom pleaded guilty to the remaining two and on them was fined £30,000. (He let it be known that he would have great difficulty in finding the money, but it was widely believed that the difficulties would be overcome, which they soon were.) But whatever he may or may not have done vis-à-vis the law, he had without question improved the sector of British industry that he had entered, and long after he had disappeared from the business, the prices of washing machines remained where he had forced them.

# 10

# Point of order

As the mood of political cynicism and despair deepened, and outlets for its expression were more eagerly sought, they began to be found in increasingly exotic quarters, and to take on shapes increasingly ominous from the point of view of the established providers of outlets for political expression. What gave these custodians of regularized dissent cause for anxiety was that, however extreme the disillusionment with traditional forms of political dissent might become, the equally traditional extremist groups were not the beneficiaries of the disgruntled popular will. Communists, and a variety of Fascist splinter-groups, offered their wares stridently and incessantly, but they had no electoral success under their own colours, and even Independents, who had once served a valuable political purpose, seemed to have disappeared for good. The public began instead to turn to new political groupings, or old ones in new guises, whereat the other party managers began to look pale as they sensed a genuine political threat to their ascendancy, and their sighs of relief were loud and sincere as each new wave of enthusiasm broke and dissipated harmlessly on the shores of traditional politics.

It began in 1962, with the first of a series of sensational by-election results. At Orpington, which might have stood for ever as a definition of middle-class Conservative solidarity – it was the home of Orpington Man, a creature which many would have thought worthy to stand alongside Piltdown Man, Neanderthal Man and Peking Man as another example of a species that in its day seemed set to survive for ever – they suddenly found themselves representative of everything most volatile and least stable; as, indeed, had Piltdown Man.

The cause was a Liberal parliamentary candidate, Eric Lubbock, who caused a considerable sensation by turning a 1959 Conservative general election majority of nearly 15,000 into a 1962 Liberal by-election one of nearly 8,000, and this, moreover, on a poll vastly higher (over 80 per cent) than in most by-elections.

Immediately psephologists, pollsters, analysts, commentators, investigators, apologists and explainers poured into the town to examine and question Orpington Man, to tap his political knee-jerks and test his political water, to find out what made him behave in so unorthodox a manner. The Liberal Party naturally claimed that it was the superior attraction of their policy and candidate, but this view was not widely accepted outside its ranks, and there was much agreement that the Liberal success at Orpington was a kind of social equivalent of the slow, and continuing, geographical success the party was having in the Celtic fringe; for just as in Scotland, Wales and Cornwall people felt themselves, with or without justification, neglected and exploited by the Moloch of Westminster, so at Orpington the middle class, which likewise felt that its interests were being intolerably neglected, had struck out in the only way available, by voting Liberal. Since the Liberal policy was sufficiently elastic to accommodate at the same time those who wanted a more right-wing Government, those who wanted a more left-wing Government, and those who wanted, for a wide range of entirely disparate reasons, a Liberal M.P., all were enabled to do so with satisfaction and a clear conscience. Whatever the complex web of reasons, Orpington elected one, and thus forged the first link in a long chain of political events.

The most immediate of these was the instillation into Mr Macmillan of the fact that his Government was doomed, and his tenure of Downing Street with it, unless he acted. This led in turn to the July massacre of half his Cabinet ('the wrong half', Mr Wilson was fond of saying, unkindly but also inaccurately), which in turn led to a deep and inarticulate feeling among the public that the Tories had lost both their nerve and their relevance and had better go. But the revolt of Orpington Man had another consequence, at that time almost unrecognized, which cast a much longer shadow and was not to be seen clearly until much later in the decade, this being its destruction of the traditional assumptions of permanently reliable political loyalty. As it happened, there was to be no wave of Liberal Orpingtons, largely because no suitable by-elections presented themselves soon enough afterwards to ensure that the impetus was maintained, and although the Liberals did improve their position at the ensuing General Election, they did not do so sufficiently well to persuade many that their band-wagon was at last rolling in earnest. This fact was combined with the vacillating behaviour of the Parliamentary party in the crucial twenty months of the 1964 Labour Government, when there was a Parliamentary majority varying between four seats and one; with the damage done to the party's standing and credibility by the violent action and even more violent language of a group of Young Liberals; and finally with the resignation as leader of the party of Jo Grimond and his replacement by the engaging but much less substantial figure of Jeremy Thorpe; the result was that the Liberals were unable to reap the reward of their unexpected good fortune in being in the right place, Orpington, at the right time, March 1962.

But where Orpington Man sowed, a far more primitive political anthropoid began to reap. The most startling political development of the entire decade was the rise and astonishing success (however short-lived it was to prove) of separatist Nationalism on the geographical, as on the political, fringe of Britain.

The modern Scottish and Welsh Nationalist movements had long been able to command the emotional, and strictly verbal, allegiance of hundreds of thousands, perhaps millions, of Scots and Welshmen, who were always willing to sign a petition, answer a Sassenach or Sais questioner with impeccable Celtic sentiments, or even paint 'HOME RULE NOW' on a lonely boulder normally seen only by the grazing sheep and cattle; they were not, however, usually to be persuaded to do anything more vigorous, even to the extent of voting for the Nationalist candidates.

The dragon slumbered, as did the thistle, and they were not awakened even by the extraordinary behaviour of Rutland, England's smallest county, which, faced with a plan by the Local Government Commission to merge it with its neighbour Leicestershire, instantly stood to arms under the slogan 'RUTLAND WILL FIGHT, AND RUTLAND WILL BE RIGHT' and campaigned for its ancient borders to such effect that the Government retreated in total disorder, leaving the campaigners master of the field. Only when Orpington demonstrated that social separatism could be achieved through the ballot-box did the Celtic subconscious realize that national separatism could follow the same example. There was then a period of gestation while this news slowly grew to maturity within the womb of the Sixties; it then emerged a bizarre, hybrid monster, to terrify its parents almost as much as it terrified the Labour and Conservative Parties, not to mention the English.

The scale and rapidity of the change in the fortunes of the Nationalist Parties, and the regard in which they were held, can be measured by the figures provided by those incurable realists, the bookies; just before the Carmarthen by-election of July 1966, which saw Gwynfor Evans, the Welsh Nationalist candidate, returned, it was possible to get 2,000 to 1 against his victory, though it appears that nobody actually put any money on at those odds. The day before Mrs Winifred Ewing's by-election victory at Hamilton in November 1967 the pencillers were offering 4 to 1 *on*, and there were no takers at that price either. In London, with increasing nervousness, the leaders of the main parties began to say that these were protest votes, as indeed they were, and to maintain that they would return to their traditional allegiances at a General Election, which was exactly what happened early in the new decade; but eventually such remarks as those of Merlyn Rees, a junior member of the Government who in March 1967 had said that 'Welsh Nationalism shows many of the traits of Fascism' (and he a Welshman!), and of Edward

Heath, Conservative Party Leader, who at about the same time described Nationalists as offering 'flower politics for flower people' (and he a Broadstairs man!), suddenly began to be thought in poor taste, and both parties began energetically, if not frantically, to search for credible policies for Scotland and Wales that would enable them to draw the Nationalists' fire without actually conceding the Nationalists' claims, a search not made any easier by the fact that the Nationalists, the heady but, as it proved, delusive scent of victory in their nostrils, rejected every proposal put forward.

The Nationalists carried to even greater lengths than the Orpington Liberals the policy of allowing those of all shades of opinion to believe that it was their particular world-view that the party and the candidate shared, while assuring those of entirely contradictory outlook that the same was true for them. To this day, nobody knows whether the Scottish Nationalists, for instance, are broadly speaking on the Left or the Right in political matters, and the heroine of their great 1967 by-election triumph, Mrs Winifred Ewing, has not only been careful to suggest that she is both, and indeed neither, but gives a distinct impression that if she were ever forced into a position in which she could not choose but answer the question, she would be able with complete sincerity to say that she does not know.

At one point it was alleged that the Scottish Nationalists, or some of them, were enthusiastic supporters of the Smith regime in Rhodesia, and thought it should be given immediate independence. (This recalled, for spectators with long memories, the similar atmosphere around the Orpington by-election, in which some of the most extreme right-wing voters in the town were wholeheartedly for the Liberals.) At this, a party spokesman said with unfortunate clarity that 'No statement has ever been issued on behalf of the Scottish National Party relating to Rhodesia.' This admission that the party had no view on a subject as important as Rhodesia typified the dilemma of such an organization, its whole hope of survival being to conceal from its potential followers its beliefs, if any, on all matters of major public controversy, lest some of those potential followers should prove to hold contrary ones. In the circumstances those who searched for any practical and recognizable policy which the party might be expected to pursue in an independent Scotland seemed certain to be disappointed. As for the party's day-to-day activities, other than electioneering proper, these rarely seem to deal with any matter more weighty than its demand, in August 1968, that one of a series of postage stamps should be withdrawn from sale, as one of the series (which were of reproductions of a number of well-known British paintings) was an anonymous portrait of Queen Elizabeth I, not recognized by Scottish Nationalists as Queen of Scotland. The offending stamp was not withdrawn and another grievance against brutal foreign oppression was born in Scottish hearts, while the Prime Minister made things no better by tartly pointing out in the House of Commons in answer to a question by Mrs Ewing, who had been demanding that he visit Scotland more often, that 'At the airport on my last visit but one, I saw some of your supporters, cheerful and enthusiastic, whose only contribution was to hold the flag of Scotland upside down.'

For their part, the Welsh Nationalists had a similar problem, if problem it was, to which was added another and more urgent one, this being the attitude of the main nationalist body–Plaid Cymru–to those extremists who thought it right to use violence in the sacred cause. When in 1968 a bomb planted by Nationalist extremists seriously injured an R.A.F. warrant officer, Mr Gwynfor Evans, momentarily the party's sole M.P., denounced the 'vicious and degrading cult of violence' with such admirable promptitude that only four clear days elapsed between the explosion and his condemnation of it. It was not, however, always so. Earlier in the decade, for instance, Mr Evans himself had said that he had 'great sympathy and admiration' for two men convicted of sabotage at the workings of a Welsh reservoir that was designed to carry good Welsh water to the black heart of Liverpool, and he had to be prompted more than once, after entering Parliament, to denounce the wild men in the valleys.

As the decade moved towards its end the Nationalists found

themselves in something like the same position as had the Liberals after Orpington, unable to capitalize fully on their electoral advance because of the failure of sufficient Scottish and Welsh M.P.s to die, and thus create parliamentary vacancies to be filled at by-elections. A certain amount of frustration, even nervousness, resulted, and in the case of the Welsh Nationalists the inability of the orthodox Plaid Cymru to register any more really striking successes by constitutional means led the extremists to attempt to do so by less orthodox ones.

The Free Wales Army had long existed, and its members had as long taken pleasure in dressing up in odd bits of what they imagined were military uniforms, the better to indulge in what they imagined was military drill. From time to time one of them got hold of a bit of gelignite or a detonator (these last, of course, hardly more difficult to come by in mining country than three-leaf clovers), and soon blood-curdling stories were going about concerning what they intended to do with this massive armoury. Most of the time the intrepid resistance fighters had to content themselves with operating clandestine radio-transmitters on which they broadcast occasional calls to the Welsh to rise against the English, in doing which they were wont to liken themselves to those who broadcast clandestine messages against the Nazis in wartime Occupied Europe. The comparison could hardly stand close inspection, however, being between offences punishable on the one hand by torture and death at the hands of the Gestapo, and on the other by a fine not exceeding £10 for the first offence, and not exceeding £50 for any subsequent offence, following conviction under Section I of the Wireless Telegraphy Act, 1949.

Matters were not helped much by the growing insistence, borne along on the wave of nationalism, that the Welsh language must be revived and strengthened, and taught in the schools instead of dreadful foreign tongues. The fact that the vast majority of Welsh people spoke little or no Welsh and showed no desire to learn any, or to have their children learn any either, made no difference. At any rate, if it did, the difference was one which only caused complaints that Welsh children were being deprived of their cultural heritage, though the amount of genuine literature in Welsh was small, and additions to it of any merit rare. That this was the case could be seen each year at the Eisteddfod, where, amid much dressing-up and chanting, a Bardic crown was awarded to, say, a school-teacher in horn-rimmed spectacles and what he believed to be Druidic robes. The crown was awarded for, as it might be, an enormous poem in rhymed octosyllabic couplets about an ancient Welsh chieftain who had done little of note other than to sell his army to the English for cash down; the poem would be discussed for a few days or weeks in a small circle in Wales, and thereafter never be seen again, nor its author heard of.

However, with the constitutionalists quiescent, the militants had the field to themselves. After a time a series of bomb explosions, or at any rate bomb-plantings, took placc. The first major onc demolished, fortunately with no loss of life, a building in Cardiff named the Temple of Peace, which was blown up the day before a discussion was to takc place there, attended by, among others, the Earl of Snowdon, on the plans for the Investiture at Caernarvon Castle of Prince Charles, in fulfilment of a vow made by the Queen when she dubbed him Prince of Wales. The next major explosion was the one already mentioned, which left an R.A.F. officer partly disabled for life. Not long after that, a bomb was found in a left-luggage office at Cardiff station; when experts were called in to dismantle it, they announced that if it had gone off it would have demolished much of the station and killed anybody who happened to be in the vicinity at the time. Credit, or discredit, for the outrages and attempts was variously apportioned and claimed, but the identity of the bombers remained unknown, and a good deal of unease was generated in consequence, particularly since threats now began to be heard, suggesting that the Prince of Wales himself might be the next, or the ultimate, target.

For what might be termed the militant but non-violent section of the unorthodox Welsh Nationalists had chosen the Investiture of this harmless and engaging young man as the focal point of their activities. They objected, it seemed, to the rule over them of a foreign prince, though the prince in question was neither foreign nor a ruler over them; in addition, they objected to the idea of having a Prince of Wales at all.

Further objection was taken to the enrolment of Prince Charles at the University of Aberystwyth for a course, lasting seven weeks, in Welsh language and literature, though those who objected to this seemed unable to make up their minds whether they did so because the course was too short or because the Prince should never have taken it at all. His arrival at Aberystwyth, accompanied by a formidable security force (headed by Superintendent Jock Wilson, whose presence instantly exposed the unstable nature of the Celtic Alliance by provoking as a complaint additional to all the others that he was a Scot), was heralded by a hunger-strike on the part of a group of four students, who were believed to have gone almost entirely without a square meal for nearly three days to demonstrate the intensity of their nationalist passion.

At the same time posters and car-stickers began to appear in Wales opposing and ridiculing the idea of the Investiture, though since the words on these were naturally in Welsh it was feared that many of those whose blood they were intended to stir failed to understand the point, as must have been the case with an even higher proportion of those whose blood they were meant to freeze. There was even talk of an attempt to sabotage the ceremony by violent means, and an assiduous *Daily Mirror* reporter actually claimed to have heard talk of an attempt at assassination. But all this seemed suddenly less impressive when a Gallup Poll taken in Wales revealed an overwhelming majority of the Welsh people in favour of the Investiture. The authorities, however, were taking no chances, and as the campaign against the Investiture got under way, and the prospects of more bomb-attacks seemed to grow, prosecutions were launched against a group of men who were alleged to be, and for that matter boasted of being, concerned in the running of the Free Wales Army. The prosecutions took place under the Public Order Act of 1936, which forbids, among other things, the management of an organization using or displaying physical force in promoting a political object. The charges seemed impressive, and the accused began to take on the appearance of very desperate men, until the case actually started, when, though they were undoubtedly guilty as charged, they began to cut less impressive figures; it came out that much of the evidence consisted of statements they had made on television programmes, their hunger to appear on these being apparently unassuageable. Nor was the picture of a sworn blood-brotherhood of desperate men much improved when it also came out that the organization was infiltrated by the police to such an extent that it was a nice thing whether there were more policemen or genuine members in the ranks.

The Investiture was a great success.

By now the division between the constitutionalists and the extremists was wide and unbridgeable, the former declaring that the latter were a lot of silly children playing with dangerous toys, the latter declaring that the former were as many silly grown-ups playing with Parliaments. But by now too, up and down the land, men were seeking new nationalisms in the oddest and most remote corners. In the west the ancient Cornish tongue was suddenly rediscovered, and an organization called 'Mebyon Kernow' in it – or 'Sons of Cornwall' in English – declared that it wanted nothing less than a separate Cornish State, though it did not go on to specify whether, when full independence was achieved, it would withdraw from NATO or join the United Nations; it did, however, say that it would put up separatist candidates in Cornwall in the next general election, and so potent was this heady wine of nationalism becoming that several members of more orthodox political parties hastily joined the organization in the hope of keeping their bread buttered on both sides. So far, there have been no reports of bomb outrages in Liskeard or Falmouth.

* * *

And yet, for all the absurdities on the Celtic fringe, those who remembered Orpington and could see the connection were not disposed to dismiss the Nationalist enthusiasm entirely, though it was only sensible to regard the truly Nationalist feeling in it as a mere top-dressing, which provided the character and flavour of the movement without necessarily expressing the fundamental truth in what was affecting its supporters.

These had clearly been moved by the restless air of the decade, that grew more restless as the decade wore on. It had many names: cynicism, alienation, affectlessness. It had many results: violence, the new arts, the student revolt. It had many causes: affluence, poverty, war, peace. Common to all its forms, though, was the feeling that events were slipping from the individual's grasp, that somewhere a computer was inexorably beckoning human beings towards the mouth of Moloch, that decisions were taken not by elected representatives, nor even by identifiable oppressors, but by forces unknowable and unrecognizable that did not themselves know what they were about, or why. Late, perhaps too late, the people had begun to wake up to the enervating effect of the way of life they had, over the years, chosen, with its increasingly impersonal flavour and its increasingly distant connection between cause and effect. The hungry sheep looked up, and were not fed, or if they were, were fed things that no longer satisfied their stomachs, though they did not know why, and in many cases did not even realize that it was so.

This was happening in industry, in education, in social relations. But in no field was it more true, and the realization of it more bitter, than in politics. The voters voted for one party, in the vague belief that it would do certain things that they wanted done. As much the prey of vast impersonal forces as the electors, the party failed to do these things, and fell instead to blaming the voters for their failure. The voters sighed, and turned that party out and put in its rival. Again the dark clouds rolled across the sky, the trivial, paper-bound thunderbolts fell casually from them, and this party too was helpless, its endeavour blunted, its aims forgotten. The voters began to panic; it seemed as though diabolical forces were in charge, as though nothing happened when the instructions were given; it was as if thirty million electric-light switches had been turned and no light had come on in thirty million lamps.

The search for identity was not conducted only upon the stage; even in the polling-booths people asked: 'Who am I?' Clearly 'I' was not Conservative, not Labour, hardly Liberal; these were no more than words, indeed than sounds signifying nothing, having been for so long only systems whereby results might flow from causes, and unrecognized as such until they ceased to be. Identity, political identity, was something else; it might be that of a striker, grasping, head down, at the only thing that seemed stable – money. It might be that of a student, demanding that society be destroyed immediately, and the debate on what would replace it postponed until the job was done. It might be the marcher, carrying a banner like a kaleidoscope, the device on which seemed to change half a dozen times between one end of the street and the other, so that its bearer seemed to be protesting now about one shifting, meaningless abstract called 'Vietnam', now about another called 'Biafra', now about yet another called 'The Bomb', and none of them conveying to banner-carrying demonstrator or banner-reading passer-by anything but a feeling of generalized unease.

* * *

In truth, it was a very uneasy decade, and in it the whirling fragments of the almost cosmic explosion that had broken up so many of Britain's traditional attitudes and beliefs, the tensions and contradictions of these most tense and contradictory years, produced a state of national metaphorical weightlessness akin to that experienced physically by astronauts outside the earth's gravitational force.

As, beneath the surface of the Sixties, strange things bubbled and seethed, so, beneath the thinning crown of Enoch Powell, two conflicting ideas began to dance, slowly at first, then more and more quickly, until both burst forth to make him the most controversial politician of the decade, and to leave him, as it ended, balanced on a cliff-edge from which he might at any moment ascend to a mountain-peak of triumph, or tumble to irreversible ruin.

Powell had long been uneasy at the course of Conservative politics. When Macmillan fell, he was involved in a last-minute attempt to stop Sir Alec Douglas-Home succeeding to the party leadership, and when the attempt failed he refused office under a Prime Minister regarded as being of an insufficiently modern stamp to lead the Conservatives, particularly into an election in which the Labour Party would be led by Harold Wilson.

It is very unlikely indeed, as a matter of fact, that Mr Powell's reason (whatever may have been true of Macleod and the others involved in the stop-Home movement) for remaining outside the new Government had anything to do with Douglas-Home's quaint and old-fashioned image, particularly since the alternative proposed by the 'plotters' had been Butler, who was the archetype of everything Powell had by then come to hate and reject in Conservative philosophy; it is much more probable that Powell, having been persuaded to join the Butler forces by his belief (though he can scarcely have thought the question very important) that the Conservatives were less likely to win an election under Douglas-Home than under Butler, seized joyfully on the excuse their failure provided him with for staying out of the administration entirely. Indeed, ironically enough, Douglas-Home's ideas were far closer to Powell's than were Butler's.

For Powell, by the mid-Sixties and to a considerable extent much earlier, had persuaded himself that Conservative economic policy was, in its fundamental assumption, indistinguishable from that of its Labour rival, and equally pernicious. Ever since 'Butskellism', that economically bipartisan hybrid of the Fifties (made up of half a Labour chancellor, Hugh Gaitskell, and half a Conservative one, R. A. Butler), Conservative economic policy had been interventionist, and the party's leaders committed not only to the belief that Government action *could* affect the economic situation but that it *should*. This belief Powell had gradually come to reject, until by the end of the decade his rejection of it was so complete and so extreme that it had reached with him the point of obsession, and almost of mania. It would hardly have been surprising if he had begun to advocate the removal from the public sector of the police force, the armed services, and the fire brigade, and the handing over of these institutions to private companies to run at a profit or to close down if they could not be made to pay. In short, Powell by the end of the Sixties had returned, as far as economics was concerned, to the most extreme position held in the nineteenth century by such proto-Powells as Nassau Senior, and in an earlier decade of the present century by Professor Ludwig van Mises. This strange position was arrived at by Mr Powell, ironically enough, because of his rigorously logical mind, which, once it had seen good reason for taking one step, could see no good reason for not taking another, nor, that step taken, for not taking the next. Eventually he was objecting strenuously to any Government attempt to give any kind of economic direction or aid to privately owned firms. All attempts at an incomes policy or appeals for restraint, any proposal for keeping prices down or for fixing proportions by which wages should be allowed to increase, any official body set up to pronounce upon questions of national economic planning or to help the rationalization of particular industries – all such steps were denounced, in increasingly severe terms, by the man who now came to believe that any attempt to interfere, in the slightest way, with the 'laws' of supply and demand was not only doomed to certain failure but was actively harmful, and even, in some mystical moral-economic sense, wicked.

Further and further out he was driven by the relentless pressure of his own logical, classics-trained mind, until it seemed that no party, no group even within any party, could hold him; as a gesture to his own conscience he entered the election for leader of the Conservative Party which followed the resignation of Sir Alec Douglas-Home, and may well have been satisfied with the fifteen votes he got out of the three hundred cast in all, if only because it must have demonstrated to this extraordinarily ascetic figure, a kind of political Savonarola, that a man who preaches doctrine so right and true that all others must reject it for fear of facing reality cannot expect to attract any considerable following.

But there was another side to Enoch Powell. As he grew more and more deeply into the realization that he could not in good conscience take office in a Conservative Government pledged, and even intending, to follow the paths of State economic interventionism, he began to be troubled by the thought that in that case he could never aspire to lead the country into the paths of economic righteousness at all. Casting about in both the national scene and his own subconscious for something that might give him a personal following with which he could, should circumstances favour it, appeal over the heads both of the Labour Party and of the leadership of his own party to the electorate, he hit, in his own mind, upon what must have been deeply embedded racial feelings about those of a colour different from his own, and simultaneously upon the widespread fears and resentments produced in the minds of many others by the influx of coloured immigrants into Britain during the decade. Thus armoured with the belief that in Britain black and brown people should not be permitted to mingle too freely or too numerously with white, lest terrible though unspecified national harm should follow, he found himself in a position to play upon the fears and resentments of others in order to gain a substantial, passionate and vociferous following, which needed only an improbable but not at all impossible combination of political circumstances to carry him towards the political power he craved, as all fanatics crave it, in order to do people good whether they wanted such good done them or not. (It was not only, or even mainly, on the Right that such feelings existed during the Sixties; by the end of the decade it was becoming very fashionable on the Left to talk of 'repressive tolerance' and to argue that the mass of the people were so deceived by the infinitely cunning capitalists who controlled them that they could not see where their true interests lay, and would therefore have to be forbidden to choose, in their ignorance, for themselves. Truly, in the Sixties the longest way round was still, sometimes, the shortest way home.)

And so Powell began a campaign, increasingly fanatical in its nature, and increasingly wayward in its use of facts,[1] to persuade the country that it was gravely threatened by the coloured immigrants, and that only he was willing to face the truth. His first major speech on this subject, which threatened Britain with rivers flowing with blood and offered some titillating stories about excreta (an obsession with which, among those convinced that certain identifiable groups are threatening them, is a not uncommon psychological disorder), caused him to be ejected from the Shadow Cabinet on the grounds, as Mr Heath put it in announcing his decision to sack him, that it was 'racialist' in tone, and the dismissal must have come as a relief, since it severed the formal link between him and a policy-direction that he had entirely rejected, and also left him free to pursue his cause entirely unfettered by the need to keep in some semblance of step with his party's leaders; from then on, he pursued it assiduously and with masterful timing, and by the end of the decade it was by no means certain that it would not, at some future time, carry him to supreme office, nor was it certain that the rivers would not flow with blood. But it was certain that if they did, he would be as responsible as any man.

* * *

It was not, after all, so surprising. In this two-headed decade it was not surprising that the backward-looking head should

[1] See, for instance, his claim, during a television discussion with David Frost that the Milner-Holland Report on London housing supported, in 'case after case similar in its details, similar even in the excreta', his claim about the bad behaviour of coloured people in 'taking over' white streets. The claim was false, the report going out of its way to emphasize that bad behaviour was not a racial matter, and the actual 'case after case' listed in it containing only six examples, out of forty-seven, which described bad coloured behaviour towards white residents.

become embittered, disillusioned, resentful of its forward-looking partner. The memoirs, political and military, the volumes of warning and of dreadful prediction, the truths that surrounded Britain like the sea – these were influences that could only lead to, or at least chime in with, the growing feeling of despair and alienation. Welsh and Scottish Nationalists took the high road; those who saw in Mr Powell a saviour, a true prophet, took the low. At the crossroads stood Mr Wilson and Mr Heath, urging the nation forward, down the road that led to their ideas of the future. Some peered down the road and did not like what they saw; others looked at Wilson and Heath, and liked what *they* saw even less. The woodwork seethed.

Yet there was still a place, in the Sixties, for an older political tradition. On polling day in the March 1966 general election the London borough of Hampstead looked quite likely to collapse under the weight of people pouring into the area from outside, all bound on one errand, all united – strangers as well as brothers – in one cause, a cause that had by then become something like a symbolic crusade for many, and a crusade which summed up one aspect of the Sixties to horrid perfection. The purpose of the throng which milled about the streets of Hampstead that night, getting in each other's way, knocking on doors that had already been knocked on, applying the law of diminishing returns in an acute form, was to get Henry Brooke removed from the House of Commons, and it is a measure of their achievement that the fact that they succeeded, that what had only a year or two before been one of the safest Tory seats in England returned in 1966 a Labour M.P., was less remarkable than the fact that, at a time when the pressure of the two Harolds had almost entirely emptied politics of principle, and public apathy about principle was growing so rapidly, such a feeling should have taken hold of so many people. For many, that evening, turning Brooke out of Parliament had nothing to do with support for the Labour Party or disapproval of the Conservatives; it had nothing to do with politics at all, and the invaders included many people who were normally quite apolitical,[1] but who were simply determined that Henry Brooke's tenure of the Home Office should be brought to an end.

The Home Office had for many years had a succession of dreadful chief ministers and even worse permanent officials, until it had become a byword for ignorance, obstinacy, brutality, fanaticism and various combinations of these, together with a reluctance to admit error and a willingness to go to great lengths to avoid admitting error and to mislead or deceive those who wished to reveal it. Under such men as Major Gwilym Lloyd George and David Maxwell-Fyfe its reputation had in no serious way mended, while modern techniques of evasion and concealment had greatly improved its chances of getting away with its misdemeanours.

And now the Home Office was in the hands of Henry Brooke. His political career had begun, in a lamentably prophetic manner, with a passionate defence of Chamberlain in the famous debate of May 1940 that finally brought the Government down and Churchill to the Premiership. ('I know', he had said on that occasion, 'that people who speak as I am doing are labelled "yes-men" ... The men who win wars are the men with burning hearts and cool heads ... It is because I see that combination present in the Prime Minister that I would rather trust him to lead to victory than any other man ... I support him, and I am ready, if it so befalls, to go down to failure with him, confident that I by my speeches and actions shall not have betrayed the country.'[2]) He continued his career in an even more characteristic fashion when, as he predicted, having gone 'down to failure' with his leader, he sank into back-bench obscurity from which he was not to emerge until long after the war.

But Brooke came into his own when he was appointed Home Secretary by Macmillan, and achieved in a mercifully short

[1] They included one man, active on that occasion and in this cause from mid-afternoon until the polls closed, who was so apolitical that he had never used his vote, and did not even do so on this occasion, his residence being in another constituency.

[2] *Hansard*, May 7th, 1940.

tenure of office a series of decisions unequalled for their pigheadedness, it is safe to say, by any of his predecessors, so that one of Parliament's most familiar sights was that of his pasty face over the dispatch-box, explaining away his department's latest blunder, latest turpitude, altogether unable to understand why one Labour M.P. described him as 'the most hated man in Parliament'.

His first notable achievement took place in the first week of his tenure of the Home Office (which had begun, the superstitious may care to note, on a Friday the thirteenth), when he proposed to deport a West Indian girl who had stolen from a supermarket goods worth slightly less than two pounds. It was her first offence, but Brooke, when pressed, replied: 'I am not prepared to look at this case again'; he then did, the girl having spent six weeks in prison while he was doing so.

From there Brooke went on to bigger things, his next notable coup being the case of Robert Soblen, a convicted American spy who had escaped and got to Britain. Soblen, having asked for political asylum in this country and been refused it, was then ordered by Brooke not only to leave the country but to be sent back to the United States, despite the fact that no extradition proceedings had taken place and Soblen could have gone, and wished to go, elsewhere. (Soblen solved the problem by committing suicide while awaiting return; and the corpse was sent back to the United States.)

Occasionally there was a comic interlude, as when Brooke, having refused permission for Georges Bidault to enter Britain and told the House of Commons 'I have no grounds for thinking that Mr Bidault is now in this country', was shortly afterwards able to watch a television interview with Bidault that had been filmed in Britain more or less at the moment at which Brooke was giving his assurance to the House, and petulantly said: 'My permission for him to enter the country was neither sought nor granted.' Rather less comic was his performance in the Challenor case, in which a number of policemen, one of whom had been insane at the time, had planted and manufactured evidence and committed perjury to convict innocent men, and throughout which Brooke, on behalf of his department, had prevaricated and wriggled until some of the innocent men had spent over a year in prison though the truth had long since become apparent. Nor were there many laughs in his conduct in the case of Chief Anthony Enahoro, who was sent back to Nigeria to face certain imprisonment and (for all Brooke knew) possible execution, on political charges; the British courts, appealed to by Enahoro, had asked for an assurance that Enahoro, if he was returned, would be able to have counsel of his own choice to defend him, and Brooke told both Parliament and (by affidavit) the courts that he had satisfactory assurances on this score, despite the fact that he already knew from Nigeria that Enahoro's counsel, Dingle Foot, would not be allowed to enter Nigeria.

And so on polling day 1966 something that had been quietly dying in British politics came to life again, for the last time in the Sixties (perhaps for the last time ever); that is, the translation into directly political terms of a profoundly felt, even if not articulated, moral conviction. The conviction was that there should be no place in the House of Commons for Henry Brooke; the result, with one of the biggest swings over the 1964 and 1966 elections of any constituency in the country, finally vindicated the Hampstead constituency from the general – and generally valid – charge that such issues no longer played any part in elections. But so swift-moving were the currents of the decade, and so entirely of another era was Brooke and his conduct, that within a year of the 1966 election it was difficult to believe that he had ever existed as Home Secretary, that such behaviour, such attitudes, could ever have been allowed to rule. The two faces of the decade could not have been more exactly pictured than in the portrait of British politics with, and then without, Henry Brooke.

One of Brooke's wheels came an ironic full circle. Enahoro was imprisoned on his return to Nigeria, but, after a coup which displaced the regime that had imprisoned him, became a member of the successor Government. Almost at the end of the decade, six years after his own betrayal by Brooke, it fell to his lot to rule on the case of a Russian seaman, who jumped overboard from his ship in Lagos harbour, swam to a British freighter and to demonstrate (he spoke little English) that he wanted asylum touchingly drew a Union Jack before the captain. Enahoro had him returned to the Soviet ship, justifying his conduct, itself worthy of Brooke, in a manner that showed he had learnt all too well how the game was played. He 'understood' that the sailor had 'no political motive'; it seemed that he was 'merely resentful at the way he had been treated by his officers'.

11

# The machine stops

Political cynicism strode on, quickening its pace; and no wonder. Attempts were made from time to time to authorize the presence of television cameras in the House of Commons, to bring the sight of the legislature at work into the homes of the people and thus forge stronger links between voters and voted-for, to the lasting benefit of both. A system of continuous televising of the entire proceedings being too expensive, among other things, to contemplate, the advocates of the proposal settled upon an edited daily version of events in the House.

The proposal was put by a variety of advocates to the Government, which decided that it was essentially a matter for the House, and accordingly arranged for an experiment in which the House would be televised in closed circuit, so that Members could make up their minds about the effects of having cameras present, and also on the kind of thing that would be made out of the day's televising.

To the astonishment of many, the proposal had run from the start into the most virulent opposition from many Members of Parliament, who, as is usually the way with determined opponents of a scheme only half-heartedly advocated, were able to gain the day. Among the arguments these used against the modest proposal was the contention that members conscious of the television cameras would tend to 'play to the gallery', that they would compete fiercely for screen time on days when public interest in Parliament's proceedings might be thought to be at its height, and that they would tend to join in debates in which they had little personal interest, just in order to keep themselves before the public, a set of charges which tended to leave somewhat dazed those observers who knew how the House of Commons, collectively and severally, already behaves. It is, however, only fair to the opponents of the plan to point out that although the more shrewd and far-sighted of them had instantly seen the true objection, which was that the knowledge by the mass public of the way in which the House of Commons almost invariably misconducts itself on important political occasions might lead to a total collapse of confidence in Parliament, or even to revolution, most of those who rejected the idea did so on the grounds that they sincerely believed that for the public to be allowed to see and hear their representatives at work was at best an impertinence and at worst a serious breach of Parliamentary privilege.

At any rate, when the House came to debate the proposal formally, it was defeated by one vote in an unwhipped division, and Parliament's reputation stood secure from the prying eyes of the nation. Shortly afterwards, by the happiest of ironies, the chief and most implacable opponent of the measure, the Labour Chief Whip, Herbert Bowden, left Parliament and, raised to the peerage as Lord Aylestone, was appointed Chairman of the Independent Television Authority, in succession to Lord Hill, who had moved from the post to that of Chairman of the Governors of the B.B.C. and was a man cast in much the same profoundly and unshakeably conservative mould as Lord Aylestone. It was now very unlikely indeed that any further serious pressure would come from either of the broadcasting organizations to persuade Parliament to change its mind.

Was it surprising, the increasingly desperate rejection of the traditional forms and resources of politics that went on throughout the decade? The people were, in the Sixties, in the grip – increasingly powerful, too – of forces which knew and cared nothing about individuals and their hopes and wishes and fears. The advance of modern technology, with all the problems it entailed, meant that more and more people found themselves measured against templates that were designed, because the social machine would not work otherwise, only for the average, the standard, the passive. As the Post Office declared that it would demand a surcharge for envelopes of a size outside certain specified limits (this being only a preliminary to a refusal to carry such envelopes entirely), so Ministries, Government plans, party policies, industrial concerns, nationalized industries, local authorities and others all found themselves unable to cope with the particular, geared as they were only to the demands of the general.

Stealthily the computer advanced, vanguard of the technological revolution, hailed as the cure for all mankind's ills and denounced as the baleful force which would first enslave and then destroy us all. At the beginning of the decade the chief argument about computers concerned the relative merit, cost and reliability of the British and American varieties, and the Government was urged to support the struggling local computer industry instead of buying American equipment. At the end of the Sixties this argument persisted, but no longer occupied the chief place in the minds of those who thought about such things, who were now increasingly worried, as well they might have been, at the problems that the extensive automation and computerization of more and more areas of life brought with them. Nobody seriously feared that mad computers would presently break loose and take over the world, despite the attempt to do so made by Hal, the lovable, gleaming, and sadly dated fellow in an otherwise most imaginative science-fiction film, *2001*. But more and more anxiety was being expressed by those who received telephone bills for £99,999 or for nothing at all, those who found themselves against their will on mailing-lists the addresses in which were stored by computers and could not be found when the recipients protested and demanded to be pestered no more, those who resented the continuous decline in the individuality of the accountancy provided by such institutions as banks, large shops and other suppliers of goods and services.

Gradually more and more people came to realize not only that far too many organizations, institutions and commercial bodies had installed computers long before they had either the trained staff or the back-up facilities to make them work harmoniously, but that the errors of omission and commission made by the computers or their fallible human operators, multiplied by the extreme difficulty and even, in some cases, impossibility of tracing and correcting such errors, had led by the end of the decade to a situation that was coming to resemble E. M. Forster's short story, *The Machine Stops*. In that picture of the future the world is run by a sealed system which is entirely self-correcting, so that when it goes wrong there is no way in which new impulses, designed to prevent deterioration and breakdown, can be injected from outside the system, and no initiative left outside it to make the effort. But it was part of the times, times in which the people were told that progress was good for them, even when—*especially* when—it hurt.

What was progress, what regress? None could say for certain. One, however, professed to, as the pace of change quickened, continued to quicken, throughout a decade of change and of preparation (or lack of it) for even greater change. Over much of it there loomed the figure of Anthony Wedgwood Benn, ministering priest (or maintenance engineer) to the great god Technology, whose worship, by the time the Sixties ended, had for many (especially Benn) become the State religion in succession to an effete and despairing Church of England; while in holes and corners small groups of worshippers of gods even older than those of the Anglican persuasion met and prayed for hand-made goods, unspoilt countryside, inefficiency, peace and quiet, unmetalled roads, natural fertilizers, respect for tradition and the immediate demise of Benn and all who thought like him. Benn, one of the most inexorably characteristic figures of the decade, was a prognathous teetotaller who all too predictably became Minister of Technology in Mr Wilson's Government, after an interlude in which the post had been filled by Frank Cousins—the nation's leading Luddite—though not for very long. Benn flung himself into the Sixties technology with the enthusiasm (not to say language) of a newly enrolled Boy Scout demonstrating knot-tying to his indulgent parents. Presently the entire land echoed to his pronouncements, and many shuddered at his vision of a hygienic, remote-controlled, automated future, the shudders becoming more pronounced as the technology with which the public already came in contact showed more and more signs, as the decade moved towards its end, of total breakdown.

The truth of the matter was that, during the Sixties, passion for automation and automatic control of industrial and social processes, including the collection and storage of information, had far outrun the capacity of the concerns subjected to their installation to handle them. (Thus the central book-distribution system formed by a number of publishers produced far greater delays in finding and dispatching a wanted book after computers were installed than before, and the same pattern could be found in many other areas.) This state of affairs did not, however, prevent Benn from painting, in ever more exciting colours, his dream of the future, though the more he sprinkled his language with 'jolly goods' the more his vision was belied by the actuality.

* * *

But earlier in the decade Benn had fought a battle with profound symbolic significance for the country, and very considerable practical significance for its political life. The death of his father, the first Viscount Stansgate, automatically elevated him to the peerage. His father, at the time he was offered his peerage, had consulted his eldest son, who would one day inherit it, and who offered no objections. That son, however, was killed during the Second World War, a fate which could not of course have been foreseen at the time Stansgate agreed to be ennobled, and the second son thus became the heir to the viscountcy, and in the course of nature inherited it. Benn, however, passionately desired to continue his career in the House of Commons, and may even have had dreams (indeed, may have them still) of achieving the one political post that all were agreed could no longer be held by a member of the Upper House, namely that of Prime Minister. Some years earlier, during the post-war Labour Government, a like fate had befallen Quintin Hogg upon the death of his father, the first Viscount Hailsham, and Hogg had asked the Prime Minister, Attlee, whether he would consider legislation to enable the eldest sons of peers to avoid automatic elevation to the peerage on the death of their fathers; Attlee refused, and Hogg, little dreaming that his turn would come, and in the most bizarre circumstances, over ten years later, accepted his fate.

Benn fought like a whole company of King Arthur's knights; first he maintained that unless he accepted the Writ of Summons to the House of Lords he was not a member of it, and therefore remained a member of the House of Commons. Barred on the Speaker's orders (the unhappy custodian of the door which he approached informing him that instructions had been given to repel him by force if necessary) and his barring confirmed by the House's acceptance of a report from the Committee of Privileges declaring him ineligible to sit in the Commons, he took his case to the people and fought the resulting by-election against a Conservative opponent. The people of Bristol, perhaps remembering that their city had once been represented by a man of so independent a temper as Edmund Burke, returned him with a large majority, but an electoral court, asked to adjudicate on the validity of his election (Benn fought his own case before the court, with considerable panache), ruled his election invalid and the runner-up the true holder of the seat. The surrogate victor most gallantly promised that if legislation were passed which would enable Benn to stand and be elected he would vacate the seat at once, on the grounds that the voters had shown that it was Benn they wanted and it was not his fault that they could not have him. At this, and after much argument, a Select Committee of Parliament considered the matter, and advised that legislation be introduced to allow reluctant peers to disclaim their ennoblement. It was; though a clause was inserted in the bill which would have prevented peers from taking advantage of it until after the next ensuing general election. This would not have worried Benn, especially since he had his Tory opponent's promise to vacate the seat when the legislation was through; but it would have entirely altered the face of British politics for years to come, though nobody could foresee that at the time. As it fell out, however, the House of Lords, sensibly enough, could see no reason to delay relief to the man who had battled so long for it, and struck out the delaying clause. This action was accepted by the Government, the bill was passed, Benn renounced his peerage, the Conservative member for Bristol South-West immediately honoured his promise and resigned the seat, nor did the Conservatives or the Liberals put up a candidate at the ensuing by-election, the second in the constituency in just over a year. And thus an anachronism that had stood the test of centuries suddenly collapsed under the assault, skilfully and courageously planned and executed, of one determined man.

The unforeseen by-product of Benn's campaign, and of the Government's decision to accept the Lords' amendment and bring the bill into force as soon as it passed both Houses, was that both Lord Hailsham and the Earl of Home were in a position, when the crisis of the succession to Harold Macmillan broke out, to step down and reach for the crown – Hailsham declaring his willingness to do so on the very day Macmillan's intention to resign was announced, Home waiting until the necessary head of steam had built up behind his own candidature to let it be known that he would, if chosen, renounce his earldom. (This curious accident of history was given another odd twist by the fact that if Macmillan's departure had been a little longer delayed, neither Hailsham nor Home would have been allowed to renounce his peerage, as the bill gave peers who were already members of the Upper House when it was passed only twelve months to make up their minds whether to take advantage of its provisions, or else thereafter for ever hold their peace.)

But the more foreseeable effect of the Peerage Act was to make many wonder, when it was through, how on earth the ancient rule had stood for so long in the face of common sense. As so often in the Sixties, a principle which had not been seriously questioned for centuries was abandoned as soon as it *was* questioned, since in a decade that saw the hereditary principle under attack as never before, and—more significantly—with no serious defenders to say a good word for it, it could hardly be maintained that if it was wrong for a man to inherit power, it was right provided only that he did not wish to. Yet only in this shifting and uneasy decade could the time, the man and the circumstances have come together to topple so impregnable-seeming a fortress, and the decade must share the credit with Wedgwood Benn.

* * *

But there were other things the decade had to share with him. There had been a stream of warnings about what technology was doing to man, from Rachel Carson's *Silent Spring*,[1] which pointed to a future literally poisoned by chemicals, to the *enragés* of the French student revolt of 1968, who were protesting against a soulless society bound to the racing wheels of the machine. In the United States, where by the end of the Sixties the crisis was at its most acute, this argument had got mixed up with others, from the increase in crime to the continuing injustices suffered by the Negroes, and was thus in danger of disappearing altogether from view, though in fact it was at the bottom of practically all the unease that America was feeling, as she slowly began to recognize the dangers in thinking only of the present and so storing up terrible trouble for the future. But in Britain the same deep crisis existed, though its overt expression was far less violent, less extreme. All the same, it was there; protests against the mechanical and repetitious nature of most industrial work were nothing new, but in the past they had always been coupled with protests against the poor material rewards the work had provided. Now, for the first time, the system was under attack in circumstances of unique prosperity, for by the Sixties in Britain the average industrial worker was better off than ever before, and a very substantial number lived in conditions of material comfort absolutely unprecedented in the country's history. And yet dissatisfaction persisted, or was making itself manifest for the first time. The

[1] Hamish Hamilton, London, 1963.

growing revolt against traditional political forms, which resulted in such strange phenomena as the Nationalist votes in Wales and Scotland, took other shapes in other fields. The explosion of liberated sexuality, for instance, resulted not only in a vast increase in tolerant attitudes and possibly practices but also in a kind of sexual uncertainty, illustrated by the rapidly increasing popularity of 'drag' or transvestite performances, which by the end of the decade had secured countless footholds even in working-men's clubs (until then the last bastion of traditional entertainment), and the interchangeable 'unisex' fashions adopted by young people. Many had no idea what was happening to them, knowing only that they were at once excited and alarmed; in the circumstances it was not surprising that many rejected all traditional forms of guidance and authority, and sought their own, inward Nirvanas.

The argument about the use of cannabis had reached deafening proportions by the end of the Sixties, and the passions unleashed by a heavily publicized newspaper advertisement, signed by a wide variety of artists, entertainers and medical experts, urging the removal of the legal penalties against its use, together with those provoked by the more cautious advocacy of a liberal attitude to it offered by the Home Office's own advisory committee, suggested that there was much more to the argument than appeared on the surface. Cannabis was one form of retreat, or withdrawal, from a society which had become for many too noisy, too ugly, too selfish, too mechanical, too unimaginative, too uncaring of individuals, too materialist, too majority-oriented, too standardized in every way.

The technological standardization of life in the Sixties produced for many a dilemma that was insoluble by traditional means. The retreat into the use of drugs, like the search for mystic certainty with Maharishis and Ché Guevaras, or practical certainty with the sudden enthusiasm for political absolutists like Mao Tse-tung, was an attempt to find a way out of the trap which had started to close as long ago as the Industrial Revolution and which was now closing very rapidly indeed. What was sought was real purity, physical and emotional, so that there was, for instance, a sudden increase in the incidence of vegetarianism, especially among the young, and the word 'macrobiotic', applied to food, made its appearance to denote food untouched by anything artificial, by any refining or colouring or chemical process or substance. At times it went even further, and elixirs, the claims for which only just stopped short of those made for similar panaceas in earlier centuries, and that only because of modern laws against over-extravagant advertising, began to make their appearance, frequently under pseudo-scientific names. Paradoxically, sexual promiscuity, or at any rate the theoretical argument for it, can be seen as part of the same search, involving as it did the rejection of all artificial constraints on emotion and conduct; the new heroes of the young did not include Jean-Jacques Rousseau, but the first sentence of the Social Contract might have been their motto, as they sought to throw off the chains of externally applied discipline, of organization and of formalized interdependence, of the traditional, hierarchical forms of society (it was not by accident that 're-structuring' became one of the keywords of the young in the latter part of the decade).

For some the search took the form of a new kind of apostolic poverty, and a new tribe of wandering holy men (and women) appeared, some of them being the children of wealthy and aristocratic families, who went from place to place on foot, or with a horse and cart, living as best they might free from the fetters of place and possession. The rejection of possessions – the sign of the society that many found so unsatisfactory – was the more understandable when some of the more appalling manifestations of affluence were examined. The nadir in the advocacy of conspicuous consumption was reached by the advertisements in the colour supplements, and ultimately in the editorial pages of the Sunday papers in which the colour supplements were folded, so that features such as 'Look!' in the *Sunday Times* and 'Ego' in the *Observer*, with their strident weekly advocacy of the purchase of ephemeral rubbish, were enough to turn the stomach of the most materialist of their readers. The harmless word 'trend' suddenly took on new meanings as the practitioners of this kind of turnover-worship began to hunt more and more frantically for the latest gewgaw, the latest toy, the latest fashion in trash, with which to tempt the increasingly jaded palates of their readers; the whole movement was summed up in the *Observer* colour supplement feature on Lorenzo de Medici, who was described on the cover as the 'inspiration of the affluent society'.

It was the artificiality of such mock-life that was rejected; all around there was an increase in the artificial, the pre-packed, the product designed to meet a demand that was created simultaneously (much of the work of Len Deighton, for instance, whose *London Dossier*,[1] with its glib and flashy glamour, was really an extreme form of his immensely successful novels, not to mention his cookery column – significantly presented in the form of a strip-cartoon – and indeed his prose). In these restricting circumstances it was not surprising that the Sixties saw the rise of the cult of the psychedelic, or mind-expanding. Drugs such as LSD which expanded, or which were believed to expand, the consciousness, and other practices for which a like effect was claimed, were increasingly popular during the Sixties. Interpersonal physical contact was extolled, and the inhibition existing in Britain against touching, assaulted; forms of non-verbal sound expression were likewise used increasingly to break down the unnatural and inhibiting barriers and let the mind expand.

Much of the new popular music had, or was designed to have, a like effect, as indeed was some of the more 'serious' music of the decade – a decade in which, in any case, barriers between the arts, and between different forms of the same art, were being continually overturned (the electronic and random sounds introduced by such composers as Stockhausen, whose contact with anything previously recognizable as music grew increasingly exiguous as the decade progressed, could have been dismissed as yet another of the artistic blind alleys up which music and the other arts had constantly wandered in their long history, had it not been for

[1] Cape, London, 1967.

the absolutely unprecedented phenomenon that they packed concert-halls wherever they were performed).

The theatrical Happening, which consisted of more or less random behaviour, also flowered during the Sixties (curiously, it had been introduced at the beginning of the decade but had not caught on; only towards the end did it suddenly meet a demand for its presumably mind-expanding qualities), and a troupe of players from the United States, the Living Theatre, caused a considerable sensation in London with their performances, a great part of which were spontaneous when not actually random – their musical equivalent was a group called the Exploding Galaxy, and they had in common not only the free, swirling quality of their artistic expression, but also their communal life-style, which was more like that of some simple, primitive-communist sect than anything previously recognizable as appropriate to the creative and performing arts, even in their more eccentric forms of expression.

The more familiar theatrical and cinematic forms, faced with such techniques, struggled to keep up; one of the ways they did so was to adopt, not without a good deal of self-consciousness, many of the attitudes that went with the abandonment of conventional restraints, and which almost inevitably issued, as far as the performing arts were concerned, in the portrayal of increasingly explicit sexual activity, a tendency that was made easier in the Sixties by the almost total collapse of all forms of censorship, that of the theatre being formally abolished by Act of Parliament, and that of the cinema being virtually abandoned where sexual relations were concerned and retained only for the more extreme or aberrant forms of violence. Nudity having proved successful on the stage when *Hair* was staged as the first London theatrical production to be mounted after the censor's office disappeared, it presently became almost obligatory, as did the use of words and expressions that would previously have been censored; eventually in the cinema the sex act, previously confined cinematically to the illegal 'blue film' trade, was first simulated and then, it was reported (from Italy), performed in actuality. On the stage things had gone further, if it was possible to judge from the fact that the entire cast of a New York 'off-Broadway' production were arrested after the performance and charged with, among other things, 'consentual sodomy' (which must, the times being what they were, have given some producer the thought that non-consentual sodomy might be even more interesting).

All of this, of course, was very far from the intention of those who sought, whether through Indian sages, drugs, sexual experimentation, group-rituals, random music and unconstricting clothes, the expansion of consciousness. But these originators were learning to their dismay the lesson that trade follows the flag, no matter who shows the latter. The theatre and the cinema speedily discovered that there was much money to be made from adopting and portraying the more relaxed attitudes of society, and the fact that the relaxation in question was also being twisted into more commercial shapes was ignored both by those who found it good business and those who used it indiscriminately as a stick with which to beat the more genuine manifestations. Similarly, the movement to a new, freer kind of clothing swiftly became big business, and Carnaby Street and the King's Road, so far from containing the temples of innocence and youth, were filled from end to end with hard-headed businessmen and women, calculating to the last penny how best to cash in on the demand for new clothes on the part of young people who at last had the money to pay for them. Even the liberated politics of the decade was not free from commercial exploitation; the tomb of the martyr himself was rifled, when a multi-million-dollar Hollywood epic on the life of Ché Guevara was made, starring Omar Sharif.

* * *

There were more traditional forms of increasing relaxation in society, of course, these not strictly psychedelic; the Sixties in Britain produced an extraordinary number of legislative reforms, which carried to extraordinary lengths the new spirit of tolerance and its codification in the law.

The abolition of capital punishment, for instance, was eventually achieved; strictly speaking it was at first only for a five-year experimental period, though it was made permanent in the last days of the Sixties. The reform of the savage laws against male homosexual behaviour, repeatedly attempted and repeatedly frustrated, also went through, with comparatively little opposition (though that very strident), and it was difficult to believe, only a short time afterwards, that such penalties for such acts had ever existed. Not long afterwards the law on abortion was no less radically amended, though there the fight was more bitter and prolonged, and wild charges continued to be flung about, indeed were flung about with increasing frequency and vociferousness, after the Act had been passed. London was dubbed 'the abortion capital of the world', on the grounds that there were now more legal abortions being performed than previously, though since this state of affairs was precisely what the Act had been designed to bring about, it was not easy to see the logic in the protests at the fact that it had succeeded in its purpose. Finally, at the very end of the decade, a new Divorce Act was passed, which gave Britain the most humane and reasonable divorce laws in the world, and it was particularly significant that the impetus for the new legislation had come from the Church of England, which had urged the abolition of the concept of the 'matrimonial offence' and its replacement by that of the 'irretrievable breakdown' of a marriage, which was precisely what the new Act established, adding provision for divorce by mutual consent of the partners after two years of separation, and by unilateral application on the part of one of them after five. It was, incidentally, noticeable that all of these measures were introduced not by any Government, but by back-bench Members of Parliament.

It was the continuous pushing back of the unexpected, unfamiliar frontiers, and particularly by the young, that dominated the later years of the decade, though it was only towards its very end that serious attempts to study and understand the phenomenon began to be launched. That proper investigation was needed was shown not only by the increasing numbers of young people involved, and the suggestion that for the first time in history a generation had appeared which might not change its ideas or even behaviour when it got to adult years, but also by the way in which the destruction of old rules and structures took on a form so extreme that it seemed to take the destroyers right round the circle and back where they began. There was much comment, for instancc, on the fact that, although the contraceptive pill had by the end of the decade made unwanted pregnancy more easily avoidable than ever before, the illegitimacy figures continued to rise, until investigation suggested that there was a growing number of girls who rejected the use of that or any other contraceptive method, ostensibly to add the excitement of danger to that of sex, but perhaps out of a subconscious desire, which would fit well into the search for purity, simplicity and absolutes, to avoid anything which might come between the individual and his or her search for certainty and absoluteness.

* * *

And yet, amid all this, technology marched on. Partly in order to further Britain's involvement in her inevitably European future in general, and her entry into the Common Market in particular, road-signs began to be changed for the Continental style, and eventually the change to decimal currency, and after that to metric measures, was decided upon, and the first steps taken before the end of the decade. In vain were voices raised against these developments, as they were against the introduction of permanent 'Summer Time' to bring British hours into line with those of Continental Western Europe, against the replacement of named telephone exchanges, obtained by use of a lettered dial, by numbers, reached by an all-figure dial, and against the use of stylized 'postal codes' for addresses – all of these things being seen (rightly, as a matter of fact) as further illustrations of the way in which life was becoming standardized, made to fit specifications that allowed less and less for individual tolerances or eccentricities. But there was no serious expectation that the movement could be halted, or even seriously slowed down. In the circumstances it was hardly surprising that the spoliation of the countryside and the ruin of the towns went on, during the Sixties, at a constantly increasing pace, Governments, local authorities, speculative builders, industry and the armed forces vying with one another to see which could destroy the greatest tracts of beautiful and undisturbed woodland, knock down the largest numbers of ancient and interesting buildings, pollute the biggest stretches of clear and fish-laden water, befoul the highest proportion of wild and natural coastline, ruin for the maximum number of people the enjoyment of nature and of man's achievements. The enemy was powerful, ruthless and swift, and his Fifth Column, the motor-car, was everywhere, weakening resistance and spreading alarm, and thus making conquest easy. At regular and frequent intervals plans were produced to control the motor-car, to render it harmless, to nullify the adverse effects it had wherever it spread and colonized. The faster the plans appeared, the faster the motor-cars bred, so that there were always a million more owners to resist any solution that would inconvenience them, and to urge alternative solutions that would inconvenience others. It was decided that there were too many vehicles in the already congested centres of cities (the congestion was caused by vehicles, so that the principle of decongestion was at bottom one of removing vehicles to make room for vehicles), and parking meters sprang up like ugly weeds along the pavements of city streets, to the immense indignation of the residents, who had been used to parking their cars outside their houses without fee or fear. With the meters came traffic wardens, equipped with uniforms uncomfortably reminiscent of *vespa vulgaris*, or the common wasp, and no more popular with those they stung for two pounds a time. By the end of the decade the number of cars in the country was approaching fifteen million, and the number of plans designed to deal with problems they posed sometimes seemed scarcely fewer.

The plans differed very widely in their nature. One involved the fitting of an electronic device to every car, and of further electronic devices to the roads, so that each vehicle might be electronically followed, the number and duration of its visits to the congested areas logged, and taxes and other fees levied on the owners accordingly. Another envisaged a network of light railways along the pavements of all the streets of the central areas of the cities, along which automatically propelled and guided vehicles would run, so that visitors would be encouraged, or even compelled, to leave their own cars at home and use public ones.

The most famous of all the plans was that drawn up by a committee presided over by Professor Colin Buchanan, which reported in 1963,[1] was eagerly discussed at all levels, and died a few weeks later, never to be resurrected. The Buchanan Report, indeed, illustrated perfectly the fate of all such studies, all such recommendations, together with the reason for their invariable doom. Nobody in authority at any time had the smallest intention of putting any of the plans into effect, since the amount of money they would cost could in no circumstances be provided. The Buchanan Report, for instance, proposed what would have amounted to the demolition and reconstruction of the whole central area of almost all major cities and most minor ones. The committee examined what would be involved in solving the actual and foreseen traffic problems of Newbury, a town of some 30,000 inhabitants, and came to the conclusion that to build even the principal network of roads proposed would cost four and a half million pounds; they then made a similar study of Leeds, with a population of approximately 500,000, and arrived at a figure of over ninety million pounds; finally they turned their attention to a small section of Central London, but wisely did not indicate what their radical (and, it must be admitted, exciting) plan would cost, though some idea may be gathered from the fact that it was estimated that one method of reconstructing Oxford Street, envisaged as part of the simplest and least extensive form of their plan, would cost twelve million pounds.

Since it was clear to the most casual glance at the problem that none of these plans would in practice be adopted, it may be asked

[1] *Traffic in Towns* (H.M.S.O., London, 1963).

why then they continued to be commissioned, undertaken and enthusiastically received by a succession of Ministers of Transport. 'We are nourishing at immense cost', said the introduction to the Buchanan Report, 'a monster of great potential destructiveness. And yet we love him dearly.' In that antithesis the whole problem was laid bare; the plans were designed to deal with the motor-car's destructiveness, but the final truth, that we love him dearly, would ensure that no such plans would be put into effect. So each Minister of Transport could leave office with the satisfaction of knowing that a wise and far-seeing plan for dealing with the growing challenge of the motor-car and its effect on the environment had seen the light of day during his or her tenure, and with the added satisfaction of knowing that, at no extra cost, the plan had been, after its initial discussion, safely ignored. Where all, or most, own motor-cars, or intend to own them or aspire to own them, the tone of public debate on the environment of cities and countryside will be set by the motor-car; in a short space of time the emphasis will shift from the discussion of methods of preventing town and country from being ruined by the car and its demands to the discussion of methods designed to adapt country and town to the demands of the car. Just such a situation, in which the environment of the motor-car took clear priority over the environment of the human being, arose with the plan put forward by the Greater London Council for a new road structure for London. This involved the building of a network of motorways through and around the central area, at a cost estimated by the council at something over a thousand million pounds and by the opponents of the plan at one thousand five hundred million, so that, given the normal multiplication of the costs of all such projects by a factor of at least two over the most pessimistic original forecast, the final cost would hardly be less than three thousand million and probably very much more.

At a time when the housing shortage, so far from diminishing, seemed to be getting worse, the plan involved the demolition of at least 15,000 houses and the consequent addition of some 45,000 people to the numbers of those awaiting new homes; it also involved the destruction of beautiful or historic or peaceful enclaves of urban life within the mass of the city, at such places as Cheyne Walk, Belsize Park, Blackheath Village and Canonbury. Furthermore, the melancholy example of the two major 'flyovers' on the motorway from London to Heathrow Airport, which had resulted in continuous streams of traffic roaring past the houses bordering the motorway only a few feet from their windows, was to be followed with the new G.L.C. system, so that those unlucky enough to own or live in houses close to the proposed route but not actually on it would find themselves almost overnight living not in the quiet residential area they were used to, but in the midst of stench, fumes, noise, vibration and prying eyes. The opponents of the scheme argued that the economic benefits to be derived from it were grossly exaggerated, that the misery and uproar vastly outweighed any benefit, social or financial, that might accrue, and that no thought had been given to the long-term needs and problems of London. To all of these complaints, and more, the appropriate elected representative of the people, a Mr Vigars, retorted: 'You cannot have an omelette without breaking eggs', though – as has always been the custom with those who have used this expression to justify every atrocity in history – he had apparently failed to consider what would be the position if the eggs were broken but no omelette resulted. Vigars had, incidentally, taken the precaution of hiring, at a fee of £15,000, the very same Professor Buchanan who had produced the once-famous report, to be a consultant to the G.L.C.'s project, the thought doubtless occurring to those responsible that Buchanan's name was sufficiently respected to overawe all opposition. Alas, no such thing happened; Buchanan's name had clearly been forgotten as completely as his report. The opposition redoubled its efforts and its fury, and eventually had the precarious satisfaction of seeing the scheme postponed (a postponement that seemed likely to last until the end of the century) on the grounds that funds were insufficient for it to be completed according to the original timetable.

What nobody could explain in any of the numerous cases that

from time to time arose was the cause of the obstinacy and determination that those in charge of the spoliation of the land brought to their unlovely work. In countries with a lower standard of integrity in elected public servants and their professional advisers it would have been easy to explain it in terms of corruption, but such lapses were genuinely rare in Britain. Yet the determination to persist in a decision once arrived at, however high the cost in logic, natural justice, and damage to the interests of others, and however low the return, seemed so great that a kind of madness appeared to possess those responsible.[1] They pursued their goal with a lack of consideration, either for the people or the principles involved, that posed one of the greatest problems in democratic control, and – in view of the frequency with which those responsible turned out to be members of local authorities – raised considerable doubts as to the wisdom of the policies of 'devolution' and 'regionalism', which became fashionable, at any rate as words, in the Sixties. The briefer the little authority in which proud man was dressed, the greater the pride inside it seemed to swell. It was, for instance, during the Sixties that coroners, those public officials with the least actual authority but considerable opportunities for publicity, surpassed themselves in the frequency, irrelevance and impertinence of their *obiter dicta*; and perhaps the fierceness with which minor unpaid local governors and minor ill-paid local officials pursued what at times seemed a savage vendetta against the public interest and common sense, suggested that they were uneasily conscious, or subconscious, of the fact that the decade had seen a further weakening of their position, a further diminution of the power they could exercise. And perhaps they feared, with justice, that the demands of the future would diminish it still further.

The demands of the future were not always met, however; sometimes the backward-looking tendency of the Sixties triumphed, nor was it always possible to feel that such triumphs were unjustified. For a long time the volume of air traffic into and out of

[1] This at times seemed true in the literal sense, as a study of the Crichel Down affair of the Fifties revealed.

London (Heathrow) Airport had been growing, and it was expected to grow even faster in the future. Temporary relief had been obtained with the extension of Gatwick, but the strain on Heathrow continued to increase, and since it was one of the worst-planned and badly run airports in the world, total collapse was predicted some time in the Seventies and there was every expectation that the prediction would be fulfilled. It was therefore determined that a third London Airport should be built, and the choice for the site of it fell upon Stansted, in Essex, one of the few remaining areas of that now hideous county that had not been already irredeemably ruined by the inexorable twin-pronged thrust of the enemies, ribbon development from London and industrialization. Stansted already had an airport, which did only a little business; it was proposed to extend it vastly and make it suitable for a very large proportion of the increased traffic that would be wanting to land near London in the next decade.

Instantly a huge campaign of protest and propaganda was launched. The decision had been made in a particularly clumsy way, at least one report of the Ministry's own inspectors having been overruled, and the objectors concentrated much of their fire on a demand for a new public inquiry. At the same time they argued both that no new airport was needed for London, and that Stansted was quite unsuitable for the urgently needed new airport; from this it may be seen that logic was not the strong point of the protesters' case, and from the fact that they solemnly declared that historic churches fifteen miles from the proposed runway would fall down if the thing were built (fifteen miles being the distance from Heathrow to Westminster Abbey, which had shown no signs of falling down in all the years Heathrow had been in operation) it may be gathered that caution was not their leading characteristic either. Nor, for that matter, was altruism, for they were only suggesting, when all was done, that the mess, noise, uprooting and destruction inevitably attendant on the building of any new airport should be taken away from them and used to smother some other, equally inoffensive, part of the country.

Yet the campaign grew to avalanche proportions, and it sometimes seemed that not a car in the land was without its window-sticker bearing the legend 'Say NO to Stansted'. By a happy accident, the Minister responsible for the original decision, Mr Douglas Jay, disappeared from the Government while the row was at its height, and his successor as President of the Board of Trade, Mr Anthony Crosland, took the opportunity to bow to the storm, appoint a new commission to inquire into the whole range of alternative sites, and gratefully accept the commission's report, which excluded Stansted. It did, however, include several other possibilities, and shortly afterwards 'Say NO to Wing' and 'Say NO to Nuthampstead' were to be seen on cars, and smaller versions of the Stansted campaign were rolling vigorously. But support for the newly threatened areas from the happily relieved Stanstedians was nowhere in evidence: Jack, it seemed, was safe in the lifeboat.

# 12

## The walrus ...

Politically, the Sixties were in a sense the perfect refutation of all determinist theories of human behaviour and economic and political activity. The stamp was put on the decade by two Harolds, Macmillan at the earlier end and Wilson at the latter. In all ways but the most important there could not have been two men less alike; in style, appearance, oratory, background, political antecedents they had nothing in common. Only ambition for power, skill in its pursuit, and a ruthless energy in the struggle to keep it, united them, but united them with bonds so strong that they cast their shadow over the whole decade, and may well have etched that shadow permanently into Britain's public life. Hugh Gaitskell, trapped in the iron web of his own integrity, could never take the measure of Macmillan; Alec Douglas-Home, floating on the lethargic sea of his own simplicity, could not for a moment compete with Wilson. It is idle to speculate what might have happened had Gaitskell died sooner or Macmillan resigned later, so that Macmillan and Wilson could have been matched for longer than the few brief months their leadership of the two parties overlapped; idle but attractive. For it would have been such a match as British politics had never seen before, and the whole character of the times would have been summed up day after day as these two men, who between them managed to empty the decade of political principle and scour the vessel, battled to keep or to gain power—the only thing, in the end, which interested either of them.

One played the part of the last aristocrat, Beachcomber's Lord Shortcake of Boulton Wynfevers, advancing through life with a paralysed shuffle, an assortment of facial tics, a voice which was the distilled essence of all the confidence-tricksters who ever went home and entertained the children after the day's work was done. The role assumed by the other was that of the purposive, technologically-equipped, full twentieth-century citizen, leaning forward when he walked, like a man trying not to fall over if the bus starts with a jerk, his voice the ingratiating wheedle of the toucher who wants yet another fiver to tide him over until payday, and will do anything to get it. Up the greasy pole they had both struggled, stamping on others' fingers as they went by, dropping sand in the eyes of those trying to get a fingerhold below them, at desperate moments leaning downwards with a knife and plying it energetically. Neither would let go of his hard-won power without a desperate, even a mortal, struggle.

Macmillan must have been one of the most extraordinary men ever to appear on the scene of British politics, let alone in the office of Prime Minister, and the extraordinariness consisted in the difference between the appearance and the reality. Watching him and listening to him on any public occasion after he became Prime Minister, it was almost impossible to believe that he was anything but a down-at-heel actor resting between engagements at the decrepit theatres of minor provincial towns, his ability minimal for anything but hoodwinking fools by the thousand and the million. The very word 'hoodwink' seems like some Joycean echo of a coherent description of him; the eyes were *hooded*, they seemed to hover always on the verge of a *wink* at his fantastic good fortune in being set down in the country of the blind, where none could see through him. The platitudes of his oratory, the vulgarity of his demeanour, the apparently limitless willingness to debase himself before the glittering prize of supreme office—these were the elements that together made up a man of whom the perceptive spectator was compelled to say, as soon as he had completed another performance and left the scene, that he did not, *could* not exist, that he must have been imagined.

And yet it could not be; the record spoke against such an explanation, and spoke too loudly to be ignored. The methods by which he became Prime Minister, and stayed Prime Minister thereafter, were not for the squeamish, and still less for the unable; behind the absurd, fly-blown façade there was a real mind and a ruthless will. Sir Anthony Eden discovered as much; R. A. Butler found it out just too late; it baffled Hugh Gaitskell; it enraged George Brown; it cast down Iain Macleod. Only one man took the full measure of this astonishing truth, and that man the one who knew what Macmillan was made of for the best of all reasons; Harold Wilson was made of the same stuff. Between them, then, Walrus and Carpenter, they divided up the Sixties.

When the Sixties began, Macmillan was packing for his tour of Africa, a tour that was to prove momentous in its implications; he left England when the decade was less than a week old, and returned only a few weeks later, in which short space of time he had affected a political revolution of momentous implications, though – as we shall see – the implications were not at first apparent, and some people have not noticed them even yet.

He had always been in his element at the Commonwealth Prime Ministers' Conference, presiding over its dream-like deliberations, uniting in at any rate a show of harmony its bizarre assortment of wholly disparate elements, showing them the garden at Ten Downing Street (he had once done the same, with great effect, for a delegation of trade union leaders during the negotiations over a threatened strike, the militant unionists ending up by eating out of his hand as docilely as the ducks at the garden's end), soothing ruffled feelings, explaining things to Mr Diefenbaker, avoiding conflict, postponing pain. The group photograph taken at the end of the ritual gathering – like the end-of-term picture when the whole of the Sixth is leaving – in which, year by year, the black and brown faces outnumbered more and more heavily the white ones, is remarkable enough whoever presides over it; Sir Alec Douglas-Home, for instance, looked strangely dominant (he is shown pointing out something to Jomo Kenyatta, while Mr Menzies turns his eyes heavenward), Wilson uneasy. But Macmillan, relaxed and genial, gave the impression of being immensely well satisfied with his achievement in having got through another of these extraordinary gatherings without anything untoward having happened, except for the occasion in 1961 when South Africa refused to reapply for membership of the Commonwealth after becoming a republic rather than accept dark skins in the High Commissioners' residences in Pretoria. (Later this policy was relaxed to the extent of accepting an ambassador from Malawi, but the schizoid national condition of South Africa was perfectly exemplified by the fact that he was given a house specially reconstructed so that the door opened at the back, lest the white occupants of the neighbouring houses should accidentally meet him in the street, and a high wall was built round his garden, lest he should accidentally catch sight of his neighbours, or they of him. A parallel case of national psychosis in the Sixties occurred in Peking, where, after a mob burnt down the British Legation, the authorities refused to admit that the incident had ever taken place, and continued to deliver post to the empty and blackened shell.)

Macmillan's progress through Africa was in some ways the most amazing performance of his entire career as Prime Minister, possibly of his entire life, so perfectly did it blend the two Macmillans, the ridiculous and the real, and so clearly did he revel in the activities of the first while getting on with the business of the second. What the Africans made of him will never be known and can scarcely be guessed at; it is a wonder that they could be persuaded to refrain from cooking and eating him.

In Accra he rode in a surf-boat paddled by chanting Africans in caps, vests and striped trousers, like some parody of a Boat Race crew, with him as a parody of the cox. In Salisbury, rogue to rogue with Sir Roy Welensky, he managed the almost incredible feat of getting the better of that astute Lithuanian despite the fact that Welensky had, when they met, a transcript of a talk that Dr Banda, then in jail, had had with his legal adviser, Dingle Foot; the conversation, which had been 'bugged' on Welensky's orders, revealed that all Macmillan's protestations about his firm resolve to keep the Central African Federation in being were false. In South Africa he was led round by Verwoerd like a stuffed bear on wheels, prevented from meeting any Africans other than hand-picked ones, and shown a 'model' township, like left-wing visitors to Stalin's Russia being taken over the specially kept wing of a concentration camp. He was also made a tribal chief of the Bantu, the ceremony of induction involving his being dressed in a leopard-skin; he was also officially installed as 'son-in-law of the tribe', which meant that he had to be carried about throughout the ceremony, as the feet of the tribe's honorary sons-in-law are not permitted to touch the ground. (In view of the fact that there were many who believed Macmillan's feet had not touched the ground for years this was a considerable irony, though presumably one which escaped the Africans, or possibly which did not.)

In Cape Town, however, his feet touched ground briefly but decisively, when he made what has been known ever afterwards as the 'Wind of Change' speech, in which he said unambiguously that Britain could no longer support South Africa in her policy of totally barring all advancement in society to Africans, but managed to spread the speech, unambiguous though it was, with so much butter that he fairly hypnotized the joint assembly of the two Houses of the South African Parliament, to whom it was made, into believing that it implied support for them, and he was cheered when it was over. Only afterwards, when they read it, did the South African legislators awake from their trance and discover that Macmillan had said:

> Nothing we do in this small world can be done in a corner or remain hidden ... it has been our aim, in countries for which we have borne responsibility, not only to raise the material standards of living, but to create a society which respects the rights of individuals – a society in which men are given the opportunity to grow to their full stature, and that must in our view include the opportunity to have an increasing share in political power and responsibility; a society in which individual merit, and individual merit alone, is the criterion for man's advancement whether political or economic ... in countries inhabited by several

> different races, it has been our aim to find the means by which the community can become more of a community, and fellowship can be fostered between its various parts ... It is our earnest desire to give South Africa our support and encouragement, but ... there are some aspects of your policies which make it impossible for us to do this without being false to our own deep convictions about the political destinies of free men, to which in our own territories we are trying to give effect.

The delayed sensation of the speech was even greater, though more diffused, in Britain than it was in South Africa, where the Prime Minister, Dr Verwoerd, replied to it a month later by accusing Macmillan of 'appeasement of the black man', and adding:

> I cannot help thinking back to before the war, when a British Prime Minister had tried appeasement with a German leader, but, because the British people felt it impossible to accede to the claims of this German leader, because they could not be justified on moral grounds, they had been prepared to involve themselves in war

– sentiments which none of his hearers felt it would be tactful to sour by pointing out that in the war in question Verwoerd had supported the other side. But in any case Verwoerd was shortly in no position to have his history tidied up for him, as a fortnight later the massacre of sixty-nine unarmed and fleeing Africans at Sharpeville took place, and three weeks later still Verwoerd was shot and seriously wounded, events which so far from persuading South Africa to bow before the wind of change provided her with what she saw as abundant evidence that it must not be allowed to blow at all.

Macmillan by then was already alarmed at the genie he had let out of the bottle, and the Government contented itself with expressing its 'deep sympathy with all the people of South Africa at the recent tragic events', while the English Folk Dance and Song

Society declared its reluctance to undertake a tour of South Africa, arranged earlier, if its members' safety could not be guaranteed. A few months later the Congo was in chaos, gleefully welcomed by the South Africans and their allies in Britain as evidence that black men would revert to savagery as soon as the governing hand of the white man was removed.

The significance of the Wind of Change speech was much greater in Britain than in Africa, for in Africa, whatever the sensation, it had no actual effect, whereas in Britain its purpose was to make clear for those, particularly in Macmillan's own party, who still had not realized the fact, that the Empire was at an end, and all that remained was the winding up of its business, the disposal of its assets, and the organization of fittingly solemn funeral rites, to be followed at a discreet interval by the erection of memorial tablets. That the Conservative Party should turn its back on Africa and accept a new destiny elsewhere, with all that such a change implied for the changing status of Britain, was something so improbable that it would have been impossible to predict only a few years earlier, and much of the confusion that has resulted since, particularly over the seizure of power in Rhodesia, stems from the fact that although Macmillan was responsible for recognizing the strength of the wind of change and the inability of Britain to do anything but scud before it in the general direction of Europe, he lacked the nerve to say that that was what he was about, and instead did good by stealth, and blushed to find it fame. The British Empire had not existed for very long, by comparison with some of the empires that the world had seen, and its African possessions were among the most recently acquired. Yet the speed of its dismantling, once the decision was taken, was extraordinary, and it was in the Sixties that the process of complete abandonment of British sovereignty over Africa was completed, having started only in 1957 with the granting of complete independence to Ghana—an event which was itself only five years later than the Mau Mau rebellion in Kenya, which had seemed to confirm the intention of Britain to maintain her dominion for ever. Whether Macmillan consciously took in advance the decision to leave Africa will never be certainly known, and it may be that he simply found himself floating on the tide and feeling responsible for it. But the effect was the same. 'I did not', Winston Churchill had said, 'become His Majesty's Prime Minister in order to preside over the dissolution of the British Empire.' Macmillan did, and to this day there are those among his erstwhile followers who cannot forgive him for putting down the White Man's Burden with a haste that suggested he had found a poisonous snake sticking out of it.

Again, what a contradiction between the appearance and what must have been, *a posteriori*, the reality behind it! He who walked through life in the guise of the Last Aristocrat, the last bastion of the Victorian age into which he was born and the Edwardian in which he grew up, who bore upon him all the marks of the nobly born, not excluding his claim to be a crofter's grandson, who embodied a world of permanence and of resistance to change, who belonged to the Athenaeum, the Carlton, the Turf, Pratts, Bucks and the Beefsteak, who accidentally started a fashion when he appeared on a television programme in dinner-jacket and cummerbund but forgot to flip his bow tie up again after turning down his collar – so that within a few weeks huge numbers of impressionable fools were deliberately wearing their dress ties under their collars – who revelled in the adulation of his silliest supporters, he who seemed born the last Englishman and the last Emperor, he it was, even he, who dissolved the British Empire. It was, to say the least, an unexpected role.

And yet he would not say what he was doing. He put on a ridiculous hat and went to the Khyber Pass, a more ridiculous one and went shooting on the grouse moors, an even more ridiculous one and went racing at Ascot; he went on a tour of the Commonwealth and did an old-time music-hall soft-shoe-shuffle in the middle of Downing Street on his return; he appeared on television with President Eisenhower and indulged in a cross-talk act of such unimaginable mutual idiocy that there must for some hours have been moves among their colleagues to have the pair of them committed; he shuffled and staggered and puffed and panted; and yet, behind it all, the Last Aristocrat was moving with all deliberate speed towards that land-mass which Britain had spurned for so long, with the excuse of her imperial possessions and the attention she had to pay them.

* * *

The Sixties were profligate with themes and arguments that illustrated the nation's crossroads dilemma. None did so more completely nor more vitally than this of the Common Market. Britain's reluctance to commit herself to a European role went back to before the Sixties, of course; it was Churchill, for instance, who, after years of urging just such co-operation, effectively scuppered the plans for a European army, and the Iron and Coal Community had found Britain unwilling to join even earlier. But it was in the Sixties that matters came to a head, when Britain was faced at last with a real choice: to throw in her lot economically with the continent to which she was bound geographically (and soon, if all the decade's talk of Channel Bridge or Channel Tunnel were to come to anything, literally too) or to remain on the outside, mourning the Empire that was gone and the 'special relationship' with the United States that was going. And just as Harold Macmillan was the man who turned the Tory head away from Africa, so it was he who turned it in the direction of Europe. Great was the turmoil inside his party when, soon after the decade had begun, he launched Britain's attempt to join the Common Market, appointing Mr Heath to be his emissary. Many of the old Empire wing, who had not noticed that the Empire was no more, were horrified at this threat to merge Britain's economic sovereignty with a grouping of foreigners, many of whom cooked strange things, and in olive oil too. Yet this was not, for the Tories, a strictly Left-Right split, any more than it was in the Labour Party, where only the fellow-travelling Left were opposed as a bloc to Britain's entry, fearing that it might ultimately strengthen and unify Western Europe politically as well as economically, which indeed was the idea. Many ancient combinations were broken up by the Common Market issue, and even the Liberal Party, first to adopt the cause of Britain's entry as party policy, was riven by it. But the division everywhere was between those who knew what currents of history were hurrying Britain through the Sixties, and those who did not know, or who, knowing, refused to believe that the currents were inevitably stronger than the swimmers, and urged the latter to turn round and strike out for the safety of a familiar shore.

Macmillan knocked on the door, and had it slammed in his face by de Gaulle. Long before the negotiations were finished, indeed before they were well under way, it was clear that de Gaulle would veto Britain's entry, but by then Macmillan had staked too much on the attempt, and it had to go on to the final, bitter humiliation. On the other side of politics Harold Wilson, soon to inherit both the leadership of his party and the responsibility for trying to take Britain in, sat on the sidelines and cultivated his own interests, characteristically finding himself, shortly afterwards, attacking the Tories for their willingness to accept whatever conditions the Common Market partners, or even de Gaulle alone, might see fit to impose, while preparing his own far more abject (and equally unsuccessful) first attempt to get in.

When, shortly before the decade ended, de Gaulle himself departed the French scene, hopes ran high yet again, and a third attempt was prepared, with much gloom at the prospect that it would end like the other two. But by then the Common Market had become the talisman of the decade, the key that would turn in all the locks that had so baffled Britain for nearly ten years. Most of the original reasons for going in had been forgotten, but the effort went on, like the crew of a space-ship in a science-fiction story who learn that their home planet has been destroyed and must go on in their orbit for ever, despite the fact that they can now see no positive reason for doing so. Over the entire effort there brooded the massive Establishment figure of Lord Gladwyn, tireless in writing letters to the papers, in preparing memoranda to strengthen the fainthearts, in making speeches to convert those who were still to be convinced. Europe, now identified with the future, was the goal; but no provision had been made for an alternative route to the future, indeed the energy to seek one was conspicuously lacking. So as the Sixties ended the future itself hung in the balance. But the long debate had provided Britain with a powerful weapon with which to defend herself against the assaults of reality, in the person of General de Gaulle, to whom all Britain's failures could be confidently ascribed.

For as it was with individuals, so it was with nations. Britain had once ruled the waves, and now ruled them no more; Britain had once held dominion over palm and pine, and now every palm and pine concealed a sniper, determined that the British should leave; Britain was once the world's workshop and the world had been willing to wait outside her door for the opportunity to buy her manufactured goods, whereas now the world made its own goods, and even exported them to Britain, and waited no more outside her door, instead sending letters of complaint about delivery-dates and the poor quality of her merchandise. In the circumstances it was not surprising that Britain should look for reasons outside herself. (A new cause of failure was added to all the traditional ones, and individuals speaking on behalf both of themselves and of the country were to be heard blaming people with black faces for being the cause of every ill the flesh, including the flesh of the body politic, is heir to, arguing, for instance, that the coloured immigrants lived on National Assistance, thus helping to beggar the country, and also took, by unfair means, the jobs of the indigenous, though it was never satisfactorily explained how any man, even a black one, could manage both feats at once. But it was generally recognized among the more sophisticated that these enemies were insufficient to explain Britain's decline. There had to be something bigger, more powerful, less worn, to act as the hostile force imperilling our prosperity, security and self-confidence.)

In the circumstances it can be seen that the elevation of de Gaulle into the head and fount of all Britain's troubles was inevitable from the moment he took office. For one thing, he was so obviously unlike our own leaders, particularly Harold

Macmillan; where de Gaulle proudly proclaimed the destiny of the French nation, Macmillan, by nods and winks, proclaimed the end of the British. Moreover, Britain's national difficulties, particularly her economic ones, seemed to be bound up increasingly as the Sixties wore on with France. Soon de Gaulle was behind every fall in the value of the pound, every widening of the trade gap, every failure on Britain's part to secure new and trusted allies, every decline in the quality of an ancient alliance.

The French were blamed for everything; at one point, a temporary meat shortage in Britain caused complaints that 'our' meat was being exported to France, and the *Daily Express* published a photograph of a man wearing a beret and with his napkin tucked in his collar – sure signs both of his Frenchness – eating meat, the caption being designed to arouse horror and indignation in every loyal British breast, or at any rate stomach.

But Macmillan, of course, had other meat to fry. In the political life of this man of many ambiguities, one ambiguity stood out. It was the identification of the patrician Macmillan with the brashest and most indelicate of all the slogans of the decade, the famous 'You've never had it so good'. The more assiduous students of Macmillan's style knew that beneath the fastidious exterior there lurked a vulgarian, and somehow his attempts to ape the idiom of the masses, as in his claim that 'There ain't gonna be no war', or 'Exporting is fun', seemed not patronizing but genuine, enabling him to get away with behaviour that would have caused Sir Alec Douglas-Home to die of embarrassment if he had attempted it, and would have made even Mr Wilson, who really was sprung from the people, though not quite so low down on their ladder as he liked to imply, freeze in mid-banter.

But when, late in the Fifties, Macmillan said: 'Most of our people have never had it so good', the phrase ran through the country, and through the public consciousness, like fire, and every attempt by his opponents (inside his party as well as opposite it) to limit it, to point out that the future had a claim too, that what goes up must come down, and that a series of inflationary economic policies must in the end be paid for, only made the slogan, and the thinking that lay behind it, more popular. For it was true.

In the inflationary days of Macmillan's administration those who got left behind in the rush to keep their incomes ahead of their outgoings suffered considerably, but they were a minority, and most of them either voted Labour anyway or were of unshakeable Conservative loyalty; most people, however, until the air began to escape from the balloon, had no complaints about their new-found affluence, and all appeals to them to put aside material things and think of spiritual ones fell, not surprisingly, on deaf ears, since very few people were willing to part with the security and material well-being they now had for the first time in their lives. Great was the fury of the Labour Party at seeing their clothes so blatantly stolen, their philosophy having for so many years been one of alleviating the lot of the poor, who until so recently had comprised the bulk of the population, and the result was the extraordinary spectacle of the Left denouncing affluence as though it was some kind of disease, and a contagious one at that (which, according to orthodox Keynesian theory, it presumably was), and vainly urging the people, like biblical prophets, to turn aside from the things which were done in Tyre and Sidon. Curiously, they were joined in this appeal by the forces of the Right, which not only disapproved of the poor becoming less poor, on the grounds that it would unsettle them and sap their fibre, but held to the belief that austerity was in itself beneficial, and in a few cases actually practised it themselves.

Yet there was no evidence that the people shared this view, or even understood it. Never had there been so many investors of small sums buying shares on the Stock Exchange; never had any industry expanded at the dizzying rate attained by the growth of Unit Trusts, the poor man's portfolio. Ever with its nose cocked to the wind, the *Daily Mirror* appointed a City Editor for the first time early in the decade, perhaps alerted to the need for one by the astonishing last-minute rush of 'small' money, on the eve of the 1959 general election, into shares that would do well in the event of a Conservative victory. He proceeded to give advice to his readers, who might vote Labour for the most idealistic of reasons but were not averse to making money on the Stock Exchange, however often and however vociferously it might be denounced as the temple of Baal, if somebody would only show them how to. 'The luxuries of the rich', said Macmillan, 'have become the necessities of the poor', and in the exaggeration there was truth embedded, as was mordantly pointed out in a cartoon in the *Spectator* by Trog, on the morrow of the 1959 election, which showed Macmillan seated at the Cabinet table with the other chairs filled by washing machines, refrigerators and cars: 'Well, gentlemen', he is depicted as saying, 'I think we fought a successful campaign.'

Later the plump chickens came home, not so much to roost as to have their necks wrung. The delights of affluence did indeed prove sour, though not because they sapped the people's fibre, as had so dismally been predicted, but because they were not accompanied, at anything like the speed at which the private affluence grew, by the creation of a background against which the affluence could be enjoyed in true comfort. 'Private affluence and public squalor', Professor Galbraith's phrase, was used to describe the United States, yet in a different way it applied to Britain too. The more the nation acquired the comforts of life, the more uneasy it became at the ugliness and drabness of most people's surroundings, without understanding why. Most British industrial towns have remained unrelievedly hideous since they first began to grow in the nineteenth century, and very little was done, in the Macmillan Sixties, to alter that state of affairs. Most industrial work is of almost unbelievable dullness, relieved only, if at all, by the companionship of the factory or workshop; nothing was done to change that either. Of what use were new curtains if the factory chimneys a few yards from the windows in which they were hung still poured filth into the atmosphere as they had done for a hundred years? Of what use was a new fishing-rod if the only rivers for miles around were polluted beyond any possibility of containing fish by the effluent from the chemical plant upstream? Of what use was even the car, if its only use was to escape from the weekday surroundings into the country, and thus emphasize the need for the escape?

When they got the chance, the people turned on the man who had encouraged their affluence and rent him. Before the end Macmillan began to feel the criticism of his policy that previously he had airily dismissed, and had taken to saying, quite untruthfully, of his famous slogan: 'I was not making a boast but giving a warning.' It was he who should have heeded the warning, and did not. In the end Trog had his revenge when the Profumo scandal broke: he depicted a wall with, painted on it, the famous slogan, in the form 'We've never had it so good', while Macmillan scurries away, paint-pot in hand, having just changed the final word to 'often'.

* * *

Of all the strange incidents of this strange man's career, none was stranger than his participation in a wholly unnecessary election, in which success was by no means assured and would in any case have brought him no power and little credit, and failure would have been, though unimportant, humiliating.

In the first months of the decade Lord Halifax died, and the question arose of his successor as Chancellor of Oxford University. Macmillan was a Balliol man, with all the traditional reverence for that college and the university of which it is a part (or, as many of its alumni seem to think, the whole) that Balliol men seem to acquire so effortlessly, and he also enjoyed, or suffered from, that nostalgia that understandably affected so many of his generation who went from Oxford straight into the First World War, a journey which cruelly emphasized what all feeling men must have realized, that a world had ended in the summer of 1914, and which in Macmillan's case, as in so many others, was even more emphasized by the number of those who went with him but did not return.

This feeling never left him, and he put it into words on more than one occasion, speaking of the *douceur de vivre* in that golden and vanished world. In the circumstances the temptation to allow his name to go forward into the election for Chancellor of his old university must have been strong; what was surprising was that he allowed himself to succumb to it, and risked damaging the symmetry of the dream by losing the contest. The first (and, as it turned out, only other) nominee for the post was Sir Oliver Franks. He was supported by an impressive array of Oxford notables, he would have carried out the duties of Chancellor (which are few and of no great significance) with discretion and without disturbing anybody, and he was expected to be returned unopposed. Those who expected this outcome were surprised, in many cases disagreeably, to learn that Professor Hugh Trevor-Roper, whose appointment as Regius Professor of History had been made on Macmillan's advice and whose skill and relish for academic politics was renowned, had appointed himself campaign manager for Macmillan's rival candidature, at that time unknown to the prospective candidate, and was determined to see his man not only accept nomination but win the election. Accordingly, while Macmillan was making his 'Wind of Change' speech in Cape Town, Trevor-Roper was collecting support in Oxford, and before Macmillan got home had formally invited him to stand, indicating as he did so what support he might expect. Macmillan accepted.

The voting, conducted according to ancient ritual which must have baffled foreign observers even more than the election itself, resulted in the victory of Mauricium Haraldum Macmillan over Oliverum Shewell Franks by 1,976 votes to 1,697, a mathematical anagram that did credit to Professor Trevor-Roper's organizational abilities. At the ceremony of induction of the new chancellor, Macmillan was in his element, making a speech in dreadful dog-Latin mugged up for the occasion, though some slight suspicion was cast upon his constantly iterated professions of 'true and deep affection for Oxford' by the fact that throughout the proceedings he wore his mortar-board back to front.

When, shortly afterwards, the new chancellor had the opportunity to nominate the recipients of honorary degrees, he showed his loyalty to his friends and willingness to pay his debts, together with what on the face of it seemed a somewhat macabre sense of humour, by nominating Selwyn Lloyd to be Legum Doctor, Honoris Causa. (It must have reminded many of two more of Macmillan's recommendations for awards, made only a few months before for the first New Year's Honours List of the decade, but without the whimsical element implicit in Selwyn Lloyd's elevation to academic distinction; these were a Barony for Sir Evelyn Baring, who had been Governor of Kenya at the time of the massacre of eleven prisoners at the Hola Camp, and from whose Press office had first come a hastily concocted and wholly false suggestion that the men had died from drinking contaminated water, and a Companionship of Honour for Alan Lennox-Boyd, who had been Colonial Secretary, and therefore constitutionally responsible for conditions in such camps.)

Franks got his revenge, though he probably did not think of it as that, some years later, when he was appointed to be the Chairman of a Commission appointed to inquire into the constitution, organization and functioning of Oxford University, and produced a report which made a number of very sharp criticisms and pointed recommendations; these it would have been his duty to reply to, if not indeed to resist and obstruct, if the election of Chancellor had gone the other way. This was an irony that Macmillan, by then in retirement, no doubt relished, though he wisely left the replying, resisting and obstructing to those more immediately involved in Oxford affairs, who showed themselves, led by the Warden of All Souls, to be fully equal to the responsibility. Certainly, to this day nothing has been done to implement the Franks Commission's proposals.

* * *

Macmillan's nerve was good, having been tempered early in the First World War, his service in which he was wont to invoke; when he lost it, however, he did not do so with half measures, but fell into something like total panic. He lost his head in 1962, when his Government fell upon hard times, whereupon seven of his colleagues lost theirs, and Jeremy Thorpe, surveying a sight that resembled the last act of a Jacobean play, the stage covered with the political corpses of seven senior Ministers, sacked in a single day to keep the wolves from Macmillan's own sled, commented: 'Greater love hath no man than this, that he lay down his friends for his life.'

The first rule in such situations is to find a scapegoat, and Macmillan picked on Selwyn Lloyd, a kind of Fido Achates, who had trotted obediently at the heels of Eden, and thereafter even more obediently at those of Macmillan. As Chancellor, Lloyd had faithfully carried out Macmillan's policy; a scapegoat, however, was the role which Selwyn Lloyd might have been born to play, and Macmillan needed one for the Government's disastrous slump in popular support. Selwyn Lloyd fitted the bill to perfection. Along with Lloyd went the Earl of Kilmuir, who never forgave Macmillan for his abrupt dismissal from an office (Lord Chancellor) he could hardly be said to have adorned; Lord Mills, an old friend of Macmillan's who had been given Ministerial office, amid general astonishment, some years before, and instantly vanished without trace, so that the first many people knew of his membership of the Government was when he left it; Harold Watkinson, a Minister of Defence whose extraordinarily high abilities were of the kind that everybody talks about in retrospect, since at the time they do not, for some unaccountable reason, spring much to mind; John Maclay, undistinguished even by the standard of Scottish Secretaries; David Eccles; and Charles Hill, baggy-trousered clown to Macmillan's ringmaster, who had long outlived the memory of the reason he had been given office in the first place, which was his immense popularity with radio audiences, for whom he had been, in his capacity of Radio Doctor, an invaluable source of information about such matters as minor disorders of the bowels. (Hill, amid considerable amazement, became Chairman first of the Independent Television Authority, and then of the B.B.C. He too never forgave Macmillan.)

Macmillan's new Ministerial team was designed, and might have been reasonably expected, to bring back the retreating public confidence in time for a massive upsurge of electoral support in the forthcoming general election. In fact, matters turned out quite differently; the slaughter was seen by so many people to be the act of a desperate man, and left so much resentment among the victims and their friends, that, although Macmillan easily survived the immediate crisis it provoked, it turned out after all to have been a politically fatal error from which he was never to recover. And when he fell, he fell like Lucifer, never to hope again.

He fell, in the most spectacular circumstances, during his party's annual conference, in 1963, when his decision to retire, following his discovery that a blocked prostate gland necessitated an immediate operation followed by a considerable period of convalescence, was actually announced from the platform at a session of the conference in Blackpool.

It was a traumatic moment for the Conservative Party, for Macmillan, and for the contenders for the succession, together with their supporters and campaigners. But it was also a traumatic moment for Britain, and once again emphasized the curious nature of the decade, poised as it was between past and future. Ever since the modern Conservative Party had emerged in the nineteenth century, its leaders had been chosen by a mysterious and undefinable process. Sometimes the new man had 'emerged', as the expression had it, as though he was a kind of Botticelli Venus or Excalibur sword. Sometimes, more prosaically, he was a compromise candidate between two rival, deadlocked ones with more or less equal support. Sometimes—as was the case with Macmillan's own succession to the Premiership—he was chosen by the members of the Cabinet. The choice of Macmillan's successor was to mark the last occasion on which so grave a matter would be left to the interplay of such subtle forces, of 'soundings' and 'voices', of 'constituency opinion' and 'the knights from the shires'. Such methods had no place in the future towards which Britain was inexorably moving, and it was fitting that the Sixties should have seen them used for the last time and then abandoned for ever, even if it is possible to wonder whether they would have been abandoned if it had not been for the extraordinary circumstances that, at the moment Macmillan made his fateful announcement, there were no fewer than six possible candidates for the succession, each of whom, moreover, had a real chance, and each of whom had real supporters.

Yet the method used to select one of them, and the way in which that method was employed and its constituent parts manipulated, and the aim of those doing the manipulating, made it sure that the 'customary processes' were being used for the last time, so bitter were the recriminations, so prolonged the disputes, so clouded the truth, in what finally happened. A few months later Randolph Churchill published a version of the events under the title *The Fight for the Tory Leadership*,[1] which was described by Iain Macleod in a long reply to it in the *Spectator* (of which Macleod was briefly editor during the Sixties) as 'Mr Macmillan's trailer for the screenplay of his memoirs'; but though Mr Macleod was engaged, in his article, in being waspish about Churchill's heavily Macmillanized version of the events of the previous October, and also in demonstrating the way in which (another of his phrases) the 'magic circle' which controlled the destinies of the Tory Party operated, he was doing more than this. He was determined to see that new methods were devised for the future. 'The procedure which had been adopted', he wrote ominously, 'opens up big issues for decisions in the future. That everything was done in good faith I do not doubt—indeed, it is the theme of this review to demonstrate it—but the result of the methods used was contradiction and misrepresentation. I do not think it is a precedent which will be followed.'

Nor was it, for when, a year after succeeding Macmillan as Prime Minister, Sir Alec Douglas-Home led the Conservative Party to the narrowest electoral defeat of modern times, the first major action he took when the dust had settled was to sweep

[1] Heinemann, London, 1964.

away the 'customary processes' for ever and replace them by a direct, secret ballot, confined to the membership of the Conservative Party in the House of Commons, and the next major action he took was to resign the party leadership and preside over the first, historic use of the new machinery. This, it should be noted, was used to choose between three candidates – Heath, Maudling and Powell – none of whom could possibly be described as being a member of any 'magic circle' whatever, thus giving rise to the suspicion that the matter could have been left to the customary processes after all.

The newspapers and magazines at the time and for long afterwards, and a crop of books later still, and the reviews of those books when they were published, discussed and analysed the fateful days and hours of the Conservative leadership crisis, together with the dramatic meetings, the significant telephone calls, the pledges, broken and kept, the crossing of intentions and the double-crossing of colleagues. It was, not even excluding the struggle between Wilson and Brown for the succession to Hugh Gaitskell ten months earlier, or the two elections of mid-decade, the most richly entertaining of all the political activities of the Sixties, but more to the point it was also perhaps the most typical of the decade. Never again in the Sixties was politics to be so personal, never again were the activities of individuals in moving the levers of power to be so important and the vast impersonal forces of destiny of so little effect by comparison, never again were the cleverer players to beat the less clever so unarguably, the more ruthless triumph so completely over the less, never again were the dangers of underestimating an opponent in politics to be so clearly and – for the losers – so sadly demonstrated. Whether one accepts the thesis of Randolph Churchill that the Earl of Home 'emerged' during the crisis as the only man who could unite the Conservative Party, form a Government and command a majority in the House, or whether one cleaves rather to the thesis of Iain Macleod, which was that 'From the first day of his Premiership to the last, Macmillan was determined that Butler, although incomparably the best qualified of the contenders, should not succeed him', or whether one accepts the view of Mr Quintin Hogg (as Lord Hailsham had again become) which he put forward in two most interesting articles in the *Sunday Express* (the first of which appeared a fortnight after he had rather rashly declared that he had no intention of adding to the accounts of the leadership contest then circulating an account of his own), which was that everything that occurred was 'perfectly honourable, perfectly straightforward, and reflects, I believe, nothing but credit on the principal characters concerned', those without direct political or emotional involvement in the business could, at the time and for long after, simply enjoy the show.

There were certainly some spectacular acts in it. There was, for instance, Hailsham's announcement, at the end of a long and rambling speech, prepared far in advance but delivered, by chance, on the day of Macmillan's decision to step down, that he was going to renounce his peerage so as to be available for selection as Prime Minister, which was greeted by a demonstration described by one of his opponents as reminiscent of a Nuremberg Rally. There was Butler's increasingly wan appearance as the frenzied week in Blackpool wore on, and his characteristic throwing away of his chance at the final Saturday rally by making a speech of exceptional flabbiness ('Conservatives have always believed in the British people ... We must not rush forward in a moment of thoughtless euphoria. But neither should we dawdle in a fog of defeatism and cynicism ... A Programme for Peace is above all a Programme for People, for peace is what people care about most'), unrelieved even by the civilized Augustan wit of which he is capable. There was the mounting excitement of the days in London, when the glare of the conference arc-lights could at last be turned off and the knives plied under the cover of a decent obscurity; the midnight meeting, when it was too late, of the group of senior Conservative Ministers who could have stopped Home and insisted on Butler; the eleventh-hour chance that, by sticking together and refusing to serve under any but Butler, they could have pulled it off even after Home went to the Palace, followed by their inevitable betrayal by Butler himself; the growing astonishment, in the final hours, as it became apparent that it was indeed to be Home. There followed the deadly attack by Wilson on this 'elegant anachronism', the Fourteenth Earl, and the riposte ('I suppose, when you come to think of it, Mr Wilson is the fourteenth Mr Wilson') by Home, which was to be the last time he seriously scored off his opponent, and was in turn followed by the realization, in the months that followed, that Home was simply not equipped for the position. And yet finally there was the 1964 election, in which, after a campaign by the Labour Party designed to secure the greatest possible advantage from their presentation of the contrast between the parties as one of the future against the past, the dynamic grasp of the demands of the modern age against the static belief in the virtues of the old ways, the Tories under Home nevertheless ran the Labour Party under Wilson to a margin of only four seats, and then had the chagrin of seeing the margin widen to a hundred when they had for the first time employed the machinery of the democratic future and chosen as their leader a man they thought fit to match its demands.

Few things in his career became Macmillan like the leaving of it. The Stag at Bay with the mentality of a fox at large, he ended exactly as he had begun, by doing down Mr Butler with weapons that were not, or (according to the view of the matter taken by the observer) were, worthy of the man wielding them.

It is not easy to summarize Macmillan and his tenure of the Premiership, and probably not profitable either, in view of the comparatively short time that has elapsed since he stepped down. One of the most fascinating characters to bestride the stage of British politics since Disraeli, whom in some ways he closely resembled, Macmillan has to his credit the foresight that enabled him to turn his party's head away from Empire and towards Europe, away from the past and towards the future. And yet he would not or could not say clearly to his party and the country what time of day it was, and in consequence was led into such amazing adventures as his startling comparison of Mr Dean Acheson with Hitler (when Acheson had said, in the course of a most friendly appraisal of Britain, that she 'had lost an Empire and not yet found a role'), and his final mad fling when, thwarted of his wish to see Hailsham succeed him, he insisted on Home, almost as if he had been determined to smash everything he had so laboriously built over the previous years.

# 13

# ... and the carpenter

And so, after a brief interregnum, Britain entered upon the reign of the second Harold. For those with sufficiently long memories it was already clear how the wind would blow. Few of the intra-party political battles of the decade so well symbolized the strain imposed on the Sixties by the effort to face the future while staring fixedly at the past as the struggle within the Labour Party, during the opening months of the decade, over Clause Four of its constitution. This pledged it 'to secure for the workers by hand or by brain the full fruits of their industry, and the most equitable distribution thereof that may be possible, upon the basis of the common ownership of the means of production, distribution, and exchange'. The prose style of the notorious pledge, which seems to tremble on the very edges of a discussion of the respective roles within society of the workers, the peasants and the intellectuals, dates it fairly precisely, and even if it did not, the days when the workers by hand, at any rate, needed any assistance to secure the fruits of their labours, and indeed of other people's, were long since over by the beginning of the Sixties. Moreover, the Labour Party had abandoned any intention it may have had once of nationalizing everything; all that remained, after the party had lost the 1959 election by an even greater margin than the previous two, was to complete the task of modernizing this one small part of its appearance and outlook by unstitching the ancient words from its banner. To this end, therefore, Hugh Gaitskell bent his best endeavours, only to find, to his amazement, that great sections of the party instantly rallied to the defence of the albatross around the party's neck.

Into the twentieth century he was determined that the Labour

Party should go; the Labour Party would have none of it, insisting on remaining within the nineteenth. It was about this time that Harold Wilson began seriously his campaign to supplant Gaitskell as leader of the Labour Party, and by encouraging the defenders of Clause Four he made Gaitskell's position more difficult, though Wilson naturally did not believe in the doctrine any more than his chief did. In 1963, however, Gaitskell died, and Wilson succeeded him as leader. Whereupon he found himself locked in combat, for the same modernizing purpose, with the same ancient and embattled forces in Labour policy and philosophy.

Wilson's career has been characterized for so many years by what Lord Radcliffe, in another connection entirely, coined a fine phrase to describe as 'an undeviating lack of candour' that it is possible to find, for every unambiguous statement of his beliefs or attitudes or policies, an equally unambiguous statement of exactly opposite convictions or intentions. Indeed, an entire book has been composed of such contradictions.[1] And in the end the fact that Wilson had given far more hostages to fortune than any other politician of modern times, in the shape of the repeated betrayal of everything he had ever said he stood for, helped to bring him down. The one-eyed man reigned successfully over the country of the blind until his subjects recovered their sight; and then there was a reckoning.

His success, indeed his entire career, cannot be understood without understanding the intensity of his ambition to become, and having become to remain, Prime Minister, together with an ability to disguise from himself almost (though not quite) entirely the strength of that ambition and the extent to which he has been willing to go in its pursuit.

Every politician needs ambition, of course, if he is to succeed and advance, and since without such success and advance he will be unable to put into effect policies which he believes the country needs and will benefit from, no criticism can be levelled, on that score alone, at an ambitious politician. Every politician too

[1] *The Politics of Harold Wilson*, by Paul Foot (Penguin, Harmondsworth, 1969).

knows that sometimes it is necessary to trim those very policies to remain in office or the race for it, since without doing so it will cease to be possible to put into effect even the residue of his proposals; only the naive will criticize an ambitious politician for that either. Finally, every politician knows that it is sometimes necessary, for the same purpose, to do one thing while claiming to do another, and to say that one thing has been done though in truth a very different thing has been; to this course also small blame should be attached, and little usually is.

Yet the extraordinary thing about Wilson is not that he took these principles, or lack of them, to lengths undreamed of by almost any other politician alive or dead, but that he did so in a manner which virtually invited the public to lose its confidence in him, and still managed to retain a following and also a reputation as an almost infallible winner of elections, so that right up to June 1970 not only his own party but his opponents and the voters seemed convinced that he would achieve the unprecedented feat of winning three successive General Elections. But the voters had the last word, and with it gave their verdict: that he was a man of straw.

Many theories have been put forward to explain this phenomenon. His brilliance, his prodigious memory, his knowledge that most people have a less comprehensive memory (which usually enabled him safely to contradict himself, on major issues of policy and principle, within a period of only a few months), his ability to control an organization as diverse, as split, as the Labour Party – all these and more have been offered as the qualities which enabled him to attain his ambitions. Yet the truth was surely simpler. If there was any one moment at which he could have been said to have won the 1964 election, it was at the meeting at which the baby cried. It cried and cried, and would not be comforted, while its mother grew more and more embarrassed and the rest of the audience more and more restive, irritated and amused. Eventually, her face very red, the mother rose to leave the hall with the infant heckler. Instantly Wilson broke off his speech and swung round on her. 'Don't take him out, madam,' he cried; 'this election is about his future.'

It was genius; more to the point, it was widely reported; more to the point still, it was true.

For, just as the picture of Macmillan as 'a faded, attitudinizing, Turf Club bummaree' (which is what Malcolm Muggeridge called him) was, though perfectly accurate, neither the whole picture nor the most important part of it, so the picture of Wilson as a ruthless, scheming, unprincipled man activated by self-interest was also, though accurate, incomplete and less important than the rest of the authentic portrait.

The clue to Wilson, and his achievement, can be found in his now famous 'technology' speech at the Labour Party Conference of 1963. Within a week of his making it Macmillan resigned, but the speech was so perfectly conceived as the instrument which would finally topple the crumbling Tory Party that it might have been written after Macmillan's decision rather than before, and indeed after Sir Alec Douglas-Home had succeeded to the Conservative leadership.

In the cold light of the decade's end the speech does not make particularly impressive reading. For one thing, too many of the phrases which set the conference on a roar have since become not merely clichés but parodies of clichés ('... the conscious, planned, purposive use of scientific progress ... '). For another, the promises in it were belied as rapidly and completely as Wilson's other promises. Yet its timing was perfect, and its content, for the time, no less so; and both were indicative of Wilson's instinctive political genius. And it was this genius which, when all the more lurid but irrelevant details of his character and career have been put on one side, carried him to the summit of his ambition.

For in that speech Wilson did what Gaitskell, over Wilson's ambition-governed obstruction, had wanted to do but failed: he brought the Labour Party up to date. Without spelling out what he was doing (spelling it out would have ruined the object of the exercise entirely, as it would for Macmillan, in precisely parallel circumstances, when he turned his party away from

Empire), he announced that the Labour Party was no longer the party of labour, of the 'workers by hand and brain', of the 'grass roots' and the 'Methodist influence', of the nationalization of the means of production, distribution and exchange, of the international brotherhood of man, of Socialism. From now on, the Labour Party was to be the party which understood the modern world and its reality, and could work within it; which would operate the economic system as it existed, but to ends which it believed more just than those attainable if the system were left to itself; which would take as its model Scandinavian social democracy and as its exemplar the recent transformation of the German Social Democratic Party from a Marxist-based movement, doomed to perpetual opposition, into a social-engineering party, to reap the reward of its enterprise at the end of the decade; which, in short, had buried Clause Four and everything else which smelt of it, and buried it not as Gaitskell would have buried it, with bands and processions and mourning and speeches, but with the quickness of the hand that deceives the eye. Truly, Macmillan and Wilson were soulmates of the Sixties.

Wilson reaped *his* reward exactly a year later, when he won the election by the narrowest margin of the century; seventeen months later his judgment of what the country wanted from the Labour Party was confirmed when he won the election by one of the widest. The country wanted not socialist theory, but adjectiveless practice; and it was Wilson's achievement not only to divine this (Gaitskell had done as much), but to deceive his party into swallowing it.

But it could not last. In the end the vision faded, blotted out by the defects in Wilson's own character. He had given, for a time, a tremendously effective impression of action, which turned out on closer inspection to be only activity. His insistence on personal Government, on making his own personality and reputation the test of his Government, worked while he was seen as the kind of man the new age needed to represent it, the image with which he had won the election against Douglas-Home by emphasizing the contrast he presented with the effete scion of another class and another age. But Wilson, in the last analysis, was a man who lacked political weight, and when, during the run-up to the general election at the turn of the decade, he lightly suggested that the public would vote for him again as 'the lesser of two evils', he spoke more seriously than he realized, and was wrong.

'A lot of politics is presentation,' he said privately during a crucial discussion on one of the most important political crises of his Premiership, 'and what isn't presentation is timing.' This masterly analysis of his own character could hardly have been improved upon by his worst enemy, and it was not surprising that as disaster followed disaster, each disaster was presented as a political triumph, devaluation, for instance, being a great opportunity for exporters, and the surrender of industrial reform a statesmanlike agreement between the Government and the T.U.C.

He had always had a temptation to remove himself from the hard world of reality to the more inviting shores of fantasy. From time to time, for instance, he began to be possessed of a profound belief that both East and West were only awaiting the signal from him to lay down their arms for ever. At the same time he was for ever imagining himself to be like, or even to be, President Kennedy, and when Kennedy was assassinated he began to identify himself, *faute de mieux*, with Kennedy's successor: 'I'm a Johnson,' he squeaked on one occasion; 'I fly by the seat of my pants.' And this tendency to self-deception led him at times into the wildest adventures, wholly foreign to his normal cautious character. For although his credibility, by the end of the decade, was by no means what it had been at the beginning, he was game to the last. He too had his finest hour. Two of them, to be precise.

* * *

The Sixties were not quite without their more old-fashioned excitements. In the spring of 1967 Britain experienced all the heady excitement of war with none of the danger, and her political leaders all the pride of victory with none of the responsibility. The Fleet Air Arm and R.A.F. flew bombing missions for the first time for many years, and acquitted themselves with distinction and without loss or casualties; the Navy lived up worthily to its high traditions; the Army showed that its modern, scientific approach to its work had proved successful. Civilian morale was high, and there was a noticeable return of that spirit of comradeship on which many had remarked during the Blitz in 1940, sometimes dwelling upon it long afterwards with a plea for its rediscovery and deployment against the more humdrum enemies of falling production and an adverse balance of trade; at its height, strangers were to be seen lending one another their evening newspapers in trains, and the headlines in those newspapers, and still more in their morning sisters, entered enthusiastically into the spirit of the times, and called up images of war that they had long believed utterly forgotten.

The occasion for this massive recollection in tranquillity of the days when the blast of war had blown in Britain's ears was the grounding, on a reef off Cornwall known as the Seven Stones, of a huge oil tanker, the *Torrey Canyon*, en route for Wales. Trying to make a difficult passage between the reef and the Scilly Isles, the ship, which was almost exactly the same length as the *Queen Mary*, went aground and stuck fast. This in itself would not have much mattered, had it not been for the fact that in going aground the ship had torn a hole of considerable size in her hull, and the 120,000 tons of crude oil she was carrying began to seep inexorably into the sea, and to be carried on the prevailing currents, driven by the prevailing winds, no less inexorably towards the shore.

The time was Easter, and the holiday season in Cornwall and Devon would soon be at its height; suddenly, along both the southern and northern coasts of Britain's south-western peninsula, a disaster of wholly unprecedented magnitude loomed, involving the ruin or even total destruction of the local marine life, birds, fishing and holiday industries, and ultimately the prosperity of the entire area. Though the problem of oil pollution of seas and shores had long been a pressing one, it generally arose in the form of the discharge by passing vessels of unwanted fuel oil; and although there had been previous cases of oil tankers accidentally discharging part of their cargo nothing even remotely approaching disaster on this scale had occurred before, anywhere in the world.

The Prime Minister had never had such an opportunity before, and was not to have one again until right at the end of the decade. The wreck of the *Torrey Canyon* brought out the best in him, as it did in all Britain, and once again it was clear, as it had been with Churchill in 1940, that the hour had found the man, and that the nation, which to an outsider might have seemed sunk in lethargy, was going to respond.

Almost as soon as the oil had started to leak from the stranded ship, a Navy vessel, H.M.S. *Clarbeston*, had set sail for the area with a thousand gallons of detergent to spray on the oil, and a tug, the *Sea Giant*, was making for the wreck with 3,500 gallons more. (Ultimately it was calculated that 600,000 gallons were used in the fight, but these were early days.) The oil, however, continued to pour out of the ship, and the Government, knowing like all Governments that the first thing to do in a crisis is to set up a committee, duly set one up, under the chairmanship of the Government's chief scientific adviser, Sir Solly Zuckerman, which was asked to consider what steps could and should be taken. Shortly afterwards, Mr Wilson himself appeared on the scene. His arrival did not immediately indicate that the situation was so grave that he had decided to take personal charge; it was his custom to spend his holidays in the Scilly Isles, and he was on his way there for Easter. Travelling by helicopter from the mainland to the Scillies, he was taken to see the wreck, on a kind of sixpence-round-the-lighthouse journey, and there saw for himself the extent of the danger, which was considerable, as the patch of oil that had flowed from the ship now extended over an area of some 700 square miles and was estimated to contain some 30,000 tons. (The first oil reached the mainland on the following day.) Next day, under the strain of the heaving from the attempts at salvage and of the pounding from the waves, the

*Torrey Canyon* broke into two pieces, which on the day after became three, and another 40,000 tons of oil washed out of her.

It was time to act, and Mr Wilson did not hesitate, now that the time had come. He ordered in the planes.

The Navy and R.A.F. had not had an enemy to bomb for some time, and no doubt welcomed this opportunity to show what Mao Tse-tung's airborne hordes could expect if they dared to show their yellow faces, in battle order, off the coasts of Britain. With the shore and cliffs at Land's End and on the Scilly Isles black with sightseers who had scrambled for the best position from which to see the fun (they included the Prime Minister), the Navy Buccaneers went in to the attack. The first plane dropped two bombs, of which one missed and the other failed to explode; first blood to Mao Tse-tung. Thereafter things improved, and soon there was a huge cloud of impenetrable black smoke, shot through with flames, pouring from the ship; the smoke eventually rose to a height of eight thousand feet.

After the Buccaneers, the Hunters; these, because of the difficulty of setting unrefined oil on fire, dropped highly inflammable aircraft fuel into the conflagration to keep it burning. But there was still oil unburned in the ship and it continued to pour out, so the next day further squadrons of the gallant lads in blue joined the battle, which raged all day, and included, ominously enough, the dropping of napalm bombs. This curious fact, revealed by accident, aroused some feeling, not on the grounds that it was somehow improper to use napalm on an empty ship (though there were probably those so conditioned to protesting at the sound of the word napalm that they would have taken to the streets in a demonstration if they had noticed), but that nobody had previously known that Britain possessed any napalm. Many wanted to know, understandably, what it was kept for, as the likelihood of its coming in handy to set stranded oil tankers on fire could hardly have occurred to those responsible when it was being ordered; no answer was forthcoming, however, and further speculation was quelled, or at any rate diverted, when the Prime Minister flew over the battle area while the smoke was still billowing upwards, on his way back to London at the end of his Easter break.

The Navy was already in action; the Air Force had written another glorious page in its history; now it was the turn of the Army. (First, however, it was the turn of the Treasury, which wrote another glorious page in *its* history by offering, as its contribution to the battle, the sum of a thousand pounds; this proved to be a good deal short of what was eventually required, which was some two million.) Troops were mobilized and dispatched to the north and south coasts of Cornwall. Army lorries thundered through the night carrying huge tins of powerful detergent. Ordnance factories turned out pumps and sprays. Bulldozers scooped up contaminated sand. Three hundred boys from the Junior Leaders' Regiment of the Royal Corps of Signals went into action, manning telephone switchboards and calling up fresh supplies of detergents, foam-blocks, shovels, leather-shavings, amphibious vehicles, nets, hoses and anything else that ingenuity could devise and Sir Solly Zuckerman's committee be persuaded to approve. (Among the suggestions from the public rejected earlier had been one to float the wreck off the Seven Stones by stuffing her with tennis-balls.)

In time, and at a frightful cost in money, disruption of military training-schedules, ruined clothes and holidays, broken ankles and dead birds, the battle was won; Mr Wilson had rallied the nation, and saved it from the Hun, or at any rate from eighty thousand tons of crude oil. Gradually the stains were cleaned from the beaches and the promenades; the oil was scooped up and burned, the polluted sand was ploughed up and cleaned or dumped out of harm's and sight's way; the R.A.F. studied the lessons of the fight and no doubt concluded that Mao Tse-tung could be dealt with too, a sentiment in which they were presumably joined by the Army and the Navy; and by the time the summer holiday season arrived, the episode was a thing of the past, and lived on only in the reminiscences of the locals who had been present at the fight, much as for many years after the war Londoners would tell each other how close to them the closest bomb had fallen, and as elderly Irishmen still tend to tell strangers what befell them in the Dublin General Post Office at Easter 1916.

'We will fight them on the beaches ... we will never surrender.' With those words, a quarter of a century before, Winston Churchill had called Britain to her duty, and to glory. Were those words perhaps dancing somewhere at the back of Mr Wilson's mind, as he directed the battle on this occasion? True, he had said, in criticizing the Macmillan Government in 1961 for their handling of the economic crisis of that year: 'I myself have always deprecated ... in crisis after crisis, appeals to the Dunkirk spirit as an answer to our problems'; but then, he had said in 1964, when defending his own Government's handling of the economic crisis of *that* year: 'I believe that the spirit of Dunkirk will carry us through', so the matter can be argued either way. But Mr Wilson had tasted glory (he was to taste it again); and the public had responded in a way which astonished many shrewd observers. The mood should not have come as a surprise. Beneath the surface longings stirred which had been undisturbed for many hungry years. The extent of these longings was great, greater than any realized; they lay there, dark and secret, forming a huge pool of unsatisfied desire, as the pools of thick oil lie beneath the dry sands of the deserts, unknown until the wells are drilled and the black tide comes gushing forth. There were many elements in the longings, and few of them were ever clearly defined in men's minds; they were none the less real for that. Over twenty years before there had been the end of the war, and glory enough for all in the hot hours of cheering and dancing in the streets; but twenty years was twenty years, enough for VE-day babies to grow up and start families of their own and for the parents of the VE-day babies to forget the crowds, and the cheering, and the flags, and the victory that had drilled through the sandy crust of rationing and utility furniture, patched clothes and patched houses, drabness and bombs and the telegrams that informed the recipient of the regrets of the War Office, the victory that had drilled through all these and down into the thick black pool of rejoicing in Britain's greatness, and let it erupt into the air in a great, uncontrollable, roaring sea.

Since then there had been nothing much to cheer about, apart from an occasional coronation. The partisan cheering of Election Night was not the same thing at all, and besides, it was too frequently interrupted by more mournful sounds, such as those of the drunks vomiting into the gutter and the cars driven by other drunks colliding with each other and with lamp-posts. The forced and improbable merry-making of Guy Fawkes' Night was no substitute, either, and as for New Year's Eve, it only emphasized the fact that another year of Britain's decline had passed, so that it was hardly fanciful to imagine that the dedicated enthusiasts who regularly, on the last night of the year, threw themselves and others into the fountains of Trafalgar Square were doing so in a subconscious desire to find some waves, however remote and peaceful, that Britannia still ruled. Indeed, there was nothing much to cheer about in the streets of London.

So when in 1966 England won the World Cup for Association Football (the trophy, one of the most hideous artefacts Western Man has ever produced in his long history of bad taste, had been stolen before the competition began, but unhappily recovered before it ended), hundreds of thousands of people poured into the streets of Central London, on foot and in cars, to celebrate. Perhaps, weighed against the end of Empire, the slackening pace of industrial production, the shrinking scale of politics and the politicians, the waning national energies, the trivialities of art and science, perhaps in the scale against these things winning a keenly contested football match was not a very great achievement. But then it had been a considerable time since Britain had done that either.

The victory had been won, all the way from the earliest qualifying rounds of the competition, amid the familiar chorus of complaints against the players, officials, referees and supporters of other countries. 'GO HOME, THUGS!', the *Daily Sketch* had courteously cried at the Argentine footballers, found guilty of indiscipline on the field, though the records obstinately showed that the England team's record of fouls was among the worst, and many and bitter had been the complaints that the English players were having to struggle not only against the eleven members of the opposing team but also against a vast army of secret partisans, supposedly impartial but dedicated implausibly to the ruin of England's chances by any desperate means, it being accepted that in a fair contest England must either win the match or, in the parlance that the sportsmen had picked up from the politicians, gain at any rate a moral victory.

'Old men forget; yea, all shall be forgot But he'll remember with advantages What feats he did that day'—or at least what feats he wrote about in prose scarcely less over-emphatic than the cheers of the evening which followed. 'All were heroes,' wrote *The Times* ('This story shall the good man teach his son'); 'none more so than Moore as he drove his side on, than the little flame-haired Ball, a real ball of fire this great day' ('Then shall our names, familiar in his mouth as household words'); 'than the intelligent Peters, than Hurst, who crashed in two goals in extra time' ('Harry the King, Bedford and Exeter, Warwick and Talbot, Salisbury and Gloucester'); 'this indeed was a storybook ending' ('Be in their flowing cups freshly remembered'); 'If there are no substitutes for gods, equally there are no substitutes for courage and temperament' ('And gentlemen in England now a-bed Shall think themselves accurst they were not here'); 'Thus the 1966 championships were crowned worthily' ('And hold their manhoods cheap while any speaks That fought with us upon Saint Crispin's Day').

Later in the day Henry's after-battle admonitions—'Be it death proclaiméd through our host To boast of this or take the praise from God Which is his only'—were forgotten, as the streets of London seethed and heaved with a marching, cheering, flag-waving, horn-blowing, rattle-wielding, bell-ringing, drum-banging, cymbal-clashing, traffic-jamming, glory-remembering, victory-celebrating crowd, who at last had something to march, cheer, wave, blow, wield, ring, bang, clash, jam, remember and celebrate about.

And yet, in the headache-ridden morning, or worse still, the dry-mouthed hour before the dawn, many must have realized that nothing had changed, that nothing was better for England just because the World Cup had been won, that the nation which chooses to live by the football shall perish by the trade-gap, the sterling crisis, the failure of national purpose, the loss of identity, the cohesion and determination of her enemies and commercial rivals. Certainly none had had time for such thoughts the night before, as the crowds went mafficking about the streets, again and again breaking into a ritual chant that had once signalled something of wider national meaning: 'Eng-land, Eng-land, Eng-land'. Eng-land, indeed!

* * *

The past, as we have seen, haunted this decade as few had ever been haunted before. Sometimes it seemed as though the ghosts would never be laid, the buried splendour never cease to shine out from the unquiet grave. Nor were there wanting voices to insist that it was not dead but sleeping only; there was even an organization called the League of Empire Loyalists, though when they were asked how they could be loyal to something which, for good or ill, had ceased to exist, they were unable to say. Others, no less eccentric but rather more sophisticated, declared in effect that although all signs of power and influence had vanished, the substance had not; without any evidence being adduced to prove it, the world was said to be awaiting a 'moral lead' from Britain (it was interesting that this view was not the exclusive property of the forces of the Right; it was, after all, the belief on which the Campaign for Nuclear Disarmament was based), and wherever one looked there were necromancers to be seen trying to call spirits from the vasty deep, and challenging the past to stand up and be counted.

At length, as was inevitable, the past arose and took the

present by the throat. 'History', said Marx, 'repeats itself; the first time as tragedy, the second time as comedy.' The tragedy of Suez, played in 1956 to a very mixed reception from critics and public alike, was revived in 1969 and this time played with a lighter touch, the scene being changed from the Middle East to the Caribbean and the *dramatis personae* no less radically revised, now including such memorably named figures as Mr Jeremiah Gumbs, the Reverend Freeman Goodge and Mr William Whitlock; furthermore, on this occasion, in deference to the wishes of the more nervous patrons, nobody was killed or wounded.

Mr Wilson wanted more excitement. In this, it must be said, he was not alone; few men are entirely untroubled by dreams of striding, in a white uniform ablaze with medals, sashes and orders, up to the palisade, from there to storm the enemy's headquarters, single-handed, under a hail of fire. The battle of the *Torrey Canyon* had been a great success; it was time for another such triumph.

On the earlier occasion Mr Wilson had sent in the planes, and tasted blood, or if not blood then crude oil. But the opportunities for a British Prime Minister to practise Imperial Napoleonics by the end of the Sixties were necessarily limited; the Empire which had once straddled the globe, accounting for a third of the world's population, was now reduced to a tiny handful of islands and enclaves, its total population far smaller than that of London and two-thirds of it provided by the single territory of Hong Kong. The rest lived, under a wide variety of different forms of Government, in Fiji and the Virgin Islands, in Pitcairn and Montserrat, in Ascension and St Helena, in Ocean Island and Tristan da Cunha, in the Solomons and the Seychelles, in the Cayman, Turks and Caicos Islands, in Gibraltar, the Falklands and Tonga, so that although it remained true that the sun never set on the British Empire, the coral strands it warmed were now, though still scattered over the globe, reduced to an area that could be comfortably fitted into roughly half of the total acreage of England and Wales.

On the whole the inhabitants of these territories were peaceful and tractable, and where they were not, as from time to time was the case in Hong Kong, the situation was generally so delicate that use of the iron fist would have been inappropriate and dangerous. In the circumstances Mr Wilson might never have had the opportunity to know of battles, sieges, fortunes, of most disastrous chances, of moving accidents by flood and field, of hair-breadth 'scapes i' the imminent deadly breach, and might have gone to his grave without having made the flinty and steel couch of war his thrice-driven bed of down.

Fortunately the opportunity presented itself in the West Indies. This string of islands, sun-blessed but otherwise not rich in natural resources, had long since fulfilled all the necessary conditions for complete independence, except one: many were quite unable to survive economically as self-contained nations. Various schemes for various Caribbean Federations were devised, and some were tried but found wanting, as the inhabitants proved no more immune from the natural suspicion that poisons the relations between man and man than those of Europe, which is saying a good deal. Three of the smaller islands, none the less, formed an uneasy partnership; these were St Kitts, Nevis and Anguilla, and when they had come together in as much harmony as they could muster they were awarded what was called 'associated status', a sensible enough condition in which they were entirely responsible for their internal affairs, but left foreign policy and external defence to Britain.

Unfortunately, for reasons which were obscure to start with and became much more so subsequently, the inhabitants of Anguilla resented having to associate with those of St Kitts; more, they claimed that they were being ill-treated by them, or at any rate that they feared oppressive domination by the Kittittians (as they were charmingly known), who were far more numerous than the Anguillans and Nevisians put together, and who therefore were in a position, by the exercise of undoubtedly democratic processes, to have their own way.

Accordingly the Anguillans announced that they were leaving the tiny federation and setting up in business on their own. No provision for secession had been made in the instrument under which the territories had come together, but the Anguillans might have pointed out that there was good precedent for the break-up of a federation once generally agreed to be permanently established, the Central African Federation (consisting of Zambia, née Northern Rhodesia, Malawi, née Nyasaland, and Rhodesia, née Southern Rhodesia) having been hastily dismantled at the very beginning of the decade when it had proved more embarrassing to the British Government to keep it together than to pull it apart, even though, as things turned out, the subsequent developments in Rhodesia proved a great deal more embarrassing still.

Later events are shrouded in a mystery made ever more impenetrable by the increasingly implausible explanations offered in Britain by the Government. Ignoring these as unworthy of serious consideration, what seems to have happened is that the Government, acting on a mixture of faulty intelligence and a complete inability to make up their minds what they ought to do for the best, determined that they would eventually, if the secession did not come to an end of its own accord, bring it to an end, on behalf of the dominant Kittittian branch of the federation.

Having, in the traditional method of British Governments during the Sixties, ignored the problem in the hope that it would go away, Mr Wilson decided abruptly to act after Mr William Whitlock, a junior Minister then appearing for the first and last time on a wider stage than that to which he was normally accustomed, visited Anguilla, ostensibly to make contact with the self-styled President of the island, Mr Ronald Webster, and explain to him the error of his ways. The visit ended precipitately when four shots fired from a point some miles away from the British party rang out, and Mr Whitlock thought it best to re-embark; nor did he stay upon the order of his going.

On Mr Whitlock's return claims began to be made that Anguilla was in the hands of the Mafia. Mr Whitlock's own later gloss on the claims about the Mafia presence was the statement, referring to some of those close to President Webster, that

'We have no proof that in fact they are members of the Mafia, but the general feeling throughout the Caribbean is that they are somewhat like Mafia characters.'

From fully paid-up *Mafiosi* to people thought by a carefully undefined general feeling on the part of no less carefully unspecified persons to be somewhat like Mafia characters is a long step, but by the time it was taken Mr Wilson had cried havoc and let slip the dogs of war. In the utmost operational secrecy, the only chink in which was caused by prominent announcements on the front pages of every national newspaper and in all radio and television news bulletins, two companies of the Parachute Regiment were made ready to leave for Anguilla, accompanied by a substantial detachment of policemen; the inclusion of these last was said by scofflaws and ribalds to be due to the fact that Mr Wilson had been as badly informed about the traffic conditions on the virtually roadless island as he had about its defensive potentialities.

Matters were not helped by the calling in of the Chiefs of Staff for the planning of Operation Sheepskin (as, with devastating candour, it was called), their participation being for a short time thought by some imaginative people to indicate an imminent nuclear attack. Anyway, with fanfares of secrecy and under cover of a blaze of darkness, the great armada left for the Caribbean, and some days later, under a withering fire of curious stares from the bewildered and wholly unarmed islanders, charged heroically up the beach, the effect of so magnificent an action being very slightly diminished by the fact that the first boat to reach land was the one containing the Independent Television News camera-crew. However, nobody can be in any doubt that, if there had been any resistance, the British troops would have behaved with the courage rightly expected of them by any who knew of the glorious pages written by British arms throughout history, and it can scarcely be held against the troops themselves that they were greeted, not by bombs and bullets, but by a number of native ladies. At first it seemed that their haste to see the fun had been such that they had not even stopped to remove their curlers, and were consequently photographed fraternizing *en déshabille*, no doubt to the great displeasure of their more old-fashioned relatives; it subsequently transpired, however, that this was a normal, and indeed fashionable, mode of dress in that part of the world. Having landed the troops there, Generalissimo Wilson began to learn the bitter lesson that comes to all military adventurers sooner or later: that, in Napoleon's words, you can do anything with a bayonet except sit on it. While the Government hastily sought reasons for having sent in the troops, and further reasons for keeping them there, they announced that the Anguillans would in no circumstances be returned against their will to the dominion of the Kittitians. At this the purpose of the operation became even more obscure, as the sole reason for the trouble on the island, which had led to the invasion, was the reluctance of the Anguillans to suffer Kittitian rule, so that it could be, and was, asked why it had been necessary to send armed forces to put down a rebellion the object of which the armed force was promptly pledged to uphold. But to this question the Government made no reply.

With this we may leave the subject of the War of Whitlock's Nerves, though perhaps not before remembering that ancient Jewish joke about the young man who is for ever strutting about in a peaked cap and a smart blazer with silver buttons, calling out 'Splice the mainbrace!' and 'Abaft the binnacles!' and similar nautical expressions, until somebody says to him: 'To your mother you're a captain, and to your father you're a captain; but to a captain are you a captain?'

# 14

## Heard great argument

In the circumstances it was not surprising that prophets of doom abounded, numerous as weeds in a graveyard and about as cheerful. Imperial sunsets burned in a thousand lowering skies; declines and falls flowed, avalanche-like, by; the nation, having been threatened with murder often enough, was now warned of suicide; 'her God forgotten, and her history', she

> was reeling then at the height of her dissolute triumphs ... Today, clung round by demons, a hand over one eye, with the other staring into horrors, down she flings from despair to despair. When will she reach the bottom of the abyss? When, out of uttermost hopelessness – a miracle beyond the power of belief – will the light of hope dawn?[1]

Never, said some – like James Barlow, writer of thrillers, who sat out the Sixties in growing horror and, as they ended, departed these shores for those of Tasmania, where the apples come from, never to return. *Goodbye, England*[2] he called his farewell, and a regular soldier's farewell it was, too. Debauched by lechery – 'a working-class boy expected his girls to have sexual intercourse (often standing up)' – England was doomed all right, ripe for seizure by the Communists, who had already taken over the press (as was shown by the papers' failure to print Mr Barlow's letters in support of Mr Ian Smith and the Rhodesian U.D.I.), the B.B.C. and even Parliament. The impending disaster had its effect as

[1] Thomas Mann, *Doctor Faustus*, translated by H. T. Lowe-Porter (Secker and Warburg, London, 1949), Epilogue, p. 510.

[2] Hamish Hamilton, London, 1969.

cause, too, and many a girl was to be seen walking down the King's Road 'in a topless dress, collecting dust and flies and bits of bus tickets on her breasts'. In Tasmania, it seems, boys are 'still *shy* and nervous about meeting girls', even, it seems, girls whose breasts are free of dust, flies and bus tickets, and who are entirely unwilling to have sexual intercourse standing up.

Mr Barlow galloped off furiously in all directions; but even those who would never seek to sweep the bus tickets off a lady's breasts went as far in their own particular direction. Dr Paul Einzig, for instance, whose name in German means 'unique', and no wonder, came to the conclusion in his *Decline and Fall?*[1] that it was all the fault of the working classes, who would not work. *Why* they would not work was simple, too: the Welfare State had sapped their initiative, rotted their moral fibre, kept them from cradle to grave and generally been their ruin. Thus, in the late Forties, when the Welfare State was being constructed, the Housewives' League and Sir Herbert Williams and their like had warned the nation of the dangers of making the poor too comfortable, and many a jeer was heard at the expense of those whose horizon was bounded by free spectacles, free wigs, and free false teeth; sometimes it had seemed as though the poor should go bald and blind, and mump their slops with toothless gums, in order that their ancient, sturdy virtues might be retained.

The warnings, in those days, had not been heeded, and now, it seemed, twenty years later, the chickens–bewigged, bespectacled and betoothed–were coming home to roost.

> For many years after the initiation of the Welfare State there were daily S.O.S. messages broadcast by the B.B.C. –indeed sometimes there were several of them before each news bulletin–calling on Mr or Mrs So-and-So, last heard of in some working-class district a number of years ago, to contact such and such a hospital where their father or mother was dangerously ill. Presumably in the

[1] Macmillan, London, and Macmillan Co. of Canada, Toronto, 1969.

majority of such cases the sons or daughters, having moved from their former residences, had severed all connections with their old parents, and had not even sent Christmas cards with their new addresses, just in case they might be asked for financial help which would be awkward to refuse. That wouldn't do at all, to meet such appeals. If they relieved their parents' misery they might not be able to afford the washing machine or the more expensive T.V. set on the possession of which they had set their hearts. Let the old folk live on their pension the best way they can. Such S.O.S. messages have been much less frequent in recent years and it is to be hoped that the decline in their frequency means that in this respect at any rate the demoralizing effect of the Welfare State on family ties has been wearing off during the last few years.[1]

But the Barlows and the Einzigs, though they went further than most, as far, indeed, as the land where gingerbread houses were as common as real ones, only went *further*; many, though they stopped well short of such strange country, still poured grave warnings into heedless ears.

Throughout the decade the books poured out, warning and recommending, exhorting and condemning, admonishing and insisting, telling us what we must do to be saved and informing us that the end was nigh, in some cases that the end was nigh even if we did what we must to be saved. Mr Max Nicholson told us what was wrong with *The System*,[2] Mr Samuel Brittan insisted that *Left or Right* was a *Bogus Dilemma*,[3] Anthony Sampson analysed the *Anatomy of Britain*,[4] and a group of writers, under the direction of Arthur Koestler, asked whether what they were seeing before their eyes was *Suicide of a Nation?*[5] With the question-mark a nice dilemma posed itself; if the nation survived,

[1] Op. cit., pp. 120–21.
[2] Hodder and Stoughton, London, 1967.
[3] Secker and Warburg, London, 1968.
[4] Hodder and Stoughton, London, 1962.
[5] Hutchinson, London, 1963.

the question-mark was the proof that the possibility of its survival had always been in the editor's and contributors' minds; if it did not, then with any luck its writhings, after swallowing the fatal dose, would be insufficiently prolonged for further editions to be called for, and even if these went on almost indefinitely, they could be put forth without the punctuation. As the decade ended the death-throes still seemed to be going on, and showed every sign of doing so for another decade at least; on the other hand, no further edition had been called for, so that honours were more or less even between words and question-mark.

This symposium of dissolution was dressed for its book-form publication in a dust-jacket bearing a parody of the royal coat of arms, the lion old, bloodshot and docile, and the unicorn replaced entirely by an ostrich with its head buried in the sand (the erroneous belief that ostriches practise this conveniently metaphorical behaviour being a myth as incradicable, in the minds of British writers, as the equally baseless belief that lemmings rush down to the sea and deliberately drown themselves); the colours in which the jacket was tricked out were a particularly cruel parody of red, white and blue, consisting of a central band of white flanked by a strip of the palest, most faded blue, and a bilious, bloodless pink.

Inside, awful diagnoses rubbed shoulders with even more awful prescriptions. Goronwy Rees deplored the amateur quality of British business managers; Michael Shanks deplored no less the low annual growth-rate of British industry; Andrew Shonfield deplored most of all upper-class manners and the inefficiency to which they led. Cyril Connolly looked back on the decline of the Empire, and supposed that television is 'the greatest single factor for change in people's lives'; Alan McGlashan put it all down to sexual repression at English public schools; Elizabeth Young put it down to the public schools in general. (Alas, regardless of their doom, the little victims played. Despite the looming disaster, rising incomes for most kept pace, and more than pace, with rising prices; woe to him who lived on fixed earnings, who had no cost-of-living bonus, an increase in whose pension was never quite opportune. But to the rest, no woe; weal, rather, and much of it. The line was drawn at the average income, and to earn more than the average, to be above the line, was the goal of all, as, in another field, the line was the *Financial Times* Index of stock exchange share-values, and no share, no unit in a unit trust, was worth looking at unless it showed that it could consistently 'beat the index', that is, increase in value faster than the average share. How could all incomes, all shares, rise faster than the average, how could the index be beaten by every wage-earner and every investor? This arithmetical philosophers' stone was sought eagerly, and for many it seemed that it had been found, while those whose incomes had to lag further and further behind in order that there should be sufficient numbers earning more than the average were the first to realize that King Lear was right when he said that nothing will come of nothing.)

* * *

There were also, of course, the books by those who had themselves been participants in the events on which they commented. Early in the decade the memoirs of Lord Avon, who in the Fifties had, as Sir Anthony Eden, briefly and ingloriously been Prime Minister, were published under the title *Full Circle*[1] and serialized in *The Times*. Implacably unreadable, they were designed to justify his handling of the 'Suez Affair', and to brand all those who had disputed Britain's role at the time, or who had failed to give him the support he felt was his due, as unworthy opponents, treacherous colleagues or uncomprehending foreigners, a task which, understandably, proved to be beyond his powers, though connoisseurs of political malice relished his summing-up of the part played in the affair by Macmillan, of whom he said, without naming him but with the utmost exactitude: 'There are always weak sisters in any crisis, and sometimes they will be found among those who were toughest at the outset of the journey'; while connoisseurs of political and indeed literary naivety relished

[1] Cassell, London, 1960.

no less his mournful admission that 'We were not successful in our wider objective; we did not bring about Arab-Israeli peace.' The book, when published, was received with the kind of embarrassed hush that follows a tasteless reference to one lately dead, and fell like a stone into a limitless sea of public indifference.

But the most remarkable volume of British political memoirs to be published in the Sixties was the slimmest and least remarked upon. To start with, it was remarkable because every word of it was clearly written by the author. Not for him the help of ghosts or devils, gratefully acknowledged or carefully concealed, or of researchers or of those without whom the book could never have been written; it was plain (in both senses of the word) that Reginald Bevins had written *The Greasy Pole*[1] unaided. *Ars est celare artem*; if so, Bevins was an artist of rare stature, for his book is artless (also in both senses of the word) to a degree which suggests that it was written at a single sitting, published in haste, and repented, if at all, only at leisure.

The memoirs of the fallen rarely make comfortable reading, especially if they fell because they were pushed; such documents are read with least comfort by those who did the pushing. The peculiarly gamy flavour of the political memoirs of Lord Kilmuir, for instance, came from the fact that he seemed concerned not only to demonstrate that Harold Macmillan had been wrong to sack him – the prevailing view, which was that he had been abundantly right to do so, and could be faulted only for delaying the dismissal for so long, could hardly have been expected to commend itself to the victim – but to damage Macmillan's reputation to the utmost extent for his unforgivably foolish disposal of so admirable, hard-working, efficient and loyal a colleague. In the event, of course, the reputation that was damaged was that of Kilmuir, and the prevailing view shifted still further, from surprise that he had lasted so long in the seats of the mighty to astonishment that he had ever been allowed to sit in them.

Bevins escaped this fate, though his book was a sustained cry of rage and pain at the monstrous treatment the Conservative Party

[1] Hodder and Stoughton, London, 1965.

had meted out to him, because his complaints, though no less subjective in origin than Kilmuir's, were so obviously not designed to bring in the petty harvest of revenge. What they *were* designed to do, though they failed to reap this harvest either, was to steer the Tory Party away from the paths of expediency and sin, and back into the paths of duty and righteousness. 'My prediction', said Bevins, 'is that Christopher Soames will be the next leader of the Tory Party if the Party runs true to form'; he had the embarrassing experience of seeing Edward Heath elected the next leader of the Tory Party exactly six weeks after the publication of his book. But the burden of his words was twofold; the first strand was best put in this pungent comment on the choice, as the previous Tory leader, of Sir Alec Douglas-Home:

> The message that has gone out to the world is that in 1963 the Government party in Britain selects its leader and the country's Prime Minister through the machinery of an aristocratic cabal. In this ruthlessly competitive, scientific, technical, industrial age, a week of intrigues has produced a result based on family and hereditary connexions. The leader has emerged – an elegant anachronism.

These words were spoken, as a matter of fact, by Harold Wilson, not by Bevins; but the sentiments were undoubtedly those of Bevins too, for his railing at the leaders of the Tory Party, though it lacked the rhythm and shape of Wilson's, was based on the same charge, that it was dominated by a magic circle of Etonians and landed gentry; nor are these political clichés clichés only, for Bevins used both, quite specifically, in his horror at what was happening to his party, saying: 'A Party ... led predominantly by a group of Old Etonians ... makes a bad joke of democracy'; and, of a week-end at Chequers: 'Only Ernest Marples and I were without landed estates, Ernest because he had no use for one and I because it was beyond me.'

The other principal theme of Bevins's book was the charge that the Tory leadership was too ready to give way before any pressure that was sufficiently strong, regardless of where the right might lie. In this, as in much else, he showed himself naive, at any rate for one who had served under Harold Macmillan, perhaps the greatest master in recent years of the policy of recognizing that, if politics is the art of the possible, it must also consist, to a considerable extent, of knowing when to bow to the inevitable, before which household god Macmillan, particularly in the later years of his Premiership, had been known to bow with increasing frequency and promptitude.

But Bevins had voiced aloud and for publication sentiments which have always, where the Tory Party is concerned, been spoken behind the hand and in private. The whole basis of the party's composition and social attitudes on the one hand, and approach to the realities of political life on the other, came under attack in his book, which was virtually an invitation to the party to repudiate both its leadership and its policies. In the circumstances the claim on the very first page of his book, to the effect that 'I am not finished yet by a long chalk', must be regarded as unduly optimistic.

The torrent of political memoirs and critiques followed a similar torrent, which had poured a little earlier, of military memoirs and analyses. The memoirs were of the same kind in both cases; almost every one was the author's *apologia pro vita sua*, and not very apologetic either. For every Macmillan, Kilmuir, Hill, Eden, Griffiths, Mosley, stridently proclaiming that he had never been wrong on any major question of policy, and insisting, like a cartoon-businessman telling his secretary that his wife doesn't understand him, that it was only his colleagues' obstinacy, cowardice, lack of vision or ignorance of his own worth that prevented him from settling all his party's and country's problems, there had been a corresponding military commander to insist that he never lost a battle except through the incompetence of his superiors or subordinates or both, and that if only the strategy and tactics had been left entirely to him the Second World War would have been over by Christmas, and Christmas 1938 at that.

But there was an important difference between the work of the political *analysts* and that of the military ones. The political ones –

Ronald Butt,[1] Samuel Brittan,[2] Bernard Crick,[3] Henry Fairlie,[4] Ian Gilmour,[5] Max Nicholson[6] – argued that there was something wrong with the structure and operation of the political system in Britain. On what it was that was wrong, and what ought to be done about it, no two analysts agreed, while many vigorously contradicted and condemned the rival theories of some or even all of their fellows and found their books being very unfavourably reviewed by those very fellows in consequence. But all were agreed that the present state of affairs was unsatisfactory, and that by examining that state of affairs, and making recommendations as to how it might be improved, we might yet be saved, provided of course that the obstinacy, cowardice and lack of vision, which was unfortunately the chief characteristic of those in a position to put the recommendations into effect, could be got over – a thesis which suggested that the analysts, if they ever moved into the seats of power themselves, might prove as convinced of their own invariable sagacity and rectitude as any of those who had previously occupied such seats.

No such opportunity was given to the military commentators. It was, after all, scarcely possible for a stream of fat books, or even for a few slim ones, to be produced on the lamentable state of our armed forces, their structure, command and performance, together with recommendations for their reorganization and improvement. The commentators, analysts and historians therefore had to be content with the past. It seemed as though there was no battle or campaign in either World War that could not be mined for its ore of drama and the precious metal of hindsight that, after the appropriate smelting processes had taken place in the mind of the author, the ore could be shown to contain. With the exception of John Terraine, who set himself, with almost admirable perversity, to the hopeless task of refurbishing the devastated reputation

[1] *The Power of Parliament* (Constable, London, 1967).
[2] Op. cit.
[3] *The Reform of Parliament* (Weidenfeld and Nicolson, London, 1964).
[4] *The Life of Politics* (Methuen, London, 1968).
[5] *The Body Politic* (Hutchinson, London, 1969).
[6] Op. cit.

of Haig, and succeeded only in revealing that Haig was in fact worse than he had been previously thought even by his most implacable enemies, most of the younger school of military historians – Corelli Barnett, Alistair Horne, Alan Clark – after sitting at the feet of the father of them all, Liddell Hart, had come firmly, and not surprisingly, to the conclusion that the British troops in the First World War were what Ludendorff had called them, that is, 'lions led by donkeys', one of them, indeed, calling his study of the leaders *The Donkeys*[1] to put his view of the matter beyond doubt.

When they turned their attention to the Second World War there was less unanimity, but their varying views were nevertheless made to yield a rich crop of old, unhappy, far-off things, so that at times it seemed that no battle had ever been won except by the blunders of the generals of the enemy, and then only because their blunders were greater than those of the generals of our side, a thesis which anybody who had read any military history, other than that written by the commanders themselves, could readily believe. But the point was that throughout the military books there ran a thread of unmistakeable nostalgia that was almost wholly lacking in the political books. Nor was this an accident, or a reflection of a difference in temperament between political and military critics; it was, rather, an indication of a growing conviction that the traditional war of the past would never come again between evenly matched major powers, because nuclear weapons had so transformed the military situation that future wars, even if they did not involve the use of such arms, would be conditioned by the fact that they existed. By a bizarre accident, the Second World War had become 'the war to end war' – to end, that is, both the war of attrition and the war of the Blitzkrieg. There had been exceptions, of course, even to this rule; the Vietnam war was a war of attrition, the Arab-Israeli war of June 1967 was a war of Blitzkrieg, and the Korean war was both. But the last great pitched battle, the last battle which could and did have books written about it, was Dien Bien Phu, which ended the

[1] Alan Clark (Hutchinson, London, 1961).

French involvement in South-East Asia and began the American. So the military men in the Sixties wrote about the battles of the past in the belief that they would never have an opportunity to write about the battles of the future, and the battles of the future became part of the province, not of military analysts and commentators, but of the scientists, the computers, the simulators, the exponents of game-theory, and ultimately of a genial and alarming creature from the outer space of an I.Q. of over 200, Dr Herman Kahn, who thought unthinkable thoughts about nuclear war, and not only thought them but published them, only to find himself portrayed, in a unique reversal of the normal technique of the caricaturist, as much *smaller* than life, under the name and title of Doctor Strangelove.

# 15

## To the barricades!

Not long before the decade began, the play[1] which more than any other announced a new kind of attitude, a new kind of drama, even a new kind of actor, had given the language of politics and sociology a new phrase. 'There aren't any big, brave causes left,' John Osborne's Jimmy Porter had said, contrasting his own lack of hope and belief with the zeal of his father's generation, when the Spanish Civil War was the biggest and bravest cause of them all. What was there now, the argument ran, in its place? To what mast could idealists nail their colours? What cause could inspire the idealism, the self-sacrifice, the double standards, the betrayal, that the Spanish war had provided in such generous measure? None, none.

Less than half a decade later the Sixties were upon us, and although Jimmy Porter's famous dictum went on being quoted for some time – in some quarters, all through the decade – no slogan has ever been so entirely falsified so quickly. In the Sixties, indeed, there were so many big brave causes that disillusion (the ultimate repository of all hopes for all such causes) rarely had time to set in properly over one cause before a new fashion in causes had sprung up, to be eagerly embraced in its turn, and many an intellectual digestion was ruined by the variety of the dishes and the huge size of the portions.

The decade was littered, from beginning to end, with Causes. The first of the decade was one of the strangest and most tragic, though the stir it caused in Britain was nothing much by the later standards of the Sixties. Amid preparations for the end of the Empire, the Congo loomed as an awful warning, though there

[1] *Look Back in Anger.*

were two distinctly opposed views as to what it was an awful warning of. The Belgian colonial empire, one of the worst of modern satrapies, had stood like an oak against the gathering storm. Then, at the very beginning of the decade, the mighty oak had shrunk to a sapling almost overnight. The Belgian authorities changed during a period of a few weeks from an attitude of uncompromising refusal to countenance a hand-over of power to one of precipitate surrender of it. Immediately before the change of policy Belgium had been considering thirty years as the appropriate length of time needed to bring the Africans of the Congo to a condition suitable for independence; abruptly, thirty years became six months, and in conditions of carefully fostered chaos power was handed over to a hastily assembled group of Africans. Complete collapse followed. A recrudescence of tribalism, savagery of every kind, the breakdown of all normal facilities, bitter struggles between rival groups and rival leaders—in an extraordinarily short time, the shortness of which exemplified, according to taste, either the unfitness of Africans to govern themselves or the unfitness of the Belgians to govern others, the Congo had broken down so completely that the Belgians fled from the task of restoring order as precipitately as they had run away from that of continuing to uphold it. Various battling factions arose, and an attempt was made to separate one of the provinces of the Congo (Katanga) and establish it as a separate State. It was then that Dr Conor Cruise O'Brien made his first appearance on a world stage as United Nations representative in the area, determined to crush the Katanga breakaway. (O'Brien was a fascinating figure, very much a man of the decade. After the Congo he turned up in Nkrumah's corrupt and despotic Ghana, which he left in plenty of time to maintain his undoubted innocence of complicity in Nkrumah's dictatorship, and then in New York, where he was soon to be seen participating in university troubles, protesting vigorously against the United States Vietnam policy, and again leaving, this time for his native Ireland, long before the tear-gas and bullets began to fly on American campuses. Later still he decided to give his own people the fruits of this wide experience of political affairs, and stood for the Dail in, so to speak, the Labour interest; he was returned easily, though the Labour Party as a whole did poorly, and he was soon being spoken of as a future Prime Minister of the Irish Republic. Indeed, there was no telling where this most agile of rope-dancers might turn up next, or in what guise.)

Atrocity stories began to seep out of the Congo, as is usual in such situations, and—as is no less usual—gangsters of various kinds began to arrive there, calling themselves 'mercenaries', selling their services to the highest bidder and being frequently portrayed in Britain as heroes saving civilization from its enemies. Eventually the Congo calmed down. Only the kidnapping, two-thirds of the way through the decade, of Moise Tshombe (who, after the failure of his Katanga revolt, had fled, then returned in triumph as head of the whole country, and was later ousted from that position and forced to flee again) and his incarceration, followed by his death in an Algerian prison, served to remind the outside world of the extraordinary, tragic and pitiful story that had so aroused its conscience at the beginning of the Sixties. Perhaps the most practical view of the whole tangled story was that of the B.B.C. television representative, real or apocryphal, who was said to have stepped off the aeroplane at Elizabethville airport into a scene of appalling horror, with refugees, desperate to get out, milling hopelessly around, and who, mindful both of the atrocity stories and of what would make good television, went briskly down the line of ashen, numbed and silent women crying: 'Anybody here been raped and speaks English? Anybody here been raped and speaks English? Anybody here been raped and speaks English?'

It was the first of the events of the Sixties to provide a cause for indignation in Britain. But the earlier years of the decade, and their strange atmosphere, were difficult to recall by its end, so rapid and complete had been the changes in between. Even the Cuba missile crisis of 1962 seemed very far off. Yet during the crucial days, when many seriously believed that the world was on the brink of a war of annihilation, and some of the leading campaigners for nuclear disarmament fled to Ireland in the belief that they would there stand a better chance of survival, observers from elsewhere might have concluded that the country had lost its senses entirely. Such a conclusion would have been mistaken; but there was much to support it, if the observers had judged by the agitation of those who, in some cases, were demonstrating, in the name of the Campaign for Nuclear Disarmament, for Cuba's right to have nuclear missiles upon her territory. As the tense hours went by, the excitement, at any rate among the excited, grew more and more feverish. Mass marches, mass Trafalgar Square demonstrations, were planned, and amazement was expressed, in the usual circles, at anyone dissenting from the prevailing view that the Americans were wholly to blame for the crisis and the Cuban and Russian Governments not only innocent but admirable; it may, indeed, have been the first mass-organized anti-American episode of the Sixties.

* * *

As Britain, ever more rapidly throughout the Sixties, lost her former power and influence, so the vigour and vociferousness with which she told others what to do increased. 'He who can, does. He who cannot, teaches.' Britain, in the Sixties, had no wars to fight, no hunger to sustain, no national shame to face, no decisions to make except her own. In the circumstances it was natural that all her phlegm and self-control in the face of other people's misfortunes (Czechoslovakia, for instance) should combine with all her self-righteousness in the face of other people's difficulties (America's race problems, for instance). The Bomb, Cuba, Vietnam, the Congo, Biafra—all these and a dozen more provided ample opportunity for the exercise of both.

The greatest, or certainly the noisiest, cause of the entire decade—noisier, indeed, than any cause since the end of the Second World War—was, of course, Vietnam. Under the Vietnam umbrella there sheltered from the hard rain of the cruel world's reality a wider variety of groups and individuals than even the

Campaign for Nuclear Disarmament had brought together beneath the ample cassock provided by the extra-canonical activities of the Reverend John Collins. Pacifists and military strategists, Christians and atheists, wise men and fools, honest men and knaves, Stalinists and Trotskyists, these and dozens of other varieties of *homo protestans* all came together in the Sixties, in every corner of the free world, to declare that it was wrong for the Americans to seek to prevent the Communists of North Vietnam from engulfing the territory of South Vietnam, and in many cases that it was also wrong for the Government and people of South Vietnam to seek to prevent themselves from being thus engulfed.

It was like E. M. Forster's description of the Fifth Symphony of Beethoven: 'All sorts and conditions are satisfied by it ... the passion of your life becomes more vivid, and you are bound to admit that such a noise is cheap at two shillings.' Moreover, making a noise about Vietnam was free.

At least it was free in Britain – free, that is, of the risks attendant upon the Vietnam War in the United States, which included the ultimate risk of being called up to fight in it. In Britain, however, no such danger threatened, and full rein could therefore be given, without qualms or backward glances, to the passion, which seized Britons in the Sixties in quantities, and at an intensity, never previously attained, for calling the tune while others paid the piper.

In the United States – and also in Japan and West Germany and other countries with rather more robust methods of combating disorder – there was the additional danger that those who took to the streets in protest against the American action in Vietnam might end up lying in the gutters with a truncheon-fractured skull. In Britain the rather smaller risk of this unpleasant outcome of an afternoon's marching was underlined by a scene recorded in Grosvenor Square, in which stood the American Embassy and which was therefore the target several times of the demonstrators. On this occasion a police cordon had been drawn up to prevent the demonstrators getting to the embassy itself; against the plump blue line the protesters heaved and pushed in vain. One such heaver and pusher, seeking a pause in which to get his second wind, decided to smoke a cigarette while in the thick of the imbroglio. To his horror he found that, so thick was the press of his comrades round him, and so firm the pressure from more of them behind him, propelling him inexorably against the police cordon every time he attempted to retire, that, having got his cigarette between his lips, he was unable, try as he might, to get his arm down again to the pocket in which he kept his matches. A police officer, patrolling behind the police line ready to spring into any breach that might appear, saw the predicament in which the demonstrator had found himself. 'Allow me,' said the gallant policeman, holding out a lighter over the linked arms of his fellows. The demonstrator lit up and inhaled; history, alas, careless as ever of the interests of those who come after, does not record whether he said 'Thank you.'

But if there was no danger, in Britain, of the Vietnam demonstrators having to *do* anything about Vietnam, and hardly any danger of their having anything *done to* them, it may be thought therefore that the entire movement was an exercise in mingled smugness and hypocrisy, and no more deeply felt by the participants than the realization – profoundly uncomfortable for those who permitted it to enter their consciousness at all – that it was only the willingness of the Americans to expend themselves in others' quarrels that made it possible for demonstrations to take place in the streets of Britain at all. This, however, would be to do many of those who felt most strongly about Vietnam a grave injustice. It is true that for many of them it *was* an exercise in smugness and hypocrisy; just as it is also true that the anti-American Vietnam protest movement throughout the Sixties was fostered, largely led, and to a considerable extent controlled, by Communists or Communist sympathizers, but this alone does not explain its widespread attraction, as the same could have been said about many another cause which did not attract a twentieth part of the support that this one did.

Vietnam touched a feeling that, in the Sixties, was exposed and vulnerable as never before. The feeling was like that which is said to overcome travellers lost in the snow: a desperate desire to lie down and sleep, though such a course of action must inevitably result in death. In the Sixties, in Britain, many—millions, possibly—found literally unbearable the thought that the world was the way it was; in particular, the reality of aggression simply could not be faced. In very different circumstances, thirty years before, a similar reality had been fled from, and for very different reasons; this time it was for the best of motives. The world *could not* be like that; the cup of cruelty, of war, of the subjection of peoples, had been filled again and again to overflowing, and just as there are some poor folk who, starting with the natural and indeed almost universal reluctance to get up and go to work, finally come to believe that there is no need to, as they have managed to put the sun out and day will never come, so there were many in Britain, and in full possession of their senses too, or at any rate of most of their senses, who started with the natural and indeed almost universal wish that Communist aggression would cease to exist and ended with the conviction that it had obliged them, and no longer did.

If, then, Communist aggression did not exist, it followed that, in the Vietnam conflict, the aggression must be entirely on the part of the Americans. Such facts as the desperate desire of the Americans to get out of the Vietnamese quagmire, and their even more desperate wish that they had never got into it in the first place, were unable to disturb the symmetry of the syllogism, and the streets of Britain continued to echo to cries of 'Americans out of Vietnam!' and the ritual chanting of 'Ho-ho-ho Chi Minh!' (one of the many mass murderers whose worship has, over the years, become fashionable and even obligatory in countries where mass murder is usually disapproved of and rarely if ever practised).

Yet the inspiration for many of the protesters, young as well as middle-aged and old, was far from base. It is not bad, but good, to think well of one's fellow-men, and although it is true that many even of the most idealistic protesters spent so much time and emotional energy loving their enemies that they could spare nothing but hate for their friends, it is also true that there is nothing ignoble in loving one's enemies.

Nothing ignoble; but much that is dangerous. In the end, the waves of protest in Britain over Vietnam broke and spent themselves as the waves of appeasement had broken and spent themselves in the Thirties: on the twin, jagged rocks of reality and of the common sense of the mass of the people. However large the Vietnam movement became, it never became a mass movement involving substantial proportions of all segments of society. And it failed to do so because something so hard that not even the bitter solvents of the Sixties could affect it remained at the core of the mass public consciousness: the realization that aggression *was* real, and that the soft answer did *not* turn away wrath. Long before the end of the decade the Vietnam protest movement in Britain had passed its peak, and in the last months of the Sixties a demonstration in the same cause, and led by the same people, as had only two years previously brought some fifteen thousand marchers on to the streets of London, could produce only a few hundreds.

It was over. The warm, comfortable feeling of gratuitous virtue that came from marching about the streets, collecting signatures on petitions, writing to the newspapers or appearing on B.B.C. television to denounce the Americans began to fade, and those whose joy it had been to experience it found that they no longer got the old kick from their accustomed dose, and began to crave a stronger, or at any rate different, stimulus.

This was provided, very happily, by the civil war in Nigeria, where Colonel (soon to promote himself to General) Ojukwu joined the ranks of those who could do no wrong and his cause was elevated to the status of a full crusade, aided by the activities of a public relations firm called Markpress, which patiently and skilfully set about selling the idea of gallant and embattled Biafra struggling for her freedom and indeed survival against the barbarous and genocidal hordes of Federal Nigeria.

The fact that Ojukwu's case was largely spurious made no difference; a savage and bloody war was undoubtedly going on, and appalling hardship and suffering were undoubtedly being experienced by the people of Biafra, many thousands, even hundreds of thousands, dying of their privations, quite apart from those who died by military action. Britain, France and Russia worked assiduously in their own interests, while proclaiming that their sole concern was the protection of the interests of all Nigerians. (A good deal of peripheral and melancholy pleasure was provided by the sight of Dr Conor Cruise O'Brien, who had espoused Biafra's cause, endeavouring to explain why secession from an African state had been, and remained, entirely reprehensible in the case of the Katangese, whose forcible retention in the Congo he had striven so hard to promote, but became admirable and even essential in the case of the Biafrans.)

* * *

But whenever, and it was rarely, a real cause involving Britain directly was discovered, the rejoicing was great among the devotees of causes. These discovered, late in the decade, a group deprived of elementary political rights, while the group itself discovered to its own astonishment and satisfaction that its plight, which had existed unchanged for over forty years, was a matter of concern to others. What happy combination of circumstances ensured that Ulster, of all places, should at the very end of the Sixties figure thus in a United Kingdom *cause célèbre* it is impossible to determine. But that the decade should have revealed a group of British subjects, in Britain, deprived of the vote itself, that twentieth-century cure-all, emphasized the symbiosis of the decade, which at the same time could show groups arguing that the vote was nothing but a bourgeois trick to deceive the wage-slaves into thinking that they were masters of their own destiny, and other groups plaintively demanding to have that which the more advanced thinkers were eager to be rid of.

The vote in question was for the local government franchise in the six counties of Northern Ireland, which had, ever since the formal partition of Ireland in 1923, been gerrymandered by the overwhelmingly Protestant ascendancy to prevent the large Roman Catholic minority achieving local rule, even in the areas (especially Londonderry) in which they were numerically in the majority. To that end, local government boundaries had been drawn and redrawn; other devices used to the same end included multiple voting, on a property or residential qualification, which, in almost Liberian fashion, enabled some of those who could be trusted to vote the right way to do so, quite legally, up to *forty* times in a single election, while others, deprived of homes of their own by the fact that new housing was allocated on a sectarian basis, found themselves without any vote at all in the same elections.

This state of affairs had continued for many years. From time to time there was some agitation in the Parliament at Westminster to put an end to the scandal, but Conservative Governments took the reasonable view that if they did so they might deprive themselves of the solid block of anything up to twelve pocket boroughs that they owned in Northern Ireland, which were always useful at election time and which, in a close-fought contest, might well decide the election, and Labour Governments took the different, but equally reasonable, line that there were no votes to be gained by them in the business, and they had quite enough trouble already without going out of their way to invite more.

Thus matters might have continued for ever, had it not been for the fact that the rumblings of discontent that were to be heard all over the world and in all communities and strata of society during the uneasy Sixties eventually reached Northern Ireland, which awoke from its ancient slumber with an abruptness that alarmed everybody concerned. Civil Rights groups sprang up overnight, and eventually, as was inevitable, violence ensued. Barriers were built across ancient Londonderry streets and from each side bricks, paving-stones and other missiles were flung, while groups marched and counter-marched. Some marched for votes and other rights for Catholics; others, particularly an extremist Protestant sect led by the Reverend Ian Paisley (later elected to the Northern Ireland Parliament and later still to the one at Westminster), to stop the Pope setting up stakes in every market-place at which to burn heretics, a practice which Mr

Paisley and his followers devoutly believed the Pope was still given to.[1]

The inevitable charges of police brutality followed, some of them being fully justified, and eventually the Prime Minister of Northern Ireland, Captain Terence O'Neill, was faced with the uninviting prospect of doing something to satisfy the demands of the minority without actually upsetting the feelings, and still less the power, of the majority. Matters were not made any easier for him by the fact that a number of members of his Cabinet, including the Deputy Prime Minister, Mr Brian Faulkner, had not for some time seemed eager to show their enthusiasm for Captain O'Neill; in the sudden flood of passion undammed by the Civil Rights campaign and the bigotry of Mr Paisley there was found an excellent opportunity to displace him. Eventually they succeeded in doing so.

But even before this there had been one development so spectacular and charming that not even the considerable disillusion in which it ended could prevent it from becoming one of the most memorable and characteristic political episodes of the entire decade. This was the election to the Westminster Parliament, in a hard-fought by-election for an Ulster constituency which had previously returned Unionist members with comfortable majorities, of one of the leaders of the student wing of the Civil Rights movement, Miss Bernadette Devlin. Herself a student at the time of the election, Miss Devlin became overnight indistinguishable, in the minds of many, from Joan of Arc, and when she took her seat at Westminster just in time to contribute, against all Westminster tradition, a fiery and uncompromising maiden speech in

[1] When the Pope's representative, in the person of the amiable Father Corbishley, was invited to preach in Westminster Abbey during the celebrations of that building's nine hundredth anniversary, Mr Paisley and a band of his followers attempted to disrupt the proceedings, and when, later on, Cardinal Heenan accepted an invitation to address an assembly of the faithful and ecumenical in St Paul's, there was fighting on the steps and even in the aisles, and the Archbishop of Canterbury was accused, both within and without, of being little better, if any, than a fifth-columnist, desirous of clamping the iron rule of Rome upon the necks of the Anglican Church.

a debate on the Northern Ireland situation, the effect on the House of Commons was astonishing to behold, many of its members writing her not just the customary polite note of congratulation, but multi-page letters. The House is not an exceptionally sophisticated place; but this could not alone account for Miss Devlin's reception, any more than her diminutive size (five feet and half an inch), her age (twenty-two) or her waif-like appearance. Nor could it have been her opinions, which were on the whole as silly as they were well-meaning. What enabled her to conquer the place was the fact that she was the first representative to be elected to Parliament, perhaps the first to the national legislature in any of the major democracies, of the younger generation's protest and revolt against conditions which they found materially adequate but spiritually impoverished. Most Members of Parliament had, quite literally, never met anybody like Miss Devlin before, nor heard, except filtered through the distorting trumpet of the newspapers and television and the clangorous echo-chamber of the young people's publicity-hunting leaders, any such voice, and when, a few months after her election, she entered the House wearing trousers, the place surrendered. Miss Devlin was soon reported to have had enough of politics and not to be seeking re-election, though if so she changed her mind and was triumphantly returned, going on almost at once to the traditional Irish martyrdom of imprisonment for the cause—an event which looked likely to precipitate something like civil war in the embattled province. But she had been the first to pass through a door that many had long clamoured to open, and the fact that the keepers of it hastened to fling it wide for her did not lessen the magnitude of her achievement.

Nor did it alter the fact that in Northern Ireland, as the Sixties ended, Mr Chichester-Clark, who had succeeded Captain O'Neill, looked no more likely than his predecessor to satisfy the irreconcilable claims of those who wanted full equality for the Catholic minority of Ulster and those who would not have it at any price.

* * *

Propaganda, in the Sixties, made no distinctions between continents. The tragic pictures of Biafran children with hunger-swollen bellies matched the no less tragic pictures of Vietnamese children with war-shattered limbs. But the Biafran tragedy, like the Vietnamese, illustrated again the vicarious nature of Britain's indignation in these ambiguous years. Both provided many good citizens with a feeling that, simply by making a noise in public, they had somehow contributed towards ending the war in Nigeria, or at least mitigating its horrors, just as they had earlier felt about the war in Vietnam, and still earlier about banning the use or even manufacture of the hydrogen bomb. 'Ban the Bomb!', 'Victory to the N.L.F.!', 'Hands off Biafra!' – the cries resounded through the air of the Sixties; and Vanessa, when she was not herself joining in the cries, smiled upon those who were.

None represented so clearly, so *representatively*, the glorious muddle into which the idealistic, the kind-hearted, the soft, the gentle, the generous-impulsed were apt to get in the Sixties as Vanessa Redgrave, who also represented, again with appalling fidelity, another and more specialized current of the decade, namely the transformation of the performing artist into a kind of oracle or sage, whose opinions on matters of politics, economics and international affairs were eagerly canvassed and solemnly recorded. And none threw herself so whole-heartedly into the bottomless pit of her own good-hearted confusion as Vanessa, whose ethereal, Excalibur-like beauty, combined with an astonishingly accomplished technique, had a memorable effect in a series of Shakespearean roles (Rosalind, Imogen, Katherina). Convinced that the Americans were responsible for all the wickedness in the world, Vanessa went about piping the pure, clear faith of the doctrine of the capitalist conspiracy to take over the world and starve its peoples into submission. Naturally her main interest was, in this respect, in the war in Vietnam, though from time to time she was found as the author, or at any rate signatory, of letters on such subjects as the conditions of the peasantry in Peru. In common with many gentle-hearted fanatics she soon became an almost more ardent partisan of the North

Vietnamese cause than the Communists themselves, and was to be seen at demonstrations wearing a pretty Vietnamese-style headband at the most becoming angle and calling, in her beautifully modulated voice, for total victory for the Vietcong.

But it was not only propaganda that worked, during the Sixties, wherever it felt there was work to do; and it was not only the muddle-headed who were stirred. There were organizations which catered for those who felt, in a rather more practical way, the altruistic desire to help the poor, the hungry and the hurt. Charities had, of course, always flourished in Britain, no country having more of them or supporting them more lavishly. But it was only during the Sixties that so many tens of millions of pounds were collected by such organizations as Oxfam and War on Want, and the more specialized agencies like Christian Action and the Save the Children Fund, to help the afflicted *in other countries*. This was a phenomenon decidedly to the credit of the decade, even if it was explicable or partly explicable in terms of the assuaging of consciences and the realization that Britain was now powerless to affect the course of world events by political action, let alone to disburse, in the form of Government foreign aid, such gigantic sums as those provided round the world by the United States; certainly it was *pari passu* with Britain's relieving herself of her imperial responsibilities, and with the shrinking of her ability to support those poorer than herself, that there arose a huge and virtually spontaneous mushroom of private generosity to take its place.

New fashions in political method, as in political causes, arose in the Sixties. The 'demo', as it had always been known in affectionate political terminology, used to be (in the Thirties, for instance, which were full of them) a homely, rough-cast affair, and even when it involved considerable violence it still seemed amateur, home-made and innocent. It was left to the Sixties to turn the humble *demo* into the proud and purposeful *demonstration* (the pet name being sternly eschewed by the Sixties demonstrators), designed not just to protest against wrong, nor even to bring down the Government, but to destroy society altogether, after which, presumably, the demonstrators would set about its reconstruction after a new and better plan.

In Britain the demonstrations succeeded in attracting many thousands of demonstrators, and to produce at any rate a good semblance of violence, directed for the most part against the American Embassy, and to a lesser extent—particularly outside London—against visiting politicians and other such figures held to be participating in activities, here and abroad, of which the demonstrators disapproved. But even demonstrations need leaders.

> I think that with twenty-five thousand people we should have been able to break through to the American Embassy and hold it against fearful odds. This would have given great encouragement to the freedom fighters in Vietnam. After it became apparent that we were not going to take the embassy we marched down Park Lane to take the next best symbol of American imperialism, the Hilton Hotel. But the police had wind of this and were standing six deep outside. Some of our supporters suggested we should storm the Bunny Club instead but during a brief discussion outside a number of demonstrators recalled that Hugh Hefner, owner of *Playboy* magazine, had taken a strong stand against the war.

By the end of the Sixties the speaker was instantly identifiable from the tone, with its air of wildly individual logic ('This would have given great encouragement to the freedom fighters in Vietnam'), its order of priorities ('the next best symbol of American imperialism, the Hilton Hotel') and its earnestness ('Some of our supporters suggested we should storm the Bunny Club, but ... Hugh Hefner, owner of *Playboy* magazine, had taken a strong stand against the war'). Many of Tariq Ali's boldest revolutionary statements had this escarpment-like shape, rising evenly and inexorably to a brave and uncompromising peak of fervour and then tumbling over the shorter side into bathos.

And yet for all his endearing absurdity, his passion for appearing on television and giving interviews to the newspapers, and his highly symbolic practice of invariably being photographed with his mouth open, this fiery and in many ways attractive young man did represent something more than the fact that he was having a hugely enjoyable time announcing, in that curiously lifeless prose that seems to be the medium of every generation of new revolutionaries, the imminent destruction of bourgeois society and its replacement by a new form of human and social organization which, though the details of it still remain unspecified, was to usher in heaven upon earth. Tariq Ali was denounced by more serious revolutionaries (or those who thought themselves more serious, which is not necessarily the same thing) and by those who disapproved of him and all his causes, but it was difficult to see what was wrong with ushering in heaven upon earth, apart from the difficulty of actually doing so, and it was noticeable that criticism of him did not usually concentrate upon this particular weakness in his argument. Despite an unfortunate difficulty in distinguishing reality from his own fantasies ('In Africa the Portuguese-controlled territories of Mozambique, Angola and Guinea are rapidly being taken over by native liberation movements'), his cheerful condonation of slaughter and atrocities committed by movements of which he fundamentally approved, his repeated announcements that he was shortly going back to live permanently in Pakistan, combined with his failure actually to do so, his bewilderment in the face of unwelcome truths that not even he could ignore ('It would be wrong to maintain that Scandinavia ... will necessarily experience a *high* level of unemployment and that this will pave the way to a socialist revolution') and his general air of being ever so slightly spurious, Tariq Ali, from the moment he sprang to national attention as President of the Oxford Union, represented for many, with some justice, the disaffection of youth – ignorant, confused and dishonest though much of it was – with a society that treated so many of its members unjustly.

It was not to be supposed that the unrest which, late in the decade, gripped much of the student body in the United States, France, Federal Germany and Italy (and to a lesser extent other countries) would leave British students wholly immune, nor did it, though as so often the student uprisings in Britain seemed a pale copy of those from whom the participants had got the idea. Nevertheless the movement reached Britain and before long was in full swing, with student 'occupations' at the Universities of Essex, Sussex and Bristol and the London School of Economics, at which last the only death so far to occur in the British student unrest was recorded early in the campaign (it was of a porter who had a weak heart but who nevertheless insisted on taking part in the defence of those parts of the school declared 'out of bounds' to the insurrectionaries, and which they were attempting to enter).

Since the conditions—of study, personal freedom, physical surroundings—were on the whole better in British universities than in those of most of the rest of the world, it could hardly be maintained that the revolutionaries were acting in protest against them—nor, to do the revolutionaries justice, did many maintain that they were. They claimed instead to be attempting to destroy the basis of society as it existed in Britain, and eventually a symposium of studies in the destruction of the basis of society was produced by Penguin Books, though it is safe to say that this could have influenced very few of the student revolutionaries, as a good deal of it seems concerned to show only how much more the authors know than the readers, and therefore consists of such improbable paragraphs as this:

> In their various ways Belinsky and Herzen, Chernyshevsky and Dobrolyubov, Gogol and Saltikov-Schedrin, Bakunin and Kropotkin, Tolstoy and Dostoievsky, Chekhov and Gorky, Tugan-Baranovsky and Plekhanov, Lunacharsky and Riazonov, together with a host of others too numerous to mention, all contributed to the cultural background of the Russian revolutionary.[1]

Thus also, the editors of the symposium may dream, may

[1] *Student Power*, Ed. Alexander Cockburn and Robin Blackburn (Penguin Books, Harmondsworth, 1969), Introduction, p. 16.

Adelstein and Anderson, Blackburn and Cockburn, Davidson and Fawthrop, Halliday and Stedman Jones, Nairn and Singh-Sandu, Tinkham and Triesman and Widgery be one day seen to have contributed to the cultural background of the British revolutionary, and some new editor of a new symposium may hope that he too will be taken to be familiar with the works of the authors whose names he so lavishly scatters on the page.

All the same, the absence of any coherent theoretical framework for the student revolution did not mean that it was any the less significant. A kind of contagious frenzy gripped many student bodies (student uprisings went in cycles, an explosion in one college triggering off similar explosions in a number of others, until that particular cycle had run its course). Worst hit was the London School of Economics, which was at one point closed entirely by the authorities, and from which a number of students and a junior lecturer were expelled for committing or approving acts of violence. Thus the ancient and erroneous popular belief of the L.S.E. as a breeding-ground for revolutionaries suddenly arose again with renewed vigour, and indignant tax-payers began once again to write to the *Daily Telegraph*, that last recourse of indignant tax-payers, to ask why they should keep these revolutionary louts in idleness. This view was also, more or less, expressed by the increasingly bizarre Minister of Education, Edward Short, who lurched through his tenure of that office, in the second half of the decade, in a series of sudden jerks, like a car being started in gear, at one moment denouncing the student protesters as 'thugs', at another screaming abuse at a publication which questioned some of the assumptions of progressive education, at yet another denouncing a suggestion by Lord Snow, that Jews might have more innate intelligence than other people, as reminiscent of Hitler and Goebbels, which had a fair claim to be the most remarkably ill-expressed point of the entire decade.

It soon seemed, however, that the student protest-movement had little mass backing, and that what it temporarily obtained in this respect was usually due to the clumsy way in which the authorities reacted. Lacking issues such as the Vietnam war or racial discrimination, which animated the American student revolt and involved many American citizens directly and almost all indirectly, the British movement found itself facing the traditionally apolitical mass of British university students, and as the decade ended it seemed that the movement, except perhaps for isolated incidents, was on the wane. In its brief career, though, it had shaken some of the traditional assumptions of university organization and method in Britain, so it can hardly be said to have achieved nothing, and the unread copies of *Student Power* further testified to the existence of a revolutionary spirit which, alas, had failed to move the mass of students to whom it was addressed.

The young, of course, had been getting out of hand for some time past, for at least as long as recorded history, which, as the recording had always been done by the grown-ups, had been in this respect one long catalogue of the crimes and follies of youth. In Britain, in the mid-Sixties of the twentieth century, a new wave of revolt broke out, a new clash between crabbed age and youth, which lay between the 'teddy boys' of the Fifties and the student revolts of the decade's end. Like all such movements there was no saying how they originated; one moment they were not, the next they were, and the passers-by had to shift for themselves as best they might. In 1964 there was a sudden rash of violent outbreaks among young people at a number of seaside towns, and a good deal of adult head-shaking in consequence, coupled with demands for the birch and other convenient remedies.

The young people in question were unfortunate in that they got caught up in the adults' longing, never so great as in the Sixties, for categories. This had started earlier with the classification into 'U' and 'Non-U' as a method of social distinction by speech-patterns—an investigation which almost immediately degenerated into a party game, played in the modish magazines, and followed by a long series of such classification-exercises, each less soundly based, and shorter-lived, than its immediate predecessor. 'In' and 'Out', 'Camp' and 'Non-camp', 'B' and 'Non-B' (in this last the distinction was between those who were, and those who were not, members of the 'broilerhouse society', in other words conformist and non-conformist) – these were among the categories, and since the lists of people and things were arbitrarily chosen and virtually interchangeable, the games were easily played. One of them that flourished briefly was 'Mods and Rockers', this being a supposed distinction between two classes of youth who might be told apart by their styles of dress (smart or casual), locomotion (scooters or motor-cycles) and entertainment (cinema or dance-hall). The violent outbreaks at Bournemouth, Brighton, Clacton, Margate and Hastings which took place during Bank Holiday week-ends in 1964, and resulted in one death, a substantial number of injuries, widespread arrests and convictions, and a newspaper and television jamboree of rare dimensions, were supposed to be clashes between the two groups, Mods and Rockers being, according to the theory, antithetical and bound to fight as soon as the critical mass was reached and an incident, generally a quarrel over girls, occurred to provoke the nuclear reaction. Newspapers, universities, social-help institutions and other interested bodies launched investigations into the phenomenon, which, whatever the degree of accuracy in the descriptions, had certainly resulted in the terrorization of the towns in question while the fighting, window-smashing and wrecking were going on, but no firm conclusions were ever come to, except – and it was a note which was to be heard more and more often as the decade wore on – that the participants were bored and their lives aimless, so that violence, particularly casual, unprovoked and purposeless violence, provided the necessary excitement and interest of which their lives were otherwise devoid.

Nevertheless the violence of the Mods and Rockers, and later of their successors in the violence-category game, Hell's Angels and Skinheads, and the argument to which it gave rise, were pointers to something far more serious, and which by the end of the Sixties was causing far deeper and wider concern: this was the apparent breakdown of the inarticulate premise on which societies such as Britain's rest, namely the acceptance, in the last resort, by all the members of it, of that society's minimum standard of authority. By the end of the Sixties authority was being challenged by the young at the universities, and challenged theoretically as well as practically, the rise of anarchistic thought being the most extraordinary philosophical development for many years if not decades. This too issued in violence, but, like the Mods and Rockers battles of the mid-Sixties, had its roots in the dissatisfaction with society felt, however unconsciously, by those who were now demanding society's total overthrow and replacement by something that would give meaning to their lives and to the lives of the masses. No Mod or Rocker would have put it so eloquently; but the plea was, at bottom, the same.

16

# Conquering heroes

It was hardly a time for heroes; yet the new forces, the new rebels, insisted on having idols. These were not the idols of their fathers, though, who one by one, during the Sixties, were leaving the stage. The new heroes included some who did not die before the decade was over, but whose friends and admirers might have been less embarrassed if they had, for they insisted, as if driven by some mad compulsion, on carrying down their white hairs in sorrow, not to say foolishness, to the grave, and would not heed Chesterton's words of warning:

> My friends, we will not go again or ape an ancient rage,
> Or stretch the folly of our youth to be the shame of age,
> But walk with clearer eyes and ears this path that wandereth,
> And see undrugged in evening light the decent inn of death.[1]

Chief among these, perhaps, was Bertrand Russell, possessor of what had been in its prime one of the most remarkable minds that had ever adorned the human race, but now fallen into a state of sad gullibility. Russell, the only really outstanding English philosopher since John Stuart Mill (it comes as a startling *memento mori* to discover that Mill, who died in 1873, dandled the infant Russell upon his knee), in the Sixties abandoned philosophy entirely, and even the critical or philosophical approach, in favour of beliefs and conduct so extraordinary that many of his erstwhile admirers were driven to the conclusion that his brain had softened now that he had come to his tenth decade, a view that might have been comforting but that was not true at all, for it

[1] G. K. Chesterton, *Collected Poems* (Methuen, London, 1933), *The Rolling English Road*, p. 204. Reproduced by permission of Miss D. Collins.

was abundantly clear that Russell's mind was still in good working order, and the only thing wrong with it was the use he put it to. 'When United States capitalists hoard food and poison it,' he wrote, in one of his milder spasms:

> they not only deprive the starving, but force the developing countries to buy food at high costs. The riches of the earth are destroyed, wasted, stolen by the few and used to murder the millions. Three thousand three hundred military bases are spread across the planet to prevent the peoples from destroying this evil system.[1]

President Kennedy and Mr Harold Macmillan he described, at the time of the Cuba missile crisis, as 'mass murderers, worse than Hitler'; he told the British people at the same time that 'You are to die because rich Americans dislike the Government that Cubans prefer'; and he got fully into his stride with this considered passage:

> The C.I.A. draws up lists of popular leaders to be assassinated. It plots to start wars. It invades countries ... In Argentina, American tanks smashed the civilian Government of Arturo Frondizi ... Brutal military putsches have been imposed upon Ecuador, Bolivia, Guatemala and Honduras ... The United Nations has become a tool of American aggression ... In the Congo, mercenary troops acting for Belgian and American interests ... have shamelessly killed ... The dregs of American militarism have been used for this purpose ... right-wing generals, with United States money, have taken control of Indonesia.[2]

Explanations for the sad decline in Russell were sadly, though assiduously, sought. Some thought they were to be found in the remorse he felt for his earlier declaration that an international settlement should be imposed upon Russia under threat of atomic

[1] Bertrand Russell, *War Crimes in Vietnam* (Allen and Unwin, London, 1968), Ch. VIII, p. 95.

[2] Ibid., Ch. VIII, pp. 97–8.

annihilation in the days when the United States had still a virtual monopoly in nuclear weapons: 'Communism', wrote Russell, 'must be wiped out.' Others attributed Russell's decline to the baleful influence exerted on him by one Ralph Schoenman, who became his secretary, then his assistant in his political activities, and ultimately seemed to have taken over the old man's mind and soul entirely. Schoenman, an expatriate American with a deep hatred of his native land, eventually gained a hold over Russell so great that old friends who tried to warn the aged Faust against his young Mephistopheles were barred from Faust's presence, while he continued to believe everything that Schoenman told him, to sign all the protests that Schoenman drafted and to act, or refrain from acting, on Schoenman's suggestion.

Fortunately Schoenman, who had fallen foul of the law in Britain once or twice, was finally barred, by Home Office *fiat*, from returning here after he had unwisely left the country, and, after a few regulation protests, Russell was at last freed from his terrible shadow, and shortly afterwards began to show signs, perhaps deceptive, but none the less hopeful, that he was recovering something of his old independence of spirit. In any case he had made, even while Schoenman's influence was at its greatest, one last contribution in his old former manner, when he published his autobiography, the first two volumes of which had been written many years before Schoenman hove in sight, and which were written with all his old limpidity of style, and all his old lucidity of thought, and for that matter all his old wit too, so that in sum the books were among the most glittering literary products of the decade, quite apart from the relief they provided from the activities of the later Russell. And it was difficult indeed to remember, let alone quarrel with, that later Russell when the earlier one was recalled with such force and poignancy in this, the prologue to his autobiography:

> Three Passions, simple but overwhelmingly strong, have governed my life: the longing for love, the search for knowledge, and unbearable pity for the suffering of mankind.

These passions, like great winds, have blown me hither and thither, in a wayward course, over a deep ocean of anguish, reaching to the very verge of despair. I have sought love, first, because it brings ecstasy—ecstasy so great that I would often have sacrificed all the rest of life for a few hours of this joy. I have sought it, next, because it relieves loneliness—that terrible loneliness in which one's shivering consciousness looks over the rim of the world into the cold unfathomable lifeless abyss. I have sought it, finally, because in the union of love I have seen, in a mystic miniature, the prefiguring vision of the heaven that saints and poets have imagined. This is what I sought, and though it might seem too good for human life, this is what—at last—I have found.

With equal passion I have sought knowledge. I have wished to understand the hearts of men. I have wished to know why the stars shine. And I have tried to apprehend the Pythagorean power by which number holds sway above the flux. A little of this, but not much, I have achieved. Love and knowledge, so far as they were possible, led upward toward the heavens. But always pity brought me back to earth. Echoes of cries of pain reverberate in my heart. Children in famine, victims tortured by oppressors, helpless old people a hated burden to their sons, and the whole world of loneliness, poverty and pain make a mockery of what human life should be. I long to alleviate the evil, but I cannot, and I too suffer.

This has been my life. I have found it worth living, and would gladly live it again if the chance were offered me.[1]

Most unlikely of all the heroes of the decade was Mao Tse-tung, god-king of seven hundred million Chinese, whose Thoughts were treated as reverentially as once were, in another context, splinters from the True Cross, and who compelled, with the aid of fearsome penalties and a regime of unprecedented severity, his own deification and worship, the Chinese people eventually

[1] Bertrand Russell, *Autobiography* (Allen and Unwin, London, 1967), Vol. I, Prologue, p. 13.

having a form of Versicles and Responses to exchange on meeting, extolling the magical and divine powers of the supernatural Chairman.

Yet, all over the world, even in places where the inhabitants were free to choose, Mao's doctrines, and more particularly his own personality, commanded a bizarre and hypnotic reverence. Lacking the romantic charm of a Castro which, however spurious, could plausibly be projected, let alone the passionate good looks and martyr's fate of a Guevara, Mao seemed the most unlikely hero of a decade as modern as the Sixties. But this view would ignore some of the most pronounced features of the decade, in particular its quest for absolutes, for Nirvanas not only spiritual but political and economic. Mao was *absolutely* mad, his policies *absolutely* ruinous, his dictatorship *absolutely* complete, the destruction of those in the West who most admired him *absolutely* certain if they ever set foot in his China. The desperate craving for certainty that affected the Sixties so much naturally reached out for the most certain certainty of all, one which rejected, in the name of pure theory, even the inconsiderable retreat from iron tyranny that had taken place in Russia since the death of Stalin. Westerners who had fellow-travelled for years, and had found the relaxation of Soviet rule psychologically disturbing, hailed with relief the emergence of a new bosom on which to lay *all* their cares; truly, the Sixties must have been in desperate need of substitute fathers to accept this one.

But if there were those who were not quite sure which side they were on, there were also some who were quite certain. It was a decade for spying and for its consequences – spy trials; it was also a decade for questioning the whole basis of military intelligence, for decrying its worth and validity, and for insisting that there were no longer any military secrets worth preserving, or that if there were Britain certainly possessed none of them. Stronger still was the argument that the intelligence services in Britain were run by incompetents or traitors, a line which was given a considerable fillip every now and again when sufficient evidence emerged to suggest that the charge might be perfectly true. Others were amused by the whole gallimaufry of agents and double agents and military information, and seemed to think that the lives which depended upon the obtaining of information about potential enemies, and upon the safeguarding of information from those enemies, were somehow not real. And mixed with all these fashions and beliefs was another fashion and another belief, this one insisting that for Britain to have military secrets, or to seek to gain those of other countries, was, in a very special sense, wrong, because Britain ought not to be in a position to defend herself, because she ought not to be defended, because (thus ran the theory in its extreme form) her enemies were right and more worthy than her of the victory.

So it was noticeable that the spies of the Sixties – Gordon Lonsdale, Peter and Helen Kroger, Houghton, Gee, Vassall, George Blake and Kim Philby (the last had, of course, done his spying long before, but was only finally revealed as a spy in this decade) – attracted much more sympathy and even respect than had been the case with spies in the past. Many of those who offered them tribute would have argued that their attitude was one of sophisticated understanding of the spy and his function (though this feeling never seemed to be extended to those caught in intelligence work *for* Britain). When Philby's memoirs were published in Britain, they not only sold a few thousand copies, but came complete with an admiring introduction by Graham Greene, who maintained during the Sixties, apparently on ideological grounds, that he would rather live in Soviet Russia than in the United States, though in fact he continued to live in the south of France. But the decade's special attitude to intelligence work was most perfectly illustrated by John le Carré's ingeniously cynical novel, *The Spy Who Came In from the Cold*;[1] and even more by its enormous popular success.

* * *

But war itself, in the Sixties, also took on a new aspect. It had lost

[1] Gollancz, London, 1963.

its glamour and romance decades earlier, of course, and settled down, in the thermo-nuclear age, to being unthinkable. But early in the decade it had all been taken very seriously, and the Campaign for Nuclear Disarmament had achieved some spectacular publicity by its annual Easter pilgrimage from the Aldermaston nuclear-research establishment to Trafalgar Square. The Aldermaston March became one of the great social occasions of the year, the left-wing equivalent of Sir Alfred Bossom's political parties or the Ascot race-meeting. (In its early days the campaign had attracted little attention and little enthusiasm; its organizers had made the mistake of launching the march in the wrong direction, *from* London *to* Aldermaston, which meant that the numbers fell away as the four days went on, rather than augmenting, as they did when the march went in the opposite direction and the less hearty or determined joined in, sheepishly or surreptitiously, at points closer and closer to the finishing-line, in some cases delaying their active participation until the front of the column was in Whitehall.)

But by the end of the Sixties such diversions seemed very quaint and unsophisticated, as the whole argument had shifted on to a philosophical basis. War was now the instrument of capitalist distraction of its own subjects, rather than (as it had long been) that of the oppression of foreign peoples in the name of imperialism.[1] New bibles, mostly as unread by the new revolutionaries as the products of the Left Book Club in the Thirties had been by their political fathers, poured out, and the works of Herbert Marcuse, Frantz Fanon, Ché Guevara and Eldridge Cleaver were constantly referred to by many who had clearly not read them, but picked up what they could from them by a kind of politico-spiritual osmosis. At the same time there occurred the rejection on a massive scale of all ancient modes of thought or conduct which were, or could be made to seem, associated with national physical defence, itself dismissed as nothing but the State's rulers' reaction to a real or supposed threat to their class interests. On the

[1] Cf. the invention of the term 'neo-colonialism' to explain the failures of the newly independent nations of Africa.

whole it was thought better to illustrate this thesis from the wars of the past, and two powerful works did so through the Crimean War and the First World War. *The Charge of the Light Brigade* argued that the notorious blunder was inevitable because of the background and character of the men in charge, and their views and outlook. It was pointed out by John Terraine that if the film had been called *The Charge of the Heavy Brigade* the thesis would have led to a precisely opposite conclusion, since the Heavy Brigade, which charged at Balaclava a few hours before the tragedy of its sister force with great success against huge odds, was led by the same men, bred in the same families and taught at the same schools. But such arguments made only a faint showing against the conviction, growing throughout the Sixties in Britain, that no war was so wrong as when Britain was participating, which was also the theme running through the one work of indisputable genius this attitude produced during the decade, Joan Littlewood's stage production of *Oh, What a Lovely War*. To the astonishment of many, and the distinct unease of those who realized where such an argument might lead, there appeared during the decade one man who took to the *Second* World War the same attitude – that it was nothing but a capitalist charade. He was Charles Wood, whose play *Dingo* made this argument explicit, and turned Winston Churchill, of all people, into the villain of the Forties.

This improbable picture demonstrated how young the young of the Sixties were, but it also led, among some at least of their elders, to the realization that those who were too young to have lived through a just war could not be convinced by mere argument that such a thing could exist.

# 17

# Wives and servants

In the field of literature the Sixties began with an attempt to stop the decade entirely and replace it with an earlier one. The attempt was foiled, but the manner of its foiling, and the ground on which the struggle took place, were so curious, and full of so many things that presaged, for those with the foresight to make the necessary extrapolations, much that was to come in the Sixties, that they deserve examination.

The Obscene Publications Act, passed in the last year of the Fifties, was designed by its sponsors (the Society of Authors outside Parliament, and Mr Roy Jenkins inside) to remedy a strange state of affairs in which many serious and reputable books were subject to prosecution for obscenity without a serious defence being possible because of the antiquated nature of the law under which they were charged. The new legislation was designed to prevent in future prosecutions of such books as D. H. Lawrence's *Lady Chatterley's Lover.* This being the case, it naturally came about that the Director of Public Prosecutions selected as the first book to be prosecuted under the new law *Lady Chatterley's Lover.*

It proved in the event to be an unwise choice from the point of view of those, and they were many, who deplored the gradual extension, over the years, of the limits of what was permissible in print and feared what it might lead to; so much so, in fact, that in order to explain the otherwise inexplicable a story began to go about that the Director of Public Prosecutions was in truth a secret sympathizer with the horizon-wideners, and had deliberately set up the prosecution of *Lady Chatterley's Lover* in order to have it knocked down and thus establish new, wider limits of tolerance.

It is, like all theories that seek to explain what must otherwise remain for ever a mystery, an appealing argument. It must, however, be discarded, since the Director of Public Prosecutions of the day, Sir Theobald Mathew, was one of those (and they were many) who, so far from wanting the limits of the permissible to be extended, would have been happy to see them shrunk so far that any literature still to be found within the constricted boundaries would have been squeezed to death, and it is indeed doubtful whether Sir Theobald had entirely approved of the contents of any book at all since the *Malleus Maleficarum*.

Whatever the reason, the prosecution of Penguin Books for the publication of Lawrence's novel (banned in Britain since its first appearance in 1928) was decided upon, though in order to improve the chances of a conviction only the company was charged, and not its eminent chairman, Sir Allen Lane, whose distinguished appearance in the dock might have had so unsettling an effect on the jury that they would have mentally acquitted him before the trial had got properly under way.

The principal change that the new law had effected was the introduction of the right to bring expert evidence about the nature of a book under indictment, so as to establish if possible the book's character as being in the interests of 'science, art, literature or other objects of general concern'. Naturally the prosecution was also entitled to bring such evidence to show, if it could be shown, that the book's publication was by no means in the interest of these important things. Both sides, therefore, had been assiduous in searching for writers, artists, psychologists, theologians, critics, teachers, moral philosophers and other eminent people who might be thought to have an expert's opinion to offer. The contents of the rival lists were, of course, a closely guarded secret, not because there might be attempts at nobbling the famous runners before the race began, but because assiduous research might have produced contradictions in their previously expressed opinions that would have provided usefully embarrassing material for cross-examination. A gasp of astonishment, therefore, on the fourth of the trial's six days greeted the admission by Mr Mervyn Griffith-Jones, for the prosecution, that he would not be calling any such evidence at all. At the time, of course, nobody knew of the prosecution's unsuccessful search for any witness of repute and standing who would say that the book was not of literary merit; only gradually and privately did the story begin to get about, one of its choicest details being the account of the contumely with which T. S. Eliot (who would have been a notable catch for the prosecution, and was hopefully approached because he had once written adversely about Lawrence) rejected the request. But the failure illustrated to perfection the difficulty in which a case against such a book inevitably puts the prosecution, for it was hardly likely that anybody of sufficient distinction to impress a jury could have seriously argued that it was without literary or other merit. (It is true that when the battle was safely over, one or two voices were raised to say that the book was worthless, chief among them being that of Mr Malcolm Muggeridge; but it was notable that Mr Muggeridge had kept very quiet while the search for witnesses was going on, though he would have been a most welcome volunteer in the ranks of the accusers.)

But even without the clash of expert against expert, view against view, approbation against revulsion, the trial was a circus so hilarious, fascinating, tense and satisfying that none who sat through all its six days will ever forget them, or begrudge the hardness of the Old Bailey seats and the way they appear to have been designed and situated to make it impossible for anything being said or done by counsel, accused, witnesses or judge to be either seen or heard.

Three things above all gave the action its memorable quality. These were the conduct of the prosecution by Mr Griffith-Jones, the demonstration of forensic skill by Mr Gerald Gardiner for the defence, and the seemingly endless parade through the witness-box of authors, scholars, academics, journalists and divines.

Mr Griffith-Jones began by asking within the first hour of the first day the famous question which will for ever be associated with his name: 'Is it a book that you would even wish your wife or your servants to read?' He then warmed to the task of demonstrating his conviction that *Lady Chatterley's Lover* was certainly not of great literary merit. Unfortunately it speedily became apparent that Mr Griffith-Jones's view of what constitutes literary merit, and what does not, was one that would not by any means command universal agreement. What at first seemed the only general principle of his outlook that could be gathered with any certainty was his belief that repetition of the same words or phrases was something that almost by itself ruled out the possibility of literary merit. To this end he seized upon two words: 'womb' and 'bowels'; and for nearly ten minutes they rang through the astounded court-room. On this point the cross-examination of Mr Graham Hough went like this:

> ' "Connie went slowly home ... Another self was alive in her, burning molten and soft in her womb and bowels, and with this self she adored him ... " I suppose that is good writing, or is that ludicrous?'
> 'Not to me.'
> ' "In her womb and bowels" – again we have got the same two parts of her anatomy coupled together within three lines – "she was flowing and alive now ... " I do not want to be unimaginative, believe me, but can one flow and be alive in one's womb and bowels?'
> 'Metaphorically I think one can.'
> 'Even metaphorically?'
> 'Yes.'
> ' " ... and vulnerable, and helpless in adoration of him as the most naive woman. It feels like a child, she said to herself; it feels like a child in me. And so it did, as her womb ... " – and so we have "womb" for the third time?'
> 'Yes.'
> '... I am asking: do you regard that as good writing, to repeat again and again "womb and bowels", "womb and bowels", and "bowels and womb"?'

'In the context, yes.'

'And it does not finish there, because if we can go on to the next page almost at the end of the first long paragraph "womb" appears?'

'Yes.'

'Then a little bit further down page 141, towards the bottom, at the end of the longish paragraph the two words "womb" and "bowels" appear again?'[1]

'Yes.'

'Is that really what you call expert, artistic writing?'[2]

The unpromising nature of this approach was to strike the prosecution after a comparatively short time. Before its abandonment, however, Mr Griffith-Jones propounded yet another theory of literature, the new thesis being that for an author to misquote another author is an infallible sign of lack of literary quality. 'In a work of high literary merit,' Mr Griffith-Jones asked Graham Hough in cross-examination, 'if you were minded to quote from somebody you would expect the author to quote it accurately?' Notwithstanding Mr Hough's brisk disposal of this startling theory – 'No, sir; from my knowledge of the habits of authors, it is the last thing I would expect, for them to quote accurately. They do it from memory and they always get it wrong' – Mr Griffith-Jones went on with the point, providing as he did so one of the minor moments of high comedy with which the trial was studded throughout.

'Just look, would you, at page 219. You see, halfway down the page he is quoting, "Lift up your heads, o ye gates, that the king of glory may come in"?'

'Yes.'

'I certainly would not expect anybody to remember what the

[1] It is the author's clear recollection, as one who was present throughout the trial, that by now the words 'womb and bowels' had ceased to convey any of their normal meaning whatever, and a fantasy presented itself distinctly, in which they became a firm of antique-dealers.

[2] Quoted from C. H. Rolph, *The Trial of Lady Chatterley* (Penguin, Harmondsworth, 1964).

actual quotation is, but I happen to have looked it up. "Lift up your heads, O ye gates, even lift up ye everlasting doors, and the King of Glory shall come in" ... Do you not think that in a work of high literary merit, if he is going to quote from the 24th Psalm he might take the trouble to look it up?'[1]

Mr Hough dealt with this gently enough – 'It isn't Lawrence quoting from the 24th Psalm, it is the gamekeeper' – but resisted the temptation to point out the enchanting fact that Mr Griffith-Jones, in his indignation at Lawrence's getting the quotation wrong, *had got it wrong himself.*

But at that point the prosecution clearly realized that the attempt to convince the jury that *Lady Chatterley's Lover* was not a work of literary merit was doomed. Instead, Mr Griffith-Jones adopted a new line of argument, and at this point an entirely new complexion came over the trial, which in effect ceased to be a trial of Penguin Books for publishing an obscene work, or even of D. H. Lawrence for writing one. It became instead a case against Constance Chatterley for adultery, and the jury was invited to condemn her for it.

As a study in literary anthropomorphism R. v. Penguin Books thus became a landmark for future students of the extraordinary way in which the law behaves. Both Mr Griffith-Jones and the judge clearly believed that the people in the book had a real existence outside its pages, that they led lives that involved actions and thoughts quite separate from those described and expressed in it, that they moved in a world as real as that of the court-room in which their lives were being discussed.[2] So intensely was this

[1] Ibid.

[2] This attitude was to receive explicit support in the House of Lords' debate on the case, when Lord Hailsham said: 'Before I accepted as valid or valuable, or even excusable, the relationship between Lady Chatterley and Mellors, I should have liked to know what sort of parents they became to the child ... I should have liked to see the kind of house they proposed to set up together; I should have liked to know how Mellors would have survived living on Connie's rentier income of six hundred pounds ... and I should have liked to know whether they acquired a circle of friends, or, if not, how their relationship survived social isolation.' On

belief clearly held by the prosecution and on the Bench that it eventually began to infect some of the witnesses, and solemn exchanges took place about the character and psychology of Lady Chatterley, about her intentions and future plans, about the likelihood, or lack of likelihood, of a stable relationship between her and Mellors the gamekeeper, about her life before the book begins.

'The chief character in this book,' said Mr Griffith-Jones to Mrs Joan Bennett,

> who happens to be a married woman, is depicted throughout this book as going and having sexual intercourse ... you don't suggest that series of adulterous intercourses shows a very strong support for marriage, do you? ... And indeed one doesn't want to speak disrespectfully of the dead, but if one is talking about what the author's views ... show, that is in fact, is it not, exactly what he himself had done? He had run off with his friend's wife, had he not? ... And it is just that type of behaviour, is it not, that is depicted in this book ... I mean a man running off with another man's wife?[1]

There was more to come. 'Do you find anywhere in the book,' asked Mr Griffith-Jones of Prebendary Stephen Hopkinson, 'a word suggesting criticism of what she is doing?' And 'The only occasions when they have any opportunity of any conversation is either just before, during or immediately after the act of copulation,' he said to Cecil Day-Lewis – a remark which drew from Mr Gardiner, in his closing address, a sharp and wounding rebuke:

> When it is said that this is a book about adultery, one wonders how there can be things which people do not see. I suppose it is possible that somewhere there might be a

---

the other hand Lord Teviot, in the same debate, complained of the book and its author that 'The story he tells is pure invention; it never actually happened', which moved Lord Boothby, in his speech, to say: 'That is the thing about fiction; it doesn't happen.'

[1] Rolph, op. cit.

> mind which would describe *Antony and Cleopatra* as 'a tale about adultery'. Antony had a wife in Rome, and I suppose there might be a mind somewhere which would describe this play of Shakespeare as 'the story of a sex-starved man copulating with an Egyptian queen' ... there are minds which are unable to see beauty where it exists, and doubt the integrity of purpose in an author where it is obvious.[1]

Nor was the rebuke unjustified; for Mr Gardiner's implication – that Mr Griffith-Jones's was one of those 'minds which are unable to see beauty where it exists, and doubt the integrity of purpose in an author where it is obvious' – must have been true, if, as was perfectly clear to anyone who sat through the trial, he felt deeply moved, not by the lawyer's indignation assumed for the sake of his brief, but by a perfectly genuine revulsion from what he regarded as an obscene book with no redeeming qualities. This feeling of his – and it is clear that the judge, with equal sincerity, shared it – stemmed not from wilfulness but from an inability to see in the book what others, of all levels of education and understanding, could see, which was demonstrated, in one of the most startling and affecting episodes in the trial when, on its third day, Richard Hoggart gave evidence. In order to explain the points being discussed, he and defence counsel read passage after passage from the book, and as they read the silence in the court deepened, the coughs and the thousands of involuntary movements that make up, on such occasions, a background of sound which is not recognized as sound at all until it ceases, disappeared. The lawyers in the well of the court, the jury in their pen, the press in theirs, the few with passes to the seats at the back, the public in the gallery who had queued for hours to get in, some of them no doubt in the vague hope of hearing at first-hand something of the kind they normally bought the *News of the World* to read about at second – all these fell into a profound, rapt silence, their attention hypnotized by the power of

[1] Ibid.

Lawrence's writing. There was not only silence, but physical stillness; along the rail in front of the public gallery, for instance, many in the first row had rested their hands; these lay, fingers linked or palms flat on the wood, absolutely immobile. No head turned, except between Hoggart in the witness-box and counsel in his pew, as they played, like a tennis match, this vast and moving rally. The fact that Mr Griffith-Jones was left *un*moved by it put beyond doubt the conclusion that his conduct of the case was wholly free of those tactical considerations which compel lawyers to put forward arguments that they do not themselves believe.[1]

Mr Griffith-Jones was to demonstrate again, before the trial was done, his manifest conviction that he was not a lawyer speaking to a brief, but a man engaged in putting down wickedness. He suggested to the jury, for instance, that the rise in crime in recent years was the result, as he put it, of 'unbridled sex', and brandished, before Mr Gardiner rose to object, a copy of the annual *Criminal Statistics* published by H.M.S.O. for the Home Office, as if to prove his point. Not long afterwards he took great exception to the argument by the defence that one of the things Lawrence was trying to express in the book was the need for 'tenderness' (it had been given in evidence that Lawrence at one time contemplated publishing the book under that one-word title). 'What about tenderness?' he asked;

> is that a theme which it is in the public good to read as expressed in this book? I will tell you how it is expressed in this book, in the words of the book itself: 'Tenderness, really—cunt tenderness. Sex is really the closest touch of all. Cunt tenderness.' That is the tenderness that this book is advocating through the mouth of one of its chief characters.[2]

This raised—it could not help but raise—the terrible question: in what way did Mr Griffith-Jones's subconscious mind wish a cunt to be treated, if not with tenderness?

[1] So, of course, was the conduct of the defence by Mr Gardiner.

[2] Rolph, op. cit.

A few moments later still Mr Griffith-Jones came to the passage which, in the post-trial discussion of its implications, caused most controversy, largely because of a most entertaining and exhaustive article by Mr John Sparrow, Warden of All Souls, in *Encounter*, which took Mr Griffith-Jones's view of the meaning of Lawrence's words and brought all his (Sparrow's) considerable forensic skill to bear on the attempt to prove it. The passage was the one that came to be known in the ensuing argument as 'the night of sensual passion' – a phrase which occurs in the book. It has been quoted too often to need repeating,[1] but what gave it, as Mr Griffith-Jones read it, its special piquancy, was the way in which he wove into it as he went, with a sinister emphasis, a pretence that he did not understand the meaning: 'Not very easy, sometimes, not very easy, you know, to know what in fact he is driving at in that passage ... '

Now Mr Griffith-Jones's assault on the jury, with this very strong suggestion that Lady Chatterley and her lover had committed buggery in the night of sensual passion – an assault reserved, with remarkable will-power, to the closing hours of the trial – had much the same outward effect, though more briefly, as had the series of passages that defence counsel and Richard Hoggart had read to each other earlier, that is, it stilled and hushed the court completely; but in this case it was caused by the shock effect of Mr Griffith-Jones's innuendo as to Lawrence's meaning. It had no effect on the jury's verdict; but its subsequent effect, lovingly detonated by Mr Sparrow, was, in every sense of the word, sensational.

The burden of Mr Sparrow's argument was a dual one, the first part being concerned with his demonstration that the passage did indeed mean what Mr Griffith-Jones suggested, the second with the possibility that, if it had been made more explicit

[1] Or possibly not: ' ... it pierced again with piercing thrills of sensuality ... though a little frightened, she let him have his way ... burning out the shames, the deepest, oldest shames, in the most secret places ... the same on the Greek vases ... the deep, organic shame ... was roused up and routed by the phallic hunt of the man ... to find a man who dared to do it, without shame or sin or final misgiving! ... ' (Penguin, Harmondsworth, 1960).

and perhaps introduced earlier, it might have resulted in a different verdict, or at any rate that it was arguable that it *should* have done. The controversy that followed seemed, no doubt to Mr Sparrow's intense satisfaction, to be not so much between him and his opponents as between two sets of the latter, namely those who denied that the interpretation put upon the passage by Mr Griffith-Jones and Mr Sparrow was the correct one, and those who insisted that it was, but was too obviously correct to be worth making such a fuss about.

But, although the trial itself was a circus that had somehow got stuck at the opening parade, and thus consisted only of the sight of the acrobats, trapeze-artists, animal tamers, trick-cyclists and clowns marching around and around to the strains of the 'Entry of the Gladiators', and for all the joys, recollected in tranquillity, of the House of Lords debate on the subject, the trial of Penguin Books for the publication of *Lady Chatterley's Lover*, and the arguments which surrounded the trial before, during and after the actual proceedings, provided no bad collection of symbols for the decade that was just beginning. It was, as the prosecution said, a test case, and, although by that was meant a test only of the new Act, on which the Royal Assent was hardly dry, it turned out to be a test of very much more, a test in fact of whether there had been a change, not only in the law of the land but in a vast body of largely unspoken conventions and unwritten rules about public taste and what it will, and will not, tolerate. Of course the two go very much together, for laws which control matters concerning the tolerance of opinion and its expression must be, in a real sense, a reflection of public opinion on the matters concerned, and this remains true in a much wider context, including actions in the field of moral behaviour.

Assuming – and it is, of course, a large assumption – that the theory of the jury-system, that the twelve good men and true actually do represent the people in general from whose ranks they are drawn, is soundly based, it follows that if they acquit Lady Chatterley of the charge of corrupting and depraving those who read about her, the people are not convinced that she will do any harm outside the decorous covers in which she was wrapped by Penguins. And it is not only the Statutes that follow the changing pattern of public opinion, for they, in any case, only do so after an inevitable lapse of time; it is the enforcement of existing law, too. It is quite possible that if in 1960 some of the books published since had been put out, either by Penguins or by some other reputable publishers, for general sale, a prosecution might have had more success. But in these things it so often turns out that it does not matter in the long run who goes through the hedge first; what counts is that a hole in the hedge has been made, and thereafter all, or many, may stream through it. As we shall see, the signal defeat in this case of those who would confine the limits of the permissible, at the hands of those who would extend those limits, was by no means an end of the matter, for several more 'test cases' followed at intervals during the Sixties, in one of which the prosecution was successful, and in another of which it looked for a time as though it had been, and that the clock which had been set going in December 1960 for good or ill was stopped or even set going backwards. But the truth of the matter was only that the law-enforcement agencies are also subject to a time-lag between a change in the climate and in the pattern of their own activities, and in any case no absolutely tidy pattern can ever be established.

The fact remains that the decade which began with the prosecution of Penguin Books for publishing *Lady Chatterley's Lover* had seen, before it ended, the publication, with no prosecution or threat of it, of books such as Philip Roth's *Portnoy's Complaint*,[1] William Burroughs's *The Naked Lunch*,[2] and a number of others of which it is fairly safe to say that they would have been very lucky to escape conviction if they, and not Lawrence's hedge-breaking work, had been the subject of the 'test case' in 1960.

All the same, it is not at all easy to say exactly what has been accomplished, except in the most superficial terms. For Mr

[1] Cape, London, 1969.

[2] Calder and Boyars, London, 1964.

Griffith-Jones and Lord Teviot what has been accomplished is the ruin and corruption of the country; for Messrs Calder and Boyars, who published one of the books most sensationally prosecuted in the wake of *Lady Chatterley's Lover*, a healthy freedom of expression has been established; for Penguins it has been the opportunity to do full justice to Lawrence by publishing his one remaining unpublishable book, an opportunity which was taken at once, and, aided by the prosecution, so enthusiastically accepted that to date it has sold some four million copies; for the 'back-street pornographers' so frequently referred to in the course of the trial, nothing; and for the public at large?

It is said that successful generals, looking back at the end of their lives at their greatest battles, tend to wonder what they were all about, and why so much fuss and blood was spilt, and what, if anything, remains of the high purposes with which the battles were fought and of the great achievements that were declared at the time to have resulted from them. Some of the participants in this battle must feel, and may feel increasingly, a sense of wonder at the passions roused, the tenacity displayed, the sense of doom or salvation felt. Their subsequent histories alone provide much material for such wonder: Mr Griffith-Jones became a judge; Mr Gerald Gardiner became Lord Chancellor and, taking office with high ideals and selfless ambitions, proved in the event a considerable disappointment; Mr Roy Jenkins achieved high Government office; Mr Noël Annan became a Lord; the Bishop of Woolwich was called an ass by Lord Hailsham, and wrote *Honest to God*; the writers who gave evidence went on writing, the teachers teaching, the critics criticizing, the priests preaching.

* * *

But it was not to be supposed that the forces of righteousness and virtue, so signally defeated by those of depravity and debauchery, would be content to accept their defeat with equanimity, like the defeated General Samsonov after the battle of Tannenberg, who said: 'The enemy has luck one day, we will have luck another' and shot himself. The Director of Public Prosecutions did not shoot himself, any more than did Mr Mervyn Griffith-Jones, or Serjeant Monahan, the literary bloodhound of the Metropolitan Police, whose nose could sniff smut at a hundred paces. Within a few weeks of the prosecution and acquittal of Lady Chatterley, one of the most curious cases to be decided for many a year came before the courts, and went before it was finished all the way from the magistrate's court to the House of Lords, where it was decided wrongly.

It concerned a man named Shaw, an entrepreneur who in other contexts might have been one of those constantly praised by politicians and held up to others for emulation as the kind of merchant venturer so sorely needed if Britain was ever to modernize her industrial ways, seek new methods of commerce, and build those better mousetraps which will ensure that the world beats a path to her door. Shaw had noted the passage of the Street Offences Act in 1959 and had seen how it had made illegal, and virtually stopped, public soliciting by prostitutes in the streets. He had also observed the methods that prostitutes had adopted in order to continue their trade despite the new legislation; these included the use of small advertisements on the display boards kept by newsagents and other shopkeepers, innocently worded advertisements in local newspapers that would convey to those on the alert for such things what was being offered, and in at least one case a large neon sign in the window of a fashionable London street, reading 'French Tuition'. Shaw concluded that the prostitutes, their customers and he could all be benefited if he were to publish a register containing the details of the women who offered such services in London, together with the nature of the special facilities offered by the more adventurous among them. This he accordingly did, and shortly afterwards *The Ladies' Directory* made its appearance, selling for two shillings a copy. In it prostitutes advertised themselves and their wares, paying for the right to do so rates which varied from two guineas for a quarter-page without photograph, to ten guineas for a full-page, illustrated. The ladies described their charms in their own words and implied their varied willingnesses, with such references as 'Corr.,' to indicate that they were willing to practise flagellation ('corrective treatment'), or 'Full wardrobe', to suggest that they were willing to dress in any mode desired by the client.

Shaw was arrested and charged with publishing an obscene libel, with living wholly or partly on the earnings of prostitution, and with conspiring to corrupt the morals of the subjects of our liege lady the Queen. On all three counts he was found guilty, and began a series of appeals, in the course of which that habit of the English judiciary, of making the law conform with their idea of what it ought to be, was given full reign.

The relevant section of the Act which prohibited living wholly or partly on the earnings of prostitutes defined such an action as that of a man

> who lives with or is habitually in the company of a prostitute or who exercises control, direction or influence over a prostitute's movements in a way which shows he is aiding or abetting or compelling her prostitution.

No evidence was produced to show that Shaw had done anything to bring him within this provision. Nevertheless he was found guilty, and his conviction was upheld on appeal both to the Court of Criminal Appeal and to the House of Lords, the last body deciding unanimously that a man would come within the Act if he supplied for money anything to prostitutes for the purpose of their prostitution which he would not supply but for the fact that they were prostitutes. Thus did the judges manage to make two offences grow where only one had grown before; they later produced a third, when they rejected Shaw's appeal against conviction on the charge of conspiring to corrupt public morals.

No such offence was known to any Act of Parliament, ancient or modern; it was a charge at common law, and rested on the proposition that although to corrupt the public morals might not be criminal, to conspire to do so might be. The device of bringing a charge of conspiracy, for which penalties were generally higher than for the simple crime in furtherance of which the conspiracy was alleged, has long been used in the courts, though usually in the case of two or more defendants, since in the normal use of language one person cannot *conspire* to do anything, though he can *intend* to. Nevertheless, the charge was brought against Shaw, and upheld by the House of Lords without any claim that its members were doing anything other than impose their view of the public good on the law; one of them, Lord Simonds, put this without ambiguity when he said:

> Let it be supposed that at some future, perhaps early, date homosexual practices between adult consenting males are no longer a crime. Would it not be an offence if, even without obscenity, such practices were publicly advocated and encouraged by pamphlet and advertisement? Or must we wait until Parliament finds time to deal with such conduct? If the common law was powerless to act in such an event, we should no longer do her reverence. But her hand is still powerful and it is for Her Majesty's Judges to play the part which Lord Mansfield pointed out to them.[1]

The record of Her Majesty's Judges is such that a *dictum* of this kind must strike a chill into the hearts of all who wish for reforms in the law and are thus told that it will be for the judges to decide which reforms shall be permitted and which shall not. But Lord Simonds went even further shortly afterwards, saying:

> In the sphere of criminal law there remains in the Courts of law a residual power to enforce the supreme and fundamental purpose of the law, to conserve not only the safety and order but also the moral welfare of the state, and it is our duty to guard it against attacks which might be all the more insidious because they were novel and unprepared for ... It matters little what label is given to the offending

[1] *The Times* Law Report, May 4th, 1961.

> act—an affront to public decency, a corruption of public morals, the creation of a public mischief, or the undermining of moral conduct.[1]

From this judgment Lord Reid dissented, thus:[2]

> There are wide differences of opinion today as to how far the law ought to punish immoral acts which are not done in the face of the public. Parliament is the proper, and the only proper place, to settle that. When there is sufficient support from public opinion Parliament does not hesitate to intervene. Where Parliament fears to tread it is not for the Courts to rush in. In my judgment the House is in no way bound and ought not to sanction the extension of 'public mischief' to any new field, and certainly not if such extension would be in any way controversial. Public mischief is the criminal counterpart of public policy, and the criminal law ought to be even more hesitant than the civil law in founding on it some new aspect. The Courts cannot now create a new offence of a new kind of criminal conspiracy.

Nevertheless Shaw went to prison for nine months, and not long afterwards another court, perhaps encouraged by this decision, decided that a prostitute was breaking that provision of the Street Offences Act which forbade her to ply her trade in the streets if she stayed wholly within her home but beckoned to passers-by through the *closed* window.

Thus emboldened, the forces of virtue and purity might have been supposed to mount their chargers at once and gallop off furiously, no matter whither. But they waited almost three years before venturing on another major trial of strength, and then, almost like members of the same school or regiment gathering to commemorate some anniversary, much of the same cast assembled as had played leading roles in the prosecution of Lady Chatterley. There was Mr Mervyn Griffith-Jones, who had so distinguished himself in the earlier case and had so recently

[1] Ibid.

[2] Ibid.

distinguished himself even more in his zeal against Stephen Ward; there too were the literary witnesses ready to say their bit in defence of innocent words which others would insist on considering guilty.[1] There also was Mr Jeremy Hutchinson for the defence, who had been second-in-command to Gerald Gardiner on the earlier occasion. And the trial of *Fanny Hill*, like that of Mr Shaw of *The Ladies' Directory*, also involved considerable agility on the part of the prosecution if they were to evade the difficulties in which they had been put by Parliament. The agility of the righteous, however, should not be underestimated; on this occasion they succeeded in evading Parliament's intentions to such good effect that Parliament was compelled to amend the law to make such evasion impossible in the future.

The particular loophole discovered and exploited in order to put poor Fanny Hill in her place (her particular offence, as Lady Chatterley's had been adultery, was that, being a woman, she did at divers places and times *enjoy* sexual intercourse, and not only did so, but made it plain that she did so) concerned the distinction between Sections 2 and 3 of the Obscene Publications Act. Lady Chatterley had been charged under Section 2; Penguin Books having obligingly co-operated with the police in furnishing evidence of publication, they were charged accordingly, and were the only defendants. Section 3 was designed to catch booksellers who specialized (there are many such) in pornographic books, it being reasonably supposed that in the case of some of their wares it would be impossible, or very difficult, to track down the publisher, certainly before the work was in general circulation. But the existence of Section 3 meant that a reputable publisher could find his books in the dock through the prosecution of a bookseller who might be anything but reputable. This created several excellent opportunities for the forces of righteousness. In the first place the bookseller would generally be far less disposed, or able, to mount a proper defence of a book which for him might be only one among thousands, and cause

[1] Though in fact *Fanny Hill* contains none of the 'four-letter words' that figured so prominently in the *Lady Chatterley* trial.

him little loss if the court ordered its forfeiture; in the second place if he were an obviously shady figure, running one of those establishments in which the level of erotic stimulation in the works available grows greater as the customer passes farther into the shop, he would obviously not cut a very sympathetic figure in court; and in the third place the task of a publisher wishing to intervene with a defence of his book in the case of a prosecution of a bookseller would be made far more difficult, since he might not even get to hear of the prosecution until it was over, and even if he did the bookseller might not be at all co-operative with the publisher's efforts to stand by his book.

This being the case, the publishers of *Fanny Hill*, Mayflower Books, sought to take the same co-operative action as had Penguins and give evidence of publication to the authorities, so that they might be proceeded against with all deliberate speed and dignity. The authorities, however, blandly said to Mayflower's solicitors:

> It is because your clients have acted throughout with a proper sense of responsibility and took immediate steps, on being informed that search warrants were issued, to stop any sales to the public that it was decided that the prosecution would be oppressive in the circumstances.

And so it came about that the prosecution of Fanny Hill took place in the form of R. v. Gold, that being the name of the bookseller. The proceedings, however, took in the event much the same form as in the prosecution of Lady Chatterley, which was not surprising in view of the fact that in this case, too, the case for the Crown was in the sure hands of Mr Mervyn Griffith-Jones. 'It was put to you with horror', said Mr Hutchinson (for the defence) to Peter Quennell, his first literary witness, 'that these girls had enjoyed sex immensely. Does that horrify you?' 'It horrifies me less', replied Mr Quennell, 'than it does Mr Griffith-Jones.'

The defence was, it must be said, in one difficulty with *Fanny Hill* that they had not had to face with *Lady Chatterley's Lover*.

That book, so far from being pornographic, was written with an intense moral purpose. But *Fanny Hill* had been written by John Cleland as unashamed pornography, and great were the knots in which such distinguished figures as Marghanita Laski, Peter Quennell and Montgomery Hyde tied themselves in order to demonstrate the uplifting nature of his gay, pornographic and wholesome book. Mr Quennell insisted on the book's historical value as a portrait of the epoch; Miss Laski on the fact–which would have struck Cleland dead with astonishment if he had heard it in his lifetime–that the book insisted that sex was most enjoyable in marriage; Mr Hyde that the book taught that vice should be eschewed and avoided.

These things were difficult to maintain, and the defence did well to maintain them. But if the nature of the book made it difficult to defend on the grounds of its being justified in the interests of science, literature, art or learning, that was as nothing compared to the pit that the prosecution had dug for its own feet. Mr Griffith-Jones had insisted unswervingly throughout the Lady Chatterley trial that the intent of the author did not matter and could not be discussed (a view in which he had been ably seconded by the judge), for in the earlier case it was essential for the prosecution to keep Lawrence's intent out of the case, as it had been so undeniably moral. In this case they longed to bring Cleland's intent in, as it had been so undeniably commercial; but the door they had so firmly closed stared them in the face, and they were reduced to arguing that, in the words of the Act, the book's effect taken as a whole was such as to tend to deprave and corrupt persons who were likely, having regard to all the relevant circumstances, to read it. So the difficulty the prosecution had had in finding witnesses to testify against Lawrence's book was doubled and quadrupled in this case and Mr Griffith-Jones once again had the ignominious task of announcing that he was not proposing to call any witnesses. In the circumstances it was only the fact that there was no jury that allowed the prosecution to win at all. But the result meant that the two major literary trials since the passage of the Obscene Publications

Act had resulted in a score of one each between the forces of light, truth, purity and reason on the one hand and those of darkness, falsehood, corruption and evil on the other. It was clear to all concerned that there would, sooner or later, have to be a decider, and the opposing teams, as they waited for extra time to begin, sucked lemons and nursed their bruises.

The decider, played some three years later, was full of suspense, and not until the last moments of the match was it clear who would win; indeed, the losing side prematurely claimed the victory, only to have it snatched from them almost as the whistle blew, to their understandable confusion, misery and rage.

The book chosen as the venue for the final encounter was *Last Exit to Brooklyn*,[1] a dreadful, savage and shockingly moralistic book about a corner of New York where, to quote the British publishers, 'nothing matters except the precarious dollar and the pleasure of inflicting violence on someone weaker than oneself'. The language used by its characters, however, is certainly not the kind one would want one's wife or servants to read, nor is the brutality the sort one would wish them to undergo, or even hear about. But the authorities might never have moved in the matter had it not been for the action of those in charge of a most reputable avant-garde booksellers' called Better Books.

The first shots in the encounter were fired by Sir Charles Taylor, the Member of Parliament for Eastbourne and one of those granite survivals from the Jurassic Age which are occasionally to be found sticking up out of the more recent deposits. How he came to read the book is one of the great mysteries of the decade, but the effect it had on him he hastened to communicate to the House of Commons with a demand that proceedings should be started at once against it. The force of his plea was somewhat diminished, however, by the fact that he refused to identify the book, and since not even the Director of Public Prosecutions could be expected, Herod-like, to prosecute

[1] H. Selby, Jnr (Calder and Boyars, London, 1966).

all the books published in the previous six months in the hope that he would thereby catch the one that had so upset Sir Charles, the matter might have got no further, had it not been for the action of a group of M.P.s, led by Tom Driberg, who had deduced from Sir Charles's description what book he was talking about, and put down a motion on the Commons order-paper congratulating the authorities for taking no action in the matter. This considerably raised Sir Charles Taylor's temperature, as may well be imagined, and when Better Books, alerted by the growing controversy, hastily put advertisements in newspapers and magazines quoting with enthusiasm Sir Charles's apoplectic denunciation of the book and urging its immediate purchase, Sir Charles's self-control snapped. He enlisted the aid of another back-bench Conservative, Sir Cyril Black, who, if Sir Charles Taylor is a survival from the Jurassic Age, may be described as one of the original Pre-Cambrians, and between them they launched a private prosecution in a magistrate's court.

Not surprisingly, given the precedent of the magistrate's decision in the *Fanny Hill* case, the publishers, a firm of good repute called Calder and Boyars, were convicted. But by now the law had been amended, following the uproar that the authorities' conduct in the *Fanny Hill* case had caused, to allow publishers in such cases to insist on a trial by jury under Section 2 of the Act. This they did, and battle was at last joined for the third and deciding time.

When the Old Bailey cast assembled once more, one familiar and much-loved face was missing. Mr Mervyn Griffith-Jones had, alas, been transferred to the Bench. There was another major difference: on this occasion the prosecution had at last managed to find some people of standing to testify against the book. It was a somewhat mixed bag, and some of the testimony sounded a trifle odd; Captain Robert Maxwell, M.P., for instance, denounced the writer of the book, and its publishers, as being animated by nothing but the basest commercial motives, a moderately surprising charge to be made against a firm which was in the habit of publishing, from literary zeal, works which certainly made them no money at all, and a charge which was all the more astonishing coming from a publisher who, whatever else he might have been in business for, was utterly devoted, very properly, to the maximization of profits in every possible way. The Reverend David Sheppard also gave evidence against the book, but, as befitted a man of his cloth, ignored the commercial aspects and concentrated on the moral, insisting that the book, among other things, tended to portray homosexuality in an attractive light. This charge gave many cause to wonder, as the homosexual character in the book is portrayed as living, because of his condition, a life of desperate and unrelieved misery, and dying, also because of his nature, a death of appalling savagery. But what with Captain Maxwell, and what with the Reverend Sheppard, and what with Sir Basil Blackwell, proprietor of the famous Oxford bookshop—who testified that the book had depraved him because his memory and mind were 'impaired, vitiated and defiled by the language and conduct in the book', so much so in fact that he felt he was 'seriously hurt' by it and wanted after reading it to go away and cleanse his mind—the publishers were found guilty.

Great now was the rejoicing in the camp of the godly, and deep the gloom in the ranks of the unrighteous. It was widely supposed by both sides that the success of the prosecution in this case would now lead to a series of further prosecutions either instigated privately by such guardians of the moral will as Sir Charles Taylor and Sir Cyril Black, or by the Director of Public Prosecutions, encouraged as he must have been by his unexpected success just as he was giving up hope of ever again achieving a conviction. But rejoicing and gloom were changed in a trice to gloom and rejoicing, and the two knights went limping off the field, attended by the Director of Public Prosecutions, when the publishers, having launched an appeal for funds to enable them to appeal against the verdict, collected enough money and saw the conviction quashed in the Court of Criminal Appeal.

By a narrow, and hotly disputed, margin, the victory had finally gone to those who wanted literature to be more explicit, while for those who wanted it to be less so, or at any rate no more so, there was nothing but the sour taste of defeat. Moreover, the defeat seemed final, for by the decade's end it appeared that the authorities had entirely abdicated their function in this field, so that with the exception of a strange account of a Victorian rake's progress called *My Secret Life*, the publisher of which was prosecuted in circumstances that insistently recalled the conduct of the authorities in the early stages of the *Fanny Hill* case, no other work of which it could be argued, however implausibly, that it was of literary or other merit, had been the subject of a prosecution, and, as if to celebrate the hard-won freedom, *Portnoy's Complaint* appeared unscathed in Britain and no question of prosecution arose, despite the fact that it consisted very largely of descriptions of a series of acts of masturbation. (The book was said to have sold half a million copies in the United States within a few weeks, so popular, it seemed, were accounts of masturbation.)

In the last months of the Sixties *Fanny Hill* was republished, unexpurgated. No prosecution followed; the authorities' surrender seemed, for the time being at least, to be complete.[1]

* * *

In the beginning, we are told, was the Word. Many and strange were the shapes words had taken, the uses to which they had been put, the effects they had had. In the Sixties the last question, of the effects words might have, was the most important, the one most eagerly discussed, the one that aroused most and fiercest divergence of views.

Some held that a word was in itself without weight or substance, having, so to speak, position but no magnitude. These declared that words, however many and of whatever description, could do nothing but arouse in the hearer responses that were part of him, not of the word, that the word itself could not

[1] Though there were signs, early in the Seventies, that they were rallying their forces for another round.

create a response, and that the response was therefore independent of the existence of the word, the word being guiltless, since it was presumed incapable of forming a guilty intent.

Others insisted that this view was the merest playing with words, and that a word inevitably took on the shape, colour and intent of the mind which selected it and gave it breath. Of this group, some went further and insisted that the word in turn might, or even would, shape and colour the mind and intent of its hearer, so that he would be to that extent a different man after reading or hearing it, though some contented themselves with declaring that this contention was as yet not proven.

We have seen how, very early in the decade, the two opposing views of the nature of the word met in open battle, and how the victory went to the party that held the word to be innocent until proved guilty, and possibly even afterwards. We have seen also how the defeated party rallied their forces, regrouped, and counter-attacked, winning battles in their turn and also losing further ones, so that the fortunes of the war swayed this way and that, and none could predict its final outcome.

The most spectacular battle, however, took place almost exactly half-way through the decade, and on ground that had before, and has since, seen no such combat. Late in 1965 that same Kenneth Tynan whom we have met before in these pages was taking part in a discussion on a television programme, being shown, live, late in the evening. Part of the discussion turned on the permissible limits of liberty that, in an ideal world, would frame the stages of our theatres, like an invisible proscenium. Tynan was all for the maximum possible degree of artistic freedom, freedom, that is, not only to say, but to do; for he was not only of the party which believed that the *word* could do nothing to its hearers that the hearers had not already done to themselves, but was also of much the same mind as regards the *act*.

Now this was ground wider, and less firm, than the ground on which the battle of the word had been fought, and many who held it no sin to say the word were quite unable to agree that he who did the thing was equally blameless. Tynan, however, was consistent in this at any rate, that he believed sauce for the hearer and speaker to be sauce for the seer and doer. Asked, therefore, by the interlocutor on the fateful television programme what, hitherto forbidden, he would like to see performed on a public stage, he declared that he would like to see a play in which two players would take part in sexual intercourse or, as he put it, would fuck.

Now many objections could be raised against this modest proposal, not the least powerful of which is the question of what happens on days when there is a matinee as well as an evening performance, let alone on those occasions (such as Boxing Day) when the play is given thrice. But the argument which broke out immediately, and raged with considerable violence, concerned not Mr Tynan's suggestion but the words in which he had clothed it, so that the battle took place after all on the more familiar ground of the word and its effect.

It raged for weeks, though the combatants most fiercely determined that Tynan had done great evil were curiously divided between those who argued that this conduct might have harmed any who–all unexpectedly–had heard the terrible and unfamiliar word in the privacy of their own homes, those who declared that his behaviour was the merest childish exhibitionism, as the word in question was already known to every man, woman and child in the country and they thought nothing of it, and those who managed, by a considerable effort, to maintain both views at once.

Eventually the storm blew itself out, but some years later–at the very end of the decade, in fact–many were astonished to discover that Tynan had meant his suggestion seriously, whatever his intent might have been in using the word he did to describe it, for it was announced that he was shortly to journey to New York and there help to present a play in which members of the cast would at any rate closely simulate the act in question. Mark, however, the sad ending to this story, for long before Tynan could, so to speak, mount his own spectacle, two plays were already to be seen in New York, in one of which the members of the audience were invited to come up upon the stage and have sexual relations with such members of the cast as took their fancy (the play being called *Dionysius '69*), and in the other of which (*Che!*) such acts took place as eventually caused the entire cast to be arrested after the performance and charged with public indecency, lewdness, corrupting a minor and sodomy, the two works between them suggesting strongly that Mr Tynan had been taken at his word, and indeed his action. Nothing daunted, he went ahead with his own show, *Oh, Calcutta!*, which was presently a huge popular success in the United States, though the critic of the *New York Times* said gloomily of it that it was 'the kind of show that gets pornography a dirty name'. But soon it was on its way to London.

# 18

# Transmedia and the message

'Science announced nonentity, and art admired decay'; it seemed that one at least of the problems of the Sixties was not new, since those words, from the dedication by G. K. Chesterton to *The Man Who Was Thursday*, had been first published in 1908, and the decay of art he was referring to was the decadence of the Nineties. Nevertheless there were two crucial differences between the devastating collapse of form in the arts in the Nineteen Sixties and the exhaustion of form by elaboration in the Eighteen Nineties; first, in the Sixties of this century the arts were, or seemed to be (it came to the same thing), dominated by the new forces, new movements, to an extent that had never previously been true; and second, there was nobody of both repute and ability about to point out that many of the new Emperors had no clothes. Still less was there anybody in sight who could readily distinguish between the clothed and the unclothed Emperors, so that, as is commonly the way at such times, the unclothed flourished mightily, and seemed to reproduce as rapidly and easily as amoebas. Never was there a time when it was so easy for a painter to get his work exhibited, a composer his music played, a novelist his books published. In New York, for instance, a sculptor, seriously considered and favourably appraised, was in the habit of telephoning to a supplier of stone blocks, ordering one of a specified material and approximate dimensions, and having the supplier deliver it direct to the gallery at which the artist's work was to be exhibited, where it was catalogued, placed on show and sold to a member of the public, and all without the artist having seen, let alone worked upon, the exhibit.[1]

[1] This information was given to the author, in a television interview, by Sir

This was, admittedly, exceptional, though exceptional only in the length to which the artist had gone, not in his choice of direction. Much that was happening in the arts in the Sixties was taking the same direction, and it will not do, as many did, to denounce it all indiscriminately – music, painting, writing – as the daubings and howlings and scribblings of degenerates, and even if it *would* do to reject it thus, there would still remain the question of what had caused the degeneracy, and what, if anything, might be done to arrest or reverse its progress.

Long before the Sixties, the pre-war ogres of music had become drawing-room pets; Stravinsky was being commended for his old-fashioned harmonies, where once his unbearable discords had started riots in concert-hall and theatre, Schoenberg was discussed as a severely orthodox Jewish traditionalist, Berg and Webern were being whistled in the very streets. By the time the music of the Sixties was being widely heard that was no longer surprising, since one work by Stockhausen consisted of readings, in random order and to random vocal sounds, unaccompanied by instruments, of *The Thoughts of Mao Tse-tung*, and it was clear that the days in which the music of Bartok was considered inaccessible were not merely over, but would never come back.

In the visual arts things had gone even further, and more rapidly.[1] Even at the beginning of the decade there were those who became incoherent when contemplating the work of Jackson Pollock; by its end the same people were using what they now thought of as his pleasingly symmetrical designs for their drawing-room curtains.

---

John Rothenstein, late director of the Tate Gallery. When asked why no voice was raised in fundamental criticism of such things, Sir John offered the ingenious and plausible – but ultimately unsatisfying – explanation that those critics who had denounced the early work of the Impressionists, and whose folly was still remembered, had made their successors wary of perpetrating similar follies.

[1] Almost all of the artists of the Sixties (musical and visual) mentioned in this section were foreign, not British; but their dominance of these aspects of the British scene was virtually complete. There was no comparable British composer, and in the visual arts only Richard Hamilton and Peter Blake made anything like a comparable stir, though of course there were less 'revolutionary' artists (David Hockney, for instance) who had considerable success and influence, too.

What many of the artists who made such a stir in the Sixties, and caused such havoc among categorizers, had in common was a determination to blur the line between art and reality until it disappeared completely, though this was by no means to be confused with those artists of an earlier day who had attempted to *reproduce* reality with increasing fidelity, for the Rauschenbergs and Liechtensteins, the Reinhardts and Le Witts would not at all have liked being compared to W. P. Frith, especially if they had known who he was. When Robert Rauschenberg, sensing that the days of his poverty were coming to an end, and sensing rightly too, took the humble bed in which he slept in his sparsely furnished room, tidied it, splashed paint over it in a deliberately random manner and exhibited it at the Venice Biennale, he had lit such a candle as by God's grace would never be put out. More to the point, he won the first prize, and more to the point still, he aroused in many others the thought that if they too splashed paint on their beds with sufficient vigour and abandon, they too might win the first prize at the Biennale, whereat there was such a splashing of paint on beds in humble artists' studios in London and New York, Paris and Rome, as drove many a landlady into screaming hysterics, without producing the desired result in money or fame. But Rauschenberg's 'Bed' was the precursor not only of a host of imitators, but also of a wave of artistic enterprise that, before the decade was finished, had swept the board, and reduced even normal abstract painting to the level of old-fashioned Academy portraiture.

Roy Liechtenstein, for instance, sought his inspiration in the popular comics that had for so long entertained children on both sides of the Atlantic, and exhibited giant blowups of the vigorously designed onomatopoeic 'Pow!', 'Bam!' and 'Aaargh!' with which they were spattered, together with such iconographical elements as pistols, blondes and space-ships, all done in the violent and simple colours of the originals. By now Rauschenberg had moved on to his even more celebrated 'Monogram', which was a long-haired goat, stuffed, its face battered, and a motor-car tyre fitted round its waist; at about this time too Andy

Warhol was exhibiting meticulously painted giant-size tins of Campbell's Tomato Soup; later – these having proved popular – Warhol took up his stance at a supermarket and signed the tins right off the shelves for the customers. Each time, imitators appeared, just too late, lacking whatever it was in the inspiration of the originator that had enabled him to catch the public imagination as he had. And, just as it was possible to be too late, it was also, even in the Sixties, possible to be too early; when, right at the beginning of the decade, Yves Klein exhibited in London a series of works entitled 'Monochrome Propositions', which consisted of canvases covered in an even expanse of a single colour, applied (as far as examination could discover) with a do-it-yourself paint-roller, he had little success, but right at the end of the decade Ad Reinhardt's 'Ultimate Paintings', which were the same things, were highly prized, and John McCracken's 'There's No Reason Not To', which was a perfectly regular plank of blue polyester resin 10′ long, 1′ 8″ wide and 3″ thick, was to be found leaning against a wall in the Tate Gallery.

Every artistic endeavour must owe something to its predecessors, and the 'pop' artists of the Sixties, the artists who aimed at an art which, in the words of the introduction to a London exhibition of their work, 'makes no direct appeal to the emotions, nor is it involved in uplift, but instead offers itself in the form of the simple, irrefutable object' ('I refute it *thus*,' said Dr Johnson, kicking the stone) owed, and in some cases even acknowledged, a debt to Marcel Duchamp, who almost half a century earlier had invented, if anybody had, the art of thc 'ready-made'. Duchamp had exhibited such things as a waistcoat on a hanger, a pocket chess-set, a door which had once been that of his studio, a hat-stand, a urinal, and a birdcage containing sugar-lumps and a thermometer and entitled 'Why Not Sneeze?' But there was a gaiety and vigour about the work of the best of the artists of the Sixties that Duchamp, perhaps because he was lonely, there being no other following the same road when he started out along it, lacked. What infused the work of the 'irrefutable minimalists' was a brash confidence that they were in the vanguard, and the vanguard of a genuine new cultural march, so that it was the more traditional artists who soon began to feel, and even to seem, eccentric. Even the excesses and excrescences that gather inevitably on such movements, such as the sculptor referred to earlier, and the films which Warhol began to make, one of which consisted of a single unchanged long-shot, lasting eight hours, of the Empire State Building, could not stop the march.

In music, things in the Sixties went even further, the rejection of form having been accomplished with a completeness that seemed excessively savage for the circumstances, and the equivalent of the 'irrefutable object' in the visual arts being established with an even more complete abandonment of traditional tools and techniques than in the case of the visual arts; a 'prepared piano' used in the works of John Cage, for instance, bore even less resemblance to an unprepared one than John McCracken's blue plank leaning against the wall to a painting with a frame round it.

As the visual artists had had their Duchamp, so the musicians had had their Erik Satie, and at one London concert of the new music proper homage was paid to this forerunner of theirs with a complete performance of his 'Vexations', which consists of four bars of piano-music repeated *da capo* for twenty-four hours without a break. It might have been thought that that was as far as music could go, but apart from the fact that Satie did not have the benefit of the science of electronics, or of the tape-recorder, which were pressed into service in the search for new sounds in which the new music might be composed, he, like Duchamp, lacked the inexorable thrust of those who know themselves to be part of a victorious army. Not so John Cage, whose best-known work of the decade is probably 'Four Minutes, Thirty-Three Seconds' and consists of the pianist sitting immobile on the piano-stool, with the piano closed, for precisely that length of time. Cage explained that the sounds heard in the concert-room when the work is being performed – such as the scrape of a chair, a cough, the rustle of a programme, an aeroplane passing outside – are part of the music too, or even the whole of it; but those who wrote off Cage as merely another louse on the locks of music were hard put to it to explain what had driven him to persist in this kind of work for years before recognition came his way. When it did, though, he continued to plough exactly the same furrow as before:

> Cage's concerto for piano and orchestra, which was performed in last night's programme, had been started before any of the audience were allowed to enter the hall. The players are given a selection of more or less precisely notated sounds to produce: they can play any, all, or none of these, in what order they wish (and so, presumably, the programme-sheet rightly included the name of a performer who was neither heard nor seen). There is no reason why the work need ever end, or perceptibly begin, though in the event the pianist, Richard Toop, did leave his keyboard and conduct an ending.
>
> Whether the significance is the concatenation of sounds or something else Cage and his followers refuse to decree.[1]

Cage, ridiculous though he was, had put the essence of the new music for his less ridiculous comrades as baldly as E. C. Goossen (the author of the essay from which the statement about the 'irrefutable object' is taken) had done for the visual arts. 'A sound', he said, 'does not view itself as needing another sound for its elucidation – it is occupied with the performance of its characteristics.' Thus it seemed that every note, or sound, might or even should be considered separately, and the listener who sought for connections between one and another – connections of harmony, rhythm or melody – would be disappointed. A much more serious musical figure of the Sixties, Pierre Boulez, put it like this: 'Purely thematic writing has no future. It was adapted for certain kinds of situations: the situation is over when a theme can take place.' So indeed one might think, in view of the performance of a work (not by Boulez) for woodwind instruments which was played by musicians standing around a tank of tropical fish on the

[1] William Mann, *The Times*, January 15th, 1968.

sides of which unscored music-paper had been pasted, so that as the fish swam about in it they appeared momentarily, whenever their position coincided with one of the lines of the stave, to be notes, and were promptly played by the musicians. But Boulez – who ended the Sixties by being appointed conductor of the B.B.C. Symphony Orchestra – though he was not as random in his composing as that, nevertheless had abandoned almost all the conventions of music except rhythm, and even from rhythm he had stripped most of the continuity, so that whereas once it had been difficult for a listener to a piece of music in a new idiom to pick out the themes, with Boulez it was difficult to pick out even the physical shape. And yet, just as the irreducible minimalists of the visual arts gave sign that they were conscious of their position in the mainstream, so the new composers clearly had the same sort of confidence.

Boulez, Messiaen, Xenakis – these could, if they had been so minded, have pointed to the crowded concert-halls that frequently greeted a programme of their works. The generally acknowledged master of them all was Stockhausen, whose earlier work, though advanced enough, to be sure, aroused no suspicion that he was playing games with his followers, but whose later ones included such items as a work for solo percussion in which the score is spirally bound, so that the player can begin anywhere and go on until he gets to where he came in, when he can stop if he is so minded; another in which part of the music is printed on a transparent ruler, pivoted at one end, which the players are invited to swing across the relatively fixed part of the score and play the result; another – the famous 'Gruppen' – which demands three orchestras, each equipped with a conductor, for its performance; and yet another which requires no fewer than four orchestras and four choirs to boot. Asked to explain himself, Stockhausen was wont to talk of macrostructure and microstructure and to describe his 'Microphonie I', in which

> he has a tamtam (a rimless Chinese gong) which two players strike or touch to make it sound, while two others move

> microphones round its surface picking up sounds and superimposing a second layer, and then a filtering machine collects and varies these to make yet a third layer of structure in rhythm, dynamic and timbre.[1]

'I hesitate to call it music,' said the music critic of the *Daily Mail*, describing a work the principle of which was that 'notes and noises from players in different parts of the audience would combine with the same sounds electronically distorted and fed back through loudspeakers, with occasional additions of pre-recorded tapes', but to this charge, if indeed it was meant as a charge, the composers of the new music had a complete reply, because they, when they had gone far enough, not only hesitated to call the result music, but resolutely refused to, insisting that it was a new order of art entirely, and that music as it had hitherto been was over, having been replaced by sound.

With all this and more (a great deal more) there went a deliberate breaking of the compartment walls in which the different arts had for so long been segregated, though it was not the search for that *Gesamtkunstwerk* of which Richard Wagner dreamed which animated those involved in the process. Suddenly, a new word—'transmedia'—appeared, under whose kindly and umbrella-like aegis anything, anything at all, became art, just as for John Cage anything had become music.

Temples sprang up to accommodate this new worship, chief among them in Britain being the Institute of Contemporary Arts, which had once been a staid harbinger of the avant-garde situated in Dover Street, but which acquired a new and revolutionary director, Michael Kustow, and palatial new premises, formerly part of the German Embassy, in the Mall. The I.C.A. threw itself into the art-and-revolution business with such vigour and enthusiasm that in no time at all it had spent its considerable Arts Council installation grant and also its year's subvention of twenty-five thousand pounds and was anything up to thirty thousand pounds in debt and calling loudly for more public

[1] William Mann, *The Times*, December 10th, 1965.

money, its leaders noticing no incompatibility between their revolutionary aim, which was to overthrow everything 'bourgeois' about society, and their demands for larger subventions to enable them to proceed with their work. Madame Defarge to all this was the amazing figure of Jennie Lee, Minister for the Arts, whose creed was summed up by her when, at the opening of the I.C.A.'s new gallery, she defended the exhibition, which was called 'The Obsessive Image' and dealt largely in violence, death and eroticism, by saying:

> Now let us have some humility. What do you expect to see here, pretty pictures of country cottages with roses round the door? What you see here tonight is what life is all about and we have all got to play our part to help artists to portray this. What is happening here tonight is not just something national but international and it is something for us to be proud of. You do not particularly have to like, or understand, what is on show here. I might not particularly like or understand it, but I am not going to set myself up as an art critic.

Panic and emptiness! Panic and emptiness! Not only was Jack as good as his master, but sound was as good as music; nay, the simultaneous blaring of six random-tuned radio sets (a work by John Cage) was as good as Mozart if not better (because less bourgeois), and a papier-maché thumb four feet high (the centrepiece of the I.C.A. exhibition at which Jennie Lee had made her impassioned defence of the new art) more real than Titian. 'Environment' was all the cry, and soon it had almost eclipsed 'transmedia' as the password to the innermost mysteries of the new, revolutionary art, and at the I.C.A., as was inevitable, an 'environment' was built and put on show, consisting of a huge plastic tube which was both exhibit and exhibition room, since visitors entered it and walked about inside. 'The show is not the show, but those who go' had come literally true.

Meanwhile the popular arts had been busy too. Procol, O Procol Harum, profani! The Beatles had started something, or more probably something had started with the Beatles, that showed by the end of the Sixties no sign of stopping, or even slackening off. The growth of pop-music groups – many, no doubt, inspired by the gigantic commercial success of the Beatles to believe that the lightning might strike them too, if they only formed fours and began to perform, but many, also, clearly in the business of self-expression – was the most extraordinary phenomenon in the world of entertainment of the whole decade; long before its end there were literally thousands of them, in Britain and America, and though many flourished only briefly, many displayed surprising endurance, and in any case there were always ten to take the place of one which fell. Some were almost as famous, and successful, as the Beatles; some were known only to the most devoted aficionados. But all added to the atmosphere of the decade, and the isle was full of noises as never before, coming from, among others, the Rolling Stones, the Bee Gees, the Monkees, the Doors, the Cream, the Mothers of Invention, the Seekers, the Who, the Small Faces, the Pretty Things, the Animals, the Pink Floyd, the Scaffold, the Grateful Dead, the Tremoloes, the Family, the Supremes, the Holding Company, the Four Tops, the Led Zeppelin, the Shadows, the Exploding Galaxy, the Editors, the Fugs, the Gods, the Kinks, the Hermits, the Paper Dolls, the Breakaways, the Greaseband, the Casuals, the Amen Corner, the Big Sound, the Flirtations, the Herd, the Marbles, the Status Quo, the New York Public Library, the Hollies, the Foundations, the Electric Havens, the Four Seasons, the Bachelors, the Seychelles, the Love Affair, the Fifth Dimension, the Three Dog Night, the Equals, the Vagabonds, the Marmalade, the Mindbenders, the Moody Blues, the Mirettes, the Tuesday's Children, the Plastic Penny, the Procol Harum, the Troggs, the Fruit Machine, the Union Gap, the 1910 Fruitgum Co., the Beach Boys, the Fairport Convention, the Vanity Fair, the Harmony Grass, the Aces, the Young Tradition, the Nice, the Dubliners, the Tinkers, the Fleetwood Mac, the Incredible String Band, the Web, the Little Free Rock, the Blodwyn Pig, the Liverpool Scene, the Spooky Tooth, the Third Ear, the High Tide, the Mamas and Papas, the Carnations, the Pacemakers, the From Genesis to Revelation, the O'Hara Express, the Pentangle, the Chickenshack, the Blind Faith, the Fourmost, the Searchers, the Four Pennies, the Bar-Kays, the Unit Four Plus Two, the Hedgehoppers Anonymous, the Applejacks, the Box Tops, the Edison Lighthouse, the Blood, Sweat and Tears, the Vibrations, and the Rada Krishna Temple.

The bulk of the output of all these, including that of the Beatles themselves, vanished, quite rightly, down the memory-hole of instant oblivion. Yet something remained, and in any case no such mass movement can be without significance, nor can a hundred thousand young people turn up in Hyde Park, there to listen in an orderly and peaceful fashion to a concert by one of the groups (the Rolling Stones), unless they are part of a shared experience wider than the sounds which they find pleasing. What that experience might be, none of their elders could say, and they were themselves too inarticulate, and usually too contemptuous, to explain. But it could not be denied that they were serious, if any evidence could be derived from the fact that one of the earliest priests of the movement, Bob Dylan, sang in the tones of a medieval flagellant charging the sins of mankind with responsibility for the ravages of the plague, and that his most popular song consisted of an unmistakeable, and far from comforting, vision of the apocalypse:

> I've stumbled on the side of twelve misty mountains,
> I've walked and I've crawled on six crooked highways,
> I've stepped in the middle of seven sad forests,
> I've been out in front of a dozen dead oceans,
> I've been ten thousand miles in the mouth of a graveyard,
> And it's a hard, and it's a hard, it's a hard, and it's a hard,
> And it's a hard rains are gonna fall.
>
> I saw a new born baby with wild wolves all around it,
> I saw a highway of diamonds with nobody on it,
> I saw a black branch with blood that kept drippin',
> I saw a room full of men with their hammers a-bleedin',
> I saw a white ladder all covered with water,

I saw ten thousand talkers whose tongues were all broken,
I saw guns and sharp swords in the hands of young children
And it's a hard, and it's a hard, it's a hard, it's a hard,
And it's a hard rains are gonna fall.

I heard the sound of a thunder, it roared out a warnin',
Heard the roar of a wave that could drown the whole world,
Heard one hundred drummers whose hands were a-blazin',
Heard ten thousand whis'prin' and nobody listenin',
Heard one person starve, I heard many people laughin',
Heard the song of a poet who died in the gutter,
Heard the sound of a clown who cried in the alley,
Heard the sound of one person who said he was human,
And it's a hard, and it's a hard, it's a hard, it's a hard,
And it's a hard rains are gonna fall.

I met a young child beside a dead pony,
I met a white man who walked a black dog,
I met a woman whose body was burning,
I met a young girl, she gave me a rainbow,
I met one man who was wounded in love,
I met another man who was wounded with hatred,
And it's a hard, it's a hard, it's a hard, it's a hard,
It's a hard rains are gonna fall.

I'm a-goin' back out 'fore the rain starts a-fallin',
I'll walk to the depth of the deepest dark forest,
Where the people are many and their hands are all empty,
Where the pellets of poison are flooding the waters,
Where the home in the valley meets the damp dirty prison,
Where the executioner's face is always well hidden,
Where hunger is ugly, where souls are forgotten,
Where black is the colour, where none is the number,
And I'll tell it and think it and speak it and breathe it,
It'll reflect from the mountain so all souls can see it,
Then I'll stand on the ocean until I start sinkin',
But I'll know my song well before I start singing,

And it's a hard, it's a hard, it's a hard, it's a hard,
It's a hard rains are gonna fall.[1]

Not many of the groups' songs had the genuinely poetic quality of that. But very many of the players and singers, and huge numbers among their audiences, would have sensed something of what Dylan, and the movement he somehow led, meant by his vision.

* * *

All revolutions devour their children, and none so voraciously as revolutions in entertainment, of which there were many in the Sixties in Britain. By the end of the decade it was difficult to remember, so far had things progressed (or, as some would have said, retrogressed), the extraordinary effect that had been caused at its beginning by a four-man stage revue called *Beyond the Fringe* and a weekly television programme called *That Was The Week That Was.*

The former abandoned the cosy, congratulatory air that had dominated intimate revue until then, and for the first time in such entertainment included the audience in its targets. The show was received with raptures and ran for several years, though long before the end of its run it had suffered the inevitable fate reserved in England (at any rate until the end of the decade) for rebels, namely affectionate absorption into the bosom of the Establishment that they are supposed to be out to destroy. Eventually the Queen went to see it, and was reported to have laughed heartily.

But those were also the days in which a television programme provoked questions in Parliament every week. *That Was The Week That Was* reached eventually an audience of over twelve million weekly, and entirely altered the pattern of Saturday-night behaviour for them while the run continued. Again, the items which caused the stir, such as a guide to comparative religion done in the style of *Which?* reports ("This handy little faith ... optional extras ... if you want Transubstantiation you can have it, if you

[1] 'A Hard Rain's a-Gonna Fall' (Dylan) © 1963 by M. Witmark & Sons. Used by permission of Warner Bros. Music. All rights reserved.

don't you don't have to ... '), now seem mild and harmless, as indeed they mostly were then, but the climate at the beginning of the Sixties was so different from what it was at the end that such things caused an uproar out of all proportion to the offence actually caused, or even to that intended.

A bishop attacked the programme with a savagery that was not at all diminished when he admitted, in something of an anti-climax, that he had never actually seen it; an Anglican clergyman denounced it as a poisonous conspiracy against all that was best in British life, describing the enchanting Millicent Martin as 'a repulsive woman with a grating voice' and another member of the team as 'a thick-lipped Jew-boy'; Members of Parliament on both sides of the House called for its suppression, calls which were redoubled in numbers and intensity when the programme included an item, called 'The Silent M.P.s', which drew attention to those Members of Parliament who held the record for the longest period spent without speaking in the House; the letters columns of the press, then the feature pages, finally the very editorials, were crowded with fury against the filth, sedition and blasphemy that, to many viewers, the programme consisted of almost entirely. In this instance the change between one end of the decade and the other is the more marked because it took place in the B.B.C., an institution which at the beginning of the Sixties was still known as 'Auntie', to signify its kindly though stern authoritarianism, an attitude which in turn stemmed from the Presbyterian rule of its first Director-General, John Reith. At the beginning of the Sixties Reith's influence had been long a-dying, and the Director-General of the day, Hugh Carleton Greene, who had sensed much earlier than most figures in positions of comparable responsibility which way the wind of the times was blowing, probably did more than any other individual in the B.B.C., before or since, to bury Auntie's Presbyterian ethic for ever, if only by allowing (for a considerable time, at any rate) such creative figures as Donald Baverstock the freedom they needed.

Now it is not necessary to be a Marxist to recognize that the new B.B.C. and the new theatre were symptoms rather than causes, and that the revolutions they underwent were all part of the birth of the new world that emerged during the Sixties, just as the outraged roars of displeasure that greeted them represented the groans of the assembled husbands and fathers experiencing sympathetic labour-pains and demanding analgesics or even the immediate reversal of the processes of birth that had just started. But, as is the way with births, the processes once started are irreversible, and indeed had been since the moment of conception, though exactly when that took place, when the seeds were sown of the changes which dominated the Sixties and which produced in so many fields the strains and tensions of a society that was trying to look forwards and backwards at the same time, it would be very hard to say. All that can be said with any certainty, indeed, is that neither the theatre, after *Beyond the Fringe*, nor television, after *That Was The Week That Was*, was in any doubt about the direction in which it would now be looking, and by the end of the decade the powers of theatrical censorship exercised by the Lord Chamberlain's office had been abolished, and hardly anything was considered too extreme or offensive to be shown on television. And since revolutions, having devoured their children, are reluctant thereafter to admit their paternity, lest they be accused simultaneously of infanticide and cannibalism, so by the end of the Sixties there were few among the avant-garde who would have accepted that they had any precursors, still less that they owed a debt to those two path-finding entertainments—just as, in all justice, it must be said that those involved in *Beyond the Fringe* and *TW3* were reluctant to accept that they too were evolutionary descendants grown imperceptibly out of such older forms as the *Gate Revues* and *Tonight*. Thinking his thoughts in retirement was the extraordinary figure of Lord Reith, whose influence on the B.B.C. had been direct, and on the theatre vicarious and representative, and who finally broke a long silence with an amazing television conversation with Malcolm Muggeridge in which he appeared a profoundly disappointed and embittered man, as well he might. Revolutions devour not only their own children, but other people's, too.

In the circumstances it was not surprising that the artists of the mass popular means of entertainment began to be regarded, and to regard themselves, as the men who had stamped their sign-manual on the decade. Man of the Sixties! How many coveted that title, sought it, wooed it, pursued it! How many – sportsmen, actors, politicians, businessmen even – thought, as they basked in what proved to be their few short months of fame, that it would last, that it would be they who set the tone and pace for the decade, who would one day have an Era nicknamed after them! How many were disappointed, how many have still to be disappointed, their fames ephemeral, their names forgotten utterly, gone to graveyards, every one! The Sixties, in Britain, did not lend themselves to such type-casting; they were jealous years, they hoarded their favours, offered them and withdrew them, letting the recipient think he was the chosen man of the decade, only to prove as fickle as human beings when, a few months later, another happened along.

Yet one young man would perhaps be offered the title by many judges – not yet, but when the dust and the anxieties have sufficiently settled for us to see the decade's shape more clearly. Perhaps David Frost grasped earlier than most the quality of the Sixties. Always one jump further on than where he was expected, ever exploiting a new medium, a new technique, a new hairstyle, Frost divined by a remarkable instinct what the age demanded, and gave it. At the beginning of the Sixties he was unknown; at its end he was better known than anyone in the country except the royal family, and the Prime Minister himself would fain wait upon him at breakfast, in the hope that some of the publicity might rub off.

One of the first to make his name in the new wave of entertainment which began its mass appeal with *That Was The Week That Was*, Frost also realized very early the possibilities that were offered by transatlantic commuting in the interests of entertainment. Films and plays, and their stars, had of course gone back and forth, creating reputations in both continents, for many years; Frost was the first to take to the United States a reputation made with a single television series, and there make another reputation, a faithful copy of the first, and then bring that one back, until none could tell any longer which was original and which was copy. Seeing soon afterwards the chance of extending his reputation by means of the written word, and realizing with the acumen of one twice his age the uses to which experts and collaborators could be put, he became newspaper columnist, then author. New television series, cisatlantic and transatlantic, followed, each an advance on the one before; now he was interviewer-in-chief to the decade, bidding the great and the small to his studio; and all came when they were bid. Anon he would be a television executive, and bustled about helping to arrange a consortium to put in for, and obtain, the valuable London region week-end franchise when the independent television contracts were redistributed; soon his programme was going out on three nights a week, and now it was making and unmaking reputations, here exposing before millions the villainy of a Dr Savundra, there introducing to millions the likeability of a George Brown.

A classless, unregional accent and a decent, engaging personality left him lacking only one thing, but that the thing the decade was most short of—weight. His talent, although often denied, was undeniable, his wit sharp and ready, his judgment shrewd, his eye for the gap in the line opposite excellent; yet by the end of the Sixties he had said no memorable thing, left no imprint on the age. Rather had the memorable things been said to him, or about him, or beside him, while the age left its mark on him. Still, Prime Ministers and Cabinet Ministers and Shadow Cabinet Ministers, entertainers, writers, judges and criminals, scientists, lunatics, and men in rebellion against the Crown—all were grist to Frost's mill, all obeyed the summons to his presence, until, as was perhaps inevitable, royalty itself scorned not to appear on the David Frost show, when Prince Charles, the heir-apparent himself, did so. The O.B.E. was now not far off, the Knighthood not much further; as the Sixties ended, David Frost had indeed established a claim to speak as the decade's representative. Young enough to remain for many more years in the public eye, flexible enough to move on again and yet again, aggressive enough to battle on behalf of the future yet wise enough to keep on his side those who feared it, with all the most modern techniques for getting audiences and keeping them, David (as we may presume to call him, lest we be constrained to call him Dave) at the close of the Sixties could reflect, and probably did, that he had done well out of the decade, and that it had done none too badly out of him.

# 19

# Pillars of society

Was nothing sacred? Nothing was sacred. The restlessness of the decade, the dissatisfaction with what existed *because* it existed, took many forms but was unmistakeable in them all; from the revolutionaries who wanted to destroy society for much the same reason as Mallory gave for wanting to climb Everest, to the middle-aging television 'personalities' who aped the fashions of the young and thus looked ridiculous both to the young and to their own contemporaries (to say nothing of their elders), the story was the same. Whatever was, must not be; whatever was not, must. It was like a kind of gigantic national game of spiritual Postman's Knock, with General Post being called every time, so that it sometimes seemed as if everybody was rushing from one place to another, or one attitude to another, or one mood to another, only to rush on, or sometimes back, as soon as they had arrived.

This restlessness, this dissatisfaction, produced many effects large and small, and no area of life was free from its influence. It was in the Sixties that the Monarchy, the function and place of which had not been seriously questioned for nearly three-quarters of a century, became again a subject for debate; so much so that before the decade was out the royal family themselves had joined in. Indeed, if one were to seek a single example of the speed and inexorability with which Britain had changed during the Sixties, to stand as symbol of all the changes, the revolution in attitudes to the Monarchy might well serve.

The first royal occasion of the Sixties was one perfectly in keeping with a view of royalty which had disappeared almost entirely by the decade's end. In the very first days of the decade Romance, which was to become increasingly scarce as it wore on, raised its beautiful head, with the engagement and marriage of Princess Margaret. Five years earlier she had made the nation's heart beat as it had not beaten since the romance of her uncle twenty years before had cost him his throne, when she had decided, after much heart-searching and a discussion with the Archbishop of Canterbury, not to marry a divorced man. Now, after a courtship kept with what turned out to be ill-advised perfection from the outside world, her engagement to a young and fashionable photographer, Antony Armstrong-Jones, was announced. The news came as a surprise to everybody; particularly chagrined at their failure to hear about it before the world did were the gossip-columnists, who from the moment of this exposure of their missed scoop determined to have their revenge. Presently paragraphs began to appear which on the face of them were unexceptionable, but which carried an unmistakeable flavour of hostility.

An opportunity soon arose to turn dissatisfaction to rich and fruitful account, when the best man, after a campaign of innuendo and gossip, cried off on the grounds of ill-health and was replaced. Millions, unskilled at reading between the lines of the gossip-columnists' code, suspected little of what was going on, and for them the marriage took place in an atmosphere of metaphorical orange-blossom that had not been seen in Britain for decades. The night before the wedding – fortunately a warm one – thousands slept along the route the bride was due to take to Westminster Abbey, and the following day the route was packed with uncountable hundreds of thousands, come to see the fairy story right to its end, as the golden coach, drawn by four white horses, passed by.

The wedding marked the high point of that ancient adulation of royalty that had caused so many stern moralists to declare that it was nationally unhealthy, though the moralists who thought of the Monarchy as 'the gold filling in a mouth of decay'[1] did not make entirely clear if what they were advocating was extraction of the teeth and their replacement by some kind of

[1] The phrase was coined by John Osborne.

Scandinavian plastic ones. Certainly the feeding of the hunger for news of royalty had long been a profitable business for newspapers and magazines, and the empty intimacies of 'Crawfie', who had been the Queen's governess and spent the years of her retirement selling her memoirs and her comments on royal matters (until she came a cropper by describing the Trooping of the Colour in considerable detail in a year in which it was cancelled at the last moment, too late for the magazine in question to take Crawfie's account of it out of its pages), undoubtedly commanded a wide sale and an eager public. It was in the Sixties, however, that the cult withered and died, and before the end of the decade the announcement by a large newspaper group that it was to bring out a magazine called *Majesty*, exclusively devoted to the doings of royalty, was greeted with incredulity, and shortly afterwards, when it became apparent that there would be neither advertising nor sales sufficient to keep alive, it was quietly abandoned. It was another sign of the way in which a healthily sceptical maturity stole upon the country in the Sixties, and no doubt the royal family themselves welcomed the opportunity it provided to spend a little less time on display in the goldfish-bowl. Long before the decade ended even the B.B.C. had ceased to give minor news of the royal family precedence in their news bulletins over major matters of domestic or international affairs.

The marriage of Princess Margaret and the Earl of Snowdon, and the attitude of the less reputable newspapers to it, was also the beginning of the end for the old-style newspaper gossip-column, with its nose, as well as its eye, to the keyhole. The second choice for best man at the wedding fell upon a distinguished surgeon, Roger Gilliatt, and his then wife, Penelope, had been fired by the gossip-writers' attitude to the wedding to write what turned out to be one of the most remarkable and influential articles ever to appear in a British magazine. Backed by the proprietor of the *Queen*, a wealthy and well-connected young man named Jocelyn Stevens, who had himself suffered from the attention of the gossip-writers, Mrs Gilliatt wrote a series of detailed analyses of the characters, methods and achievements of the leading members of the trade, lavishly illustrated with examples of their practices, and decorated with cuts of the apologies, extracted under threat of legal action, that so frequently appeared in their columns.

The effect of the article was almost immediate; the two worst offenders—'William Hickey' of the *Daily Express* and 'Paul Tanfield' of the *Daily Mail*—were drastically changed, both in personnel and style, and the ferreting out of the details of private lives, in which they had so long specialized, came to an end, so that both columns now deal harmlessly in the doings of debs and the trivia of the trivial.

Again and again, the people of the Sixties were taken by surprise at the speed with which change itself was changing. The oldest British institution of all, the Monarchy, which had seemed, when the decade opened, least likely to change, was by the time it closed hurling itself against the yielding walls of the future as though trying to make up for a dozen centuries of resistance to innovation. Not long after the Sixties began, and on the announcement of Lord Snowdon's appointment as a photographer with the *Sunday Times*, a cartoon appeared in the *Spectator* which, in the format of the front page of the *Sunday Times*, depicted the artist's conception of the Snowdon family-album thus exposed to public view, with snaps of corgis, royal hands waving from Rolls-Royces and the like. It was the first time royalty had been caricatured, even affectionately, in any but revolutionary journals, since Max Beerbohm's version of Edward VII, and the cartoon excited considerable comment, in print and elsewhere, not only in Britain but abroad. Long before the decade ended the royal family was being caricatured as savagely as it had been at the time of the early Georges; Gerald Scarfe's monstrous physical distortions, for instance, were being applied to the Queen, and the artist[1] who had started it all with the Snowdon album summed up what had happened when, towards the end of the decade, he produced another cartoon in which the Queen, sitting amid scenes of immense splendour, ornateness and expense, and reading

[1] Trog (Walter Fawkes).

a newspaper report of a speech by her consort, is saying: 'Philip, why do you keep on harping on waste and inefficiency at the top?'

On rather more fashionable advice than many thought them likely to be offered, the royal family abruptly decided to give themselves a new public image, more in tune with the decade than the combination of mousiness and rigid protocol that they had lived with for so long. Suddenly, from, roughly, the moment that the formal investiture of the heir-apparent as Prince of Wales was decided upon, a torrent of intimate and authorized publicity about the royal family began to pour out. Some of it, like Dermot Morrah's creepy-crawfie biography of Prince Charles, was still stuck, like a fly in amber that had begun to ooze with the heat, in the ancient servilities of the courtier, prose and all. But most of it used with skill and shrewdness the most modern techniques of that salesman of images, the advertising man, high priest of the image-conscious Sixties, and the campaign culminated in a full-length television documentary on the lives of the royal family which, a full year in making, portrayed them with an intimacy never before attained except in the unreliable below-stairs gossip that had been peddled for so long.

Perhaps more remarkable still were the two direct television interviews, with the Duke of Edinburgh and Prince Charles, which respectively preceded and followed the documentary film. The Duke faced a trio of journalists and answered questions about his work, his position, his attitudes, which only a year or two before would have been unthinkable, and the Prince went further, discussing with an engagingly self-deprecating air questions about the kind of girl he might marry.

Then, just too late to do anything about it, the royal family realized that mingling itself with the people could not be a one-sided process, that the people would mingle with royalty too, once the door had been opened; he who descends into the market-place inevitably finds himself rubbing shoulders with the shoppers. Immediately an argument broke out about the wisdom of the decision; did not the divinity that doth hedge a king disappear when the public got so close to him? Obviously it did, and the decision to abandon any attempt to preserve it promptly raised, without its apparently having been foreseen on the part of those responsible for the decision, the question of the Monarchy's relevance and usefulness. Before, its defenders could have argued in the last resort that it was both irrelevant and, in any practical sense, useless, and that this was its strength; it served as a mystical-magical symbol, a repository of the nation's history and a remote and cloud-wrapped fount of sovereignty and honour. But now, when in the Sixties it had stepped off the plinth in a brisk and utilitarian fashion, many began to weigh and measure it by utilitarian standards, and its relevance and usefulness were being judged by entirely different principles of cost-effectiveness. No serious republican movement arose, but at last there was a real possibility that the Monarchy might one day wither away. Such was the effect of this extraordinary change-ridden decade. And as far as royalty was concerned, the symbol of the decade's end, as Princess Margaret's wedding had been that of the beginning, was the Queen's decision, at the time of the last Christmas of the Sixties, to dispense with the Monarch's annual broadcast to the nation, a tradition which had been unbroken, in peace or in war, since it was first instituted by George V in 1932.

* * *

There were other institutions, younger than the Monarchy yet in some ways as close – even closer – to the people's hearts. And they too felt the effect of these shaken and ambiguous years. One such was the family Dale. They had first made a mark on the national consciousness in the late Forties, when Mrs Dale had started her famous Diary. The longest-running radio serial of all, *Mrs Dale's Diary* (or *The Dales*, as it was known from 1962 onwards – the first, ominous, sign that even the unchangeable might change) had gone on tinkling, teacup-like, in five million homes, day after day for over twenty years. Now, in 1969, it stopped, struck down by the fell hand of the B.B.C., whose spokesman explained with breathtaking impudence that 'We have run out of story development.' The announcement came like Lytton Strachey's description of the news that Queen Victoria was dying:

> When, two days previously, the news of the approaching end had been made public, astonished grief had swept over the country. It appeared as if some monstrous reversal of the course of nature was about to take place. The vast majority of her subjects had never known a time when Queen Victoria had not been reigning over them. She had become an indissoluble part of their whole scheme of things, and that they were about to lose her appeared a scarcely possible thought.[1]

Petitions sprang up all over the country: Save the Dales was their message. On the backs of cars appeared labels: SAVE THE DALES. Plans for a kind of Dales-in-Exile were made, for a Free Dale Government to be set up in some neighbouring country (Radio Luxemburg, perhaps) against the day when the liberation should take place. All in vain: the B.B.C. stood firm, and the Dales went.

But twenty-one years do not pass without memories. There were the memories of the oldest inhabitants, who could remember the early days of the serial, and the relentless triviality of everything and everyone concerned. It had gone on thus for a decade, and more than a decade, and it seemed it might go on thus until the end of time. So indeed it might have done, had it not been for the desire, so strong in the Sixties, to change anything that had not been changed for some time. In 1962 the Dales moved from their genteel London suburb, perfectly named Parkwood Hill, to a less genteel, semi-industrial town, less evocatively christened Exton, in East Anglia. Then it was that *Mrs Dale's Diary* became *The Dales*, and her famous opening line – 'I'm very worried about Jim' – was heard no more. Then too, more serious things began to happen. Hitherto no topic more serious than needlework

[1] Lytton Strachey, *Queen Victoria* (Chatto and Windus, London, 1921), Ch. X, p. 309.

or measles had been allowed to obtrude upon the Dales' gentility and detachment, and if in the real world there were elections, controversies, economic crises, national scandals, the Dales knew them not. The B.B.C., as was well known, was dedicated to impartiality, at any rate in the sense understood by the Irish judge who declared that he would lean neither to partiality on the one hand nor to impartiality on the other. All the same, there were those who, though not demanding that the Dales should actually take sides in controversial matters, felt that the family ought at least to know that they existed. Nervously, like a townee dipping his toe into the sea on the first day of his holiday, the Dales tried controversy when they moved to Exton, and, like the same townee finding the experience very much to his taste, leapt bodily in with cries of glee, and thereafter proceeded to hurl themselves about with abandon, splashing everybody within sight. The colour-problem, a variety of sex-problems (at one point one of the characters was found to be a homosexual, which in the early days of the serial would have been about as likely as an acute attack of paedophilia by Dr Dale, and Mrs Dale actually experienced the menopause, where previously she would have been unlikely to be allowed to experience indigestion), international affairs, economics – all these were discussed, in their latter-day maturity, sophistication and freedom, by the newly liberated Dales.

It could not last. Once the character of the Dales had changed, once they were no longer fixed in their nexus of genteel know-nothingness, they began to wither and fade, like those inhabitants of the legendary land of Shangri-La, who remain eternally young while they stay there, but once they set foot outside speedily age, shrivel and die. After only a few years the decision to wind up the Dales as soon as it could conveniently be done was taken, and Dr Dale had a heart attack, so that the thing could be brought to an end at any moment by simply giving him another, and fatal, one. A year later the blow fell; Dr Dale was to retire and the programme was to come to an end. Outcry followed, but it was to no avail, and on April 25th, 1969, the Dales took the air for the last time. And so they passed over, and all the teacups tinkled for them on the other side. Rest, rest, unperturbed spirits; you were too frail for the Sixties, and when injected with their rich, red blood it killed you. You should never have been allowed, let alone encouraged, to quit the featureless Fifties where you belonged, if only some way could have been found of prolonging them, and you, for ever.

Meanwhile the Archers went on.

The bifocals with which the nation peered at the decade—up for one view of it, down for the opposite—were used again and again to watch television, that most demotic of the arts, most popular, most often denounced, feared, praised, welcomed. Was it a soporific, lulling the viewers into mindless complacency, satisfying them with capsuled opinion, making them an easy prey to a conspiracy of ruthless men (or, more likely, machines) that was trying to turn them into fully automated robots, broiler-house chickens without will or personality? Or was it a mind-expanding, life-enhancing force, opening new windows, providing new sensations, broadening the experience and understanding of the people, and turning them instead into a new breed of giants—mature, sophisticated, knowledgeable and well-balanced?

Two television series stood out, in the Sixties, from the run of programmes, to typify, with only a little nudging and pushing to persuade them into the starting-stalls, the dichotomy of the decade. In one corner was *The Power Game*, epitome of the ruthless world that would make or break our own; in the other *The Forsyte Saga*, a leisurely unfolding of an old chronicle of human passions.

Both exerted a huge fascination over vast multitudes; sometimes in ten million homes ten million television sets were tuned to them, and double that number of watchers silently enrapt. The respective fascinations of the two programmes (even more characteristically, *The Power Game* was the product of the commercial channel, *The Forsyte Saga* of the B.B.C.) were almost unbearably symbolic. On the one hand was the awful spell cast by power ruthlessly exercised, the deep, secret thrill of seeing the powerful lord it over the weak. Sir John Wilder, with the handsome flat face and roughened voice of Patrick Wymark, drove hard towards what he wanted; it might be women or drink or recognition or money, but above all, subordinating all his minor desires to its terrible attraction, was power. A horrid report came from Sweden, one of the countries to which the series had been exported, that there the wives of business magnates nagged them to be more, not less, like Wilder, and if the report was true it suggested that Sweden was in an even more riven state than Britain, even more unable to make up her mind whether to go forward or back, for in this country, with considerable discretion, neither British businessmen nor their wives would admit to identifying themselves with the characters in *The Power Game*, while many went so far in the direction of caution as to deny that they ever watched it. 'I want the boy to tear his father's guts out,' said Sir John Wilder, driving a wedge between the generations in an effort – successful, of course – to destroy his business rival, Caswell Bligh, by suborning his son, and a million hearts stirred guiltily at the thought that they too wanted this lamentable result, wanted it all the more in fiction because they did not dare, or could not, want it in real life. How comforting, how agreeably disturbing, to be told that nature was indeed red in tooth and claw, particularly human nature! And yet how true, in the Sixties, it was! Imagine Sir John Wilder not as the head of Elbertson's Merchant Bank, but as a symbol of all those forces, so powerful and inexorable, that swelled and thrust through the decade, composed of foreign competitors for Britain's markets, new motor-roads that roared and bulldozed their way through people's homes, the vast, impersonal interplay of market trends and monetary systems – was it any wonder that Wilfred Greatorex, chief writer of the series, admitted that before it began his wife used to call him Wilfie, but that after it had started to achieve its enormous success she began to call him Greatie?

And then, on the other hand, the gracious world of Galsworthy's Forsytes, a struggle between generations in which nobody would dream of saying 'I want the boy to tear his father's guts out', but a world which, for outward show at least, rested on an assurance so complete that the people in it could be described as resenting death itself, and regarding it as 'contrary to their principles and an encroachment on their property'. What might they have said about the modern scale of death-duties!

A world still being born; a world still, incredibly, passing away. And how great the fascination with both! Would Sir John Wilder's extra-marital affair bring him down? What were the ethical considerations in the insistence by Soames Forsyte (played with great strength and restraint by Eric Porter) on 'exercising his rights as a husband'? These questions were debated at a million breakfast-tables, in a million offices, in a million pubs. On one side, power; on the other, respectability; between the two oscillated the needle of public taste, public awareness. The producer of *The Forsyte Saga* summed up its theme in the words 'disturbing Beauty impinging on a possessive world', by which he meant that the closed, charmed circle of the Forsytes, presenting such an iron front to outsiders, could yet be penetrated by the worm of human passion and eaten away from within. Yet what a world to contrast with the real one of the Nineteen Sixties, where far more disturbing things than beauty impinged on possessive worlds. Even by the end of the decade it was not entirely clear whether Britain would go forward with Wilder or back with the Forsytes, and the argument had got bogged down in a discussion of which would be better, as if there was any choice.

* * *

In the circumstances it was not surprising that many goods, many evils were ascribed to television, with greater or lesser plausibility, in the Sixties, and by their end it was in a seriously schizoid condition, induced by the rival claims of those who denounced it as pernicious or praised it as health giving.

Among the former was Mrs Mary Whitehouse, who had come, half-way through the decade, to the conclusion that the B.B.C. was, and the commercial companies would be if they were not watched, conspiring to subvert the morals, destroy the faith and overturn the established institutions, of the country. Skilled in the art of lobbying behind the scenes while fussing in front of them, she had by the end of the Sixties built up her Viewers and Listeners Association into a body which was being taken seriously at any rate to the extent that her views, on television in general and controversial programmes in particular, were given widespread coverage in the newspapers. From the start she had received a sympathetic hearing from the I.T.A., the chairman of which at that time was Lord Hill, a man willing to listen to complaints and even act upon them, particularly when they came from people or bodies able to cause trouble; in return she was markedly sympathetic to the products of the commercial channels, which in any case were far more completely filleted of material likely to cause offence, or for that matter thought, in the viewers, than to work of the B.B.C., which, under the wily and on the whole most courageous leadership of Hugh Carleton Greene, had right at the start of the decade struck out for the shores of the future. Behind the stalking-horses of television violence, of television sex (in which field she seemed, like Mr Muggeridge, to regard the real thing as at best a necessary evil, to be dispensed with entirely as soon as a reliable method of parthenogenesis should be devised), and of television swearing, Mrs Whitehouse went about the work of challenging all those who were themselves challenging the received ideas, the conventional wisdom, the Establishments of thought; and the more she disclaimed any wish to impose censorship on television, the more it became clear that her arguments, if accepted, could lead to nothing else.

Supported by a job lot of Members of Parliament, Mrs Whitehouse and her organization hammered away at the world, the flesh and the devil, particularly the flesh, and she was almost the only person to express pleasure and satisfaction when Lord Hill was appointed Chairman of the Governors of the B.B.C., clearly hoping, and not without good reason, that the corporation would from now on be, or be compelled by its chairman to be, more receptive to her views. And this hope was not long in being fulfilled, if Lord Hill's first major policy pronouncement ('... definite obligation not wilfully to depart from a standard of good taste ... the seamy side of life is not the whole story ... a balance must be struck ... a large proportion of our audience are deeply offended by overt references to or portrayals of sexual behaviour ... ') was anything to go by.

More serious charges were levelled at television during the Sixties; a decade as uncertain of itself as this one could hardly be expected not to worry about the function in society of a medium with such supposed capabilities as television. A good deal of the worrying that ensued took the form of charges that it was being used, or misused, to try before the court of public opinion individuals who had done nothing to justify prosecution before less notional courts, or even who were, or might be, prosecuted for the offences they were being accused of on television. Hand in hand with this charge went another, this one largely brought by the politicians: it was to the effect that television interviewers were being too aggressive, too hectoring, with the elected representatives of the people. Such men as Robin Day were particularly liable to this kind of attack, his incisive manner ('Oooh,' Frankie Howerd had said in a memorable aside, 'those *cruel* glasses'), and refusal to accept an obvious lie as a conclusive answer to his questions, having caused much pain to some of those he was interviewing. This charge in turn slopped over into the further complaint (at first sight contradictory) that television was paying too little attention, whether favourable or unfavourable, to the politicians, and the phrase 'the trivialization of politics' began to be heard, though mostly from the politicians. In a brilliantly composed, though less brilliantly logical, lecture, which attracted much attention, Mr R. H. S. Crossman developed this theme at length, and since he had long been known as one of the sternest critics of television's claim to comment on politics as well as report the activities thereof, and since so politically controversial a subject could hardly have been developed in such a manner without at any rate tacit agreement from the Prime Minister, it began to look as though the future of television in the area of public affairs would be increasingly cabin'd, cribb'd, confin'd, bound in to saucy doubts and fears. This represented yet another aspect of the obsession that some leading politicians, notably Mr Wilson, had with their television and other 'images'—of all the vogue-words of the decade perhaps the most significant, more so even than 'trend'. For two-thirds of the decade television had been pushing further and further out the frontiers of the areas in which it felt free to express opinions. (Occasionally it suffered a reverse, as in Granada's attempt to mount a politically balanced studio discussion, during the 1964 general election, of the party political broadcasts, which had over the years grown into a symbol, if not indeed a definition, of political dishonesty and irrelevance; the programme was to go out from the studio immediately after each party's offering, and the idea was instantly vetoed by a horrified Lord Hill. But television, nevertheless, was always taking three steps forward for each two back.) The last third of the decade saw the first significant reversal of this general advance; the departure of Carleton Greene from the B.B.C. director-generalship, which was inevitable from the moment of the appointment of Hill to be chairman, suggested that the retreat might become a rout during the Seventies. There were fears that Hill, with a comparatively colourless director-general in the person of Charles Curran,[1] would begin in earnest the process of dismantling the achievements of Greene and those who had built television into so large an edifice that its shadow had begun to frighten the authorities on whom it fell, and these fears were not much allayed when Curran, in his first newspaper interview after his appointment, said that his idea was 'the extension of freedom' and instantly qualified that by adding: 'But within that ideal, I think of C. P. Scott's remark: "Comment is justly subject to a self-imposed restraint."'

Rows broke out with increasing frequency after the half-way mark was passed in the decade; sometimes behind the scenes, as

[1] Not to be confused with the journalist and (from time to time) M.P. of the same name, who could hardly be described as colourless.

when, on a late-night programme, a picture of Mr Wilson was shown, and the question asked: 'How can you tell when he's lying?', and promptly answered: 'When his lips are moving'; sometimes on the spotlit stage, when Dr Savundra appeared on a programme with David Frost—another of those criticized for the inquisitorial tone he sometimes adopted—and was charged, *coram populo,* with the criminal offences which he had undoubtedly committed, and for which he was actually tried, and convicted, shortly afterwards. Savundra cut a figure so unpleasant that the normal sympathy of any audience for the victim of a television bullying was instantly alienated, particularly since Frost had taken care to pack the audience with a number of Savundra's victims, including widows whose husbands had been killed while insured with Savundra's firm and who had found that there was no insurance forthcoming. But after Savundra's conviction the trial judge was so injudicious as to issue a public rebuke and warning to Frost and his associates on the programme, charging them with possibly prejudicing the trial, and threatening terrible dooms if such behaviour should be repeated. Since Savundra had not been charged at the time of the programme, and since inquiries made of the authorities on behalf of Frost had elicited the fact that there was no objection to it by those charged with the investigation (and possibly prosecution) of him, Frost was easily able to wave his lordship down, and no more was heard of the matter. But there could be no doubt that the affair was symptomatic of a gradual encroaching on territory which Frost and those who thought like him had assumed to be safely secured, as the jungle creeps in on a clearing or settlement if the vigilance of the inhabitants is for a moment relaxed. For most of the decade television had thought it was safe, in its dash for freedom; in the last few years of the Sixties the jungle began to creep back.

What irritated many of the stockade's defenders was the fact that the public in whose name the jungle waged its never-ceasing war frequently made clear that they would prefer to fight their own battles. At the beginning of the decade, when such programmes as *That Was The Week* were breaking genuinely new ground, there were regularly hundreds of protests from viewers during and after the programme; half-way through, when the *mot de Tynan* was pronounced, there was another such flurry; but when, near the end of the decade, a programme depicted with savage seriousness an institution for mentally disturbed children called Warrendàle, and showed one of the children undergoing the special and highly controversial methods of treatment that Warrendale practised, repeatedly screaming 'fuck', not only did nobody protest, but the London *Evening Standard* celebrated the event by achieving the breakthrough that had long eluded the popular newspapers, and printed the word. Nobody gave the paper up, and shortly afterwards the *Daily Mail* said 'crap', with a like effect, or lack of it, and was followed shortly afterwards by the *Daily Mirror* with 'shit'. The world went on.

* * *

For the other medium of mass communications was no less affected by the troubled air of the times. In the search for certainty the most unlikely holes and corners were invaded, and the most surprising characters discovered in them, behaving sometimes in the oddest way. Journalism had been changing before the Sixties began, changing probably more than at any time since the introduction of the popular newspaper in the 1880s. The changes were largely the result of the impact of television on the press; not only had the struggle for advertising revenue become much more acute, but the true nature and function of the newspaper in a television-dominated market was increasingly under discussion. Somehow the press had to find some way of presenting the world that would wrest back from television the advantage of immediacy, or replace it by a counter-advantage of a kind that television could not match. The written word was discounted more and more, almost as if newspapers' managements and editors were determined to prove Marshall McLuhan right; by the end of the decade the number of journalists whose chief drawing power lay in their prose style had fallen catastrophically, and the movement to convert newspapers into a kind of static television screen, despite the obvious contradiction which this implied, had gained a momentum that seemed very impressive, but was quite unable to halt the gradual and irregular, but inexorable, fall in circulations. The new methods claimed, as it were, to add brightness to writeness, and their apotheosis was the purchase by Lord Thomson of *The Times*, that bastion of everything unchanged and unchanging in English life, and its rapid transformation into something far more like a magazine than any newspaper, let alone than the particular newspaper it had been. Change, indeed, must have been the word for the Sixties, if *The Times* itself, which had resisted so many pressures in its time and exerted so many more, which had even escaped unharmed from the dreadful embrace of Lord Northcliffe, even when he went raving mad in the proprietor's chair, should fall into the ever-open jaw of the Canadian upstart, peering mole-like through his pebble-lenses and collecting newspapers, with a satisfied chuckle, as another man might collect postage stamps or post-Impressionists. The changes in *The Times* were gradual, but their pace increased, and they were all in the same direction. It was a direction that had long since been taken by the *Sunday Times* (Lord Thomson had bought that in the Fifties from Lord Kemsley, who had thereupon retired into an obscurity from which he emerged once or twice a year to deny, with some pain, that he was dead, whenever a reference to him as 'the late' appeared in print, which it did with some frequency until he finally did die and thus solved the problem for ever) and thereafter by the *Observer*, and finally by the popular papers, starting with the *Daily Mail*.

For the decision had been taken. The newspaper could compete with television in the 'global village', only by giving more and more the background that television was unable to present visually until the sights it would have presented were no more to be seen. A Cabinet crisis broke; a City takeover battle raged; a scandal in the art-world was revealed; a major decision was taken abroad. All these things could be shown, even if only symbolically, on the screen; but the comings and goings in the smoke-filled rooms, the secretly recorded meetings of plotters, the pressures and persuasions, the advice tendered and accepted or rejected – these could not be shown, because by the time they were known about they had already happened, and, short of reconstructing them dramatically, a technique which even the more fanatical television producers generally shrank from, there was nothing to be done that *only* television could do. So the newspapers set to and found out how it had happened, and who had made it happen, and why, and whenever they could not find it out they dressed up speculation and called it fact. Whole pages of the *Sunday Times* took on the air of a racily written blue-book. The *Observer* printed one of the most remarkable newspaper features of the entire decade, a meticulous account by Roy Jenkins of a City battle between two aluminium-producing giants. The *Daily Mail* got the message, no doubt via the medium, and led its popular rivals into the same business with its 'Newsight' background feature; the *Sun* caught the prevailing tide, and its 'Probe' performed the same service as the other features it resembled. Last of all came the *Mirror*, with 'Mirrorscope', most thorough and varied of all; and the *Mirror*, in the very last months of the decade, was the first of the popular papers to plunge into the deep waters, until then charted only by the *Sunday Times* and *Observer* and *Daily Telegraph*, of the colour supplement, which proved a massive and costly failure.

Those in charge of the supplements had made no bones about it, at any rate in private: they were bait for advertising, looking ahead as far as the days, right at the end of the decade, when commercial television would have advertisements, as well as programmes, in colour, and determined to get a paw in the cream before then. The *Sunday Times* even began to print advertisements in the guise of articles, and in the magazine's normal style, and even to solicit such advertising with the promise of preparing such features to the sponsor's requirements. The money rolled in.

Thus journalism strove in the Sixties to give the idea that it, and it alone, could tell the public what was really going on, while all the time it was drifting further and further from any kind of reality, concentrating on trends and fads (before the end of the decade there were sections of the Sundays that really were headed 'Trend', and 'Fad' could not be much longer delayed), and on the more and more rapidly shifting, restless turnover of fashion and opinion and fashion *in* opinion that characterized the decade; concentrating also on the trivia that passed for seriously informative explanation, and which dazzled with a display of the time, to the nearest minute and sometimes nearer, at which events in themselves quite unimportant happened, and of such scarcely momentous matters as the menu at the crucial working lunch at which the vital decisions were taken. Various claims have been made for the paternity of this movement, but the Sixties were the true parents, demanding as never before the satisfaction of unrecognized desires for certainty (to be told what clothes to wear, what music to hear, what books to read) and for pre-wrapped, even pre-digested, information.

One episode in the world of newspapers, however, served to remind everyone, but principally those who thought that nothing could dislodge them from the positions of power and influence which they occupied, that all flesh is as grass. Without any public warning, on a quiet autumn afternoon in 1968, it was announced that Mr Cecil King had been removed from the chairmanship of the International Publishing Corporation by the unanimous vote of his fellow-directors. On hearing the news many in Fleet Street flatly refused to believe it, and, when finally convinced that it was true, sat clutching the furniture, in fear that the floor and the ceiling might suddenly change places.

Nor would it have seemed more surprising if they had. The International Publishing Corporation was by far the largest periodical-publishing organization in Britain, being responsible for the *Daily Mirror* and *Sunday Mirror*, the *People*, the *Sun* and several hundred magazines, which it had acquired in job lots by swallowing successively the ailing publishing empires of Newnes and Odhams and adding their publications to its own already formidable list. The I.P.C. had great problems and difficulties; many of the magazines, for instance, were unprofitable, and as fast as that side of the business was rationalized, and publications merged or discontinued, further problems arose. Moreover, the *Sun*, a paper which was supposed to arise from the ashes of the *Daily Herald*—which it had replaced—like a phoenix, had unfortunately arisen only like a badly scorched chicken, and was confidently, even gleefully, reported to be losing sums in the region of a million pounds a year, and these increasing. Many newspaper proprietors, faced with such a situation, would have responded by amputating the gangrenous limb; but King had rashly given, when complete control over the *Daily Herald* had been gained, a pledge that it would be kept alive for at least seven years, thus giving sufficient time for it to be put on an economically sound footing, or alternatively to show itself ruined beyond any possibility of recovery. The paper was instantly dubbed 'King's Cross' and the seven years began to look very lean indeed, matters not being improved when King announced that the *Sun* would continue 'into the Seventies', though exactly how far into the Seventies not even he, perhaps wisely, was willing to specify.[1]

The situation might have continued indefinitely, or at any rate into the Seventies, had it not been for the fact that King, as eventually seems to happen to all newspaper proprietors, began to think that the Government of the country would go on better if he were to dictate its composition, nature and head; he felt, for instance, that Harold Wilson was a disastrous Prime Minister and that things would never go right for the country until he was removed. But King's increasingly direct suggestions for political changes and reforms began to worry some of his fellow-directors. In the normal course of events they might have gone on worrying indefinitely, had it not been for two things. One was the growing difficulties of the organization that he headed; it

[1] It was sold, at the end of the decade, to Rupert Murdoch, an Australian newspaper proprietor who had not long before acquired the *News of the World*.

was thought, though it was probably not put so indelicately, that he should attend to the beam in his own eye before turning his attention to the beam in the Government's.

The second element in his downfall was the fact that some of his colleagues felt that King's departure might well improve matters for the International Publishing Corporation. Gradually the directors of the organization began to gather in twos and threes to sound each other out, like members of the Resistance movement in an occupied country trying to discover whether their neighbours will join them in the heroic struggle for liberation or will on the contrary instantly betray them to the Occupying Power, with all the unpleasant consequences that would follow.

Greatly, one presumes, to the surprise of the conspirators, it became clear that the board was, down to its last member, already fully persuaded that their duty lay with the Resistance rather than with the Occupying Power, though whether this conviction had seized them before it was clear that the Occupying Power was on the wane, or—as has commonly been the case in history—soon after, never became clear.

Action having been decided on, the next step was to take it. This was not quite so easy as it sounded; the mice, after all, were unanimous in their conviction that the cat should be belled, but still found great difficulty in selecting one of their number to do the belling. Eventually it was decided that the most tactful way of proceeding would be to inform Mr King in writing of his dismissal, as a personal confrontation might have proved embarrassing. Early one morning, therefore, a letter was sent to Mr King by hand, and arrived, as luck would have it, while he was shaving, though suggestions that the conspirators hoped the news might come as such a shock to him that he would, by a happy accident, cut his throat are unworthy, and even unfounded.

It may be asked how King could have been brought down in this fashion without his having any prior inkling of what was going on; but a moment's reflection on the countless sudden assassinations or depositions of powerful rulers with which the pages of history are littered will show that the overwhelming majority of them go to their doom, like cattle to the abattoir, spared by a merciful providence or the care of the slaughterman from the agony of knowing in advance about what can no longer be avoided; the point being, of course, that each thinks, despite the example of his predecessors, that it cannot happen to him, that he alone is in an impregnable position. That some such feeling must have been present in the mind of Mr King is shown by the way in which he had himself become chairman of the organization, and which he can hardly have forgotten entirely; he, too, had organized a coup to overthrow the then chairman, Harry Guy Bartholomew – though in his case there was a more pressing reason, it being Bartholomew's normal practice, as King engagingly pointed out, to be drunk by half past nine in the morning.

So fell King, and he may have reflected as he fell that, as he had done to his predecessor, so might someone else one day do to his successor, and although he was not to be provided with so symmetrical and complete a revenge, he did live to see, in the first weeks of the new decade, his successor at any rate to some extent supplanted, when the I.P.C. was taken over by the huge Reed Paper Group, and Hugh Cudlipp became deputy chairman of the new, merged organization.

The sensation the affair caused was confined, as are most newspaper sensations, to the world of newspapers; but its effect, in that world, could hardly be overestimated. It had long been known that reporters, writers, executives and editors could be dismissed at a moment's notice under what Katharine Whitehorn has called Rothermere's Law, which states that 'Any journalist may be exchanged for any other journalist without penalty.' What was unprecedented in this situation was that it was the boss who was sacked; and if King's head could roll, whose would sit firmly in his shoulders?

With time on his hands King turned to writing his memoirs, a post as a kind of editorial adviser to *The Times* to which he had been appointed clearly not sufficing to occupy his days, and these were presently published. They were not memorable, except for the revelations they contained about his family; of whom, it appeared, some had been drunkards, some lunatics, and some had laboured under both of these afflictions.

# 20

## Brief chronicles

Two plays, first produced within two months of each other in the middle of the Sixties, summed up the tensions of the decade with almost suspect neatness, the one—Peter Shaffer's *The Royal Hunt of the Sun*—saying farewell to the faith that was disappearing or already gone, the other—John Osborne's *Inadmissible Evidence*—looking ahead in some disquiet to the emptiness that was to follow. Both, moreover, were by playwrights who had the ability to startle their audiences by the extraordinarily wide range of styles and themes they used, so that the nature of a new play by John Osborne or Peter Shaffer could never be predicted in advance. Shaffer, when he came to write *The Royal Hunt of the Sun*, had written a penetrating domestic tragi-comedy (*Five Finger Exercise*) and a pair of glittering one-act studies in myth and realism respectively (*The Private Ear* and *The Public Eye*), and was to follow his massive historical essay with a brilliant farce (*Black Comedy*); Osborne, his fame first established with *Look Back In Anger*, an account of the domestic battlefield of a modern marriage, had also tried his hand at a religious drama (*Luther*), and succeeded *Inadmissible Evidence* with an extraordinary historical play set in the decadence of the Austro-Hungarian Empire (*A Patriot for Me*). Now, with Shaffer's historical-religious pageant, and Osborne's savage study in the disintegration of an individual under the strain of realizing that his life has been meaningless to all including himself, they faced each other like jousters, at any rate as far as form was concerned; in content they were duellists, back to back as they prepared to count off the paces.

*The Royal Hunt of the Sun* tells, with no more than necessary historical liberty, the true story of the conquest of the huge empire of Inca Peru, with a population of ten millions, by a scrap of an army consisting of Francisco Pizarro and one hundred and sixty-six men in all; *Inadmissible Evidence* is an account of the trial for obscenity of a middle-aged solicitor, in which the trial turns out to be in his own mind, and the obscenity his own life.

Two more dissimilar themes could hardly be imagined; yet the plays as written have a striking amount in common. Shaffer is concerned to examine the basis of faith, and to insist that the problem be faced without the aid of a God, or of any external reference; Osborne searches into the heart of his character for a clue to human reality, for some fulcrum on which to manipulate the lever of existence. For Shaffer the universe is empty unless peopled by human attitudes:

> Fool! Look, you were born a man. Not a Blue man, or a Green man, but A MAN. You are able to feel a thousand separate loves unordered by fear or solitude. Are you going to trade them all in for Gang-love? Flag-love? Carlos-the-Fifth love? Jesus-the-Christ love? All that has been tied to you; it is only this that makes you bay for death.[1]

Osborne looks steadily at a man who at the beginning of the play has begun to doubt whether he exists, and by the end is certain he does not:

> Oh, what's the matter? I don't seem to hear properly ... Yes, we went to the party, don't ask me why, I think I'd even have rather gone home ... Of course I had too much booze, what do you think ... It was strange, as if I were there on tolerance ... Sure they're sorry for Anna and think I'm a boorish old ram but there was more, there was more to it than that ... I don't know ... Liz ... Liz ... Hullo, Liz ... I'm frightened ... It was as if I only existed because of her, because she allowed me to, but if she turned off the switch ...

[1] Peter Shaffer, *The Royal Hunt of the Sun* (Hamish Hamilton, London, 1964), Act II, Scene X, p. 73.

> turned off the switch ... who knows? But if she'd turned it off I'd have been dead ... They would have passed me by like a blank hoarding or a tombstone, or waste ground by the railway line or something ... [1]

If it be true that the spirit of a period may be detected as easily in its drama as anywhere, and if—a more questionable proposition—these two plays can stand as representative of the decade's drama, there could be little doubt as to what was happening in the Sixties. Not merely was man doubting his identity; he was questioning his very existence, and the existence of any reason for it. Seen in perspective, many of the theatrical movements of the decade—the Theatre of the Absurd, the Theatre of Cruelty—seem passing fashions, like the disintegrating music of John Cage and Stockhausen or the exploding art of Roy Liechtenstein and Robert Rauschenberg. But just as behind a Stockhausen or a Liechtenstein there is a significance that transcends the ephemeral nature of the art or the artist, and a bitter residue is left when the absurdities have been dissolved, so the theatre represented, in its disorder, the disorder that was coming upon the modern world, in religion, politics, social organization, international affairs. *The Royal Hunt of the Sun* and *Inadmissible Evidence* were plays fashioned with much craftsmanship, and the disorder in the soul of man they mirrored was by no means reflected in their construction. All the same, they were harbingers of destruction, the destruction of the moral law, though both clearly regretted what they were prophesying, just as, right at the beginning of the decade, a playwright of even greater foresight, Robert Bolt, had put it in these words, in his study of conscience, *A Man for All Seasons*:

> ROPER: So now you'd give the Devil benefit of law!
> MORE: Yes. What would you do? Cut a great road through the law to get after the Devil?
> ROPER: I'd cut down every law in England to do that!
> MORE: Oh? And when the last law was down, and the

[1] John Osborne, *Inadmissible Evidence* (Faber, London, 1965), Act II, p. 62.

> Devil turned round on you—where would you hide, Roper, the laws all being flat? This country's planted thick with laws from coast to coast—Man's laws, not God's—and if you cut them down—and you're just the man to do it—d'you really think you could stand upright in the winds that would blow then?[1]

Or, as Bolt says in his Preface to the published version of the play:

> We no longer have, as past societies have had, any picture of individual Man (Stoic Philosopher, Christian Religious, Rational Gentleman) by which to recognize ourselves and against which to measure ourselves; we are anything. But if anything, then nothing, and it is not everyone who can live with that, though it is our true present position. Hence our willingness to locate ourselves from something that is certainly larger than ourselves, the society that contains us.
>
> But society can only have as much idea as we have what we are about, for it has only our brains to think with. And the individual who tries to plot his position by reference to our society finds no fixed points, but only the vaunted absence of them, 'freedom' and 'opportunity'; freedom for what, opportunity to do what, is nowhere indicated.[2]

Many Theatres waxed in the Sixties—not theatres, but Theatres. The former were buildings where plays were performed, to audiences of generally diminishing size. The latter were schools of drama, theories on which entire seasons could be erected, to be demolished like exhibition marquees at the end, and the ground cleared to make way for another prefabricated and temporary theory. Of the Absurd, Of Ritual, Of Cruelty—these Theatres were like the works of so many seventeenth-century essayists. Each school, each theory, had its father-figure, its priest.

Of Cruelty, for instance, looked to Antonin Artaud, a minor figure from the fringes of French café-literary society who

[1] Robert Bolt, *A Man for All Seasons* (Heinemann, London, 1960), Act I, p. 39.
[2] Ibid., Preface, p. xi.

suddenly and briefly became in the Sixties a major writer and philosopher; his reputation, however, suffered even from attempts to put any of his own dramatic work on the stage, let alone a reading of his theoretical writings. He inspired for a time Peter Brook, the most gifted of all the post-war directors, but also the most given to fits and starts. Brook's Artaud phase resulted in a memorable production of *King Lear* in which the director went a long way towards justifying Goneril and Regan for the first hour, so that speculation began to rise that he had in fact gone the whole hog and made Lear the villain.

*The Wars of the Roses*, an immensely successful version of the three parts of *Henry VI*, together with *Richard III*, conflated by John Barton and directed by Peter Hall, was also much criticized for what many felt to be its gratuitous cruelty, but in this case the charge certainly failed, for the Wars of the Roses were cruel indeed by all accounts (certainly by Shakespeare's), and Hall laid mighty symbolic emphasis on the scene between A Son that has Killed his Father and A Father that has Killed his Son. Besides, the proof of the pudding was in the purgation, for Hall, greatly daring, staged all three sections of his drama in a single day, and at the end of this twelve-hour traffic of his stage, late at night, the audiences left in a condition more fresh and invigorated than that in which they had entered the theatre just after breakfast.

The Theatre of Cruelty petered out fairly quickly, which is not to say that cruelty disappeared from the stage; indeed it reached extremes never seen before outside Grand Guignol, or possibly even inside, with Edward Bond's *Saved*, the big *scène à faire* in which consisted of a baby being rolled in its own excrement and then stoned to death in its pram. (This was itself a notable advance, or something, on an earlier play of the Sixties, Fred Watson's *Infanticide in the House of Fred Ginger*—as literal a title as a theatre-goer could hope, or fear, to find—in which a baby was killed by having gin poured down its throat; this play also included what many experts in theatrical history declared to be the first premature ejaculation ever depicted on the English stage. As the Sixties ended it seemed most unlikely that it would also be the last.)

Of the Absurd, the Theatre's high priest and chief practitioner was Samuel Beckett, whose influence spread from the Fifties, when *Waiting for Godot* had impressed even those (the majority) who did not understand one word of it, but sensed its bleak and rigorous message to the effect that it is more blessed to wait patiently than to leave. Following in Beckett's wake came Ionesco, often confused with the well-known United Nations organization – a confusion which may well have pleased this highly surrealist author if he ever got to hear about it. His plays, which were both amusing and disturbing, specialized in the unreality of the conventional, and the conventionality of the unreal, so that he was equally at home in a world in which all mankind turns rhinoceros or in one in which the gigantic feet of a corpse fill almost the whole of a stage while a straightforward suburban action goes on around them. But if Ionesco and his imitators (N. F. Simpson, for instance) could stretch reality to astonishing lengths, they could not make it deep; the Theatre of the Absurd became fatally superficial, and long before the end of the decade had dried up almost entirely, with Beckett alone surviving like the grin of the Cheshire cat – a simile which Beckett made literally apt, as he eventually dispensed altogether with words, and when last heard from was expected shortly to dispense with light, stage, actors and ultimately the very theatre, his disappearing trick being rewarded, with fitting irony, by the last Nobel Prize for Literature awarded during the Sixties.

The Theatre of Ritual, which bowed before Dionysus, whose servant John Arden was, had got badly mixed up, by the end of the decade, with many of the waves that by then were crashing high on the shores of our civilization. It is possible, however, that Mr Arden was not mixed up at all, that his grim and hypnotic *Serjeant Musgrave's Dance* was the harbinger of riots and anarchies to come, and his *The Workhouse Donkey* not a confused and shapeless mess but a great pagan allegory, to be considered along with Robert Bolt's *Gentle Jack*, another play which reminded us that the word 'panic' is derived from the Great God Pan. If so, then it was Arden who was the most perceptive of all the playwrights of the Sixties, and his plays celebrated the disintegration in the decade that was gathering speed so frightfully before its end.

And yet, despite its opportunity, greater than at any time for four centuries, to reach right through society, the theatre in the Sixties turned its back on the chance and instead became increasingly arcane, increasingly remote from the new audiences it professed to want so badly to reach. It sought to find the subject-matter and the style that would provoke the desired response in audiences, claiming however that it was not interested in the audiences that had for so long filled the playhouses, but that it wanted a new one, unimpressed, involved, without preconceptions about the drama but with many about life and society. Who they were who were to compose this new audience was never unanimously agreed; for Arnold Wesker and his school it was to be the working classes; for Peter Brook and his it was to be those with a newly awakened political conscience about Vietnam and similar matters; for Tony Richardson and his it was to be the young. In their different ways they set about trying to persuade these to buy tickets, or ideally to sit in seats provided free at the charge either of the management or of the patron-State. All produced work of very varied quality, at its best powerful and memorable (*Roots*,[1] *Little Malcolm*,[2] Seneca's *Oedipus*[3]), and at its worst precious and dreary with didacticism (*Their Very Own and Golden City*,[1] *US*[4]), and all failed to persuade the new audiences into the theatre, the most spectacular failure being achieved by the most successful (in commercial terms), which was the 'tribal love-rock musical' *Hair*, an energetic deployment of the new music, the new language and the new attitudes of the young. This suffered the ultimate but inevitable indignity of being clasped to the very bosom that was meant to reject it, namely that of the traditional middle-class audiences; the producers, promoters,

[1] By Arnold Wesker.
[2] By David Halliwell.
[3] Adapted and produced by Peter Brook.
[4] Devised and produced by Peter Brook.

and participants of *Hair* had finally to recognize defeat when Princess Anne not only went, but joined in the on-stage dancing that followed the final curtain-fall and in which the audience were nightly invited to join (on the first night the warning lights had been lit by the fact that the first up on the boards were the Duke of Bedford and Zsa-Zsa Gabor). Once again the Establishment had proved itself wiser than its enemies and, instead of resisting their assaults, had opened its ranks and let them through. It had done so earlier with John Osborne, swallowing every insult he saw fit to hurl against it, as it had with Brendan Behan (who finally drank himself to death as a result—partly, at any rate—of being taken up by the wrong people).

But the more experimental the theatre became, the more 'Arts Laboratories' sprang up to preach the message that all the arts were one art (most notable of these last being the one run in amazingly happy disorder by Jim Haynes, a mystic from America who had made a notable success of the Traverse Theatre in Edinburgh and then came south bringing an even more frothing and varied diet to premises he acquired in Drury Lane); the more the theatre and allied arts insisted that they were part of the essential current of the time, that they had heard the heart-beat of history and were intent on amplifying it so that it could be heard by all; the more they declared (as towards the end of the decade they declared more and more insistently) that they were engaged in the business not merely of interpreting revolution or even participating in it, but actually of creating it—the more the audiences, or potential audiences, demonstrated, by their silent reluctance to participate, that whatever it was they wanted, it was not that. What the potential audiences *did* want was never made entirely clear, though there was no lack of voices raised to claim that they knew the answer. Nor were these voices only those of the avant-garde; in a decade that saw the most conventional of all theatrical managements, H. M. Tennent, mount Brecht's appalling *St Joan of the Stockyards* simply in order to be in the swim, it was clear that no theatrical avenue need remain unexplored. In the Sixties it was easier than ever before to get unconventional plays put on, as it was to get exhibition-space for those experimenting in the visual arts, and even to get money to back films without sure commercial prospects. The search for novelty, for experiment, for the future itself, had grown so frantic, and the fear of missing genuine talent (or even exploitable talent, whether genuine or not) by casting it out along with the rubbish was so intense, that almost nothing was rejected, and the Sixties became the decade of acceptance – the acceptance, that is, of an artist at his own evaluation – while critical faculty was abandoned by managements and critics alike in the rush to sweep the old away and usher in the new.

Never was there such a time for reputations which went up like rockets and came down like well-weighted sticks. The voracious appetite of sensation, and of the machines that fed it, especially in the realms of entertainment, saw to it that the turn-over was great. Every new actress was a star overnight, every new singer the most popular in history, every new novelist another Tolstoy, every new playwright a second Shakespeare. For a while they blazed, their talents stretched as far as they would go, and then fashion changed (or some over-eager promoter stretched the talent too far), the glorious star-burst of the rocket dimmed, and the stick began to descend.

One man only seemed to have taken the measure of the decade, and indeed, infant though he was, of half a dozen previous decades too. Alan Bennett was the least extrovert and most individual of the four members of the *Beyond the Fringe* team which had so startled theatre-going London at the beginning of the Sixties, and which had signalled the beginning of so many of those changes in manners and morals, attitudes and expectations, that had taken place by the time the decade ended. For some years after its spectacular success he had lain fallow; some television comedy-programmes, a little writing, had come from him; but all the while, within his fertile, perceptive mind, the definitive comment of the wiser heads of his generation on the England of their fathers was gestating. At the end of 1968 it was born, and it was seen that he had been hatching vipers. *Forty Years On* was widely misunderstood and dismissed, many being deceived by its brilliantly funny surface polish, as a trifle, or – others being no less deceived by the author's previous reputation – as nothing more than a series of revue sketches. In truth, however, it was much more, and properly understood offered small comfort to anybody, for it managed with astonishingly sure-footed skill the exceptionally difficult task, one which was achieved successfully by almost nobody else in the decade, of facing both the future and the past calmly, with understanding and without self-deception. In the Sixties, in Britain as elsewhere, one world was dying and another being born, and it is a measure of Bennett's achievement that in *Forty Years On* he says clearly that although it is inevitable that this should be so, and that the new world must be welcomed, if only because it will come whether it be welcomed or not, nevertheless the old world had value and substance too, and in losing it for ever England was losing something she could ill spare. This note had been touched upon briefly but unmistakeably even earlier, by John Osborne, in the play which started it all – *Look Back In Anger*. Mr Osborne – in those early days at any rate – welcomed the new world unreservedly, but he was too good a playwright to stack the cards quite ruthlessly, and too intelligent a man not to see that their stacking would in any case be unfair. So to the representative of his enemy, Alison's father, Osborne gave enough understanding to enable him to see what was happening to him and his class and generation, and to express it in such a way as to move the audience momentarily to his side. That was in 1956, and ten years later Osborne was no longer at all sure that the passing of the past was the unmixed blessing he may once have thought it; the long speech in *Inadmissible Evidence*, in which Maitland savagely denounces his daughter and her entire generation, suggested that he was having regrets at the genie he had let out of the bottle. But Bennett, with the advantage of a dozen years' hindsight, could see, and say, clearly, that it is perfectly possible, and even proper, to regret the passing of something that it is necessary should pass.

From this point of departure, he galloped off; his allegorical devices, of using a minor public school to represent England, and of setting it at the moment the old, conservative headmaster is retiring and being succeeded by a young radical one to represent the decade, both worked perfectly. What was so extraordinary about such a play from a man of Bennett's age (he was thirty-three when it appeared) was that he had put his finger unerringly on the point at which Britain had finally been forced to decide which way she would go, though she had spent the entire time since – Bennett's lifetime – desperately trying not to admit as much, and only now, in the Sixties, had begun consciously to face the reality that had been staring at her since 1940. It is Neville Chamberlain who dominates this play, which has within it another play, turning on the narrative of an anti-Munich Conservative M.P. (Bennett actually quotes Harold Nicolson's *Diaries* in the course of it) through whose eyes the Second World War is seen, interspersed with sharply pointed comments (which in turn are interspersed with episodes of great beauty and poignancy) on the passing years from the Boer War to T. E. Lawrence and from the slaughter of the trenches in the First World War to Virginia Woolf.

Bennett's school is called Albion House, with unobjectionably obvious symbolism, and its school song is the same as Harrow's, and gives the play its title as well as even more of its symbolism. Its final spoken paragraph puts the point beyond all doubt, being an announcement to this effect:

> To let. A valuable site at the crossroads of the world. At present on offer to European Clients. Outlying portions of the estate already disposed of to sitting tenants. Of some historical and period interest. Some alterations and improvements necessary.[1]

At which point the old headmaster shakes hands with the new, takes a last look round and leaves, but the curtain does not fall until, 'with full organ accompaniment and descant', the company on stage sing the first verse of Old Hundredth: 'All people that

[1] Alan Bennett, *Forty Years On* (Faber, London, 1969), Act II, p. 78.

on earth do dwell.' Before that, however, in the most piercing lines of the play, the principals have spoken an Antiphon for a vanishing England:

HEADMASTER: In our crass-builded, glass-bloated, green-belted world Sunday is for washing the car, tinned peaches and Carnation milk.

FRANKLIN: A sergeant's world it is now, the world of the lay-by and the civic improvement scheme.

HEADMASTER: Country is park and shore is marina, spare time is leisure and more, year by year. We have become a battery people, a people of under-privileged hearts fed on pap in darkness, bred out of all taste and season to savour the shoddy splendours of the new civility.

The hedges come down from the silent fields. The lease is out on the corner site. A butterfly is an event.

TEMPEST: Were we closer to the ground as children or is the grass emptier now?

MISS NISBITT: Tidy the old into the tall flats. Desolation at fourteen stories becomes a view.

MATRON: Who now dies at home? Who sees death? We sicken and fade in a hospital ward, and dying is for doctors, with a phone call to the family.

HEADMASTER: Once we had a romantic and old-fashioned conception of honour, of patriotism, chivalry and duty. But it was a duty which didn't have much to do with justice, with social justice anyway. And in default of that justice and in pursuit of it, that was how the great words came to be cancelled out. The crowd has found the door into the secret garden. Now they will tear up the flowers by the roots, strip the borders and strew them with paper and broken bottles.[1]

* * *

There were other attitudes, of course. Just half-way through the

[1] Ibid., Act II, pp. 77–8.

Sixties, the decade, or rather one aspect of it, found its Virgil, though, as befitted our particular version of the Augustan age, he used a camera to record for posterity the spirit, as it appeared to him, of the times. David Bailey had been one of the first of the new breed of photographers, those chroniclers of the times who, suddenly in demand for the photographing of clothes that were to be sold to the newly enriched multitude of girls with enough money to buy them, set up in society as its new leaders, along with the models they photographed, the designers whose clothes the models wore, the singers whose records they played on their gramophones, the managers of the models, the gigolos, the younger sons of the nerveless aristocracy among whom they moved, the hangers-on of all these, and the vast penumbra of pimps and agents and tenpercenters, whores and pedlars and actors, film-makers and playwrights and decorators, all the froth and scum that, together with the chunks of real meat, bubbled and seethed in the stew of a society that was in the process of changing from what it no longer wanted to be into what it did not know whether it wanted to be or not.

Of all these none was so successful as Bailey, none so skilfully or quickly saw the opportunities that his talent gave him, none was so readily accepted throughout the new world that was coming into being in the Sixties. The camera's all-seeing eye could pass through any door now, and on the other side of it find fame, money, girls, and sufficient publicity to ensure that the supply of all these would continue. His life and background illustrated with extraordinary fidelity (as, perhaps, befitted a photographer) the quality and character of the new world. A poor (in both senses of the word) childhood in the East End of London, its background the war and the Blitz, followed by a succession of ill-paid and degrading jobs, left Bailey with an ineradicable resentment against a society which built barriers along class lines and refused to let anyone cross them, together with a determination to cross them come what may, and a burden of fear, when he did succeed in crossing them, lest the past should come and reclaim him, emotionally if not materially.

How many felt the same about the sudden, unprecedented success the Sixties had given them! Never was there such a decade for lifting up, or – the inevitable corollary – for casting down, never were there so many nervous nouveaux riches, nouveaux célèbres. There were playwrights who had come from the north to make their fortunes in London, singers, barely literate, who had instinctively divined what it was that was demanded of them, models who knew how brief was the garland, how soon the flowers would fade. Society, its palate jading more and more quickly, demanded sharper and sharper tastes, and changed them more and more frequently; in the world that supplied society's wants the competition grew fiercer, the methods necessary for survival – emotional even more than economic – more and more brutal. The rest of society – still the majority, after all, counting heads – began to resent the success of those it saw as lacking the proper qualifications to deserve it, or to support it in the proper manner when they had got it, forgetting that the laws of supply and demand operate as much in the world of the fashion photographer, pop artist or drug-pedlar as in that of the insurance agent, the I.C.I. director or the farmer. Soon there was heard, increasingly, the high-pitched whine of those who envied the too quickly successful; when, at the decade's end, the students added their own particular brand of provocation, the envy began to turn into hysteria, even paranoia. For some time David Bailey, the easy insolence of his life, his public love affairs, his expensive cars bought out of his huge earnings, served as the universal hate-figure, and when he appeared, drunk, on a popular television programme and swore, the public's fury and resentment knew no bounds.

Exactly half-way through the decade this child of his time, having long since ceased to be satisfied with photographing fashion, decided to stretch his wings and fly higher; the consequence was an extraordinary coffee-table book called *David Bailey's Box of Pinups*,[1] which was indeed a box rather than a book, filled with large glossy prints mounted on card, of thirty

[1] Weidenfeld and Nicolson, London, 1965.

people who, in the words of Francis Wyndham (one of the most successful of those journalists who had seen that the new world of the Sixties needed commentators in prose too, and who wrote the captions to the photographs) 'in England today seem glamorous to him' and who 'make a statement about London life in 1965' having 'gone all out for the immediate rewards of success: quick money, quick fame, quick sex—a brave thing to do'.

The subjects of the pictures included a singer called P. J. Proby, whose act consisted very largely of miming orgasm, and, it was said, provoking it in a proportion of his young female audience (eventually, after actually exhibiting his genitals on stage, he was refused readmission to Britain, and was last heard of in trouble with the United States tax authorities); in the Bailey work Proby appeared, naked, in the same pose as that traditionally associated with Christ on the cross, explaining that his ambition was to star in a film about a pop singer who thinks he is Jesus Christ. Others in the Bailey collection have since committed suicide, or been sentenced to thirty years' imprisonment for murder; but what is most significant is that an astonishingly high proportion have ceased to figure in the public eye, the public consciousness, the public resentment and envy.

At the end of the decade Bailey did it again, offering his, or more precisely his camera's, conclusion on the decade to which he must have felt that he had contributed so much of its prevailing tone. In *Goodbye Baby and Amen: a Saraband for the Sixties*[1] the captions no longer consisted of the elegant ambiguities of Francis Wyndham; instead they were supplied in the thick, greasy prose of Peter Evans. The cast too was a sad come-down from that of the earlier work, many of them, it is safe to say, being entirely unknown to more than a few score people other than their fellow subjects. Brief indeed was the fame that the Sixties brought to so many, flaring up with a brightness that was doomed by its very intensity to splutter and go out. The restlessness, the instability of the decade took its toll of those to whom it gave so much, and reminded many that the fickleness of public taste was no myth,

[1] Condé-Nast, London, 1969.

and that it was fickle in the Nineteen Sixties as never before. By the end of the decade Bailey was still earning huge sums from taking fashion photographs, but it was very clear that the world of the Sixties had moved on, and left him, and most of his world, behind.

21

# Benedicite omnia opera

The arts flourished, in the Sixties, for a variety of more or less unusual reasons, and in a variety of more or less unusual ways. Most remarkable of all the *raisons d'être* the decade afforded the arts, however, was their use as a form of financial investment, akin to good industrial equities, unit trusts or a bag of golden sovereigns, and many wealthy men with no artistic inclinations had expert advisers to tell them when to buy Impressionist pictures, when to sell Louis Quinze furniture and when to speculate in Victorian china. After a time the thing went further, and features began to appear in the newspapers which recommended different kinds of *objets d'art* as likely to rise, just as the City writers appraised shares for their short-term or long-term profit-value, and indeed as the racing tipsters gave naps for the 2.30 at Epsom or the 4.45 at Aintree. The *Daily Mail* went further than almost any by not only having a regular feature on these lines but putting it in its weekly financial supplement, where it was surrounded by articles telling the uninstructed what were the best methods of raising a mortgage or an overdraft, how to distinguish between different forms of life-insurance, and when to get out of one kind of share and into another.

It was, of course, yet another sign of the final collapse of confidence in money that took place during the Sixties, when it was finally borne in upon the country that inflation was to be the general lot of Britain for ever and that no Government could or would bring it under control. Thereupon the hunt for something that moth and rust would not corrupt, nor Chancellors of the Exchequer break in and steal, and which might provide something to live on in old age, grew more and more frantic, and penetrated further and further among groups of people who had never before bothered with such matters.

The Sixties, in this pursuit, saw an astonishing rise in the hobby of stamp-collecting and even more in that of coin-collecting, which, previously confined to a small number of enthusiasts, now became a widespread national pursuit, followed by hundreds of thousands. Shops specializing in the sale of stamps or coins, or both, sprang up by the hundred, and magazines catering for those interested in the subjects multiplied. It was an apt comment on the condition of the currency in the Sixties that people should feel less happy with banknotes bearing the head of Queen Elizabeth II than with a silver coin bearing that of the Emperor Augustus, but it was so, and he would have been a stern moralist, or a very eccentric economist, who could seriously argue that the feeling was misplaced.

But the most extreme result of the desire for a secure form of investment was the appearance in *The Times* of a monthly feature called 'The *Times*-Sotheby Index', which provided, with the aid of graphs and charts, tables and averages, a record of the movement of fine art prices in the major salerooms of London, Paris and New York, and from which readers could discover such things as that the overall price of English glass had risen four times between 1960 and 1968, though Jacobite glasses had risen rather less and baluster-stemmed glasses rather more, and in which a record of the fluctuation in the rates paid for Old Masters (flower pictures 300 per cent up between 1960 and 1969, Italian primitives ditto, Dutch landscapes 250 per cent) could begin: 'Every year, the shortage of really fine old pictures, or any pictures at all by the great names, makes expensive pictures even more expensive at auction.' There were, of course, snags, as the *Times*-Sotheby Index made clear: for instance, speculators buying Northern primitives in 1967 in the hope of a rise would have been disappointed to find that their price fell by some 4 per cent, while their owners, 'long' of them (as used to be said on the Stock Exchange), cast no doubt envious glances at those who had, in the same year, stuffed a warehouse full of Italian eighteenth-century pictures and watched them rise by 15 per cent almost at once. Even more chagrined must have been those who bought Seicento pictures in 1968 and held them for the rise, only to discover that, in a year when prices in general rose by 16 per cent, and those of Italian primitives by no less than 38 per cent, their expensive investment had actually depreciated in value by 19 per cent.

Art has, over the years, been put to strange uses, and it was once fashionable, for instance, to smile at the nouveau-riche collector who could now afford a Rembrandt or a Canaletto, and must needs have one. But no J. P. Morgan, no Mrs Electra Havemeyer Webb, could ever have gone so far as those who studied the *Times*-Sotheby Index and, on the evidence it provided, determined whether they should go for a bull market in Tompion clocks or wait for a bear market in Dürer engravings, or enthusiastically stag Victorian button-back chairs despite the high storage-costs. Art has always, in the end, been the handmaid of commerce, and great had been the complaints made by the artists in consequence. But it seemed unlikely that many of the artists who provided the works that figured on the *Times*-Sotheby Index would have been entirely enthusiastic about this method of measuring the pain and grief and joy, the suffering and celebration, the sacrifice of themselves and others, the hope and despair, the poverty and riches, which had gone into their work. (They would have been even less enthusiastic about a new magazine which inevitably made its appearance in these same Sixties, which was called *The Four-in-Hand*, and which concerned itself entirely with art as a subject for investment.)

* * *

All the same, it was not all like that, even in the Sixties. 'Who prop, thou ask'st, in these bad days, my mind?' Assuredly there were not many props for the mind to be found in the arts, which were on the whole occupied in knocking props away rather than putting them in. Both functions, of course, are essential to artistic progress, and the arts have traditionally proceeded under the command of, now the prop-putters, now the prop-knockers, each artistic generation of prop-knockers finding itself obliged to undo much of the work of the preceding age of prop-putters, and a good deal of the most substantially propped work turning out to be the most flimsy when the cruel hammers get to work. If fixed standards were under attack in politics, religion, morality, it would have been naive to expect the arts to remain firm, an island of tranquillity in a stormy sea—nor did they, as from the proscenium arch in the theatre to the very instruments of the orchestra in music, the story was the same: if it looks like a prop, knock it away.

The result was much excitement, some good work and a very great deal of rubbish, together with an uneasy suspicion, which was being voiced aloud only right at the end of the decade, that some of the second category had only got there under the influence of the first and would ultimately be relegated to the third, when the prop-knockers of the succeeding wave, very properly no more deterred by the awesome reputations acquired in the Sixties than the owners of those reputations had been awed by the reputations they had arrived to find already occupying the field, had had their say.

For a thread by which to steer out of the labyrinth into which the break-up of form in the arts had plunged those who needed threads to steer by, it was often necessary to creep, more and more shamefacedly, to the most anachronistic of all the arts, the opera, which was under increasingly fierce attack at the end of the decade as an irrelevant and expensive bauble, kept up, at huge cost to the vast majority who were entirely uninterested in it, for the pleasure of the tiny handful who doted on it.

But the more opera, as an art-form, appeared absurd, moribund and socially indefensible, the more clear it became that it, alone among art-forms, provided in the Sixties that which the other arts had forsworn, and indeed ranged themselves, in deadly enmity, against: certainty. Thrice in the decade opera provided, for London opera-goers at least, experiences as intense as any art can offer, and on each occasion the work in question was one which made statements about the world and the place of man in it that flew in the face of all those relativist and disintegrative forces that otherwise dominated the arts of the Sixties, so full of certainty were they, and so full of hope.

In February 1961 Dr Otto Klemperer made a surprisingly belated debut at Covent Garden, conducting (and producing) *Fidelio*, with an international cast, recruited specially for the occasion, including Sena Jurinac as Leonore, Jon Vickers as Florestan, Hans Hotter as Pizarro and Gottlob Frick as Rocco. Already it was clear that *Fidelio*, the sub-title of which is *Conjugal Love*, the plot of which concerns an heroic willingness for self-sacrifice, and the theme of which is one of resolute distinction between good and evil, with no allowance whatever for moral ambiguities, was very far from being in accord with the spirit of the age, as also was Dr Klemperer's Gothic, architectural style, particularly in Beethoven. On the whole, although it is unlikely that such thoughts were consciously present in the minds of those who settled down, in the highly charged atmosphere of the first night, for Klemperer's *Fidelio*—or, as he would say, Beethoven's—there was undoubtedly present a feeling that a banner was being raised with an uncompromisingly old-fashioned device upon it.

They were rewarded, whatever their state of mind, with a very remarkable experience, which it is safe to say that few of them will ever forget. The very certainty of Beethoven's world lent a momentary, brittle strength to the fast-disappearing certainty of the world in which the production took place (the Cuba crisis, which may be said to have ended what little certainty the post-war world possessed, was twenty months away), and gave many in the audience the illusion that they were watching, indeed participating in, one of the climactic moments of a world in transition, and that the egg was cracking before their eyes, to emit what frightful bird? The production itself—otherwise careful, straightforward and unadventurous—contained two moments of symbolism, one obvious, one less so, that made this feeling most real. The first occurred in the opening scene of the opera, and was startling enough; the knocking at the door referred to by Jacquino

('Zum Henker das ewige Pochen') is so explicitly present in the music that producers of the opera do not normally feel it necessary to have a stage-manager actually thump, in time to the knocking in the orchestra, on the outside of the door at the back of the stage, thus underlining what is already in italics.

Klemperer, however, had not only insisted that the knocking on the door be loudly and obtrusively present; he deliberately had it out of time with the rhythmic knocking in the music, thus producing a kind of aural-visual-psychological discord of shocking, and deeply disquieting, effect that upset all preconceived notions of rhythm and order. Rhythm, after all, *is* order, and thus to shatter the illusion that order reigns over all, and to do so, moreover, in the warm, human, domestic setting of the first scene of *Fidelio*, before either the heroine or the villain has made an appearance, was a *coup de théâtre*, literally as well as metaphorically, which announced that there was something abroad in the Opera House that night which had taken the measure of what was abroad in the world outside.

The second example, as healing in its assertion of the triumph of good as the first was destructive in its claim that the universe was without form, occurred at the beginning of the final scene of reconciliation and justice. To the rage of the purists, Klemperer had reverted to the tradition of playing the *Leonora No. 3* Overture between the dungeon scene in Act II and the apotheosis which follows it. The curtain fell on the dungeon, and rose again, therefore, after twenty minutes, on a setting that consisted, significantly, of a huge drawbridge—filling virtually the entire stage area—which was, no less significantly, down. On this side, we were given to understand, was the prison, so that the drawbridge was, presumably, kept up against the intrusion of justice and liberation from outside; on the other side was the world, stretching away into the distance (though symbolically represented by a cyclorama), from which justice and liberation were to come. Come they did, in the person of Don Fernando and his forces, preceded by a standard-bearer with a huge silk banner, and over the drawbridge they marched to make all well. But before they did so, indeed before they appeared from the back of the stage (which had been raked away from the audience, so that the liberators had to climb up to the drawbridge and thus emphasize the chiliastic nature of the scene by being at first invisible), Klemperer played his second card, which took on the nature of a Last Trump. As the curtain rose, the eyes of the spectators were assailed by a burst of light from the back of the stage, the direction from which the avenging angel was to appear, so intense that it was for the moment as unbearable as, we are told, looking upon the face of God will be, and every head in the audience was simultaneously turned away in an instinctive shrinking from the dangerous freedom that it heralded. So Beethoven's most important lessons, that evil has to be conquered again and again, and that, since there is nothing but the good in human beings to conquer it with, the human beings had better nerve themselves for the battle, were driven home with irresistible force.

In between the destruction of order in the first scene and its reconstruction in the last was a memorable performance by a cast that seemed, as well they might, inspired. A series of visual and musical tableaux remains on the mind: Frick, as Rocco, singing of the importance of money with his hand thrust deep into his breeches-pocket; Hotter, stalking upstage as the curtain fell on Act I, his hands on his hips so that his cloak stood out on either side of his body and transformed him into a great black bat of menace; the prisoners in their moment of cruelly truncated freedom staring up at an empty, promise-breaking sky; the trembling embrace of Jurinac and Vickers before their duet of love and escape at the end of the dungeon scene; the hideous glee of Hotter's 'Ein Stoss, und er verstummt!'; the deadly, unanswerable accusation of Vickers as the dagger was presented at his breast —'Ein Mörder steht vor mir'; the passion and tenderness of Vickers and Jurinac as 'O namenlose Freude' swelled up; the final chorus of praise and thanksgiving; and above all, of course, the trumpet-call.

The trumpet-call in *Fidelio* consists, as a matter of bald musical arithmetic, of thirty-nine notes in the key of B flat major, but such a description hardly does justice to the fanfare itself, much less to the dramatic and psychological implications it contains. It announces that at the moment when all is lost, all is saved; that just when Florestan is about to die he is about to live; and that on the point of Leonore's sacrifice being proved vain, it is proved wholly successful. Moreover, it is immediately followed by the entry of a messenger, who says that the Herr Minister has arrived, news which Rocco greets with the words 'Praise be to God.' In these circumstances it would be hard to imagine a more concise statement of the Christian message of sacrifice, redemption and resurrection than is provided by those thirty-nine notes, and there arises immediately a puzzle, so far unexplained, about Beethoven's belief, for while it is as certain as anything in history or biography can be that his religion was pantheistic and humanist, it is no less certain, from the evidence of this scene, that it was Christian and catholic; which suggests that Beethoven was, at that moment, more Christian than he knew, or would admit to being.

*But the trumpet might not sound.* That is Beethoven's ultimate honesty, to face without flinching the terrible possibility that evil will conquer – as, after all, in the real world, in the Sixties as in other decades, it frequently did. Some in an audience for *Fidelio* find themselves, at the point at which the trumpet-call is due, in an access of terror lest the trumpet should not sound. For the ramparts of the world are not necessarily invulnerable, and one day the trumpet may be silent, Leonore's bluff called, and the end of everything at hand. This dreadful possibility Beethoven admits, and under his spell the audience, though it may know every bar of *Fidelio*, admits it too. Indeed, if it did not do so, the scene, and indeed the whole work, would be robbed of effect, and become just an exciting moment in a musical melodrama, just as, to those who accept the Christian doctrine, if the Christian God abolished free will and made the world perfect by compulsion the point of the Christian story would be likewise lost, and it would become no more than a miscarriage of justice.

So the trumpet sounded from high above the stage and the messenger from the gods came clattering down the stairs to announce glad tidings of great joy: the trumpet shall sound, and the dead shall be raised incorruptible, and we shall be changed. An unfashionable doctrine in the Sixties, but the more welcome for that.

* * *

A second, equally unfashionable, message arrived a little further on in the decade. An opera about the importance of married couples bearing children might seem, thus described, to be something out of the state art of a totalitarian society, demanding that its women breed future soldiers for the fatherland, and decorating with Nazi insignia or Orders of Lenin those who manage the greatest fecundity in compliance. Moreover, *Die Frau ohne Schatten*, certainly the most remarkable of all the operatic collaborations between Richard Strauss and Hugo von Hofmannsthal, was first produced, in Austria and Germany, in 1919 and 1920, so that it might have been taken, and perhaps by some was, as a deliberate appeal to pan-German patriotism, urged to make good the frightful slaughter of the war years. But if so, the passing years sieved out such things, as they have transmuted the Tudor propaganda in *Richard III* and the Augustan in the *Aeneid*, and left behind only the poetry and the music; so that when, in June 1967, Covent Garden mounted its first production of the work, audiences knew only that it was an opera of enormous complexity, moving on several planes at once, and crowded with symbolism to an extent which made it dangerously top-heavy, so that it was liable at any moment to topple over into the ridiculous. (At one point, indeed, at the dress rehearsal, it did; during the scene in which the little fishes, symbolizing the unborn children, fly across the stage and fall into the pan of oil on the stove, some of them missed and fell upon the floor, at which the producer, understandably, lost his nerve, so that at the public performances the scene was represented by an arrangement of flashing lights.)

The production, whether because of the massive doses of myth and symbol that the audience had to absorb, or despite them, provided for many of those present a profoundly moving experience, in which the implicit didacticism of the work was entirely forgotten and it became a great apostrophe to unselfish love and self-sacrifice, sentiments which were as irrelevant to the new art even then gathering head as were the harmonies of Strauss's music and the shimmering delicacy of von Hofmannsthal's poem.

Reducing the plot to a few lines of synopsis is a considerable task, but necessary for the reader unfamiliar with the opera. Briefly, then, the woman without a shadow is a spirit, half-human and half-immortal, married to the Emperor; his favourite falcon had seized on a white gazelle, which was transformed into a beautiful woman; she had become his Empress, attended by her nurse, the spirit of evil. Because the love between Emperor and Empress is selfish and heedless of any further purpose in love but their pleasure, she is unable to conceive or, in the symbolism of the opera, she casts no shadow. Unless by the end of a year she has so far progressed into human understanding and unselfishness as to acquire one, she will go back for ever to the wholly spirit world, and the Emperor will be turned to stone. (When the action begins, the year has only three days to run.)

Simultaneously another plot is unfolding. This tells of Barak, a humble dyer, and his shrewish wife. She is childless from selfish choice, though her shadow is proof of her ability to bear them. The Empress, desperate to find a shadow in her love for the Emperor and her fear of his impending fate, visits the dyer's wife, the Nurse acting as go-between, to bargain for her unwanted shadow. The Nurse offers the woman bribes – wealth, a handsome lover, servants – and the dyer's wife succumbs, promising to forswear children for ever and hand over her shadow. But at this very point the Empress begins to understand what, for the dyer's wife, the loss of her shadow will entail; that is, she begins to be fully human, to understand her own and the Emperor's selfishness, and to determine that she will give everything up so that the poor couple may be happy. This awakening represents the triumph of good over evil; the Nurse is defeated, and after a series of ordeals for both couples, both are united in a new unselfish love, and the chorus of unborn children, singing off-stage, brings down the final curtain on a future radiant with hope.

Such a summary by no means exhausts the structure of the plot, let alone the extraordinary, rich texture of the opera, teeming with incident and symbol. But since it was probably as much as many members of the Covent Garden audience had gathered before the curtain went up, and possibly more, it may serve. In any case, the message of the opera came over with unmistakeable power and overwhelming poignancy. The key passage occurs at the end of Act I, when the dyer's wife has given her consent to the Empress's fatal bargain. When Barak returns she tells him abruptly that they are now to sleep separately, and he, uncomprehending but resigned, lies down on the mat she has indicated for his bed. At that moment a chorus of watchmen are heard outside the house, going their rounds and singing a hymn of praise for the fruits of true love:

*Ihr Gatten in den Häusern dieser Stadt,*
*Liebet einander mehr als euer Leben,*
*Und wisset: nicht um eures Lebens willen*
*Ist euch die Saat des Lebens anvertraut,*
*Sondern allein um eurer Liebe willen!*

*Ihr Gatten die ihr liebend euch in Armen liegt,*
*Ihr seid die Brücke, uber Abgrund ausgespannt,*
*Auf der die Toten Wiederum ins Leben gehn!*
*Geheiligt sei eurer Liebe Werk!*[1] [2]

[1] You husbands and wives in the houses of this town,
Love one another more than your life
And know this: not for your life's sake
Is the seed of life entrusted to you,
But solely for the sake of your love!

You husbands and wives, who lie in one another's loving arms,
You are the bridge across the gulf
Over which the dead come back to life,
Hallowed be your work of love!

[2] Boosey and Hawkes Music Publishers Ltd, London, 1964.

At that point the power and truth of the argument were clothed in words and music that transcended their limitations, imposed by the earthly associations they have in every mind. Faith was not a plentiful commodity in the Sixties, and it is difficult to be entirely sorry. The world, especially in the twentieth century, had had too many lessons in the effects of faith and authority, and the questioning and rejection of those forms of certainty which could offer no justification but a blind understanding were, rightly, under attack as never before. Yet for all that, a moment was taken out of the struggle, in 1967, and became a rock on which the rudderless ships might tie up and the gasping crews get their breath back. *Die Frau ohne Schatten* at Covent Garden, in Georg Solti's penetrating and illuminating version, became that rock, and for that moment the song of the watchmen was a call to all mankind. Next day, no doubt, the problems of the population explosion would come flooding back, but next day was some hours off.

* * *

The third time the beating of the wings was heard in an opera house was in January 1968, when Sadlers Wells, the poor relation that had so often shown a spirit of enterprise and initiative foreign to the grand folk in the great house, mounted Wagner's *Mastersingers*.

The effect was great in proportion as it served the intentions of the composer, and since Wagner's purpose is probably clearer and purer in *The Mastersingers* than in any of the other works of his maturity, even those who knew nothing of him or his purposes, and had scarcely heard a bar of his music before, felt themselves touched by something illuminating and joyful in what became a celebration of man and the right use of his gifts. *The Mastersingers* is one of the few major post-Renaissance dramas with no villain, for Beckmesser is one of those turnip-ghosts with no real harm in them, doomed to be defeated and offering up his defeat more or less willingly as the necessary sacrifice to enable the prophecies to be fulfilled and the resolution of the conflict to be arrived at.

The chief note sounded by *The Mastersingers* is, then, this one of resolution; and no production which misses it, either in a search for hidden meanings, or because of a failure of understanding, or from the lack of capacity to carry out the composer's manifest intentions, can succeed in being more than a series of performances by soloists, chorus, orchestra and conductor, some of them perhaps very fine yet none reaching those heights attained only by the participants in a music-drama which imposes its own unity and order on the various components, and welds them, sometimes despite themselves, into a whole.

This resolution, which became a healing benediction, was what Reginald Goodall and his forces at Sadlers Wells achieved, and was symbolized in a tiny incident in the production that went almost entirely unnoticed. In all music there are few moments to compare with the frame that Wagner puts round Act II of his *Mastersingers* by his use of the Night Watchman. This figure makes his rounds of the sleeping town at the beginning of the act, singing – to a tune, and words, that Wagner took from an actual sixteenth-century example – his traditional salutation to the people:

*Hört, ihr Leut', and lasst euch sagen*
*Die Glock' hat zehn geschlagen;*
*Bewahrt das Feuer and auch das Licht,*
*Dass Niemand kein Schad' geschicht,*
*Lobet Gott, den Herrn!*[1]

The Watchman ends, with a musical gesture that fixes him and his task in the mind, by blowing a blast on his horn that startles the ear, lapped as it has been in the F major in which his song has been sung, by turning out to be a grotesque G flat. At the end of the act, after the riot has erupted in the narrow streets, reached its climax, and died away as the participants flee to their houses,

[1] Hear, ye people, and let me say to you,
The clock has now struck ten;
Watch your fire and your light,
That none may come to any harm;
Praise ye God the Lord!

the Night Watchman makes his second and final appearance; hearing the tumult from afar, he has hastened to the spot, only to find when he arrives that there is not a soul in sight, that the shutters are closed and the lights out, and that the town is clearly fast asleep. Unable to believe his eyes, he sings his song again, making what in the circumstances is a reasonable enough emendation, no doubt to take care of the possibility that the vanishing riot was the product of witchcraft; instead of 'Watch your fire and your light, that none may come to any harm', he this time sings: 'Watch out for ghosts and goblins, lest an evil spirit affright your soul', and goes on his way, again with his G flat discord, leaving the stage and the orchestra pit flooded with the radiance of the moon, and a great peace to bring the curtain down.

It is one of the greatest of all musical-dramatic moments, and the part of the Night Watchman is therefore one that even leading singers are willing to take, despite its tiny size. Nevertheless, Wagner, having used the character for his purpose, discarded him; for the Night Watchman does not appear in Act III. Somehow, however, the producers of the Sadlers Wells version – Glen Byam Shaw and John Blatchley – divined that if the great juggler's purpose was to be fully achieved, he would have to be helped even to the extent of persuading him to do something in 1968 that had not occurred to him to do for the first performance of the opera exactly a century before: that is, to bring the Night Watchman back in Act III. There being no words or music for him in the score or libretto, this might seem to pose an insuperable problem, but the producers were fully equal to it, for as each guild entered the scene in the last act, the Night Watchman was there, a kind of major-domo, to take its emblem and hang it on the ceremonial stands, and right at the end of the scene he came into his own once more, when it fell to his lot to bring forward the laurel wreath that Walther has won, so that Pogner may present it to the victor.

This curious, and almost certainly unprecedented, use of the discarded character from Act II provided a symbolic representation of the spirit of celestial symmetry that the opera at its best provides in such full measure, and that on this occasion flowed like a golden river from the first bar of the prelude to the final curtain, two moments separated, incidentally, by a full six hours, the longest *Mastersingers* heard in Britain for many years, and yet unanimously agreed to have seemed the shortest. In *The Mastersingers* Wagner achieves that apotheosis of humanism that occurs nowhere else in his work, and has too often had the curious effect of dividing many music-lovers into those who love *The Mastersingers* and detest the rest of Wagner, or love the rest and cannot abide *The Mastersingers*. At Sadlers Wells, in January 1968, there could be no two views of the matter: man, confident in the right use of his abilities, was at the centre of this musical universe, and for a moment it seemed that he might be able to use that confidence outside it in the real world too, and with its use to face the increasing uncertainties of the age that were making him increasingly lacking in confidence.

# 22

# Crimes of the times

The restless, fissured decade shifted uneasily, this way and that, as the earth's crust shifts from time to geological time. From the fissures there emerged strange things, strange attitudes; events and people once considered reprehensible now suddenly ceased to be, even became admirable, at any rate admired. Such, for instance, was the fate of the Great Train Robbers; such, also, that of the Kray Brothers.

The Great Train Robbery in 1963, in which a brilliantly organized gang stole some two and a half million pounds in cash from a mail train that was bringing it south from Scotland, inspired several books and films and an almost infinite quantity of argument. It also, however, produced a strange phenomenon, very much of the Sixties, which swelled up at the time of the robbery and again at the trial of those captured soon afterwards, reappeared when two of the sentenced men escaped from prison, was seen again when one of them, together with the one who had never been caught, was recaptured, and flourished yet again when the other escapee came within inches of being trapped and nevertheless managed to give his pursuers the slip.

The strange fact was that it became unmistakeably clear that a large proportion of the public regarded the train robbers as folk-heroes, and viewed their crime with glee, their enterprise with admiration, and their fate with sympathy. This attitude contrasted sharply with the attitude displayed by the public towards the engine driver injured and permanently disabled (by being hit over the head with an iron bar) in the raid, which was one of indifference. Only when the peddling to the newspapers by the robbers' wives of their reminiscences had become blatant, in the last year of the Sixties, was a fund started for the support of the driver, and seemed to touch a guilty nerve in the public, which subscribed to it in such numbers, and with such sums, as enabled the organizers, shortly afterwards, to present him with a sum of money almost comparable with those paid by the *Sunday Mirror* and *News of the World* to the wives of two of the criminals. (He did not live long to enjoy the comfort the fund provided, for he died in the opening weeks of the Seventies.)

Britain, during the Sixties, seemed to be so desperately in need of heroes that she was willing to accept even fake ones, even criminal ones. And there might even have been an additional feeling that her people had for so long been deprived, by the fiscal system, of the opportunity to acquire and retain substantial sums of money legally that they were willing, indeed eager, to admire those who had acquired gigantic sums illegally.

Some such view was somewhere about; certainly it was suggested by the action of the students of Southampton University, whose members, by a majority of 128 to 121, elected to honorary life membership of their Students Union Bruce Reynolds, chief organizer of the robbery and the last to be captured, the students' spokesman explaining that their action was 'a protest at the sentence which was passed on Mr Reynolds', though what Mr Reynolds thought of the honour accorded to him has not so far been revealed, and may not be until, sometime in the 1990s, he is in a position to take an active part in the activities of his fellow-students.

It was not just the train robbers. A little ere the mightiest Julius fell, the graves stood tenantless, and the sheeted dead did squeak and gibber in the Roman streets; in London, in the Sixties, it suddenly appeared that highly organized gangs of criminals had been operating for years, the facts coming to light with the trial and imprisonment of the leaders of two rival gangs. For weeks on end the headlines and the television screens were filled with those shorthand phrases that conveyed whole paragraphs of description of London's underworld, and whole chapters of implication about Britain in the Sixties. The casts were extensive, vivid and memorable; such figures as Mad Frankie Fraser and the Mad Axeman vied with the inevitable attraction of two sets of brothers, the Richardsons and the Krays, who somehow managed to give the whole scene a domestic, even cosy atmosphere, which was much enhanced by the celebrity-hunting that the Krays indulged in; they gathered around themselves a changing group of actors, boxers, politicians, and others attracted by the flashy glamour, mixed with the heavy air of imminent violence, in which they lived, and also, in some cases, by the brisk homosexual interchange that went on in this particular corner of the demi-monde.

For years the criminal activities of both gangs had been known about by the authorities, but the difficulty of getting witnesses willing to talk – a difficulty much increased by the fact that every now and again a gang member or associate who was believed to have squealed would be murdered, or nailed to a garage floor through his knees – had effectively precluded a serious attempt to bring them to book, and since both gangs had always wisely taken the precaution of having a selection of policemen in their employ (the Richardsons used to boast, apparently with truth, that any police move planned against them was known to them within half an hour), their activities might have continued for ever if it had not been for one gang overreaching themselves and starting to kill their victims *coram populo*, and the other gaining such a reputation for sadistic torture that some of their victims, threatened with further doses, decided that the chance of putting paid to them for good was worth the risk of failure. Thus was the lid lifted from a pot in which there seethed and stank a brew of essentially petty crime (the Krays usually dealt in sums of no more than a few hundred pounds, and even the Richardsons' ambitions and abilities never seemed to run to anything more elaborate than expensive clothes), carried out with a lunatic violence that was quite out of proportion to any possible gain. (There was a notable contrast here with the Train Robbery, in which only a single act of violence was perpetrated, though the crime was on a scale that the Krays and the Richardsons could hardly have conceived; certainly they could not have organized it.)

And so the Blind Beggar public-house and the process known as 'taking a shirt from Charlie' (Charles Richardson, after conducting a torture session, would provide the victim with a clean shirt to go home in, lest bloodstains should attract unwelcome attention) passed into the public domain, and thence into history and legend. All the same, they left behind, before the participants were put away for terms of imprisonment adding up to something like a couple of centuries, a curious stench, unique in modern times. The Krays and the Richardsons had had no difficulty, in the days of their tiny glory, in attracting respectable people from more or less respectable worlds, even if only from the fringes. These professed themselves, when their friends' activities were finally exposed, as shattered, or astounded, or amazed, to find in what vipers' bosoms they had nestled, what cruel misuse had been made of their innocent trust. Such protestations were greeted with greater or lesser quantities of scepticism, depending on the natural bent of the greeter; but it had long been true that the blurring of the line between petty and violent crime and unorthodox modern society had gone far. The circles moved restlessly this way and that, now touching, now overlapping; crime, soft drugs, popular entertainment, all the hanging-on and sucking-up that went on in the disordered, fragmented world of the Sixties – none could say where one area left off and another ended. 'BEING SEEN WITH THE FAMOUS: THEY LIKED THAT' was the caption to a picture of the Krays, posed in a kind of 'human pyramid' with many hands on many shoulders, with smiles from such figures as Victor Spinetti, Len Harvey, the dancing Clark Brothers (all entirely ignorant of the nature of the Krays); more to the point, however, was that the famous clearly liked being seen with them. Smart restaurants and clubs echoed to Kray or Richardson greeting celebrated friends; social functions in aid of worthy charities often had one or more present, and the charities benefited from their liberal donations; glossy magazines hymned them, David Bailey photographed them, for they seemed to him, as Francis Wyndham explained, exciting. The excitement that comes from contemplation of brutality is a fairly well-known, well-studied phenomenon. But on the whole, for some time before the Sixties, it had not been widely admitted in public by those who would be thought well of. This was the decade in which the principle of *nihil humanum* ruled with a vengeance, and men judged not, lest they be judged. Whereat the Krays and the Richardsons, contemplating the decades that stretched before them, might well have been tempted to wonder why they had been encouraged to think themselves popular and civilized, and what precisely those who did the encouraging imagined they were up to. Others, no doubt, wondered this too, but few did so publicly, the law of libel being, even in the tolerant and permissive Sixties, what it was.

But there was much worse to come. The suspension of capital punishment (later made permanent), after a campaign against it that had lasted for decades and foundered in countless frustrated attempts, had brought new problems in its wake, apparently quite unforeseen by the majority of the campaigners. These had for the most part seemed to regard the abolition of capital punishment as an end in itself, so that once it was achieved they took no further interest in the matter, indeed could see no opportunity for any further interest, any more than a man with an aching tooth thinks about the tooth once it has been extracted and the pain relieved. But it soon became clear that the legislation, though it had wiped out an ancient stain, had not left entirely clean the place where the stain had been. It now seems extraordinary that of all the abolitionists only one man, Giles Playfair, had had sufficient foresight to predict exactly the nature of the new problems that would arise once the deed was done, so obvious do those problems seem now that they have arisen. Indeed, there was no general discussion of the new problems until a case occurred—the Great Train Robbery—in which no question of capital punishment arose.

The problems, of course, are those posed by the necessity of keeping certain criminals, who before the abolition of capital punishment would have been hanged, in prison for very long periods, much longer than any previously known in modern times, and in some cases for the whole of the murderer's natural life. Murderers found, either at their trial or before, to be insane, and therefore, under English law, not subject to punishment, have always been detained 'at Her Majesty's pleasure', and housed in institutions devoted to the incarceration and care of the criminally insane. But now there was another category: murderers who were formally declared sane, who were convicted, and who were then sentenced (where once they would have been sentenced to death) to life imprisonment, to be served in an ordinary prison. Now it was generally agreed that to keep human beings locked up for thirty, forty or even fifty years was to practise a form of torture that no decent society should tolerate; yet nobody could think of anything better to do with them, and the judges, who for a century had obstructed every attempt at penal reform, seized the opportunity to impose sentences of such a length as made it clear that the faculty of imagination, of empathy, had entirely atrophied in them, so obviously incapable were they of envisaging themselves locked up in a small, stinking box for several decades.[1]

Of all the murder cases of the decade none raised these questions with greater urgency and force than the trial of Ian Brady and Myra Hindley, a multiple-murder case of Gothic horror. At the time of their conviction they were sentenced to life imprisonment, with no specific period being recommended; Brady, as a matter of fact, was given *three* life sentences, and Hindley, with even odder precision, two life sentences and an additional seven years.

The trial of Ian Brady and Myra Hindley, which became known as the 'Moors Murders' case, raised a number of questions of which that concerning the disposal of such killers was only one, and not even the most important. The killers had murdered a

[1] Most of the train robbers were sentenced to thirty years' imprisonment. The Richardson brothers got twenty-five years. The Kray brothers were sentenced to life imprisonment with a recommendation that they should serve thirty years. The spy George Blake, by an ingenious method of sentencing that involved a pretence that his spying had been divided into distinct offences, each of them separately punishable, was given forty-two years. Later the judges even began to increase sentences to nullify the effects of the belated, timid and largely abortive system of parole that had been introduced in 1967.

ten-year-old girl, a twelve-year-old boy and a seventeen-year-old youth, and done so, moreover, in dreadful circumstances. Not only did the murderers practise upon their victims sadistic tortures; in the case of the girl they tape-recorded their murder of her, from the first abominable act to the moment she died, even going so far as to put the microphone of the recording machine under the bed on which they killed her in order that they should miss nothing of her agony. In the circumstances it is difficult to see how anybody, whether involved in the prosecution or not, could have come to any conclusion other than that both killers were psychopathically insane, yet the fact is that many otherwise intelligent people preferred to accept the murderers' own claim that they were not mad (they were entitled, under the legislation that had ended capital punishment, to plead that they had done what they did because of 'diminished responsibility', but chose not to do so, insisting instead that they had not done what they were charged with at all – a fact which, given the amount of evidence against them, should have strongly reinforced the belief that they were insane) and were thus under the necessity of explaining how human beings could be capable of such actions.

The Marquis de Sade, who came in for some sharp posthumous criticism at the trial (the killers had had a library of sadistic and pornographic books, mixed up with perfectly respectable matter like Lord Russell of Liverpool's works on Nazi and Japanese atrocities, and among these were many by de Sade, which it was shown that they read frequently), gave the answer when, in Peter Weiss's powerful play about de Sade and Marat, he cries: 'I dug my creations out of myself!' He had thus suggested, what most people know to be true, that tendencies towards sadistic behaviour exist in all human beings; this left to be answered the most difficult question of all, namely why in these two people those tendencies were given full rein, whereas in most cases, fortunately for society, they are kept under control.

The answer, presumably, is that these two were what botany calls 'sports', and popular speech 'freaks' – that, just as there are people born with club-feet or harelips or no fingers, there are people born with murder in them which must come out when opportunity is offered.

Such a simple explanation would not suffice, however, for some of the observers at the trial, least of all for Miss Pamela Hansford-Johnson (Lady Snow), who wrote an entire book[1] to suggest that the killers, or at any rate their crimes, were the product of a 'permissive society' (a term which had fairly recently become fashionable) which had abolished or greatly lessened the restraints of censorship and other legal inhibitions on what might be seen or read, and at the same time abandoned many of the non-legal, self-imposed restrictions with which society had been accustomed to support those to which it gave the force of law. Her case sprang from the emotions natural to decent people faced with unthinkable indecency, but was bolstered with arguments some of which were very dubious indeed. 'It is claimed by Professor Sprott and others', she wrote, 'that there is little crime in China, especially recidivist crime, and very little juvenile delinquency, because of the moral fervour which infects the entire community and of the weight of public opinion upon the individual.' Who this Sprott is, let alone the others who agree with him, we are not told, but his claim that there is little crime in China must be one of the strangest ever made by one supposed to be an authority, in view of the fact that the present regime, on coming to full power, proceeded to murder its opponents in numbers reputably estimated at several million, and even by its apologists at one million. The claim that there is very little juvenile delinquency sounds even stranger, in the face of the activities of the 'Red Guards', encouraged by the authorities to commit countless acts of brutality and savagery; a noted pianist falling under their ideological displeasure, for instance, they broke both his hands. But the 'weight of moral fervour' apparently permits Professor Sprott to re-draw the definition of crime so that it excludes such atrocities, and thus permits Miss Hansford-Johnson to be troubled, in her contemplation of China, only by her

[1] *On Iniquity* (Macmillan, London, 1967).

feeling that the weight of moral fervour involved might be intolerable for her to bear—as indeed, if it were her typing-fingers being broken, it well might.

In such confusion was the argument mounted, that our permissive society had made Brady and Hindley what they were, and pushed them over the border between the country of the diseased imagination and the land of the diseased action. The argument ignored the fact that crimes as horrible as those committed by Brady and Hindley had taken place in societies far less permissive than ours, and had been committed by people who were unable to read, and had never heard of de Sade or the rest of the authors in the murderers' library. When, a little further on in the decade, the Richardson and Kray gangs were convicted of, among other things, elaborate tortures and absolutely wanton murders, there was no sound from Miss Hansford-Johnson, let alone 'Professor Sprott and others', to argue that the Krays and Richardsons too had become what they were, and done what they had done, because of the lack of restraint in theatre, cinema, television and books.

Nevertheless, amid all the confusion and argument and books, the main problem remained: what could be done, should be done, with the two murderers? Assuming that no advance takes place in psychiatry that would enable them to be cured of their impulses and therefore safely released, it seems certain that they will both have to stay in prison for the rest of their lives, which might well be more than half a century, and no argument that such a sentence is barbaric, and that no crime, however dreadful, can possibly justify it, can outweigh the plain fact that, unless society can be assured that they will not repeat their crimes on their release, it will never be possible to release them. Moreover, as the years go by, there are bound to be other cases in which it will never be safe to release convicted murderers, so that a nightmare vision arises, of the prisons slowly silting up with the permanently unreleasable.[1]

* * *

[1] One excuse that society might offer in palliation of its failure to think of any

Crime in the Sixties taught other lessons too. One saga that had lasted since the beginning of the previous decade came to an end in the Sixties, though opinions differed sharply as to whether it was a happy ending or an unhappy. When Alfred Hinds had been convicted in September 1953 of taking part in a robbery at Maple's Furniture Store in Tottenham Court Road, during which £38,000 had been stolen, it could hardly have been foreseen that he was destined to become a legend in the annals of the law, crime and punishment before the Fifties were finished, and even more of a legend during the succeeding decade. Alone of the five defendants at the trial Hinds pleaded not guilty and, perhaps for his temerity in doing so, was sentenced to the longest term of imprisonment of any of the convicted men – twelve years. After an unsuccessful appeal, an attempt to appeal to the House of Lords and the publication of a pamphlet protesting his innocence of the crime had had no effect, he decided to take matters more directly into his own hands, and escaped from Sherwood Prison, Nottingham, a fact which was to achieve enormous symbolic significance, as, in the succeeding years, he became more and more closely identified in the public mind with Robin Hood. For eight months he remained at liberty, during which time he sent countless letters to newspapers and Members of Parliament, insisting that he was innocent and asking for an inquiry into the case, which, he claimed, would establish that innocence. No such inquiry was set up and eventually he was recaptured in Ireland, where he had been living under an assumed name, and returned to prison in Britain.

Having, in and out of prison, become an assiduous and remarkably well-equipped student of the law, he then began a series of legal actions, in which he represented himself, and, while in the Law Courts for the hearing of one of them, managed to escape by means of a trick so simple, spectacular and improbable that

---

way out of this trap is that continual psychiatric research into the nature and motives of the 'Moors murderers' can be carried out during their imprisonment. In fact, however, no mental examination of them has taken place and there are no plans for any.

few novelists or playwrights would have dared to include it in a work of fiction. A confederate had screwed two bolts to the outside of the door to the Law Courts lavatory; asking to go there, Hinds was accompanied by two warders, but when they got to the door he stepped back, pushed them inside, slammed the door, bolted it, walked unhurriedly out of the building, and caught a tube train to the West London Air Terminal, en route to Ireland. Unfortunately he had just missed a flight to Dublin and had to go on to Bristol, whence another, later plane was due to leave, and was there rearrested.

In June 1958 he escaped again, this time from Chelmsford Prison, and was at large for nineteen months, being identified after arrest and conviction (under his assumed name of Bishop) in Belfast, on a charge of car-smuggling. Back in Britain, and prison, as the new decade began, Hinds had become a national figure and, as a decade conspicuously short of heroes got into its stride, something like affection and admiration began to surround him and his exploits, nor can it well be denied that the resource and intrepidity he had shown in his long battle with the law on the one hand and the stone walls and iron bars on the other had certainly been outstanding. After a further series of unsuccessful legal applications and demands for an inquiry (these last now supported by a growing body of public figures, including a substantial number of M.P.s) Hinds, his original sentence almost served, was cautiously released on parole, and almost at the same moment saw and took a brilliant opportunity of reopening his whole case. The policeman responsible for his arrest and conviction, now retired from the force, had published his ghosted memoirs in a Sunday newspaper, and in these he was so unwise, as it turned out, as to imply, in his account of the Maple's robbery, that Hinds had indeed been guilty. Hinds promptly brought an action for libel against him and won it, whereupon the law stirred uneasily, since it was now faced with a verdict by a criminal jury that he had been guilty, and another by a civil jury that he had not, and could find no way of reconciling the two or of resolving the conflict between them. Hinds asked first for a

Free Pardon (which was refused) and then at last won a fresh hearing before the Court of Criminal Appeal, which declined to set aside his original conviction – thus accidentally (or perhaps deliberately, having seen what a huge tin of hornets they might otherwise be opening) disappointing a number of people, convicted and unconvicted, innocent and guilty, who had not failed to notice the possibilities the law might now be providing and had filed away the information for future use. Eventually he was released in the ordinary course of events, and promptly published a book, called fiercely *Contempt of Court*,[1] in which he reviewed the thirty-one court appearances he had made in the long years since his arrest, in no fewer than seventeen of which he had represented himself, and with very considerable skill. He also did a little public speaking, before such forums as university Unions, and then gradually dropped from sight and public mind. But he had served to remind us all, in a decade that needed such reminders more than most, of what can be achieved by a man with sufficient resolution, self-confidence and ability, willing to hew out a path for himself through ground that others have given up as far too hard to break.

[1] Bodley Head, London, 1966.

# 23

## Death be not proud

Some died deaths of an appallingly symbolic kind. In the United States, Hemingway, his mind crumbling under the realization that his vein was at last worked out, killed himself with his favourite shot-gun, and thus departed a world in which men would soon begin to wonder whether they had not imagined him, so like a caricature did he and his books seem, and so rapidly did his bloodshot themes begin to appear irrelevant. In the Sixties a man could no more hope to write novels about Hemingway heroes than to write them about Battle of Britain fighter-pilots; both were too alien to the spirit of an age which was uneasy to the point of laughter in the presence of those who could and would cut out their own path through the jungle or the sky, and which demanded spiritual anonymity from its heroes as well as its victims. Perhaps the last Hemingway hero was Brendan Behan, who took his life in Britain in the Sixties, though in a slower and more self-tormenting way. Behan's youthful participation in the violent activities in Britain of the Irish Republican Army in the late Thirties had, together with the time he spent in jail as a consequence, provided him with the material for two fine plays, *The Quare Fellow* and *The Hostage*. Unfortunately his sudden, late flowering made him the victim of a society, and of some circles within it, where he could be engaged to provide the stimulus, necessary to jaded appetites, of the exotic. For these he soon found himself performing the functions of dancing bear and court jester, only to be dropped when they found a new fad, and one less likely to smash their furniture and urinate on their doorsteps when they had plied him with too much drink. Thereafter he began with implacable determination to drink himself to death, giving as his excuse in his sober moments the haunting memory of the two people he had helped to kill in the I.R.A. outrage to which he had been an accessory. These were a young girl who was looking in a jeweller's window to choose her engagement ring, and an old man who throughout his life had been a supporter of the Irish Republican cause, and even given to it such small sums as he could afford, and who was passing the same window at the time the bomb the I.R.A. group had put in a near-by pillar-box went off. Whether this story, or the story of Behan's participation in the action, was true, exaggerated or wholly imaginary, Behan told it to many, and such a memory would certainly have led many men to punish themselves to death. But whatever the motives which drove him might have been, he eventually succeeded in his object, and only a few posthumously gathered and published fragments reminded the world that it had lost yet another figure that was too big to be measured for a strait-jacket by the conventional tape-measures of the decade.

Others were destroyed by the times they lived in. One such was Vicky, the political cartoonist, a gentle, nervous spirit whose simplistic, unmalicious, Leftist faith had kept him borne up for a long time, but eventually became waterlogged with disillusion, as he began to realize unhappily that the nationalization of the means of production, distribution and exchange would not take place, and—more unhappily still—to suspect that it would not put an end to the suffering of mankind if it did. The suffering of mankind, under poverty, oppression and war, can be faced by those with the imagination to feel it without flinching, or at any rate without despair, only if they realize how difficult it is to alleviate it, and do not allow themselves false hopes of sudden dawns; what is more, it is usually only these who in practice bring about any actual alleviation in the suffering, for the dawn-hopers, if they achieve anything at all, more often than not increase it. So Vicky despaired, being unable either to help his fellow-men or to ignore them, and, bearing their sorrows upon his shoulders until the weight proved too much for him, eventually took his own life, this being the only violent and destructive thing he had ever done. Not long afterwards died David Low, the other great political cartoonist of the Thirties and Forties who, like Vicky, had also been left stranded on the shore by the receding tide of simple certainties. He too had had the irritating experience of seeing his caricature creations adopted by his victims, who, feeding on the caricature, generally thrived mightily; the shambling cart-horse, for instance, that was Low's image for the T.U.C., became an affectionate portrait of an honest and hard-working beast, and Vicky, who created Supermac from a conflation of Harold Macmillan and the popular cartoon figure Superman, in order to ridicule Macmillan's attempt to give an impression of ubiquity, omniscience and supernatural powers, had the galling fate of seeing its subject adopt even more consciously and flamboyantly the ludicrous postures attributed to him, with immense popular and electoral success. Both Low and Vicky were lost in the Sixties, which needed to be caricatured by men with crueller pencils than they wielded, for both of them were at bottom unable to hate, and there was much vigorous work to be done in the decade by men who had that ability and could use it. For a moment such a man seemed to have been found, and in the most unlikely quarter, for Timothy Birdsall, a young artist who achieved fame as the first man to draw caricatures on television, was an even gentler and more loving figure than Vicky; before his lamentably premature death at the age of twenty-eight, however, he was developing into an artist of exceptional stature, and it was not fanciful to believe that in him was lost a successor not merely to Low and Vicky, but to Hogarth. Be that as it may, Birdsall certainly seemed to have found, in his last work, a *saeva indignatio* that raised it into the regions of the memorable, the most striking in this category being one of Lord Beaverbrook feeding off a plateful of victims of his lordship's vendettas. Where Low and Vicky had always depicted Beaverbrook as a merry imp, Birdsall drew him as old, corrupt and irredeemably evil, and whichever view of Beaverbrook (if either) was the true one, it is certain that, despite his notable appetite for flattery, he did not ask for the original of *this* portrait, but reacted instead by issuing a writ for libel against the magazine in which it appeared; he died before it could be proceeded with, but so, alas, did Birdsall.

For the true spirit of the decade in drawing we had to wait a little longer, when it blossomed forth in the *fleurs du mal* of Gerald Scarfe, whose caricatures, so far from turning their subjects into lovable figures with endearing foibles, must make him a reasonably likely candidate for the position of the first man to be prosecuted simultaneously for obscenity, blasphemy and criminal libel. If Birdsall had Swift's holy rage, Scarfe appears to have inherited his disgust with the flesh, to judge from some of his monstrous, dropsical faces and bodies, the products of a deadly, though still undisciplined, genius. If, then, we could see a future Hogarth in Birdsall, it may be that in Scarfe we can recognize the heir of Hieronymus Bosch, and a Bosch, moreover, without the didacticism, which only makes the prospect more disquieting.

* * *

Even the broken-hearted clowns of ancient legend seemed to take on a modish Sixties air in their misery and downfall. Tony Hancock, a brilliant, wayward comedian, with a rare individual style based on the traditional 'little man' type made famous by Chaplin but ingeniously raised in social and income level, had had enormous popular success. But, driven by doubts and fears that pursued him like implacable hunters, he began to fail. He fell out with colleagues and script-writers, infected with an almost paranoiac certainty that nobody could help him, nobody understand him, nobody supply what he wanted. Inner failure bred outward; he tried different styles, different techniques, brooking advice less and less while he needed it more and more. Television, the demanding monster of modern entertainment, with a thousand devouring mouths where its ancestors had had only one, gaped for sacrifice. Material that would have once lasted a comedian a year, several years, was utterly used up in an evening, like the patrimony of a gambler flung away in a single session at the tables. Television giveth, and television taketh away; blessed be the name of television. To Hancock was given, and that which to him was given was also taken away. He became desperate, drank, became more desperate, divorced, married, separated, became more desperate still, drank, drank more, became yet more desperate. Eventually, in Australia, in a lonely hotel bedroom, he acted out for the last time his now awful parable of the man who cannot cope with life and fate, and so died.

No less tragic was the decline of Judy Garland. She who had once held all hearts in her hand as she sang 'Meet Me in St Louis' or 'Somewhere Over the Rainbow' had also discovered how savagely the bitch-goddess could bite. Quarrelling and making it up with agents and husbands and would-be agents and would-be husbands, she became increasingly erratic and, increasingly, in public. Temperament in a star is acceptable – even, if it will produce publicity, welcomed – but temperament in a star, once the star begins to be less starry, is not welcome, not acceptable, at length not even endurable. Performances became irregular, were cancelled, started late, were even – unthinkably, unimaginably, for those who remembered the days of glory – booed. The talent, like Hancock's, was as real as ever; the certainty that drove it had failed. Around her in her misery gathered a horrid crew, among them some of those men who, unmanned in their own riven nature, cannot help taking delight in the destruction, the self-destruction particularly, of a woman once beautiful, once femininity personified. Fame was the spur, but the spur had lost its sharpness, and now its blunt point goaded and maddened, where once it had pricked on to adulation, adoration. Moloch swallowed, belched and waited for more. (Kingsley Martin alone died exactly, in every particular, as he would have wished. Succumbing to a heart attack while, with astonishing appositeness, he was visiting Cairo and staying as the guest of the Indian Ambassador to Egypt, he had left instructions that his body was to be devoted to the use of the medical students on the spot; and so it came about that the budding doctors of the land of the Nile found themselves taking apart the mortal remains of the famous editor of the *New Statesman*.)

Still the past stirred, echoed, would not lie down and be forgotten. In the south of France there finally died in the Sixties a survival from a world not merely of a previous generation but of several generations further back. Somerset Maugham, the fissures of disappointment that ran downwards from the corners of his mouth now almost severing his chin, had sunk infinitely slowly towards oblivion and death, watched over by his faithful companion of many years, Alan Searle. The biographers and memoirists circled like vultures, waiting to drop on the fat carcase as soon as life should be extinct. Before he died, however, the aged, bitter genius turned vulture himself, and took his revenge on all the slights that fate had dealt him, from the nature of his own personality to the stammer he had never been able to control or eradicate. It is rare indeed for one of the most popular and wide-selling authors in the world to have a book rejected by the publisher under whose imprint his work has appeared for half a century, but Somerset Maugham's last work, *Looking Back*, was refused by Heinemann, and in Britain published only in newspaper-serial form, in the *Sunday Express*.

The paederast who cannot forgive a woman for forcing him to know the truth about himself is a sad figure, potentially a tragic one. Maugham was probably unique in that he had harboured the hate he bore for his wife, Syrie, on this account year after year, decade after decade, until it writhed and festered and boiled inside him and would not let him rest until he had exposed it to the world. Whore was one of the milder things he called her when he came to write the book, and it takes a remarkable twist of the mind for a man to proclaim the illegitimacy of his own child in order to do further damage to the memory of his long-dead wife.

Maugham did not long survive the publication of *Looking Back*, and his death was the signal for a wallowing riot of reminiscence, in print and out. A more or less official biography appeared from his nephew Robin,[1] a wildly organized defence of Syrie came from Beverley Nichols,[2] and slowly there emerged a picture of a world of petty corruption, amid the circle that had for years rotated around the centre of the Villa Mauresque, living off endless gossip and bitchery, pouring life and art alike into the sand, becoming increasingly remote from either. Trivial decadence is a gruesome sight, just as the large-scale kind is almost unimaginable (what precisely Dorian Gray *did* is never explained), and it was surprising in some ways that the Sixties, which were equally determined on the one hand to sweep away the past and usher in the future, and on the other to resist the future and cling to the past, did not make more of the Maugham controversy, since a spirited battle of the books could have been organized between those who wanted to condemn all the participants as irrelevant grotesques, living past their time, and those who could have plausibly insisted that the old and evil too had a right to their permissiveness and a call upon the tolerance of those who saw no reason to share their particular activities or tastes. No such battle developed, however, apart from the in-fighting in the Maugham camp itself, and the inevitable decline in his reputation that follows the death of any very successful author soon set in; it is still too early to say whether it will revive, and if so when. Meanwhile E. M. Forster lived on into his tenth decade, being honoured with the O.M. on his ninetieth birthday, and helping to shape the minds of a fourth generation as he had guided those of three already – a thought that provided a pleasing antidote to the stink from the south of France.

* * *

It was in the Sixties that a wrong first done in the Forties was in part set to rights. The victim was a man named Evans, who had been accused of murdering his wife and child and hanged for doing so. At the time, well-nigh miraculous things had

[1] *Somerset and all the Maughams* (Heinemann, London, 1966).

[2] *A Case of Human Bondage* (Secker and Warburg, London, 1966).

occurred; the inarticulate, half-witted Evans, for instance, had blossomed at one point, early in his interrogation, into a man of fluency, even eloquence, under the kindly questioning of a policeman, and confessed to the murder in terms which would have done credit to a lawyer skilled in making speeches, or even to the policeman, who had himself achieved something not far short of the miraculous with the speed at which he had managed to write down the confession as it poured from the lips of one who had previously found it difficult to put a dozen words together at a time, or to utter them when put.

At his ensuing trial Evans retracted his confession and declared himself wholly innocent of crime, accusing instead the man in whose house the family Evans lodged, a former special policeman named Christie. He, declared Evans, had done the deed, and in circumstances, involving abortion and other activities, that kept some of the less expensive Sunday papers happy for weeks. Christie, in evidence, stoutly denied Evans's accusations, and made upon the jury a good impression, so that they believed him and disbelieved Evans, who was hanged protesting his innocence to the last. There the matter might have rested had it not been for the fact that Christie, who had at the time of the trial undoubtedly murdered several women and put them in convenient niches behind the wallpaper in his house, from which he would remove them from time to time in order to have sexual relations with them *post mortem* (a practice of which he was fond), murdered some more, and in circumstances which caused the neighbours to talk. Christie fled, and was shortly afterwards arrested. The police then proceeded to examine his house in some detail, and found corpses not only behind the wallpaper but also buried in the garden, at which the same Sunday newspapers were kept happy for more weeks, so that it seemed there was always something going on at Number Ten Rillington Place to make the Sabbath more entertaining, and more profitable too.

But at this point the circumstances of Evans's trial were recalled, and his denials of guilt, coupled with his accusations against Christie. It was felt that, at the very least, the jury might have taken a less favourable view of the latter's evidence, special policeman or no, had they known at the time that he was a multiple murderer and a necrophile as well. Whereupon a huge agitation sprang up to clear the name of the dead Evans, and a lawyer, Mr Scott Henderson, was engaged by the authorities to investigate the matter before Christie, who had been found guilty in his turn, though with rather less doubt of his guilt, was due to be hanged. Henderson, who knew what was required of him, produced a report in both the time and the tenor stipulated, declaring that Evans had indeed been justly found guilty and executed, and that the fact that Christie was a murderer too was the veriest coincidence. At this the defenders of Evans's name set to and demonstrated that, for this to be true, no fewer than twenty-three coincidences, all of a startling nature, would have had to be true of the murders each had committed. Many, indeed, went close to suggesting that Henderson had said things, in his report, which not only were not true but which he must have known were not true, and it slowly and sadly became apparent that this was indeed the case, though it could not be put in terms quite so blunt until after Henderson's death, when it came as a great shock to some, though not to others, to learn that a noted Q.C. could say things which were untrue. There too the matter rested, and there too it might well have rested for ever. Many demands for a fresh inquiry were made, and, by a succession of Home Secretaries, refused. Then, like a single fine day in a prolonged series of rainy ones, a brief interval occurred in the long tenure of the Home Office, stretching back some decades, by some of the most noisome politicians of this or any other century. Roy Jenkins, a man with a reputation for a liberal outlook, was appointed to the post, and agreed to another examination of the facts in dispute. For this purpose a judge, Mr Justice Brabin, was appointed to determine whether or no Evans had been guilty of the crime for which he had been hanged, namely murdering his child. Brabin, who could hardly have done otherwise, reported that the balance of probability was that Evans had not done so, but he managed to save the face of the Home Office, the Director of Public Prosecutions and the police by saying, without having been asked to pronounce on the matter, that Evans probably *had* murdered his wife – a crime with which he had been charged but which had never been proceeded with after he had been found guilty of murdering his child and hanged, even the then Director of Public Prosecutions thinking it unnecessary to have a man hanged twice.

In the circumstances the campaigners declared themselves as satisfied as they had ever expected to be, and shortly afterwards the bones of Evans, who had been buried (as was the custom with executed felons) within the walls of the prison at which he had been hanged, were restored to the surviving members of his family for reburial in consecrated ground.

Evans's were not the only bones to be dug from a prison grave in the Sixties and reinterred elsewhere. Far more famous bones, those of Sir Roger Casement, were removed from beneath the prison yard at Pentonville, where he had been hanged in 1916, and given back to the Republic of Ireland, which had long claimed them, Casement being an Irish national hero. Thus Casement's remains were given a State funeral in Dublin, at which the British Ambassador to Ireland followed the coffin, to show that all was forgiven.

The symbolic significance of burial in consecrated ground, indeed of burial itself, clearly maintained an enormously strong grip on human imagination, being mixed up with half-held, half-forgotten beliefs about the Last Trump, and the rising of the sheeted dead from their graves which it would herald. Even many rational people could not entirely shake off these beliefs, and part of the argument that arose when, late in the decade, the surgical transplanting of hearts from one human body into another had a brief vogue, concerned the dangers that might be involved for a soul at the Resurrection if the body in which it was housed either had the wrong heart in it or no heart at all.

* * *

Yet death did nothing more symbolic in the Sixties than, exactly half-way through the decade, to carry off Winston Churchill, after a struggle which death must several times have been tempted to abandon, so resolute was his opposition, so tenacious his hold on a life which had spanned ninety years and included the achievement of a place in history that few men have attained, and fewer still in their own lifetimes. Soon after his ninetieth birthday in November 1964 he had begun the final decline, tugged along slowly and persistently by the merciless compassion of death. A week or so after the New Year he suffered a stroke, the last of many he had had, and from then on it was only a matter of time, though the time was actually more than a fortnight, and during it he seemed more than once quite capable of recovery. Eventually, however, he fell into a deeper and deeper sleep, and all over the world obituary tributes were prepared, television film edited and put together, messages and telegrams written out, and prayers offered. His family gathered at his bedside; his doctor, the faithful Lord Moran, came and went at all hours, never sparing himself in the care of his patient, who little knew that his faithful physician had for years been writing a diary of his years with Churchill, and was to publish it only sixteen months later; the Queen sent a message of sympathy and good wishes, and prayed publicly for his recovery; President Johnson and ex-President Eisenhower telegraphed their encouragement, and so did President Nkrumah of Ghana, the last perhaps reflecting that if his people believed the propaganda being put out on his behalf, which attributed supernatural properties to him, no such undignified spectacle as his own death would ever trouble them. (They did not believe it, though they kept quiet about their scepticism until he was overthrown in 1966.)

One curious side-effect of Churchill's tenacious hold on the remnants of life was the fact that it nearly ruined several British newspapers, which, night after night, had complete editions ready with his obituary and attendant material which night after night they were unable to use, together with the extra staff and distribution facilities engaged for the operation; one paper, notoriously in no position to do so, was said to be losing five thousand pounds a day while Churchill survived, and it is possible that its management had to control themselves carefully if they were not to add to the national and international prayers for the great man's recovery a prayer that he ought at any rate to make up his mind.

Day and night, the crowds stood silent in the road, as near to his house as they could get. Film and television cameras, with their cables and vans, festooned the cul-de-sac, reporters perched for their long vigil on steps and railings, and silence reigned. When a medical bulletin was issued, it was read aloud by Lord Moran or a member of Churchill's staff, and received with nothing more than low murmurs and a slight shifting of the members of the crowd from foot to foot; their numbers, however, scarcely diminished at all, and, whenever they did, were soon augmented by further arrivals.

So it went on, day and night, while the Prime Minister, Mr Wilson, announced that a promised speech on exports would be postponed 'in view of the nation's concern about Sir Winston Churchill', and even the special sittings of both Houses of Parliament, to mark the seven hundredth anniversary of the calling by Simon de Montfort of the first Parliament, were cancelled. Every medical bulletin was eagerly scrutinized by the experts for indications of the progress of the struggle, and somewhere in every news report of it there would be a note from 'our medical correspondent', explaining what cardiac irregularity meant, why the danger of pneumonia was so much to be feared, and why anti-coagulant drugs were considered useless, and surgery worse than useless, for the patient's condition.

He was a great man and had played a large part in modern history, and the British people had cause to be grateful to him, and not only the British; the anxiety when he fell ill, and the foreboding when he began to sink, were only to be expected. Nevertheless there was more to it than that, for there can be little doubt that, in the minds of millions, however little they might consciously think of it in these terms, Churchill's death signified the end of much more than his own life, and the fact that what it signified had ended for all practical purposes long before, and that Churchill's life itself had for some time been life in name only, only emphasized this truth. The point about the Sixties in Britain, after all, was that the country existed in a state of historical symbiosis, with the past and the future living off each other while contending for mastery, and the resultant strain having a deplorable effect on almost everybody, with the result that anything that could postpone the inevitable moment of separation, when we should finally know which of the Siamese twins, if either, would survive, was welcomed. And no symbol better represented the inseparable nature of the two impulses than Winston Churchill, who had represented a different kind of national unity all those years before, when the country had had only one will and he embodied it, only one aim and he articulated it, only one mind and he spoke it. Now he was going, the cement between the bricks was crumbling, and soon it would be impossible to pretend any longer that the wall would go on standing.

> What though the mast be now blown overboard,
> The cable broke, the holding anchor lost,
> And half our sailors swallowed in the flood?
> Yet lives our pilot still; is't meet that he
> Should leave the helm and like a fearful lad
> With tearful eyes add water to the sea,
> And give more strength to that which hath too much;
> While in his moan the ship splits on the rock,
> Which industry and courage might have saved?

But now the pilot was no longer living, or, if he was, it was only a matter of days, perhaps hours, before it would be necessary to face without him the loss of cable, anchor and half the crew.

Slowly, very slowly, the pilot slipped overboard, the bulletins moved peacefully towards their close, the family gathered at the bedside, those keeping the vigil in the street outside grew even more hushed and solemn, and Operation Hope Not, which had been set up, under Churchill's own supervision, twelve years previously, began to move, imperceptibly and soundlessly, into gear, preparing for the last State funeral any commoner would ever have.

But first the battle had to finish. Though the Archbishop of Canterbury, at the request of the London *Evening News*, drafted a set of prayers for the public's private use, and though no doubt these were widely employed, and though, matching his secular arts to the Church's sacred ones, Lord Moran redoubled his ministrations, there was now but one way it could go, and duly, on January 24th, 1965, the seventieth anniversary of his father's death, Winston Churchill died, and in the hour of his passing, his lifelong friend Violet Bonham Carter declared, his face had become 'a face from which all age and infirmity had dropped away, young, calm and resolute in death'.

Thereupon there occurred an expression of grief and commemoration which, in its intensity, its scope and the breadth of its international incidence, had almost certainly never been equalled before in the entire history of the world. First the messages flowed in from the captains and the kings, the presidents and prime ministers; from Germany and France, Italy and Spain, India and Ghana, Australia and Kenya, Canada and Cyprus, Russia and America, Poland and Vatican City. Three American Presidents, the Pope, the Speakers of fifty legislatures, all joined in. Around and across the world flags flew at half-mast, lights were dimmed, sport was abandoned, theatres were closed, shops shut, Parliaments adjourned, candles lit, prayers offered, tributes paid, mourning donned, sympathy tendered, history recalled. Instinctively the world was recognizing the truth behind his death: that a new world had been born, and that there was no place in it for men of his girth, men who could alter history by their own single exertions, men who, when they sneezed, caused men half a world away to blow their noses. The world had long been shrinking; it was in the Sixties, in countries like Britain, that this truth had at last been recognized, and no more forceful reminder of it could have been provided than Churchill's death. He did bestride the narrow world like a Colossus, and from now on only the petty men would be left, to walk under his huge legs, and peep about to find themselves dishonourable graves.

Meanwhile he would lie in state in Westminster Hall, the first Prime Minister to do so since Gladstone, and, it is fairly safe to say, the last who ever will. For three days without cease the column of mourners passed through the hall, the most ancient of all Britain's State buildings, which had seen more of her history than any other, and was now to see one kind for the very last time. Ten thousand, fifty, a hundred, two hundred, three hundred thousand passed by the catafalque. The queue stretched for a thousand yards, for a mile, two miles, three miles, the shuffling wait increased from half an hour to an hour, and from an hour to two hours, and from two hours to three, and from three to four. The frost deepened, the sleet began to fall, a score, a hundred, two hundred collapsed from the cold, and all the while the long, patient, silent file wound its way on and passed through the hall, where Churchill's coffin lay on a plinth, shrouded in the national flag, with the insignia of the Garter resting on it, with four tall yellow candles each pointing a trembling finger of flame at the roof, and with a silent guard of honour, changed every half hour, of four officers. Television showed it, radio described it, countless words were poured out about it, and still the tide flowed on, of people who recognized that this was something they would not look upon again, and who had come from every part of the country, and every corner of the world, to file through a door that was slowly closing, and for ever.

It was not, however, to close without formal public recognition of what it was that Churchill's death symbolized. His funeral was one of the great public ceremonies of history, comparable with the Field of the Cloth of Gold, the coronation of Peter the Great, the funerals of Wellington and of Lincoln; but it was one of the great watersheds of history too, comparable in this sense with the assassination of the Archduke Ferdinand, the shots at Fort Sumter, the execution of Charles I, the Whiff of Grapeshot, the First Reform Bill.

Never before, not even for the funeral of President Kennedy, had so many kings, queens, presidents, prime ministers, generals, high commissioners assembled to do honour to one dead man. Never before had so many unprecedented honours been paid to one man, typified by the order from the President of the United States that the Stars and Stripes, wherever it flew throughout the world, should fly at half-mast from Churchill's death until his funeral, something never done for a foreign commoner since the founding of the Republic. Before the tide of dignitaries began to flow into London, the tide of messages and tributes had flowed for days. 'It is with profound sorrow ... ' telegraphed the President of India; 'The whole German people share in the loss ... ' declared the President of Federal Germany; 'All Canadians are grief-stricken ... ' said Mr Lester Pearson; 'The Soviet people share the grief of the British ... ' wrote the Soviet Prime Minister; 'Sir Winston Churchill's death deeply affects the Belgian people ... ' announced King Baudouin; 'He was a symbol of indomitable courage ... ' added King Constantine of the Hellenes.

From Israel ('His personality will always be identified with the victory of civilization ... '), from Norway ('Churchill was not only a leader of his own people ... '), from Japan ('A great loss for the whole world ... '), from Italy ('For as long as there are free men on earth ... '), from Nepal ('Nepal has lost a good friend ... '), from Sweden ('The world has lost a strong defender of human ideals ... '), from Ghana ('The memory of his inspiring leadership ... '), from Malaysia ('An indomitable man, whose life proved that freedom is invincible ... '), from Australia ('A man of greatness has departed ... '), from France ('In the great drama he was the greatest of us all ... '), from the United States ('He is history's child ... '), the messages, tributes, statements poured in. It was as if, for a moment, the whole world, midway through a decade that everywhere was full of stresses of new worlds contending with old for mastery, had paused to remember the days when there was only an old world, and the new one was gestating out of sight. It was the correct response for the death of a man who had taken part in a cavalry charge and lived to make, in what was almost his last speech as Prime Minister, the announcement that Britain was to manufacture hydrogen bombs.

Leaders of one hundred and ten nations (almost every independent State in the world) attended the funeral service in St Paul's, thus providing the organizers with some delicate and difficult problems in the fields of both security and protocol, the importance of seeing that the Russian or American representatives, say, were not assassinated being scarcely more tractable, and for that matter vital, than the need to see that President de Gaulle, say, was not given a position that he might regard as incompatible with his and his country's dignity. In the event all went well, apart from the single horrifying moment when the bearer-party, moving up the steps of St Paul's with apparently effortless ease, were momentarily thrown out of their stride (it was afterwards rumoured that the body had shifted inside the coffin) by the circumstance of the eighty-two-year-old Lord Attlee (one of the pall-bearers) faltering, at which it looked for a few seconds as though the ultimate catastrophe was going to occur. It was, however, the frail health of Lord Attlee that gave rise to one of the most striking and memorable photographs of the day, when, waiting for his car after the ceremony, he was accommodated on the steps of the cathedral with a simple wooden chair, and sat there, bowed over his stick, remembering.

He was remembering more than most that day; but all were remembering, and throughout the land there was television to help them do so. Over half the population of Britain, twenty-five million people, watched the ceremony, and the direct transmission to other countries, it was subsequently estimated, produced a total audience of something like 350,000,000, or more than ten per cent of the entire population of the world. These saw it all, step by step of the way, from the moment when Big

Ben, early in the morning, struck for the last time that day, and then fell silent till midnight, to the moment when the cameras, perched in an eyrie high above Waterloo station, showed the train bearing the body and the family mourners to Churchill's final, private resting-place, steaming out of the station and between the houses, following it on and on and on, until it seemed as though the cameras must be flying behind the train to keep it in view so long.

The procession itself was headed by a contingent of Battle of Britain air crews, of whom he had spoken his most famous words. Middle-aged men now, yet with upright bearing, they marched, and behind them the squadrons, the contingents, the deputations, from all the branches of all the armed forces; the admirals, the generals, the air marshals; the officers bearing purple cushions on which reposed the scores of orders and decorations he had won during his long life; the family mourners; the bands; the police, the fire services, the civil defence corps.

Yet the day was won by two unexpected sights, which were to live in the minds of millions long after the hymns had died away, the commentators and reporters had said their last words, the notabilities, unoffended and unassassinated, had departed. Unannounced, a camera swung its fishy eye up towards the Whispering Gallery of St Paul's and there picked out the silhouette of the trumpeter sounding Last Post; then, as the launch carrying the coffin slid away from the pier, the cranes of London's dockland, lined up like silent sentinels, simultaneously dipped their jibs in salute.

'You saw the ceremony?'
'That I did.'
'How was it?'
'Well worth the seeing.'

More than usually so. Already it had long been impossible for anyone to use the Churchillian oratory, and the excerpts from it that were heard during the day-long transmissions sounded like quotations from some ancient writer who had lived far back in history. Already, looking down the rows of statesmen and dictators, kings and presidents, it was impossible to discern anyone of comparable stature, any who suggested the vision and breadth of understanding displayed by him they had come to mourn. Already it was clear that there would never again be a man over the last moments of whose funeral the dark velvet voice of Laurence Olivier could intone the words, from the seventeenth-century Bishop Joseph Hall, with which the broadcast ended, on the Valiant Man:

> His power is limited by his will; and he holds it the noblest revenge, that he might hurt and doth not. He commands, without tyranny and imperiousness; obeys, without servility; and changes not his mind with his estate. The height of his spirits overlooks all casualities; and his boldness proceeds neither from ignorance nor senselessness: but, first, he values evils and then despises them. He is so balanced with wisdom, that he floats steadily in the midst of all tempests. Deliberate in his purposes; firm in resolution; bold in enterprising; unwearied in achieving; and, howsoever, happy in success: and, if ever he be overcome, his heart yields last.

Next day the Sixties looked over their shoulder; the officer in charge of the bearer-party received the M.B.E., while the men who actually carried the coffin got the B.E.M.

# 24

## Two legs good, four legs better

But it was not surprising that Britain had lost her way in the world during the Sixties; man himself had lost his way, in the same decade, in the universe. Man's loss of his own identity, or at the very least his increasing uncertainty about it, proceeded apace, and fitted with a mournful precision into the mood of these years. Through many of the most notable plays of the decade, for instance, there wandered characters looking for themselves like so many Don Quixotes and rarely succeeding in their search, though the satisfaction of audiences, who had long been supposed to demand a neat and conclusive ending, seemed undiminished and even enhanced, as the heroes of, for instance, Harold Pinter stumbled through the atmosphere of menace with which he surrounded them, seeking answers to questions that were never asked, and the questions to answers that were never found. The movement had been heralded by a false dawn in the Fifties, when Nigel Dennis's *Cards of Identity*,[1] a brilliant and disquieting novel adapted with only a limited degree of success for the stage, offered a clue to the way the world was going. But nobody then realized what a torrent of Pinters and Jellicoes, Ionescos and Becketts was to follow, nor how soon. Nor, indeed, how well they would mirror a widespread public mood. If the poets are the unacknowledged legislators of the world, they need a body of knowledge and expert advice to enable them to draft their legislation, and this, as it turned out, was provided by a no less vigorous torrent of books. These were not novels, however, despite the fact that however often the death of the novel might be announced, it showed no sign of

[1] Weidenfeld and Nicolson, London, 1955.

lying down; though novels continued to be written in even greater numbers than ever before, few of those written in the same temper as the plays of identity made much mark, and experiments certainly no wilder than their dramatic equivalents were greeted with indifference, until at last (in desperation, perhaps) one novelist, B. S. Johnson, wrote a novel – *The Unfortunates*[1] – that was sold not in book form at all but in a box, the sections being loose and un-numbered and the purchasers invited to arrange them in any order they pleased before reading them, and then to rearrange them in a different order and read them again, though the quality of the book was such that a considerable effort was required to read them even once, in any order at all.

The books which caught the uncertainties of the age were not fiction at all. Suddenly ethology was the new science, and its products were on every side-table. Konrad Lorenz, Robert Ardrey, Desmond Morris and Anthony Storr were the chief prophets, and their books – respectively *On Aggression*,[2] *The Territorial Imperative*,[3] *The Naked Ape*[4] and *Human Aggression*[5] – formed the new scripture.

There had been nineteenth- and early twentieth-century writers who moralized on behalf of human beings, deriving their arguments from the behaviour of the animals but failing to realize that they had subconsciously transferred human emotions and attributes to the animals first. Thus Fabre and Maeterlinck had constructed exquisite poetic fantasies about insects and animals, though in fact they were writing about human beings. Anthropomorphism was the dominant theme of animal books, as of animal illustrations; the most famous of all animal-artists, the now-forgotten Louis Wain, drew uncountable thousands of cats and changed, virtually single-handed, the attitude of this country to the domestic cat; but all his cats were in fact human beings, and they dressed, walked and in general behaved like

[1] Secker and Warburg, London, 1969.

[2] Methuen, London, 1966.

[3] Atheneum, New York, 1966; Collins, London, 1967.

[4] Cape, London, 1967.

[5] Penguin, Harmondsworth, 1968.

human beings. (Wain died mad, his mind a battleground on which was fought out the struggle between the animal and the human instincts in man, and his work illustrating it.) Perhaps the most striking example of the attribution of human emotions and characteristics to animals that could not feel them was contributed by the once-celebrated naturalist Ernest Seton Thompson, of whom it must in strict justice be said that he was one of the most outrageous liars who ever lived; Thompson claimed to have known personally a rabbit with a sense of propriety and filial loyalty so strong that when its mother was seduced by an elderly roué of a rabbit who later 'treated her shamefully', the son sought him out and punished him for his conduct, though the nature of the punishment was never specified. (Perhaps it was a thrashing on the steps of his club.)

Such attitudes had been reinforced both by Freud and by later Freudian reaction. If the behaviour of human beings was governed by drives so deep that they were far outside our conscious control and so shameful that entire mental systems had to be set up in every one of us to suppress them, then we were indeed all animals, and the only improbable thing about the rabbit story was that the son-rabbit did not join the roué-rabbit in the shameful treatment of mother and justify it on the grounds that he suffered from an uncontrollable Oedipus complex. Or alternatively Bishop Heber had been quite right when he suggested that in any pleasing prospect it was only man that was vile, and we should do well to turn for relief from his vileness to the natural innocence of the animals.

It was inevitable that, sooner or later, men would decide that the problem could only be solved by studying the animals and reporting on their behaviour. That did indeed happen; but the wholly unexpected by-product was the lessons that the studies produced for human beings. It was almost as though Fabre and Maeterlinck had been born again, but this time upside-down; instead of seeing the animal image in the mirror held up by human behaviour, we began to see the human image in the mirror of the animals, and with much the same effect on the general reader, for however strongly the ethologists insisted that they were only describing the way the animals behaved, and it was not their fault if evolution had mixed man and animal inextricably, the message found in their work by those who needed to find it there was that they had been finally displaced from the centre of human activity itself, and that the proper study of mankind was now the great ape, the lynx, the Manx shearwater, the ox, the ass and the planarian worm – particularly, it sometimes seemed, the planarian worm, which exhibited all the signs of thought without having a brain, of memory without having any capacity for storing it, and of self-interest without having any identity. With the tricks got up to by this lowly beast, man – thinking, remembering and self-interested man – finally pronounced himself satisfied, not noticing that in identifying himself with such a nothingness he had finally dissolved his own identity altogether.

All was not lost, however; those who felt that the planarian worm did not ideally represent all that was best and most noble in man, that the idea of a planarian-worm Shakespeare, Rembrandt, Beethoven was neither probable nor flattering, were invited instead to contemplate the dolphin, to look on her ways and be proud. The dolphin, it suddenly seemed as scientists began to examine and investigate the creature, was of high intelligence and saintly disposition, a marine houyhnhnm to man's eternal yahoo. Pacific and loving, sportive and easily tamed, the dolphin was in any case an evolutionary freak, as it was descended from creatures which had reversed the normal pattern and left the land for the sea; now, it seemed, dolphins could talk too, and if only the structure and vocabulary of their language could be discovered, and communication between them and man established, they might have much wisdom to impart. In this respect the dolphin rapidly began to perform the function of the benign creature from space, filling man's unassuageable hunger for some authority outside him, something to tell him where he is wrong and how he may go right; how pleasing if the Great Teacher should turn out to be this charming fish, several specimens of which had been seen performing on television, and one of them, named Flipper, actually starring in an entire series of feature films. 'I ... heard a mermaid on a dolphin's back', said Oberon, 'Uttering such dulcet and harmonious breath, That the rude sea grew civil at her song, And certain stars shot madly from their spheres, To hear the sea-maid's music.' Now it appeared that what he heard may have been not the mermaid but the dolphin, which rapidly became the symbolic beast of the decade, displacing the lemming from the consciousness and the conversation of the smart, the sophisticated and the cynical.

The proper study of mankind was the animal kingdom; in the Sixties ethology linked hands with anthropology, and in Britain the result was received with great satisfaction. Robert Ardrey, arguing for territoriality as the basis of much human, as well as animal, behaviour, used as one of his chief examples the existence and survival of Israel, and the British attitude to Israel seemed during the Sixties to bear him out when the 'Six-Day War' between Israel and her Arab neighbours flared in 1967. There was no mistaking the extraordinary feeling in Britain of sympathy and support for Israel during the days leading up to the outbreak of the war, and still more during its brief progress. British sympathy was overwhelmingly on the side of Israel, first because, as one against many, she seemed to be the underdog, and then, when it was clear that she was nothing of the kind, because of admiration for her feats of arms.

The concept of territoriality, peculiar, in its popular aspect, to the Sixties, appeared to be ruling at a deeply subconscious level in Britain, and it found its expression in a great wave of admiration, not merely for Israel as a state, but for the Jews in general. Again and again, British Jews recorded, during and after the Six-Day War, expressions of Gentile approbation offered from strangers; even when the war had ended in total victory for Israel, and she began to behave as badly as most conquerors, so that criticism mounted in Britain, fostered by the pro-Arab propaganda groups and organizations, there was no reason to believe that British public opinion was anything but overwhelmingly on the side of Israel. Perhaps it had taken a war, fought with such brilliance and success, to convince the British that Jews were after all like other people; if so, a very persuasive thesis could, it was clear, have been argued, by the end of the Sixties, to the effect that not until the coloured peoples of Africa, the Caribbean and the Indian sub-continent had demonstrated their ability to defend their territory against hostile, and culturally distinct, forces would they be accorded the respect and acceptance in Britain that they craved.

* * *

But while man searched in himself for certainty as never before, he also quested outside himself. For men to visit stars on which there might be life, life with which they might communicate, was a project that, paradoxically, seemed to have become more remote with the development of space travel rather than less. Before, it was no trouble for a writer of fiction to have his voyagers land on planets that lay unimaginable distances from Earth, and there find, according to taste, a race of godlike beings or a savage and dangerous population of monsters. Once travel to the moon, however, became imminent, and that to Mars only a matter of a few years, men began to understand the reality of the space that separated them from any heavenly body that might conceivably contain beings sufficiently like themselves to render an attempt at communication worth while, whereat a desperate sense of frustration set in; after dreaming for so many centuries of travelling through the Universe man had been punished for his presumption in much the same manner as Tantalus, the grapes being snatched out of his reach when he had almost grasped them. Uncountable thousands of millions of years' travel by the fastest means of propulsion known to man lay between him and his fellow-creatures in space, and to add to the disappointment it was argued that, even if men discovered how to travel at the speed of light, or even faster (and to get to some of the furthest stars it would be necessary to go at speeds thousands or even millions of times the speed of light), they would return after what to them would have been only a year or two, only to find that the earth and anything on it had aged by many millions of years, this paradox being explained patiently by a number of learned men but understood by almost none of their audience.

All the same, man made himself ready for any eventuality, even preparing languages for use among the stars; Professor Lancelot Hogben, ever one of nature's optimists, invented a tongue called 'Astraglossa', no doubt in affectionate memory of the earthly language he had invented some decades before, called 'Interglossa', which was supposed, like other international languages such as Esperanto and Basic English, to bring about general peace and brotherhood, but did not.

So man was still able to astonish himself, even in the sceptical-credulous Sixties. Right at the beginning of the decade President Kennedy had, when interplanetary travel had for the first time become something more than the dream of novelists and short-story writers, announced a programme that was to culminate, at the decade's end, with a landing of men on the moon. In many quarters the whole idea was scoffed at as absurd and unattainable (though one man in Britain managed to persuade Ladbroke's, the bookmakers, to accept a ten-pound bet, at odds of a thousand to one, that an earthly traveller would stand on the moon's surface by the last day of 1969, and collected, as it turned out, with more than five months to spare), and as soon as it began to seem at any rate possible, it was scoffed at instead, especially by those for whom the denunciation of the United States had become, in the Sixties, not merely a full-time occupation but a full-fledged religion, as a typical late-capitalist waste of resources which would have been better spent on feeding the world's hungry. (This was a favourite cause of many who, in the Sixties, spent much of their time, when not denouncing the United States for starving the poor, feeding only themselves, and in some cases actually going so far as to denounce organizations like Oxfam and Voluntary Service Overseas as 'neo-colonialist' and 'white-supremacist', charges which were unlikely to have impressed those downtrodden victims of neo-colonialism who were kept alive by the organizations in question.)

But the project, named first Mercury, then Gemini, and finally, as the landing on the moon came closer, Apollo, caught Britain's imagination as few scientific or technological achievements ever had. Nor was this surprising. In a decade when such faith as there was tended to be increasingly artificial, the realization that the moon, which had sailed fancy-free through the skies for hundreds of millions of years, was at last to be violated, her cosmic dust disturbed by the foot of man, did literally inspire awe, and for the Sixties to have something awe-inspiring to contemplate was rare indeed.

As the countdown proceeded, through the journey of Apollo 9 to within sixty miles of the moon's surface, then of Apollo 10 to within nine miles, towards the final descent of Apollo 11, in the dying months of the decade, to the surface of the planet, the jokes about little green men in the moon began to fall away, and the once unimaginable had to be faced. Nor was the facing, paradoxically enough, made any easier by the fact—a miracle in its way as remarkable as the journey itself—that television brought to earth pictures of every step of the project from Apollo 9 to the final triumph, while it was actually happening. (Again, the rate at which change itself was changing was here illustrated; the first live television pictures to be transmitted across the Atlantic had been seen, to general astonishment and wonder, when the decade was already two years old, yet before it ended they were coming from the moon.)

'By heaven, methinks it were an easy leap, To pluck bright honour from the pale-faced moon.' For centuries man had dreamed of putting Hotspur's claim to the test; in the Sixties, least poetical decade yet, it happened. The astronauts of Apollo 9 had spent Christmas Day in orbit round the moon, and managed to shock the New Prigs (a breed which multiplied horribly during the Sixties) by quoting, most unfashionably, the Book of Genesis, before setting course for what they called, the pride and relish in their voices coming clearly across the 240,000 miles, 'the *good* earth'. When it became as certain as these things could be that Apollo 11 was actually going to put men on the moon, great debate broke out in Britain as to what would be, and what should be, the first words ever spoken from another planet, and one newspaper ran a contest, inviting its readers to supply them. In the event the words were 'One small step for a man – one giant leap for mankind.'

# 25

# Now we are seventy

At times the urge to preserve the past, with which the Sixties were obsessed, took on the proportions of mania. There was nothing so ugly, so dirty, so useless, so lacking in any kind of aesthetic, historical or stylistic attraction that it was impossible to find a group of people willing to solicit funds for its removal to a permanent home. Often the name of John Betjeman was attached to those appeals, and eventually Mr Eric Lyons, himself an architect, coined the phrase 'Betjemanic depressives' to stigmatize collectively those who would preserve at all costs everything from the past, be it a wrought-iron lamp-post due for replacement in Chelsea, a Victorian church in Essex complete with its 'blue-jowled and bloody' stained glass, or the celebrated Doric portico at Euston Station.

This last created the greatest preservationist furore of the decade, though it was very difficult to believe that most of those making the loudest cry about the vandalism supposed to be animating the plan to pull it down as part of the rebuilding of Euston can have ever set eyes on it. It was a product of the worst architectural decade of the nineteenth century – the fourth – and the moment the rebuilding plans for Euston were promulgated the outcry began, based apparently on the grounds that it was a product of the great 'railway age', and as such meet for retention.

The portico (it was better, though less accurately, known as the Arch) consisted of four thousand five hundred tons of granite, erected at the entrance of Euston to symbolize the Gateway to the North, which Euston, at the time of its building, was. Vast, heavy, graceless, ill-proportioned and filthy, the Doric Portico at Euston stood like Hell Gate in Housman's poem:

Wall and rampart risen to sight
Cast a shadow not of night,
And beyond them seemed to glow
Bonfires lighted long ago ...
Ill as yet the eye could see
The eternal masonry,
But beneath it on the dark
To and fro there stirred a spark ...
And against a smoulder dun
And a dawn without a sun
Did the nearing bastion loom,
And across the gate of gloom
Still one saw the sentry go,
Trim and burning, to and fro[1]

—flanked by two lodges which only served to emphasize the bad proportions of the portico, with its triforium stuck on top as an afterthought, like a small hat upon a large woman.

Yet this thing found friends and champions, who clamoured for it to be left where it was, though the whole of the Euston area rebuilding (which included not only the station itself, but also some of the nastiest slums in London) would have had to be redrawn around it. When preservation *in situ* was declared impossible, its defenders insisted that it be dismantled stone by stone and re-erected elsewhere. Examination of the problem disclosed that the cost of doing as the preservationists asked would be one hundred and ninety thousand pounds, and the Government suavely let hang in the air the question whether the campaigners would not usually be among the first to criticize Governments for extravagance and waste. At this the Betjemaniacs discovered, late in the day but possibly not too late, a firm which specialized in the physical removal of buildings by putting tracked 'skates' of steel beneath them and towing them away; thus it was proposed that the Euston portico should literally have the skids put under it, and funds were immediately solicited from the public to enable

[1] A. E. Housman, *Last Poems* (Richards Press, London, 1922), 'Hell Gate', p. 94.

this work to be put in hand; unfortunately, although the cost of this means of removal was less than for the first method suggested, being estimated at ninety thousand pounds instead of one hundred and ninety thousand, only one thousand was in hand by the time the demolition work could wait no longer, and down the thing duly came amid curses from the defeated preservationist party, though they did not have to wait long for their revenge; for the new Euston arose from the granite ashes of the old and proved to be a building quite as hideous in its own way as the Euston portico, and far less positive.

But the episode illustrated to perfection Britain's widespread habit, seen at its starkest in the Sixties (precisely because of the opposite pull in the decade, the pull that led towards the acceptance of the future and a resolve to make the best of it), of looking over her shoulder at her past. What, after all, could better symbolize Britain's past greatness than a structure which in itself commemorated the Railway Age, the years when Britain led the world in her application of the most modern methods and products? The Industrial Revolution was a British invention, and not only had Britain been the first country to build a really extensive railway network, but she sent her sons into far-off lands to build railways there, so that there are still people in Britain today deriving an income from railway enterprises in Latin America and no doubt remembering every time they receive a dividend the days of Britain's greatness. Yet it was precisely that greatness that it was dangerous for Britain now to remember, now that a new kind of greatness, or even an efficient kind of smallness, was required, and did not seem to be forthcoming. If the preservationists had had their way, the entire country would eventually have been turned into a gigantic municipal junkyard or scrap-heap; perhaps with fitting symbolism. Very fitting indeed was the symbolism of the last big preservationist campaign of the decade. It was proposed that one of the earliest iron ships built in this country, which had been rusting and rotting for decades in the Falkland Isles, should be made seaworthy, brought home and put on permanent display; the ship was called the *Great Britain.*

The preservation movement was not confined, however, to inanimate objects. Inanimate organizations too came under its aegis. The Royal Academy, which for very many years had stood like the Spartans at Thermopylae across the path of art, resisting it heroically, had fallen upon evil times. What had declined was not its repute, which had long been too low to go any lower, but its income; it was faced with the prospect of curtailing its activities sharply or even bringing them entirely to an end. In some quarters it was thought that nothing could have done the cause of art more good; but the Academicians could hardly have been expected to see it that way and they consulted among themselves as to how they might raise the wind, deciding that the best way to do it would be to get money from the nation or the Government or both. The Academy therefore announced that, of its two major artistic treasures – the marble *tondo* by Michelangelo and the drawing of the Holy Family by Leonardo da Vinci – it was going to sell one at public auction, and that the choice had fallen upon the latter.

After a time, as the Academicians had doubtless foreseen, if not intended, an agitation arose to 'save the Leonardo for the nation', and the Academy, having waited a proper length of time, so that it should not appear too eager, let it be known that if somebody would give eight hundred thousand pounds for the work they would drop their plan to send it to auction, and furthermore they would give priority, as far as intending purchasers were concerned, to those who would see that the treasure remained in Britain. At this point a committee was set up to organize the extraction from the public of the sum required. The committee had on it such respected figures as the Lord Chief Justice (Lord Parker), Mr Norman Collins and both Archbishops, and was assembled under the auspices of the *Sunday Times* and its proprietor, Roy Thomson.

The stage having been set, the cartoon was exhibited in the National Gallery, and subscriptions solicited both from visitors and from wealthy individuals and institutions. Unfortunately the money did not flow in quite as quickly as it might have done; this was partly due to the residual philistinism in Britain, partly to a very healthy reluctance to contribute on the part of those who felt that the extinction of the Royal Academy would be an almost unmixed blessing, partly to a distaste for the method the Academy had adopted to make sure that it got its money with the least possible risk, partly to a feeling among the more sophisticated of the potential contributors that there were quite enough newspaper proprietors in the House of Lords already, and partly by the curious fact, which had come to light only after the decision to sell the work had been taken, that it had been acquired, more than a century before, in rather dubious circumstances.

It should be said in fairness at this point that the Leonardo drawing was, as anyone who saw it during its period of public exhibition had to agree, a unique masterpiece, certainly worth – so far as a monetary price can be put on such things, which is not very far – every penny of what was being asked, and if only the money had been destined to go, when collected, to a more deserving quarter, few could have objected to its collection. Be this as it may, it was a fact that the money did not roll in at anything like the required rate (for a time-limit had been prudently set on the whole operation by the Academy), at which some of those involved started to get distinctly tetchy and began to carp at the nation for its implied parsimony. In particular, the Secretary of the Academy, Mr Humphrey Brooke, strongly criticized the Bank of England for giving only one thousand pounds to the appeal, which he called a 'miserable contribution', his indignation being caused by the fact that if the Old Lady herself would not give more, many financial and industrial concerns could hardly be expected to do so; Mr Brooke actually went so far as to threaten to return the money to the bank, though not quite so far as actually to do so.

Eventually the money stopped coming in almost entirely, when the appeal was only half-way to its target, and it was clear that it was not going to be met by the public. Consternation thereupon looked like breaking out, when the Government stepped in and, making a virtue out of what had by that time become the necessity of avoiding a great deal of unpleasantness, generously offered, for all the world as if it was coming out of its own pockets rather than those of the taxpayers, to make up the difference, some four hundred thousand pounds. Thus all ended happily, and great satisfaction was expressed by the Lord Chief Justice, the two Archbishops, Mr Norman Collins and Mr Roy Thomson, who was not long afterwards raised to the peerage as Baron Thomson of Fleet, to the great relief of many who were fearful of what he might get up to next.

Other national institutions also played their part in the decade. Throughout, on occasions deemed suitable, the aged Poet Laureate, John Masefield, would break into dreadful courtly verse, which by tradition was published, with visibly increasing embarrassment, in *The Times*. The embarrassment was understandable, this (on the birth of a second son to the Queen) being an example:

> Oh child descended from a line of kings,
> Born into earthly fortune, power and place,
> Unseen your blessings gather upon wings,
> A many-millioned praying shields your cot,
> The love, the hope, the promise of the race.[1]

Eventually, to the immense relief of his admirers, Masefield died, and after an unseemly wrangle about his office, many voices declaring that it ought to be abolished, and even that it ought never to have been created in the first place, Mr C. Day-Lewis was appointed to succeed him, celebrating his appointment almost immediately with verse of a nature, and on a subject, that made many regret their impulsive rejoicing at the death of his predecessor.

The poem celebrated one of the most bizarre, and symbolically significant, episodes of the entire decade. Without warning, five girls, typists in a firm making domestic heating equipment in the genteel London suburb of Surbiton (a place the mere name of

[1] Reproduced by permission of the Society of Authors.

which had provided many a hard-pressed journalist with a comic reference), declared that, after a discussion during their coffee-break, they had decided to do something about the oft-repeated exhortation by our leaders that we should all work just a little harder and that if we did so the country's economic problems would be solved. They were willing, they said, to work an extra half-hour a day for no extra wages, and by implication they invited the rest of the nation to do as much.

Instantly, springing from nowhere like mushrooms after a downpour, the slogan 'I'm Backing Britain' was born. For a few months it was to be seen and heard everywhere; even lapel-buttons proclaimed the words, proudly displayed on a background of the Union Jack. All were urged to do their bit, and the organization of prominent citizens from all walks of life that had been set up to channel and direct the universal enthusiasm took huge advertisements in the newspapers to advise the various sections of the community what they might do to help; old-age pensioners, for instance, were urged to collect silver paper, though what for was never made entirely clear.

The enthusiasm subsided, after a month or two, as quickly as it had arisen; the badges and the slogans were seen no more; the prominent citizens found other uses for their energies and the old-age pensioners presumably found *some* uses for the silver paper; and all was as before. In any case, the five gallant typists of Surbiton had very early on been told by their union that they would not be permitted to work an extra half-hour a day without the union's permission, and the union would certainly not give them permission if they were thinking of doing so without demanding higher pay in return.

* * *

Which way? Which way? Britain for ten years had been alternately thrusting her finger into the hole in the dyke and withdrawing it, unable to make up her mind whether she welcomed the inundation that lay beyond, or feared it. As fast as Prince

Philip urged the nation to pull its finger out, so fast were other voices raised begging for it to be thrust in again. Forwards or backwards? Up or down? Modernization or preservation? The future or the past? And which was which, anyway? In Alan Bennett's *Forty Years On*, the past, in the person of the retiring headmaster, and the future, represented by the incoming one, are discussing, through the medium of the school play, this very question:

HEADMASTER. Would it be impossibly naive and old-fashioned of me to ask what it is you are trying to accomplish in this impudent charade?

FRANKLIN. You could say that we are trying to shed the burden of the past.

HEADMASTER. Shed it? Why must we shed it? Why not shoulder it? Memories are not shackles, Franklin, they are garlands.

FRANKLIN. We're too tied to the past. We want to be free to look to the future. The future comes before the past.

HEADMASTER. Nonsense. The future comes after the past. Otherwise it couldn't be the future ... It's very easy to be daring and out-spoken, Franklin, but once you're at the helm the impetus will pass. Authority is a leaden cope. You will be left behind, however daring and outspoken you are. You will be left behind, just as I have been left behind. Though when you have fallen as far behind as I have, you become a character. The mists of time lend one a certain romance.[1]

[1] Alan Bennett, *Forty Years On* (Faber, London, 1969), Act II, p. 52.

In this mood, almost torn apart, the Sixties faced the future and the past at once. Long before they ended, the decision had ceased to be in Britain's control; the future was too strong for the memories – shackles or garlands – to outweigh, to outrun, to outrace. The future would have us all, whether we would or no, and whether we could take the strain or no. It might be that in the coming decade the strain would be too much, that under it Britain would collapse – economically, politically, socially, psychologically – and cease to be recognizable as Britain. It was a chance we should all have to take, whether we wanted to or not, for it was too late to call back yesterday, bid time return. Excited and disturbed, anxious yet hopeful, eating, drinking and being merry without really expecting either to continue doing so or to die on the morrow, before an audience half admiring, half despairing, Britain stumbled towards the Seventies.

How the Seventies would manage it was impossible, as the Sixties ended, to say with any certainty. But there were some clues to point the way. The rumbling about the pollution of the air, the water, the soil was one such, unmistakeable; by a happy chance, the first year of the new decade was declared European Conservation Year, and almost before it had dawned it was clear that it would consist of little more than talk, but of that a great deal. Ecology was the science, environment the prize, conservation the instrument. In the first months of the Seventies a significant news item was received from the United States: groups of students, tired of burning down their colleges in the name of peace, had decided to burn them down in the name of conservation; and since the pattern in Britain throughout the Sixties had, in such matters, followed at a fairly short interval that in the United States, it seemed likely that this would be the subject to occupy the extra-curricular activities of the students here too during the dawning decade.

And not only the students. Man's pollution of the environment had become the biggest, bravest cause of them all, and the way in which his effluents on the one hand and his scientific marvels on the other threatened to choke, poison and drown him became the great enemy, so that detergents and D.D.T., chemical fertilizers and the contraceptive pill, antibiotics and crop-sprays, began to be denounced as the monsters that would devour us all, and everywhere St Georges sprang to their chargers to save us from such a fate. There had been such St Georges for years, of course, but their warning words had gone unheeded, until they had ended up resembling so many Cassandras, mocked for their fears. But now the caponized, broiler-reared, hormone-injected chickens were coming home to roost, and the Sixties could put down their own burdens with a grateful sigh and leave this one to their successor.

It was all, we were told, a question of 'the quality of life'. Of what use were scientific advances that would lighten labour if the increased energy, the increased leisure thus provided were to be wasted in surroundings – physical, mental and spiritual – that made them worse than the labour and the effort that had been shortened, been lightened? The discoveries enabled man to combat disease, but the weapons with which he battled turned out, all too often, to be poisoned, as side-effects appeared that made the cure seem worse than the disease. New products diminished the housewife's labour by providing her with easier washing-agents, but the effluent from these choked rivers, killed fish by the million, subtly began to alter the whole ecological balance of nature. Factories poured out new plastics, cheap, sturdy and reliable, to do a thousand things in homes and offices and factories that had previously only been possible at far greater expense and inconvenience, but the plastics were biologically inert and so would not rot, non-inflammable and so would not burn, seamless and so would not tear; a dreadful vision could be seen, of the whole country vanishing under the debris of the technological society, drowned, literally, in refuse, as ten million plastic bottles a week were discarded.

Transport improved daily; methods of moving freight in 'container' lorries and trains revolutionized (to the great suspicion of the workers) the entire pattern of shifting merchandise. The new giant lorries were hailed, rightly, as the way to a better standard of living for all, and the workers who would not operate them for fear of losing their jobs were denounced as Luddites. But the lorries cracked and ruined the roads, polluted the verges with the carcinogenic filth they exuded, and brought noise-levels, long unbearable, to the point at which they became mentally and physically dangerous. The ownership of cars proliferated; another admirable sign of rising prosperity. But every car added its burden to the impossibly overcrowded roads, contributed its meed of poison to the atmosphere. Aeroplanes grew larger – at the dawn of the Seventies they were regularly carrying up to three hundred and fifty people across the Atlantic – but the tonnage of life-giving oxygen they consumed as they flew, and the tonnage of life-destroying gas they produced, were computed at terrifying levels, until it soon became clear that we were being literally poisoned from the air as well as from the ground.

Wheel after wheel was coming full circle now; at the beginning of the decade a group of public-spirited citizens living near London Airport had sought to bring a lawsuit against an airline, to compel it to make less noise, even if it had to invent a quieter engine to do so. The Minister of Aviation hastily brought in legislation that put the airlines, in this respect, above the law, and thus prevented the citizens from succeeding in their action. At the end of the decade some twenty major American and foreign national and international airlines were simultaneously prosecuted by the United States legal authorities because of their pollution of the air, and in California itself, where a great city had arisen that was planned entirely for the motor-car rather than the people, the automobile industry was warned, in legislation passed by the State Congress, that it would have to find a substitute for the internal combustion engine within two years or take its business elsewhere.

In Britain such progress was slower. When the United States, alarmed by the evidence that motor-cars were less safe than they could be made, passed Federal legislation compelling manufacturers to incorporate safety features in all new cars, the British manufacturers, who were to come under the same rules in respect of cars they exported to the United States, set up a howl that they would be ruined if they were compelled to fit, say, steering-wheels that would not automatically crush the driver to death in the event of a collision, and the Minister of Transport was actually prevailed upon to plead their shabby case with the Americans, while the manufacturers, with heavy hearts, began to think of making two models, one with the safety features for the American market, and one without for the British, who were presumably considered either indestructible or expendable.

The spoliation of the countryside went on apace and the Government deplored it, though the worst offenders were the Government and those institutions (like the army and the nationalized industries) over which the Government could exercise some, or even absolute, control; a similar schizophrenia affected the Duke of Edinburgh, who worked, and more especially talked, indefatigably and selflessly for the conservation of wild life, while the bulletins issued from Sandringham or Balmoral recorded, with depressing regularity, the stupendous slaughter he was wont to make among the wild life of the area. At the same time the Forestry Commission, once thought of as the Good Genie that would save the countryside by covering it with woods whenever man had stripped it bare, found itself instead playing the role of the Wicked Fairy, ruining and making hideous huge tracts of land by stripping them of everything natural, old and graceful in the way of flora, fauna and buildings, and then sowing them with dragon's teeth in the shape of symmetrically arranged blotches of identical conifers.

In big things and little the ruin went on, and man shrank further and further into a speck of insignificance. When the battle of the Euston Arch was lost and the new Euston arose, flat, featureless and depressing, on the ashes of the old, it was generally agreed that the new station would at any rate be efficient. So indeed it was, from the point of view of the trains, the ticket-issuing machinery, and the automatically operated timetable-boards. From the point of view of the people, however, it was less than entirely satisfactory, as was seen when somebody pointed out rather sharply that the designers had entirely forgotten to provide any seating whatever in the huge concourse, so that passengers waiting for trains or other people must sit on their suitcases, lie on the floor, stand up, or go away. It was expected that, when this oversight was pointed out, the responsible authorities would, with red faces, hastily concoct an excuse for their forgetfulness and remedy it at once. No such thing; to the general stupefaction, the authorities declared that the lack of seating was entirely deliberate and would not be remedied at all, and, when asked why, gave as their reason that 'We like a tidy station, and passengers make it untidy.' A more conclusive statement of the belief that stations exist not for the passengers but for themselves and the people who run them could not have been imagined, and a considerable outcry followed, throughout which it was clear that the authorities had not the smallest intention of abating their impudence; nor did they, and Euston Station remained without seats to the end of the decade.

As in small things, so in large. The 'Snooper Society' was another concept that was born as the Sixties died. Suddenly it was discovered that the increase in computer-controlled systems of information-retrieval, of data-storage, of service and organization, meant that more and more information about more and more people was being put away and kept, in microcosmic form that could record a million facts on a square inch of transparent tape. At the same time, as Britain progressed towards a cashless society, investigators and researchers, testing the credit-worthiness of applicants for credit, began to set up further files and registers of information, true and false, accurate and inaccurate, on millions of citizens. Questionnaires and forms, official, semi-official and unofficial, poured out in an ever-increasing stream, and the information extracted from the people by them, frequently under penalty for failure to comply, was put away—for what future use none could say, not even those engaged in collecting it. Great science, tireless as ever in helping man to ruin and destroy himself and his world, spurred forward with many wondrous inventions, some of which enabled men to listen to the conversation of others from miles away, to photograph them and record them without their knowledge and without leaving any trace, to tap their telephones and bug their bedrooms. What was once secret was now easily discovered, what was formerly private was now open to the view. None knew how this increasing invasion of privacy could be halted, and as if to emphasize the difficulty of finding any way of controlling it a Select Committee was set up, that last resort of those who would abdicate responsibility for a situation beyond them, just as a Royal Commission had been set up to examine the question of pollution and conservation.

The past was not encouraging; the future was not inviting. But the Seventies could take care of the future as best they might; the Sixties were off duty. The decade had been hurrying the country along towards the future and the Sixties' search for the past and the certainty it might contain had been desperate indeed—as a dying man grows more and more feverish with his longing to find the secret that has eluded him all his life, before life shall end for him.

The wildest of all the attempts made during the decade to satisfy the need for the past without denying the demands of the future was born on South Cadbury Hill in Somerset, where sixth-century pottery had been found which had not been made locally, which had not been imported by the Romans and left there, and which defied convincing explanation on any hypothesis other than one which accepted the Arthurian legend. Camelot, it was suggested, had been found, and a huge wave of public enthusiasm ensued. Borne up by that wave, the excavators launched an appeal for funds; substantial sums were subscribed towards the work, and the Camelot Research Committee, the chairman of which was, naturally, Sir Mortimer Wheeler, pressed forward. Considerable and continuing public interest was aroused, though the inevitable slow speed at which archaeological work progresses, together with the absence of spectacular findings, such as Excalibur, or even an arm clothed in white samite, lessened it somewhat, and there was also the inevitable attack on the credibility of the whole project by a rival academic, who said that there was not the slightest evidence that the place had anything at all to do with King Arthur, and that even if it had it would be quite impossible to prove it, and that, in general, the results were 'in no way commensurate with either the ballyhoo or the money laid out'. He also pointed out that there is no recorded use of the name 'Camelot' until the fourteenth century. This hard-headed sceptic, however, had not taken the measure of the times. Beside Cadbury Hill lie the villages of West Camel and Queen Camel, and the inhabitants, and many citizens elsewhere, went on dreaming their dreams of the once and future king, who had left them with a promise that he would return. But by the end of the Sixties he had still not done so.

# Index

# Index

# Index

# *Index*

# Index

# Index